HARPER'S NEW TESTAMENT COMMENTARIES

GENERAL EDITOR: HENRY CHADWICK, D.D.

THE FIRST AND SECOND EPISTLES
TO THE THESSALONIANS

A COMMENTARY ON

THE FIRST AND SECOND EPISTLES
TO THE THESSALONIANS

ERNEST BEST

HENDRICKSON
PUBLISHERS
PEABODY, MASSACHUSETTS 01961-3473

TO
MY WIFE

PREFACE

Anyone who attempts to write on 1 and 2 Thessalonians stands very much under the shadow of Professor B. Rigaux's massive and learned commentary. In English and German most recent commentaries have been of more slender proportions and we have to go back to Frame (1912) and von Dobschütz (1909) before we meet equivalent material. It is impossible to express my debt to these three volumes; and not to them only but to many others, in particular Dibelius, where brevity hides much wisdom, and Masson, who is stimulating in his refusal to follow the generally accepted lines of exegesis. Readers will see how much I have been influenced by these works and by the many more that have appeared in recent years. Often this influence has been unconscious and too often I may have failed to acknowledge my indebtedness to it; I hope that those whose ideas I have appropriated without explicit reference will forgive me. I have made no deliberate attempt to list names of scholars in respect of disputed points nor have I made any survey of the history of the interpretation of our letters; from time to time I have tried to indicate where material of this kind may be found. Rigaux, because of the date at which he wrote, was unable to take much account of the possible influence of Gnosticism and allied movements on these letters and I have attempted to evaluate the more recent work along these lines, in particular that of Professor W. Schmithals and Dr. R. Jewett; to the latter I am particularly grateful for he has permitted me to make use of an article, 'Enthusiastic Radicalism and the Thessalonian Correspondence', which is shortly to appear in *N.T.S.*; although I have often been critical of his view I have learnt much from it.

In view of the absence in English of any recent commentary on our letters based on the Greek text I have paid slightly more attention to grammatical, linguistic and textual points than would otherwise be expected from a commentary in the present series. I have also attempted to draw the attention of readers to separate studies of the many difficult points which arise in our exegesis. Where possible I have restricted myself to literature in English and have only referred to that in other languages when this was rendered necessary by the failure of good material in English. Moreover while I am sure that I might plead the excuse of lack of space to list everything available (and indeed I have omitted much) I am well aware that there are many studies which I have completely missed.

The translation which I have provided is not intended to meet the canons of the critic of English literature; it is rough, never elegant and oftens fails to give an exact rendering of the Greek; it is the last of these objectives which I have sought most seriously. Because of our remoteness from the first century it is often difficult to determine with any certainty what Paul really intended; on occasions therefore I have sought to give an English rendering which while ambiguous reflects, not Paul's ambiguity, but the uncertainty of our understanding of his meaning.

The Thessalonian letters by their emphasis on eschatology seem particularly irrelevant to the modern world. I have therefore tried in a concluding chapter to look at some of the issues which eschatology raises for us, but perforce this has been done very briefly and without exploration in depth.

I wish to express my thanks to the Very Rev. Henry Chadwick for his invitation to write this commentary and for his willing acceptance of its excessive length, to my friend and colleague Professor R. McL. Wilson for many invaluable suggestions, to Mr. David J. Stephens who has been working with me on 2 Th. 2.1–12 and from whose work I have profited greatly in my own study of that passage and the more general problems of the letters, to the Rev. Earl S. Johnson and Mr. Douglas P. C. Judisch for assistance in reading the proofs, to the Research Fund of the Faculties of Arts and Divinity in the University of St. Andrews for a grant towards the final typing of the manuscript, and above all to my wife for the actual typing, for helping with the proofs and for her encouragement and patience with all my work.

CONTENTS

ix

SELECT BIBLIOGRAPHY

Adeney, W. F. *Thessalonians and Galatians* (Century Bible), Edinburgh, n.d.

Bailey, J. W. 'The First and Second Epistles to the Thessalonians', *The Interpreter's Bible*, Vol. XI, Nashville, Tenn., 1955.

Barbaglio, G. 'Analisi formale e letteraria di 1 Tess. 1–3', *Testimonium Christi: Scritti in Onore di Jacques Dupont*, Brescia, 1985, 35–56.

Bassler, J. M., 'The Enigmatic Sign: 2 Thessalonians', *C.B.Q.* 46 (1984), 496–510.

Bicknell, E. J. *The First and Second Epistles to the Thessalonians* (Westminster Commentary), London, 1932.

Boers, H. 'The Form-critical Study of Paul's Letters: 1 Thessalonians as a Case Study', *N.T.S.* 22 (1975/6), 140–158.

Boor, W. de *Die Briefe des Paulus an die Thessalonicher*, Wuppertal, 1960.

Bornemann, W. *Die Thessalonicherbriefe* (Meyer, 6th edn.), Göttingen, 1894.

Bruce, F. F., *1 & 2 Thessalonians* (World Biblical Commentary 45) Waco, Texas, 1982.

Calvin, J. *The Epistle of Paul the Apostle to the Romans and to the Thessalonians* (trans. Ross Mackenzie), Edinburgh, 1961.

*Collins, R. F., *Studies on the First Letter to the Thessalonians*, University Press and Peeters, Leuven, 1984.

Deidun, T. J., *New Covenant Morality in Paul* (Analecta Biblica 89), Rome, 1981.

Denney, J. *The Epistles to the Thessalonians* (Expositor's Bible), London, 1892.

Dewailly, L.-M. *La Jeune Église de Thessalonique* (Lectio Divina 37), Paris, 1963.

---

*The volume by Collins contains all his previous articles on 1 Thessalonians. Since Collins has also supplied a very comprehensive bibliography, this list does not include articles which have appeared between the time of the 1977 reprint of this commentary and the publication of his book.

SELECT BIBLIOGRAPHY

Dibelius, M. *An die Thessalonicher I–II: an die Philipper* (Handbuch zum Neuen Testament), 2nd edn., Tübingen, 1923.

Dobschütz, E. von *Die Thessalonicher-Briefe* (Meyer, 7th edn.), Göttingen, 1909.

Donfried, K. P., 'The Cults of Thessalonica and the Thessalonian Correspondence', *N.T.S.* 31 (1985), 336–356.

Ellingworth, P. and Nida, E. A., *A Translator's Handbook on Paul's Letters to the Thessalonians* (Helps for Translators, 17), Stuttgart, 1975.

Findlay, G. G. *The Epistles of Paul the Apostle to the Thessalonians* (Camb. Gk. Test.), Cambridge, 1925.

Forestell, J. T. 'The Letters to the Thessalonians' in *The Jerome Bible Commentary* (ed. R. E. Brown, J. A. Fitzmyer and R. E. Murphy), London, 1968.

Frame, J. E., *A Critical and Exegetical Commentary on the Epistles of St. Paul to the Thessalonians* (I.C.C.), Edinburgh, 1912.

Friedrich, G. '1 Thessalonicher 5, 1–11, der apologetische Einschub eines Späteren', *ZTK* 70 (1973), 288–315.

Giblin, C. H. *The Threat to Faith: An Exegetical and Theological Re-examination of 2 Thessalonians 2* (Analecta Biblica 31), Rome, 1967.

Gillman, J. 'Signals of Transformation in 1 Thessalonians 4: 13–18' *C.B.Q.* 47 (1985) 263–281.

Grayston, K. *The Letters of Paul to the Philippians and to the Thessalonians* (Camb. Bible Comm.), Cambridge 1967.

Hainz, J. *Ekklesia: Strukturen paulinischer Gemeinde-Theologie und Gemeinde-Ordnung*, Regensburg 1972.

Harnisch, W. *Eschatologische Existenz: Ein Exegetischer Beitrag zum Sachanliegen von 1 Thessalonischer, 4.13–5.11* (FRLANT 110), Göttingen, 1973.

Harris, W. B. *1 and 2 Thessalonians* (Epworth Preacher's Commentaries), London, 1968.

Henneken, B. *Verkündigung und Prophetie im 1. Thessalonicherbrief* (Stuttgarter Bibelstudien 29), Stuttgart, 1969.

Jewett, R. 'Enthusiastic Radicalism and the Thessalonian Correspondence', *Proc. Soc. Bib. Lit.* 1972, 181–232. (This is the paper referred to on p. 19 within. Unfortunately it has never yet appeared in *N.T.S.*)

Jewett, R. *Paul's Anthropological Terms*, Leiden, 1971.

1 AND 2 THESSALONIANS

Kaye, B. N. 'Eschatology and Ethics in 1 and 2 Thessalonians', *N.T.* 17 (1975), 45–57.

Kemmler, D. W. *Faith and Human Reason: a study of Paul's method of preaching as illustrated by 1–2 Thessalonians and Acts 17.2–4* (Suppl. *N.T.* 40), Leiden, 1975.

Laub, F. *Eschatologische Verkündigung und Lebensgestaltung nach Paulus. Eine Untersuchung zum Wirken des Apostels beim Aufbau der Gemeinde in Thessalonike*, Regensburg, 1973.

Lightfoot, J. B. *Notes on Epistles of St. Paul*, London, 1904.

Longenecker, R. N., 'The Nature of Paul's Early Eschatology', *N.T.S.* 31 (1985), 85–95.

Lünemann, G. *Critical and Exegetical Commentary on the New Testament: The Epistles to the Thessalonians*. (transl. by P. J. Gloag from the 3rd edn. of Meyer), Edinburgh, 1880.

Marshall, I. H., *1 and 2 Thessalonians* (New Century Bible), London, 1983.

Marxsen, W., *Der erste Brief an die Thessalonicher* (Zürcher Bibelkommentare), Zürich, 1979.

Marxsen, W., *Der zweite Brief an die Thessalonicher* (Zürcher Bibelkommentare), Zürich, 1982.

Masson, C. *Les Deux Épîtres de Saint Paul aux Thessaloniciens* (Commentaire du N.T. XIa), Neuchâtel and Paris, 1957.

Merk, O. *Handeln aus Glauben. Die Motivierungen der paulinischen Ethik*, Marburg, 1968.

Milligan, G. *St. Paul's Epistles to the Thessalonians*, London, 1908.

Moffatt, J. *The First and Second Epistles of Paul the Apostle to the Thessalonians* (The Expositor's Greek Testament, Vol. IV), London, 1910.

Moore, A. L. *I and II Thessalonians* (New Cent. Bible), London, 1969.

Morris, L. *The First and Second Epistles to the Thessalonians* (New International Comm.), Grand Rapids, Mich., 1959. (All references are to this commentary and not to the next.)

Morris, L. *The Epistles of Paul to the Thessalonians* (Tyndale), London, 1956.

Morris, L., *The Epistles of Paul to the Thessalonians*; a much revised second edition of his volume in the Tyndale series; 1983.

Neil, W. *Thessalonians* (Moffatt N. T. Comm.), London, 1950. (All references are to this commentary and not to the next.)

SELECT BIBLIOGRAPHY

Neil, W. 'I and II Thessalonians' in *Peake's Commentary on the Bible* (ed. M. Black and H. H. Rowley), London, 1962.

Oepke, A. *Die Briefe an die Thessalonicher* (Das Neue Testament Deutsch), Göttingen, 1953.

Orchard, B. '1 and 2 Thessalonians' in *A New Commentary on Holy Scripture* (ed. R. C. Fuller, L. Johnston and C. Kearns), London, 1969.

Pearson, B. A. '1 Thessalonians 2:13–16; A Deutero-Pauline Interpolation', *Harvard Theol. Rev.* 64 (1971), 79–94.

Plummer, A. *A Commentary on St. Paul's First Epistle to the Thessalonians*, London, 1918.

Plummer, A. *A Commentary on St. Paul's Second Epistle to the Thessalonians*, London, 1918.

Reese, J. M., *1 and 2 Thessalonians* (New Testament Message, 16), Wilmington, 1979.

Rigaux, B. *Saint Paul: Les Épîtres aux Thessaloniciens*, Paris, 1956.

Rigaux, B. 'Tradition et rédaction dans 1 Th. v.1–10', *N.T.S.* 21 (1974/5), 318–340.

Roetzel, C. '1 Thessalonians 5:12–28: A Case Study', *Proc. S.B.L.* Vol. II (1972), 367–384.

Schlatter, A. *Die Briefe an die Thessalonicher, Philipper, Timotheus und Titus*, Stuttgart, 1950.

Schlier, H. *Der Apostel und seine Gemeinde. Auslegung des ersten Briefes an die Thessalonicher*, Freiberg-Basel-Wien, 1972.

Schmiedel, P. W. *Die Briefe an die Thessalonicher und an die Korinther* (Hand-Commentar zum N.T.), Freiburg, 1892.

Schmithals, W. 'Die historische Situation der Thessalonicher-Briefe' in *Paulus und die Gnostiker*, Hamburg-Bergstedt, 1965.

Schürmann, H. *Der Erste Brief an die Thessalonicher* (Geistliche Schriftlesung), Düsseldorf, 1964.

Schürmann, H. *The First Epistle to the Thessalonians* (translation of Schürmann above) and Egenoff, H.-A. *The Second Epistle to the Thessalonians* (The New Testament for Spiritual Reading), London, 1969.

Siber, P. *Mit Christus leben. Eine Studie zur paulinischen Auferstehungshoffnung* (AthANT 61), Zürich, 1971, 13–67.

Snyder, G. F. 'Apocalyptic and Didactic Elements in 1 Thessalonians', *Proc. S.B.L.* Vol. I (1972), 233–244.

Snyder, G. F. 'A Summary of Faith in an Epistolary Context: 1 Thessalonians 1:9, 10', *Proc. S.B.L.* Vol. II (1972), 355–366.

Staab, K. *Die Thessalonicherbriefe* (Regensburger N.T.), Regensburg, 1965.

Tarazi, P. M., *1 Thessalonians. A Commentary* (Orthodox Biblical Studies), Crestwood, N.Y., 1982.

Thurston, R. W. 'The Relationship between the Thessalonian Epistles', *E.T.* 85 (1973/4), 52–56.

Trilling, W. *Untersuchungen zum 2. Thessalonicherbrief* (Erfurter Theologische Studien 27), Leipzig, 1972 (See my review *Bib.* 53, 1972.)

Whiteley, D. E. H. *Thessalonians* (The New Clarendon Bible), Oxford, 1969.

Wohlenberg, G. *Der Erste und Zweite Thessalonicherbrief*, Leipzig, 1909.

Zerwick, M. *Biblical Greek* (trans. by J. Smith from 4th edn.), Rome, 1963.
(This pays special attention to the grammar of 1. Th.)

ABBREVIATIONS

Bauer   W. Bauer, *A Greek–English Lexicon of the New Testament* (translated and adapted by W. F. Arndt and F. W. Gingrich), Chicago, 1957.

Bib.   *Biblica.*

B.Z.   *Biblische Zeitschrift.*

Billerbeck   H. L. Strack and P. Billerbeck, *Kommentar zum Neuen Testament aus Talmud und Midrasch.*

Bl.–Deb.   F. Blass and A. Debrunner, *A Greek Grammar of the New Testament and Other Early Christian Literature* (translated by R. W. Funk), Chicago, 1961.

B.J.R.L.   *Bulletin of the John Rylands Library.*

Burton   E. de W. Burton, *Syntax of the Moods and Tenses of New Testament Greek.* 3rd edn., Edinburgh, 1955.

D.B.S.   *Supplément au Dictionnaire de la Bible.*

Eph. T. L.   *Ephemerides Theologicae Lovanienses.*

E.T.   *Expository Times.*

I.D.B.   *The Interpreter's Dictionary of the Bible.*

J.B.L.   *Journal of Biblical Literature.*

J.T.S.   *Journal of Theological Studies.*

K.J.V.   King James' Version.

L. & S.   H. G. Liddell and R. Scott, *A Greek–English Lexicon* (ed. H. S. Jones and R. McKenzie) Oxford, 1951.

LXX   The Septuagint.

Moule   C. F. D. Moule, *An Idiom-Book of New Testament Greek.* Cambridge, 1953.

Moulton   J. H. Moulton, *A Grammar of New Testament Greek*, Vol. 1, Prolegomena, Edinburgh, 1908.

Moulton–Howard   J. H. Moulton and W. F. Howard: Vol. II, Edinburgh, 1929.

Moulton–Turner   J. H. Moulton and N. Turner, Vol. III. Edinburgh 1963.

M. & M.	J. H. Moulton and G. Milligan, *The Vocabulary of the Greek Testament.*
N.E.B.	New English Bible.
N.T.	*Novum Testamentum.*
N.T.S.	*New Testament Studies.*
R.B.	*Revue Biblique.*
R.T.P.	*Revue de Théologie et de Philosophie.*
R.S.V.	Revised Standard Version.
R.V.	Revised Version.
S.B.T.	Studies in Biblical Theology.
S.J.T.	*Scottish Journal of Theology.*
St. Th.	*Studia Theologica*
T.D.N.T.	*Theological Dictionary of the New Testament* (a translation of *T.W.N.T.* I–VI by G. W. Bromiley).
T.u.U.	*Texte und Untersuchungen.*
T.W.N.T.	*Theologisches Wörterbuch zum Neuen Testament* (ed. G. Kittel and G. Friedrich).
T.Z.	*Theologische Zeitschrift.*
Z.N.W.	*Zeitschrift für die Neutestamentliche Wissenschaft.*
Z.T.K.	*Zeitschrift für Theologie und Kirche.*

I. PAUL'S VISIT TO THESSALONICA

A. Thessalonica

Thessalonica was the second city in Europe in which, so far as we know, Paul preached the gospel (Acts 17.1-10); he came to it from Philippi. The city was large and strategically placed on the Via Egnatia, the great Roman road running from the Adriatic to the Black Sea. It also possessed a fine natural harbour through which the trade of the hinterland had its connections with the remainder of the Roman Empire. As a result the city was prosperous by reason of the commerce which flowed through it.

Unlike many of the cities where Paul worked Thessalonica still exists as the modern Salonica; it had also a long history prior to the Pauline period. It was known earlier as Therme, or possibly this was the name of another town in the immediate vicinity which Thessalonica later absorbed; the name probably came from the hot springs in the area. Cassander, one of the generals of Alexander the Great, refounded it about 315 B.C., or founded it if Therme is not the same city, and gave it the name Thessalonica. Later with Macedonia it passed into the hands of the Romans who divided the area into four districts; Thessalonica was the capital of one of these; still later it became the capital of the whole province and the seat of pro-consular government. During the civil war after the death of Julius Caesar the city had the good fortune to side with Antony and Octavian who apparently after their victory made it a free city with its own internal government; its governing officials, of whom there were five or six, were termed Politarchs.

In social structure, religion and culture, the city was little different from others of the area. The traditional worship of the ancient deities was observed but had little meaning. Into the religious gap the mystery cults were beginning to flood with Gnosticism to follow. How far gnostic ideas had already begun to affect life and thought in our period is debatable; in so far as this relates to Thessalonica we shall be dealing with it in our notes (see also pp. 16ff); for the wider issues see R. McL. Wilson, *Gnosis and the New Testament*, Oxford, 1968. For the religious life of Thessalonica see C. Edson, 'Macedonia', *Harvard Studies in Classical*

I

Philology, 51 (1940) 125-36; 'Cults of Thessalonica (Macedonia III)', *Harvard Theological Review* 41 (1948) 153-204. There is no archeological evidence of Jewish presence in the city and apart from the N.T. there are no contemporary literary or historical references to a Jewish colony. This negative evidence should not be taken to indicate that Jews were unknown in Thessalonica; they were present in all the great cities of the ancient world and it is mere chance that no evidence other than that of the N.T. survives in the case of Thessalonica. (See Additional Note, p. 59).

B. *The Account of Acts 17.1–10*

When they (i.e. Paul and Silas) **had travelled through Amphipolis and Apollonia they came to Thessalonica; here there was a Jewish synagogue. (2) Following his usual custom Paul went into it to the Jews and on three Sabbaths argued with them from the (**O.T.**) Scriptures (3) bringing out their meaning to show** (opening and applying) **that the Messiah had to suffer and rise from the dead, and he said that the Messiah was the very Jesus whom he was proclaiming to them. (4) And some of them believed and joined Paul and Silas, and also a large number of Godfearing Gentiles, and quite a number of influential women. (5) But the Jews became jealous and took some evil men from the lower classes to help them; so they caused a riot and threw the city into confusion; they attacked the house of Jason and tried to bring them out to the crowd. (6) When they did not find them they dragged Jason and some of the brothers** (i.e. Christians) **before the Politarchs shouting that those who were upsetting civilization had come here also and that Jason had given them lodging, (7) and that all of them were acting contrary to the laws of the Emperor since they said that there was another emperor, Jesus. (8) The crowd and the Politarchs were disturbed when they heard this (9) and when they had taken security from Jason and the others they dismissed them. (10) The brothers at once sent away Paul and Silas by night to Beroea; when they arrived there they went to the Jewish synagogue.**

At first sight this account appears simple and straightforward. Paul and Silas, and apparently also Timothy (though he is not mentioned between Acts 16.3 and 17.14), after the vision at Troas crossed to Europe and came to Philippi. Here they preached, were arrested, beaten and thrown into prison; after Paul had revealed his identity as a Roman citizen they were released and requested by the city officials to leave the city. After returning briefly to the young Christian community they left and travelling along the Via Egnatia they passed through Amphipolis and Apollonia (we do not know if they stopped in these towns to preach) and came to Thessalonica (about 95 miles from Philippi). Here there was a Jewish synagogue which Paul attended as usual and on three successive Sabbaths preached to those who were present. (Some commentators, e.g. Lake and Cadbury, *Beginnings of Christianity*, IV, *ad loc.*, translate 'Sabbaths' as 'weeks', as if Paul had preached every day for three weeks; there are no compelling linguistic reasons to take it in this latter sense and if we do we create unnecessary difficulties, for: i. people would not be free to listen to Paul every day; ii. nor would Paul have been free, for he himself says he worked day and night, 1 Th. 2.9.) Worshipping at the synagogue would have been both Jews and God-fearing Gentiles. The latter, disgusted with debased pagan religion, were attracted to Judaism by its monotheism, strict moral code and, at least outside Palestine, the absence of animal sacrifice, but were repelled by its ritual laws, in particular circumcision. They attended synagogue services but rarely became Jews. Their beliefs made them fertile ground for the gospel and Acts tells repeatedly how they were among the first converts in almost every area. Luke (we use this name for the author of Acts without intending any necessary identification with Paul's travelling companion but only with the author of the third Gospel) tells us that many of those in Thessalonica became Christians, including quite a number of upper-class women. However these women were not influential enough to save the Christians from persecution (cf. E. Haenchen, *The Acts of the Apostles*, Oxford, 1971, *ad loc.*).

Since Paul was preaching in a synagogue he began from the O.T. and showed how it implied a Messiah who would die and rise again. The manner in which Luke envisaged Paul preaching and using the O.T. can be seen in the other sermons in Acts directed to Jewish audiences, e.g. Peter's at Pentecost (2.14–36) or Paul's in Antioch of Pisidia (13.16–41); 17.2f itself forms an excellent summary of many of the sermons in Acts which are addressed to Jews. Those addressed to Gentiles follow a different pattern (cf. U. Wilckens, *Die Missionsreden der Apostelgeschichte*, 2nd edn., Neukirchen-Vluyn, 1963). The Jews had no accepted doctrine of a suffering (i.e. dying; Luke often uses 'suffer' in the sense 'die'; cf. Lk. 24.26, 46; Acts 3.18) Messiah and, although the Pharisees believed in a general resurrection of the dead, no conception of a particular resurrection for the Messiah; that Jesus died would have led them to reject his messiahship; that he rose would show them the error of their rejection. As well as arguing that the Messiah would suffer and rise it was also necessary to identify him with the historical person Jesus who did die and rise.

The majority of the Jews remained loyal to their faith but were enraged at Paul's success in winning some of their number and many of the God-fearers whom they themselves had hoped to convert to Judaism sooner or later. They stirred up trouble hoping that Paul and his companions would be brought before the Politarchs and condemned for sedition. The house of Jason, where Paul and his company were apparently staying, was attacked and searched. When they failed to find Paul they took away Jason and some other Christians who were with him; these were then accused of sheltering men (i.e. Paul, etc.) who had been saying that there was an emperor called Jesus and thereby implying that the Emperor in Rome should no longer hold men's allegiance. If Paul preached Jesus as Messiah it would be natural for those who were not Jews to translate this Jewish term as 'king' or 'emperor' (cf. the 'title' on Jesus' cross). The authorities of the city did not regard the charge in as serious a light as the Jews hoped; they apparently asked for some security in regard to future good behaviour on the part of Jason and the other Christians and then let them go. That night the infant Christian community sent Paul and Silas away secretly; they went on to Beroea, where the hostility of the Thessalonian Jews still pursued them and caused them trouble (17.10–14). While we cannot be certain it is probable that Paul returned to Thessalonica on the journey mentioned in Acts 20.2, though we have no direct information of such a visit; it would in any case have been later than our letters.

C. *Acts 17.1–10 and 1 Thessalonians*

There is little in Acts 17.1–10 taken by itself which is difficult; Jason appears somewhat unexpectedly without explanation; there is no direct preaching to Gentiles other than to those in attendance at the synagogue; 17.6 implies a considerable knowledge by the Jews of Paul and his work, hardly to have been gained from three sermons; if they had possessed previous information about Paul as one who was upsetting civilization they would not have allowed him into their synagogue. It is when we compare this account with what we learn from Paul's letters (in particular the first) that we begin to doubt Luke's accuracy.

(i) We would never have deduced from Paul's own references that his stay was as brief as four weeks (long enough to enclose three Sabbaths). He tells us that he had to work day and night to maintain himself (1 Th. 2.9). He was there long enough to receive financial help at least once from Philippi (see notes on 1 Th. 2.9); it would have taken some time for the news of Paul's need to get back to Philippi (95 miles away) and then for money to have been collected and forwarded. Paul's stay was long enough for him to be able to refer to his own example (1 Th. 1.6; 2 Th. 3.7f). When Paul writes 1 Th. he has not been very long away from the community and yet the total period since his arrival has been long enough for some form of organization to appear (1 Th. 5.12), for some of the members to die (1 Th. 4.13) and for the faith of the community to become well-known (1 Th. 1.8); this can be more easily accepted if his stay was not too brief. He was also long enough there for some to have given up work (1 Th. 4.11; 2 Th. 3.11).

(ii) There do not appear to be many Jewish Christians in the community to which Paul writes; Paul does not need to give them any special attention. (We reject Harnack's view that 2 Th. was written to Jewish Christians; cf. pp. 38–40.) 1 Th. 1.9f (see notes) implies that those who became Christians had previously worshipped idols, i.e. had been Gentiles (cf. 4.1–5). There are few direct references to the O.T. such as we find in other letters where Paul speaks directly to Jewish Christians or deals with the strain between Jewish and Gentile Christians. 1 Th. 2.14 tells us that as Jewish Christians in Judea suffered from fellow-Jews so the Thessalonian Christians suffered from their fellow-citizens and these would have been Gentiles. The variant reading of the Western text of Acts 17.4, 'many of the God-fearers and a large number of Gentiles', is probably an attempt to minimize the difference between Acts and 1 Th. There is a much more general question: whereas Acts represents Paul going first to the synagogue 'following his usual custom', in Gal. 2.1–10 Paul writes as if his mission was to Gentiles alone and that of Peter and the other apostles to the Jews. In Rom. 11 he argues that he preaches to Gentiles to make the Jews jealous; did Paul preach to Jews at all after his agreement with the Jerusalem pillars?

(iii) Luke's description of the nature of Paul's preaching is not reflected in 1 Th. It may be unnecessary to argue to converts about the death and resurrection of Jesus but we might have expected a continuation of the use of the O.T.; if unbelievers could be converted through it, they could equally be instructed and supported by it. Moreover if 1 Th. 1.9f represents the form of Paul's initial kerygma it differs from that of Acts 17.2f and it differs in such a way as to be much more suitable for a Gentile audience. It in fact resembles the form of the kerygma found in Acts 14.15–17 and 17.22–31, sermons which Luke considers appropriate for Paul to address to Gentiles. In the kerygma of 1 Th. 1.9f Jesus is presented as a saviour from heaven rather than as the Jewish Messiah—as alleged in Acts.

(iv) Timothy is not mentioned between Acts 16.3 and 17.14 but Paul includes his name with his own in the address of both letters and in 1 Th. 3.2 he recounts how he sent Timothy to them; he would hardly have done this unless Timothy were already well-known to them. Indeed it is difficult to reconcile the movements of both Silas and Timothy in Acts with what we learn of them in 1 Th. 3.1–6 (see notes).

(v) Whatever 'security' was taken of Jason the Thessalonians certainly expected the return of Paul (1 Th. 2.18).

In the light of this we need to examine again the account in Acts remembering as a general principle that if we have to choose between Luke and Paul the latter is almost always to be preferred. Luke is here dependent on oral or written tradition other than the travel document, for though the account in Philippi belongs to the 'we-source' the first plural does not appear after it again until 20.5. Luke gives the correct local name 'politarch' to the city's magistrates; this varied from city to city, though 'politarch' does not appear to have been restricted to Thessalonica alone in Macedonia. He names the correct towns between Philippi and Thessalonica, though since there is only one route this is not very important. Jason appears from nowhere, suggesting his name belongs to the tradition but also that Luke and the tradition know no more about him than is told here (he is a mere name). The forcible separation of Acts 17.10 accords with 1 Th. 2.17. Against this we note: (a) Luke's account of Paul's preaching follows his set pattern for preaching to Jews and is not from the tradition; (b) his limitation of the stay to four weeks is incorrect; (c) his restriction of Paul's activity to the synagogue is not confirmed by the letters but accords with what he normally says of Paul's behaviour during the first few weeks of his stay in a town; similarly the reaction of the Jews is what we would expect from what Luke records in other parts of Acts.

We can safely assume that Luke knew Paul visited Thessalonica, that there was trouble after his preaching, that a certain Jason was involved in it and that Paul had to leave abruptly. To this Luke added Paul's preaching in the synagogue with the summarized content of his argument there, the jealousy of the Jews and probably the content of the accusation that was made against Paul (17.7 was probably a customary accusation). 17.6 as we have seen betrays internal inconsistency.

II. 1 THESSALONIANS

A. Date and Place of Writing

These two subjects cannot be discussed separately. The most widely accepted theory holds that 1 Th. was written by Paul on his first visit to Corinth (for a discussion of the priority of 1 Th. to 2 Th. see pp. 42ff). In 1 Th. 3.1f Paul says that when he was in Athens he sent Timothy to Thessalonica to bring him news of what was happening there. 3.6 implies that the letter was written shortly after Timothy's return. Acts 18.5 says that Timothy and Silas rejoined Paul in Corinth. This then is the time of Timothy's return and the letter was despatched just after this from Corinth. Although this is the normal view others have been held. In the ancient church it was believed that Paul wrote from Athens and information to this effect is appended to the letter in many MSS (A K L, etc.). If it was written from Athens we should expect the reference to that city in 3.1 to be differently expressed. This theory agrees with the preceding in placing the date of composition fairly soon after Paul's initial visit to Thessalonica. A few scholars have maintained that the letter comes from a later period, perhaps

from another visit of Paul to Corinth or Athens (during the time
of his mission in Ephesus) or even from Ephesus itself; cf.
W. Hadorn, 'Die Abfassung der Thessalonicherbriefe auf der
dritten Missionsreise und der Kanon des Marcion', *Z.N.W.* 19
(1919–20) 67–72; W. Michaelis, *Die Gefangenschrift des Paulus in
Ephesus und das Itinerar des Timotheus*, Gütersloh, 1925, pp. 27–32,
60–67 (see also his *Einleitung in das N.T.*); Schmithals finds four
letters and places them all at this later time, cf. pp. 17ff, 31ff, 45ff.

It cannot be denied that the customary view has difficulties.
The account in Acts does not suggest that when Timothy rejoins
Paul in Corinth he is returning from a mission to Thessalonica.
According to Acts 17.10ff Paul left Beroea hastily without Silas
or Timothy and was escorted by some of the Beroean converts to
Athens; he told these to send Silas and Timothy to him when they
returned to Beroea; however he had left Athens and gone on to
Corinth before they rejoined him. Acts has therefore no story of
any mission by Timothy to Thessalonica and no report of Timothy
as sent from Athens (cf. 1 Th. 3.1; on the reconciliation of
of 1 Th. 3.1–6 and Acts see on 3.1–6). Since we have already seen
that Acts is not entirely trustworthy about this portion of Paul's
travels we cannot regard this as a serious objection. There is
certainly no other part of Acts which refers to a mission by
Timothy to Thessalonica. Nor are there any later visits of Paul to
Athens on one of which he might have sent Timothy to Thessalonica. We have to suppose such a visit and mission at a later time
if Acts is correct in chs. 17, 18.

If we disregard Acts we have only the internal evidence of
1 Th.; whether 2 Th. is authentic or not it is of little help to us
in our present questions. Does 1 Th. contain any information
about the length of time between Paul's original mission to Thessalonica and his composition of the letter? In favour of a short
period between the two we may list:

(i) 2.17: Paul's desire to return was strong only for a brief period
after his departure; he was hindered and so now he writes; there
is nothing to indicate that what hindered him lasted any length
of time.

(ii) 3.1–6: Paul sent Timothy back fairly soon after he left
Thessalonica and now he writes directly after his return.

(iii) Apart from Satan's hindrance and the visit of Timothy
nothing else is indicated as happening between Paul's visit and

the letter, i.e. there is no story to be told of the continued faith of the Thessalonians, only of their conversion.

(iv) The letter is full of recollections of, and references to, Paul's visit as if nothing else of importance has taken place except their persecution; the inference is that there has been no time for anything.

(v) Paul does not mention churches in Asia Minor in 1.8 for they have not yet been founded; but Paul may only be referring to the nearest churches and 'every place' may cover Asia Minor.

(vi) If the period was long (i.e. three or four years) Paul would not have been without information all that time as 3.1 suggests; news circulated rapidly in the early church.

(vii) Repeated appeals by Paul to his oral instruction (3.4; 4.2; 2 Th. 2.5; 3.10) imply that Paul wrote not long after his visit while this was still fresh in their minds.

(viii) If the period was long Paul will have written the letter on the third missionary journey. At this time he did not have Silvanus with him; he disappears from Acts at 18.5. We must presume he worked with Paul again at a later period. 1 Pet. 5.12, if its information can be relied on, certainly implies that he was alive later than the third journey, but we cannot infer from it a renewed period of activity with Paul. Paul mentions Silvanus only in connection with churches he visited on his second journey (2 Cor. 1.19; 1 Th. 1.1; 2 Th. 1.1); in 2 Cor. 1.19 the reference is to the original visit and not to later work with Paul. Schmithals (pp. 136f) supposes that Silvanus had a separate missionary career and that Paul happened to meet up with him about the time he wrote 1 Th. But Paul refers to him in the same way as he does to Timothy who was not an independent missionary but Paul's personal assistant (cf. 1 Cor. 4.17; 16.10; Phil. 2.19–24). Surely Paul would make some distinction. Timothy was of course with Paul on the third journey and the reference to him does not call for any special explanation.

(ix) If 1 & 2 Th. come from the third journey we should expect a reference to the collection which Paul took up for the saints in Jerusalem since the other letters of this period refer to it.

(x) The primitive nature of the kerygma in 1 Th. 1.9f (see notes) suggests an early date.

(xi) The eschatological interest which Paul displays seems in part to have disappeared in the later letters and in part to have been modified in form.

As evidence that the period was longer, of the order of years rather than months, we cite (and as we do so we note that there would have been an opportunity for Paul to visit Athens when he visited Corinth on the third journey; see 2 Cor. 2.1):

(i) Sufficient time must be allowed for the news of the conversion of the Thessalonians to spread (1.7f: on 'every place', 1.8, see notes there).

(ii) The time has been long enough for churches (plural) to come into being in Macedonia and Achaia (1.8). Philippi and Beroea would be those in Macedonia, Athens and Corinth those in Achaia. If Paul has only just got to Corinth (according to the normal theory) the reputation of the Thessalonians could hardly be said to be exciting the Corinthians; it ought to be the other way round, i.e. it looks as if the churches in Achaia existed prior to that in Thessalonica; this completely contradicts the evidence of Acts. But if the period is longer then the difference in date of the founding of the churches in Thessalonica and in Corinth is not so important. On the other hand 1.9 implies that it is news of their conversion and not of their continuance in the faith which is referred to, and if the period were longer we should expect the latter.

(iii) Sufficient time must have elapsed to allow for persecution (2.14; this is not the same persecution as that of Acts 17.1–10), but this could have taken place directly after Paul's hurried departure and be almost a continuation of the persecution of Acts 17.1–10.

(iv) 5.12 implies the existence of organisation in the community; it would require some time to establish this. But our notes on 5.12 show that this organization is very rudimentary in nature.

(v) Some of the community have died and the remainder worry if the dead will have a share in the parousia. This problem would arise with the first death and there is no reason to suppose that this would take years; the expectation of life was much lower then than now.

(vi) Schmithals classes our letter with 1 & 2 Cor., Gal., and Phil., because he believes that in each Paul attacks similar opponents, *viz.* Jewish Christian gnostics; they were all written about the same time. It is very difficult to identify any gnostic heresy in Thessalonica. We attempt to deal with the particular points Schmithals raises throughout the commentary and cannot itemize them now (see also pp. 17ff). In general it must be remembered that though his opponents may make similar charges against Paul in 1 Th. 2.1–12 as in other letters this does not prove they hold similar views. Theological controversy down the centuries has led to the same type of personal abuse of opponents though the nature of the theological issues have been very different. The somewhat similar argument of W. Hadorn, *art. cit.*, that Paul was refuting a heresy involving libertinism and the denial of the resurrection which would have taken years to appear and that Paul's teaching about the resurrection resembles his teaching of 1 Cor. 15 and therefore came from the same period is equally doubtful. There are differences between Paul's teaching about the resurrection in 1 Cor. and 1 Th. (e.g. in the latter no 'transformation' of the body is taught). It is very doubtful if there was any Thessalonian heresy involving libertinism.

(vii) Paul has made several attempts to revisit Thessalonica (2.18) and this would require the passage of some considerable time. Is this necessarily so? Within two or three weeks, let alone months, various reasons, or the same reason recurring, might prevent the carrying out of a resolve. If the situation was at all awkward in Corinth the length of time to go to and return from Thessalonica might dissuade Paul from leaving Corinth. If the interval is measured in years we have to imagine a succession of opportunities each hindered by Satan with fresh reasons.

Taken overall the evidence suggests that 1 Th. was written fairly soon after Paul's visit and Corinth is most likely to be the place of writing. We do know the approximate date of Paul's visit to Corinth for it overlapped the proconsulship of Gallio (Acts 18.12). Most scholars place Paul's appearance before Gallio in the period A.D. 51–2 and 1 Th. would therefore date from about this time and the visit to Thessalonica be a year or two earlier. (See G. Ogg, *The Chronology of the Life of Paul*, London, 1968. pp 104–11.)

Many American scholars challenge this absolute dating though accepting the relative position of 1 Th. as one of the earliest, if not the earliest, of Paul's letters. Under the influence of John Knox, *Chapters in a Life of Paul*, London, 1954 (cf. also M. J. Suggs, 'Concerning the Date of Paul's Macedonian Ministry', *N.T.* 4 (1960) 60–8) they reject entirely the attempt to base a chronology of Paul's life and letters on the evidence supplied by Acts and consider that the letters alone ought to be used. For a general criticism of this approach see Ogg, *op. cit.*, *passim*, and

'A New Chronology of Saint Paul's Life', *E.T.* 64 (1952–3) 120–3; T. H. Campbell, 'Paul's "Missionary Journeys" as Reflected in His Letters', *J.B.L.* 74 (1955) 80–7. Using this method Knox argues for a visit to Macedonia prior to A.D. 45 followed by a visit to Corinth (the trial before Gallio of Acts 18.12ff belongs to a later visit to Corinth) from which (or from Athens) 1 Th. was written and 2 Th. (if genuine) shortly afterwards.

This view has been modified and developed recently by C. Buck and G. Taylor (*Saint Paul: A Study in the Development of his Thought*, New York, 1969) and we require to examine this in more detail. Their theory is based on an elaborate attempt to set all the Pauline letters in a sequence which they deduce from his developing theology and which is almost completely independent of the picture presented in Acts. While it must be allowed that Paul's thought developed Buck and Taylor are too certain of the course of its development in view of the scarcity of our evidence. There are basic structural patterns in Paul's theology which appear as early as our letters (see notes after 1 Th. 5.11); the interaction between these constants and the actual situations in the churches is sufficient to account for much of the variation we find. (For a criticism of Buck and Taylor on general grounds see J. Koenig's review of their book in *Union Seminary Quarterly Review* 25 (1970) 368–71; we shall deal only with those matters which relate to our letters.) Buck and Taylor date 1 Th. in A.D. 46 because 2.16 is taken to refer to the famine in Judea of that year and famine was one of the traditional signs of the End (pp. 146ff). The theology of 1 Th. shows that it just predates the actual first letter to the Corinthians (1 Cor. 5.9) which contained the first mention of the collection designed to meet the needs of the saints suffering in the famine. The dating of 2 Th. depends on the identification of the *katechon* (2.6f) with the Emperor Claudius and of the Rebel (2.3f) with Caligula (pp. 150ff) who just prior to his death in Jan. A.D. 41 intended to place a statue of himself in the Jerusalem temple. This nearly led the Jews to rebel and must have 'seemed to the Christians to be a fulfillment of the prophecies about the rebellion that would mark the beginning of the last days' (p. 156). Claudius by his accession had 'restrained' (*katechon*) Caligula and Paul expected on Claudius' death 'Caligula, having been revived by the power of Satan, to return and finish his work' (p. 157). Since Paul says in 2 Th. 2.5 that he had already taught the Thessalonians about the Rebel his initial visit must have been about the time of Caligula's attempt to place his statue in the temple. 2 Th. 2.2 allows us to date 2 Th., for those who believed the Day of the Lord had come were those who had calculated three and a half years forwards (cf. Dan. 7.25; 12.11–13) from the time of Caligula's murder (Dan. 11.45; 12.1–4).

Against this we argue: (i) Dan. 7.25; 8.14; 12.11–13 indicate that the three and a half years will be a time of severe trial for the saints and a period when no sacrifices would be offered in the Temple; simple observation would have told the Thessalonians that these things were not true. (ii) Paul cannot have had any inkling of the arithmetical calculations of the Thessalonians or he would have made an entirely different answer from the one he gives in 2 Th. 2.3–12. (iii) The *katechon* of 2 Th. 2.6f was a figure known to the Thessalonians before Paul wrote and therefore not introduced to meet a new problem as Buck and Taylor suppose (pp. 143, 158); how could anyone have known the *katechon* was Claudius from what Paul writes in 2 Th. without some other source of information? (iv) The identification of the Rebel with Caligula is unlikely (see notes on 2 Th. 2.3f). Buck and Taylor suppose that because the parousia is the return of Christ the parousia of the Rebel implies his return (i.e. Caligula returning from the dead); but 'return' only becomes a part of the significance of parousia at a later date (see pp. 351ff). (v) The identification of the *katechon* with Claudius is unlikely; cf p. 296. (vi) It is not as certain as Buck and Taylor believe that 1 Th. 2.16 refers to the Judean famine (see notes). (vii) The 'collection' does not belong to the period of the Judean famine; at that time money was taken to Jerusalem from Antioch; this set the pattern for the much bigger venture which is reported in the Pauline letters (cf. K. F. Nickle, *The Collection* (S.B.T. 48), London, 1966, pp. 1–73). (viii) Arguments in favour of a date of composition which places 1 Th. shortly after Paul's visit and in favour of its priority and not that of 2 Th. militate against the solution of Buck and Taylor. (ix) Their solution is also open to most of the objections which are offered to that of Knox.

B. *Occasion and Purpose of 1 Thessalonians*

It is difficult to separate occasion and purpose. In the strict sense the occasion was the news Timothy brought back from

Thessalonica but it was the content of what he said that led Paul to write and it was Paul's purpose to deal with what Timothy reported.

Paul had been anxious about the young church ever since he had been compelled to leave it and since he himself was unable to return (1 Th. 2.17f) he had sent Timothy, not merely on a fact-finding mission, but to help the Thessalonians as well as he could. Timothy has now returned, Paul rejoices at the good news he has brought and writes to the Thessalonians.

Is Timothy's oral report the sole source of Paul's information or did Timothy also bring a letter from the Thessalonians (or did they write separately?) and is Paul therefore in part replying to their letter? That the Thessalonians wrote to Paul has been upheld, especially by R. Harris, 'A Study in Letter-Writing', *The Expositor*, Vth Series, VIII (1898) pp. 161–180 and C. E. Faw, 'On the Writing of 1 Thessalonians', *J.B.L.* 71 (1952) 217ff. Paul never explicitly mentions a letter and his reference to the information supplied by Timothy is so general (3.6) that in those sections where he is quite obviously dealing with the actual situation of the Thessalonians we cannot be sure from where he derives his knowledge. Evidence that there is a source other than Timothy has been seen in: (i) The use of περὶ δέ (4.9, 13; 5.1; cf. δέ at 5.12) which in 1 Cor. 7.1, 25; 8.1; etc., seems to denote the beginning of replies by Paul to a list of inquiries made by the Corinthians, for at each point there is a change of subject both in 1 Cor. and 1 Th. (ii) The actual abruptness of the transition of subject matter at 4.9, 4.13 and 5.12 (in 5.12 only δέ is used and there is very little evidence from the content of the passage which follows to show that Paul has the concrete situation of the Thessalonians in mind; see notes on 5.12ff); the abruptness may be accounted for on the supposition that Paul is answering unrelated questions. (iii) Paul seems reluctant to discuss two of the subjects: at 4.9 and 5.1 he says they do not really need instruction; if so why does he introduce the subject, unless they have raised it to him? (iv) The use of καί at 2.13, 'we *also* thank God' (cf. 3.6); Paul thanks God in addition to their thanks which will have been expressed in their letter. (v) The frequent use of 'you know' (1.5; 2.1, 5, etc.) relates to what they have written in their letter.

The last two reasons are very weak (see notes on 2.13) but the first three have more substance. Paul may well be replying to questions the Thessalonians have raised, but they do not need to have been written questions; Timothy may have brought them back orally; they may also be answers to questions implied in the report of Timothy. In particular with regard to (i) the undoubted fact that Paul uses περὶ δέ and δέ in i Cor. to introduce fresh subjects and the probable fact that he is answering a letter are quite insufficient to imply that these phrases will always allude to a written letter as distinct from an oral report; one example of Paul's method does not create an essential pattern. So far as (iii) goes, Paul's 'reluctance' to discuss brotherly love can be equally his tactful way of suggesting that their love is inadequate and his 'reluctance' at 5.1 a sharp reminder that his instruction now goes back to what he said when he was with them. There is nothing in the evidence which excludes a letter but there is nothing which definitely enforces belief in one; i Th. can be satisfactorily interpreted on the basis of an oral report alone. If there was a letter it is impossible to distinguish where Paul is answering it and where he is writing on the basis of Timothy's report (cf. K. Lake, *The Earlier Epistles of Paul*, London, 1911, pp. 86ff).

Paul writes on the basis of: (i) what he has heard from Timothy; (ii) what from experience he knows faces young Christian communities; (iii) what he knows the condition of the Thessalonians was when he left them. He is not angry or indignant with them; indeed he is very pleased with them for they have stood firm in persecution (2.14), given an example to others in their love (1.3; 4.9–12) and have remembered Paul affectionately (3.6). Paul does not rebuke them strongly or suggest that they have departed widely from Christian faith and practice; yet, as is true in every Christian community, there is something lacking in their faith (3.10); he writes to supply this. 'Their faith required completion rather than correction (3.10). They were on the right path; what they chiefly needed was stimulus and direction (3.12; 4.1, 10)' (J. Moffat, *Introduction to the Literature of the New Testament*, 3rd edn., Edinburgh, 1927, p. 69). Consequently there was no need for Paul to be drawn into doctrinal discussion, apart from eschatology, and so what are often regarded as the great Pauline theological themes, justification by faith, life in and with Christ, the church, are absent. Some commentators take an entirely different view; information Paul has received has led him into a defence of himself against opponents; it is opposition of some kind which is the real occasion of the letter. We need then to look separately at the question of possible opponents in Thessalonica.

C. Opponents in Thessalonica?

There is a *prima facie* case for regarding 1 Th. 2.1–12 as an apologia of Paul (Frame, pp. 9f, probably goes too far when he speaks of Paul as defending himself throughout the first three chapters). In 2.1–12 Paul appeals to the Thessalonians' knowledge of him during his time with them; he had worked to maintain himself and his party so that no financial strain would fall on the young community; he had not been insincere or flattered them to win them over; he had not aimed to gain a reputation among them; instead he had acted tenderly and affectionately towards them as a nurse or a father towards his or her children. If this is an apologia whom may Paul have had in mind? The Greek Fathers tended to see the opposition to Paul emanating from heretical pseudo-apostles as in Corinth and Galatia. If it is accepted that the opposition is of a similar nature to that in Corinth and Galatia, what was that opposition? F. C. Baur and his school took the common opponents to be Judaizers; Lütgert, now followed by Jewett, takes them to be spiritual enthusiasts; Schmithals views them as Gnostics. Others dissociate the Thessalonian letters from those to Corinth and Galatia, and from this angle Frame and Milligan conclude that Jews were the opponents. Such a variety of opinion can only arise because the references in 1 & 2 Th. are very vague and because there is as yet no clear consensus of opinion as to the identity of Paul's opponents in Corinth and Galatia. Indeed the information provided in 1 & 2 Th. is so vague that it has led many commentators to doubt if it is really correct to speak of opponents of Paul at all. We can set aside certain possibilities at the outset: (i) There is no reference in either letter to controversy about the law and so Judaizers in the strict sense can be excluded. (ii) There is nothing suggesting a clear and distinct group within the Thessalonian Christian community hostile to Paul, for he never distinguishes between one group and another nor is there any stress on the need for unity.

It is not improbable that Jews would have continued the attack on Paul which marked his hurried departure from the city; in doing so they may well have made accusations against his honesty and sincerity. There were at the time many wandering preachers, teachers, magicians who made their living out of their instruction and activities; a number of these were certainly more intent on the money they received and the feeling of self-importance they enjoyed than on the truth of what they taught. If attacks on Paul could succeed in classifying him among these then his influence would quickly wane. This would not imply that the Jews themselves would have classed him among these people but only that feeling their own position threatened they would have used whatever weapons lay to hand, and Paul certainly moved around from place to place as did these preachers, teachers and magicians.

Schmithals (pp. 90–157) identifies the opponents as Gnostics similar to those he finds in Corinth (cf. *Die Gnosis in Korinth*, 3rd edn., Göttingen, 1969), Philippi (*Paulus und die Gnostiker*, Hamburg–Bergstedt, 1963, pp. 47–87) and Galatia (*ibid.*, pp. 9–46). For his view that all Paul's opponents in these churches were the same cf. *ibid.*, pp. 185ff. From 1 Th. 1.2–2.2 he infers that Paul has been accused of speaking without power and without the Spirit; there may be here a partial parallel to 2 Cor. 10.10, if κενός in 1 Th. 2.1 means 'weak' (this is doubtful; see notes on 2.1). It is however by no means clear that in 1.2–2.2 Paul is defending himself against opponents (see notes on the whole passage) and even if he is similar accusations do not imply similar opponents, especially when these accusations relate as much to conduct as to doctrine. In 2.3–12 Schmithals regards πλεονεξία as the main theme and parallels the passage with 2 Cor. 12; his explanation is forced; πλάνη in 2.3 does not need to have the meaning 'deception' nor πλεονεξία in 2.5 the meaning 'avarice'; moreover 2.3, 4 may be general and not tied specifically to the Thessalonian situation; 'money' certainly enters into the implied accusations of both 1 Th. 2 and 2 Cor. 12 but in each case it is only one element among others, and the other elements do not completely tally; the parallel then with 2 Cor. 12 is not adequately proved (see notes on 2.3ff). In the reference to tribulations in 3.3f Schmithals sees an allusion not to persecution but to trials caused to the Thessalonians by the false beliefs of the gnostic heretics; this would certainly fit with Timothy's task of strengthening and encouraging the Thessalonians (3.2b), Paul's use of 'tribulation' elsewhere (1 Cor. 7.28; 2 Cor. 2.4) does not restrict it to persecution, and false teaching can be attributed to Satan (3.5; cf. Rom. 16.20; 2 Cor. 11.14f); but the total context of the passage with the explicit reference to persecution in 2.14–16 (which Schmithals holds belongs to the same letter as 3.1ff; cf. *infra*, pp. 31f) and the implication in 3.3f that tribulation has been foretold (when Paul was in Thessalonica the heretics had not appeared, otherwise his attack on them would be much more precise) makes Schmithals' view very unlikely. In 4.3–8 Schmithals sees evidence of gnostic teaching on libertinism in sexual ethics; but the contemporary Gentile world provides a sufficient background for Paul's introduction of this instruction; some forms of gnosticism may encourage sexual permissiveness but they are not the only causes! In 5.12 Schmithals sees an attempt by the heretics to usurp the authority of church leaders; such an explanation is forced; the existence of leaders is by no means so clearly defined as Schmithals imagines; the words of Paul can be explained perfectly easily otherwise (see note). In 2 Th. 2.2 Schmithals sees a gnostic belief in the arrival of promised blessedness; his explanation requires an interiorization of 'the day of the Lord' of which Paul does not seem aware (see notes on 2 Th. 2.2).

Apart from differences in the interpretation of particular passages there are more general grounds which lead us to disagree with Schmithals: (i) If the opponents are the same as those in Corinth, Philippi and Galatia the letter must come from the third missionary journey, a position which Schmithals accepts but which we have rejected. (ii) Unlike some of Paul's other correspondence it is by no means clear that opponents actually exist in Thessalonica; the mild tone of his writing in 1 & 2 Th. is very different from that in other letters where he leaves us in no doubt that he is battling with opponents. (iii) As yet no scholarly consensus exists on the identity of Paul's opponents in other areas; Schmithals' view that they are all the same and that they are gnostic in character has not been widely accepted; cf. D. Georgi, *Die Gegner des Paulus im 2 Korintherbrief*, Neukirchen, 1964, pp. 7–16; G. Friedrich, 'Die Gegner des Paulus im 2 Korintherbrief' in *Abraham Unser Vater* (Festschrift für O. Michel), Leiden, 1963, pp. 181–215; R. McL. Wilson, 'How Gnostic were the Corinthians?', a forthcoming paper in *N.T.S.*; *ibid.* 'Gnostics—in Galatia?', *T.u.U.* 102, *Studia Evangelica*, IV, 358–67; R. Jewett, 'Conflicting Movements in the Early Church as Reflected in Philippians', *N.T.* 12 (1970) 362–90. (iv) There is considerable disagreement on the extent of Gnosticism as a defined position as early as the genuine Pauline letters; cf. R. McL. Wilson, *Gnosis and the New Testament*, pp. 48ff. (v) There is no reference in 1 & 2 Th. to the characteristic themes of Gnosticism (cf. the discussion of 'knowledge' in 1 Cor. 1–4).

The thesis of W. Lütgert, 'Die Vollkommenen im Philipperbrief und die Enthusiasten in Thessalonich', *Beiträge zur Förd. christ. Theol.* 13 (1909) 547–654, has been revived by R. Jewett, 'Enthusiastic Radicalism and the Thessalonian Correspondence', *N.T.S.* (1972). He holds that both letters are by Paul. According to his view Paul's opponents were a libertinist and spiritualist group. The evidence which Jewett marshals for this is similar in some respects to what Schmithals puts forward but there are many additional points: (*a*) The strict warning on sexual behaviour (1 Th. 4.8), as if Paul was opposing a rejection of the traditional sexual ethic. But v.8 is only one of three reasons Paul gives in support of the traditional position (see also vv. 6, 7) and amid the sexual freedom of the ancient pagan world warnings were always required because Jewish and Christian standards were so different. (*b*) 1 Th. 4.13–18 implies that the congregation 'had not only discounted the possibility of mortal death for members of the new aeon, but also lacked the traditional early Christian hope in a resurrection' (Jewett). Our notes on the passage will show this statement is untrue. (*c*) The reference to persecution in 1 Th. 3.3 implies that the Thessalonians were surprised that they should be persecuted even though the Church was born in persecution (1 Th. 1.6); they believed that they were in the new age and therefore ought not to be subject to persecution; hence Paul's need to remind them that persecution is a part of Christian life (3.3). But it is possible to be disturbed by persecution without being surprised that persecutions exist, since the persecuted may be shaken by their unexpected severity. In any case though the church was born in persecution they may have expected freedom from it afterwards just as a woman has peace after her birthpangs. (*d*) A false sense of security about the apocalyptic future is indicated by 1 Th. 5.3, 6–8 and in 2 Th. 2.2 they believe the parousia has already come. On 2 Th. 2.2 Jewett's view is the same as Schmithals' and meets with the same objections (see notes on 2.2). As for the Thessalonians' lack of preparedness there are even stronger appeals for preparedness in Matthew (chs. 24, 25) and Matthew is never viewed as writing in a context of 'enthusiastic radicalism'. (*e*) Ecstatic prophets exist in the Thessalonian community and Paul's demand that they should be tested by moral standards implies that some felt that they as ecstatics were beyond an evaluation of this type (1 Th. 5.19–22). This far overplays the problem of charismatics in Thessalonica; see notes on 5.19–22. (*f*) Paul refers to his initial visit as 'with power and with the Holy Spirit' (1 Th. 1.5) and not with words only because he has been criticized for not showing the signs of a 'pneumatic'; but if Paul was really concerned to argue that he has been a 'pneumatic' among them a mere reminder in such general terms as these would not be sufficient (cf. 2 Cor. 12.1–13). Jewett also argues that this criticism explains Paul's attempt to build up the authority of the community's leaders in 1 Th. 5.12–14; but as our notes show the position of 'leader' is not so clearly defined as such a view requires. (*g*) The 'loafers' (1 Th. 5.14; 2 Th. 3.6–15) were 'pneumatics' who claimed the right to support. Jewett here accepts Spicq's view (see on 5.14) that the Greek word indicates those who stand against God's order or the rule of nature. As a matter of principle they stood 'against the mores of their society and against the apostolic example of self-sufficient labour' (Jewett). Since Paul expressly gives up his claim to support from the community (2 Th. 3.9) it may be assumed that the 'loafers' claimed this right. There is evidence that 'enthusiasts' and 'divine men' (θεῖοι ἄνδρες) claimed the right to their upkeep (cf. Bo Reicke, *Diakonie, Festfreude und Zelos*, Uppsala and Wiesbaden, 1951, pp. 243ff; 308ff; Georgi, *op. cit.*, pp. 211ff, 220ff); Jewett closely associates his 'enthusiastic radicals' with the more widely known category of 'divine men'. But Paul may only be stressing his right in order to high-light the failure of the 'loafers' to think of the good of the community; 3.8, 10 fits this view much more closely than Jewett's. Moreover Paul on his initial visit had already laid down the principle of 3.10; had the 'enthusiastic radicals' appeared at that stage? If so we should expect Paul to have been much more precise in his accusations against them and defence of himself. (*h*) The trichotomy, body, soul, spirit, of 1 Th. 5.23 arises from a desire to emphasize the unity of man over against the pneumatics who opposed spirit to body and soul; but the phrase appears naturally against the normal Hellenistic tendency to divide man; it may have been a liturgical formulation drawn from the O.T. which proved useful against this Hellenistic tendency.

Jewett has made out a much stronger case than Schmithals but many of the points are small and really only carry weight once we assume that Paul did have 'enthusiastic radicals' as his opponents; they might easily have emerged out of the conflict between the Jewish background and substratum of primitive Christianity and the Hellenistic culture which surrounded it in Thessalonica. It must be conceded that in 1 Th. 2.3ff Paul does defend himself against charges that he has behaved as wandering gnostic or enthusiastic radical preachers or 'divine men' might have done, but does this prove that his opponents were of this type? The charges against which Paul defends himself were not only associated in the ancient world with 'divine men' and gnostics but also with magicians and cynic philosophers; his opponents might have been any of these. But do they need to have been any of these? Opponents regularly accuse their adversaries of faults which are not their own; Jews, or Christians who had been suborned by Jews, might well have accused Paul of the standard charges made against wandering preachers; the history of religious controversy shows how regularly opponents accuse one another with serious charges for which there is little or no evidence. Turning more particularly to Jewett, unlike Schmithals he believes that Paul wrote 1 Th. shortly after leaving the city: does this allow sufficient time for defined opponents to appear? Were they already in existence during Paul's visit? Certainly at that time Paul had to instruct the Thessalonians on the importance of work (2 Th. 3.10). If the opponents were clearly defined during his visit then we should expect a much more precise attack on them from Paul. Jewett brings together evidence from many different parts of the epistles to sustain his view but Paul does not himself seem to have been aware of the inner connections which are thereby created; e.g. he does not associate the 'loafers' with those who believe the day of the Lord has come (2 Th. 2.2). If 1 Th. was written shortly after Paul's visit then it is much earlier than 2 Cor.; a better, if not a water-tight, case can be made out here for 'divine men'; is it fair however to interpret 1 & 2 Th. by a much later letter directed to another city? At this point Schmithals was on much firmer ground because he puts 1 & 2 Th. at about the same date as 2 Cor.

The basic fault in the position of both Schmithals and Jewett is methodological. They assume there are opponents to be described and then they set out to discover them in every nook and cranny of the letter. While it may look theoretically easier to suppose that Paul writes against one set of opponents than that he has different groups of people in mind at different times this is not necessarily true of a human situation. Anyone who has served for any length of time as a pastor in a congregation will know that there are many groups whose criticisms, fair and unfair, have to be met, and that it is totally unjust to apply Occam's razor and say that because one hypothesis is better than many therefore it is to be assumed that all the groups are basically motivated in the same way. Human situations, let alone church situations, are rarely susceptible of such clear-cut solutions.

Instead therefore of looking for one definite group which Paul was attacking in Thessalonica we must see present a number of ideas from the Hellenistic atmosphere which were foreign to Christianity's Jewish cradle and which Paul had to refute; but it is not necessary to suppose one group consciously held together all these ideas and advocated them; whatever unity the ideas have comes from the prevailing culture and not from a definite set of people. There were also many wandering teachers and the Thessalonians had to be warned that Paul was not of their type; in addition to this there will have been pressure from the Jews who were experienced at hindering his work with accusations which would appeal in local situations. Paul will probably not have known precisely what was said against him at their instigation in Thessalonica. These different influences have produced the indefinite and imprecise nature of Paul's 'defence' in 1 Th. 2.3ff and his refutation of Hellenistic morals and beliefs. The enemy, if there really is one, is vague, and the defence can be nothing other than vague; there is no passion as there is in so many of Paul's other letters because there is no group against which Paul can be passionate.

D. Authenticity

During the middle period of the nineteenth century the authenticity of 1 Th. was contested first by C. Schrader and then by F. C. Baur and his school. (Full discussions will be found in T. Zahn, *Introduction to the New Testament*, Edinburgh, 1909, I, pp. 248f; E. H. Askwith, *An Introduction to the Thessalonian Epistles*, London, 1902, pp. 29–75; Moffatt, *Introduction*, pp. 69–73; Bornemann, pp. 300ff.) In brief their arguments against authenticity were: (i) Agreements with the account in Acts 17 imply a late date for 1 Th. since Acts was late; we have seen (pp. 3–7) that these agreements are not as extensive as is suggested. (ii) Non-Pauline vocabulary; there are non-Pauline words but these tend to be found in clusters and lead us to infer pre-Pauline traditional material (e.g. 1.9f; 4.15–17) rather than the inauthenticity of the whole letter (On traditional material generally, cf. A. M. Hunter, *Paul and His Predecessors*, 2nd edn., London, 1961); in any case the proportion of non-Pauline words is not exceptionally high (cf. p. 25). (iii) Inconsistencies within the letter itself; these can only be justified by actual exegesis and this shows that they are not as real as their proponents have believed. (iv) There are so many resemblances to 1 & 2 Cor. that these must have been used in the composition of 1 Th. There are also differences, e.g. 4.13–18 seems like an earlier sketch of apocalyptic ideas which was later developed in 1 Cor; the development which Buck and Taylor, *op. cit.*, show in Paul's theology, even though they exaggerate it, points in the same direction. (v) The absence of O.T. citations; but the extent to which Paul quotes the O.T. varies from letter to letter and is at its highest in letters like Romans where he deals with matters closely related to the O.T. and Judaism. (vi) The absence of characteristic Pauline doctrines, e.g. the law, justification by faith, life in Christ, an interpretation of the death of Christ; but in 1 Th. Paul is not arguing with opponents but like a good pastor counselling the congregation, dealing with practical difficulties, and discussing theological problems (e.g. the End) only as these emerge from the pastoral situation; his approach is therefore necessarily different from other letters which are more polemic. In contrast to this denial of the authenticity of 1 Th. we must ask: (i) Would a later writer allow the implication in 4.13–18 that Paul would be alive at the parousia? (ii) Rudimentary organisation suggests an early date (contrast the Pastorals) when forgery would be difficult. (iii) The problem of the death of members of the church (4.13–18) could only arise in the very early period.

E. G. Selwyn (*The First Epistle of St. Peter*, London, 1946, pp. 9–17; 363–466) has approached the problem of authenticity from a completely other angle. He finds considerable verbal similarity between 1 Pet. and 1 & 2 Th. and puts this down to the use by both Paul and Peter of Silvanus in the writing of the letters.

His view must be carefully distinguished from that of R. Scott, *The Pauline Epistles*, Edinburgh, 1909, pp. 215–33, who held that Silvanus and Timothy were responsible for 1 & 2 Th. which they wrote in the period A.D. 70–80 in order to continue the work of Paul. Scott attributes 1 Th. 1–3; 2 Th. 3 to Timothy and 1 Th. 4, 5; 2 Th. 1–2 to Silvanus. His theory is complicated and depends partly on a total view of Paul which would be unacceptable, i.e. that Paul was not an apocalyptic and therefore passages like 1 Cor. 15.20–25 and 1 Th. 4.13–18 cannot be by him, and partly on rather tenuous stylistic differences between the parts of the letters he attributes to Timothy and those he attributes to Silvanus. Selwyn worked from the recognised practice of ancient writers of instructing their secretaries to compose their letters after they had given them a broad outline of what they wished included—a kind of 'executive secretaryship'. He points to the continual, and unusual, use of the plural throughout 1 & 2 Th. (see pp. 26–29) and to the association of Silvanus (whom he assumes to be the Silas of Acts and 1 Peter 5.12) and Timothy with Paul in the address. In 1 Pet. 5.12 that letter is described as written through (διά) Silvanus and Selwyn assumes that this means he was an 'executive secretary'. The grounds for the latter assumption are inadequate: (i) διά in 1 Pet. 5.12 does not necessarily mean that Silvanus was a secretary; he could have been the messenger through whom the letter was sent or he might simply have been the clerk who took down 'Peter's' letter in shorthand and then copied it out. (ii) Silvanus's share in the writing of 1 Pet. is by no means certain; the letter is more probably pseudepigraphical (cf. Best, *1 Peter*, New Century Bible, London, 1971, pp. 49ff); if it is not pseudepigraphical then it is easier to account for the facts on the assumption of Petrine authorship than of executive secretaryship. (iii) The verbal and conceptual similarities between 1 Pet. and 1 & 2 Th. can be explained more easily through dependence on common catechetical, credal and liturgical material than through joint 'authorship' (see notes on 4.1–12; 5.1–22; esp. pp. 241f). Rigaux (p. 110) has shown the number of parallels between 1QS 1 and 1 & 2 Th., yet no one would suggest joint authorship. Much common material passed from Judaism into Christianity and appears in different Christian writings. (iv) 1 Pet. is itself heavily dependent on this traditional material (cf. Best, *1 Peter*, pp. 28ff; M.-E. Boismard, *D.B.S.* VII, 1419ff). (v) Selwyn failed to demonstrate a difference between 1 & 2 Th. and the accepted major letters of Paul which would have left a place for the interposition of Silvanus. (vi) The author of 1 Pet. regularly quotes the LXX, expands it and expresses himself in its words; the O.T. is used relatively rarely in 1 & 2 Th.

If we reject Silvanus' share in 1 Peter we are still left with the possibility of his joint authorship with Paul in 1 Th.—and equally, of course, the possibility of Timothy's joint authorship. Interest in such a possibility has been renewed by the work of A. Q. Morton. In a series of papers based on a stylistic analysis of the Pauline letters in which he considers variables like sentence length and frequency of commonly occurring words, e.g. *καί* (cf. e.g. A. Q. Morton and James McLeman, *Christianity and the Computer*, London, 1964), in the Pauline letters he has argued that Paul wrote only Rom., 1 & 2 Cor., Gal., and possibly Philm., of the letters generally attributed to him. He does however hold that though 1 & 2 Th. were not written by Paul they were very probably written by the same person. Using another type of stylistic analysis (*hapax legomena*), K. Grayston and G. Herdan, 'The Authorship of the Pastorals in the Light of Statistical Linguistics', *N.T.S.* 6 (1959) 1–15, have argued that our letters are Pauline. H. H. Somers, 'Statistical Methods in Literary Analysis' in *The Computer and Literary Style* (ed. J. Leed), Kent, Ohio, 1966, using still other methods of statistical analysis reaches the conclusion that all the fourteen letters of the traditional Pauline corpus are genuine. The method of statistical analysis of style is new and like many new scientific theories probably requires refinement before anything like final conclusions are obtained. If we ignore Somers as the most favourable witness for Pauline authorship and assume the results of Morton what would this mean? We must add certain other facts. The vocabulary of major terms in 1 & 2 Th. is Pauline (cf. Grayston and Herdan; Rigaux, pp. 80–94; Frame, pp. 28–37); there is general agreement that the eschatology of 1 Th. comes from an early period within the life-time of Paul and that there is continuity, if also development, between it and the eschatology of the later Pauline letters (e.g. 1 Cor.); this is supported by all the other evidence for an early date. When we add to this the implication of plural authorship as evidenced by the addresses are we not driven to the conclusion that either Silvanus or Timothy wrote 1 Th. (and if Morton is correct, 2 Th. also)? The main words and thoughts would be the same as Paul's but the minutiae of style would be different. Such a solution would be a return to the view of F. C. Burkitt, *Christian Beginnings*, London, 1924, pp. 128-32. As a solution it might also account for the general structural similarity of 1 & 2 Th. which is to some extent different from that of the genuine Pauline letters. Not being wholly convinced by Morton's arguments we have based our exegesis of 1 Th. on the assumption of Pauline authorship. If Paul was not the author and if Silvanus, or Timothy, was, what difference would this make? While we could assume that a close associate would use the same theological terms and use them in approximately the same way we could not assume that his usage of particles or grammatical constructions (e.g. εἰς τό) would be the same and we could not therefore use the genuine Pauline letters to determine his meaning in this area, i.e. we could not easily use stylistic mannerisms to determine meaning.

Closely related to the question of authorship is the almost universal use of the first plural in both letters, coupled with sudden changes to the first singular. Did Paul entrust the composition of the letter to one of his associates, who therefore wrote naturally in the first plural, and afterwards when Paul read it through he added a few emendations in the first singular? Or did Paul add emendations to a letter which he had dictated whenever he came to read it through? Or did Paul use an epistolary plural without intending to include anyone other than himself in his plural? Or is the letter actually from all three? There are only five places where the singular is found in the two letters: 1 Th. 2.18; 3.5a; 5.27; 2 Th. 2.5; 3.17; this is a proportion much lower than in any of the other Pauline letters. There are also a number of places where the plural is used which require some explanation: the use of 'apostles' in 1 Th. 2.7; the image of the mother (2.7) and of the father (2.11) and the reference to 'alone' in 3.1.

The plural 'we', when it is not a literary device concealing an 'I', exists with at least two meanings which in some languages are differentiated by the form of the word used (cf. J. J. Kijne, 'We, Us and Our in I & II Corinthians', *N.T.* 8 (1966) 171-9; A. T. Hanson, *The Pioneer Ministry*, London, 1961, p. 47): (i) where the 'we' relates only to the speakers or writers who are a real plurality; (ii) where it also includes the recipients and often an even wider group. The second of these is frequent in the Thessalonian letters (e.g. 1 Th. 1.3, *our* Lord Jesus Christ, *our* God and Father; the plural covers all Christians) and causes no difficulty. We require only to examine the first type in which 'we' is opposed to 'you' (e.g. 1 Th. 1.2; 2.1); it is found right through the letters, especially in 1 Th. 1.2–3.10 where Paul discusses his past, present and future relations with the Thessalonians. Does he include Timothy and Silvanus with himself?

What is his practice in other letters? In Phil. and Philm. he associates Timothy with himself in the address. Both are written thereafter in the first person singular; Philm. is so personal a letter that this appears reasonable. In Phil. the only exception to the general first singular is 3.17; it is not clear to whom the first plural applies; if Phil. is now in its original form and is not an amalgam of letters there is no easy reference within it—perhaps Paul intends his fellow-workers who are known to the Philippians but he certainly does not intend Timothy. In both 1 & 2 Cor. Paul associates others with himself in the address. 1 Cor. is almost entirely in the first singular but in 2.6–4.13 the plural is used with reference to Paul's fellow missionary leaders (Apollos who is certainly not mentioned in the address is included); at 9.11 the plural includes Barnabas (cf. 9.6) and at 15.11 it includes the Twelve. The plural can thus change its content from time to time; Paul knows who he has in mind; we must deduce it from the context. 2 Cor. begins (1.1–14) with the plural and probably Paul intends to include Timothy; the plural is not epistolary since 1.13b uses the singular in distinction from the plural. The isolated plural of 2.11 and the more regular plurals of 2.14ff, probably refer to Paul and his fellow missionaries. In 6.11–13; 7.2–16; 10–13; we have rapid alterations between singular and plural. Paul does not associate anyone with himself in the address of Gal.; the plural in 1.8f probably refers back to his original preaching and those who assisted him with it. There is no point in any of these letters at which it is easy to pin down Paul and say that he is using an epistolary plural.

Returning to 1 & 2 Th. it therefore seems best to reject the explanation of an epistolary plural and it would certainly be wrong to assume it is a plural of majesty; in his plurals Paul steps back into a group rather than assert himself; they represent his modesty rather than his importance. When Paul uses 'we' and does not include the Thessalonians he must then be thinking of himself and the two fellow-workers whom he names, Silvanus and Timothy. But what of those passages which are in the plural and yet Paul seems to be writing out of his own experience (1 Th. 2.4, 7, 11)? There are similar passages in other letters where Paul in the midst of a section of plurals draws on what he himself feels but states it in the plural (1 Cor. 4.10f; 2 Cor. 6.11; 7.3; 2 Cor. 3.1ff may fall into this category). Paul could not be expected to stop in his writing and consult Silas and Timothy about the metaphor which would form a suitable common denominator for all their feelings; he uses the one which comes naturally to himself and assumes they will accept it, i.e. he expresses their feelings in terms of his own. There is nothing unusual in this; everyone does it in writing letters in which they express the feelings of, say, a family group. On Paul's use of 'approved' (2.4), of the plural 'apostles' (2.7) and of 'alone' (3.1) see notes on the passages.

What now of the isolated passages in which he uses the first singular? Almost certainly in 1 Th. 5.27 and 2 Th. 3.17 we must see him taking the pen from his secretary and writing the last few sentences, and if the secretary has been Silvanus or Timothy the change is all the more natural. In 2.18 the words are so brief—and are indeed parenthetical within the sentence—that they could easily have been written in on re-reading the letter before despatching it. 3.5 is much too long for a marginal addition; it does not even read like a gloss since it does not correct or amplify what has been already said except in so far as it might suggest the plural of 3.1 was wrong; but in that event we would expect the 'I' to be antithetically expressed and the whole sentence to be placed much nearer to 3.1. 2 Th. 2.5 is shorter and might possibly be a gloss added by Paul, but with the ellipsis in vv. 3f it reads more like part of the original. A satisfactory exegesis of each of these passages is in any case possible if they are regarded as part of the original; see notes on them.

We conclude that Paul did not hand over the composition of the letters to someone else, then read them through and finally add some comments by way of amplification or correction. It is of course highly probable that he dictated them to someone, perhaps Silvanus or Timothy.

On Paul's use of the first person singular and plural cf. Milligan, pp. 131ff; Rigaux, pp. 77–80; E. H. Askwith, ' "I" and "We" in the Thessalonian Epistles', *Expositor*, Series VIII, I, pp. 149–59;

W. F. Lofthouse, 'Singular and Plural in St. Paul's Epistles', *E.T.* 58 (1946–7) 179–82; *ibid.* ' "I" and "We" in the Pauline Letters', *E.T.* 64 (1952–3) 241–5; E. Stauffer, *T.D.N.T.* II, pp. 356–62.

E. *Integrity*

In the past various scholars have suspected that one or more verses of 1 Th. were redactional additions or glosses (for references see W. G. Kümmel, 'Das literarische und geschichtliche Problem des ersten Thessalonicherbriefes', in *Neotestamantica et Patristica* (Suppl. to N.T. 6), pp. 213–27; E. Bammel, 'Judenverfolgung und Naherwartung: Zur Eschatologie des Ersten Thessalonicherbriefs', *Z.T.K.* 56 (1959) 294–315, esp. nn. 1, 2.); today most of these passages would be considered to embody pre-Pauline material. Attention has been focused most frequently on 2.16c because of its apparent conflict with the theology of Rom. 11 (see notes on 2.16).

Recently K. Eckart, 'Der zweite echte Brief des Apostels Paulus an die Thessalonicher', *Z.T.K.* 58 (1961) 30–44 (cf. E. Fuchs, 'Hermeneutik?' *Theologia Viatorum*, 7 (1960) 46ff), has argued that 1 Th. is composite and contains portions of two genuine Pauline letters plus substantial non-Pauline material; the latter he isolates as 2.13–16; 4.1–8, 10b–12; 5.12–22 (3.5 and 5.27 are linking material). He detects this non-Pauline material through: (i) its non-concrete character, i.e. it has no particular reference to the situation of the letter; (ii) in form it has a parallel structure suggestive of catechetical or paraenetic origin; (iii) elements of contradiction between these portions and genuine Pauline portions, e.g. 4.1ff discusses the need for good behaviour whereas 1.7 has said that the readers are well-behaved. Against this we may argue: (i) Some of the paraenetic material in other Pauline letters has this non-concrete nature, e.g. Rom. 12.9ff; Phil. 4.8f. (ii) The paraenetic material of the early church was in common use and shows up in many of the N.T. letters (cf. P. Carrington, *A Primitive Christian Catechism*, Cambridge, 1940; E. G. Selwyn, *op. cit.*, pp. 363ff); it would not be surprising if it obtained a stylised structure and if Paul employed it in 1 Th. since he does so in other letters (see notes on 1 Th. 4.1–12; 5.1–22). (iii) Eckart has overdrawn the parallelistic structure of the paraenetic passages in 1 Th. (iv) The passages Eckart alleges to be redactorial are full of

Pauline conceptions and words. (v) The alleged contradictions are resolved fairly easily (see notes on the relevant passages). For a full discussion and ultimate rejection of Eckart's views cf. Kümmel, *art. cit.*; W. Schmithals, pp. 91ff.

F. Unity

R. Scott (cf. p. 23) divided 1 & 2 Th. between Silvanus and Timothy but we are not at present concerned with this but with possible divisions of the letter on the assumption of Pauline authorship.

Eckart, *art. cit.*, as we have just seen, views our 1 Th. as compounded of portions from two letters of Paul to the Thessalonians with considerable additional material. The supposed first letter, consisting of 1.1–2.12; 2.17–3.4; 3.11–13, was written by Paul while he still lacked full information about the Thessalonians and was carried by Timothy to them. On Timothy's return the second letter (3.6–10; 4.13–5.11; 4.9–10a; 5.23–6.28) was written largely in answer to the information Timothy brought back. Eckart finds his evidence for the dissolution of 1 Th. into two letters in the similarity of the prayers of 3.11–13 to the conclusions of other Pauline letters (cf. 5.23) and in the element of thanksgiving in 3.6–10 which normally comes at the beginning of Pauline letters (though of course the actual address of this second letter has been dropped). We have already seen that the passages which Eckart attributes to a redactor are more probably Pauline; this in itself makes it difficult to sustain the theory. In addition: (i) This theory requires that ἐπέμψαμεν (3.2) is taken as an epistolary aorist; it is not so classed in this way by the grammarians and normally the context makes it quite clear when an aorist is to be regarded as epistolary (see on 3.2). (ii) 3.5 is difficult for this theory by reason of the sudden change in it from plural to singular and then back again to the plural in 3.6; anyone who deliberately joined 3.4 to 3.6 would not have made such a mistake (see notes on 3.5 for a full discussion); there is nothing un-Pauline about its wording. (iii) 3.11–13 would not by itself be a suitable ending for a Pauline letter; there should be either some personal references or a section of paraenesis or some greetings, or all three of them. (iv) 3.6–10 does contain thanksgiving but so also does 2.13; if Eckart is willing to leave this in the middle of one of his letters why not the former? (v) Above all the theory is unnecessarily complicated. For more detailed criticism see Schmithals, pp. 91ff; Kümmel, *art. cit.*

Schmithals himself has suggested a simpler solution (*ibid.* and 'Die Thessalonicherbriefe als Briefkompositionen' in *Zeit und Geschichte* (Festschrift für R. Bultmann), Tübingen, 1964, pp. 295-315). This is itself part of a wider theory in which he considers an editor put together a number of letters of Paul to form the Pauline correspondence as we now have it (cf. *Paulus und die Gnostiker*, pp. 175ff). In particular he finds that this editor combined four original letters to the Thessalonians into the canonical two; these were:

A: 2 Th. 1.1-12; 3.6-16.
B: 1 Th. 1.1-2.12; 4.2(3)-5.28
C: 2 Th. 2.13-14; 2.1-12; 2.15-3.5; 3.17-18.
D: 1 Th. 2.13-4.1(2)

A full discussion of this theory is more relevant to 2 Th. (Schmithals offers it as a solution to the problem of its authenticity) and we shall take it up later (pp. 45-50). For the moment we are concerned with the division of 1 Th. Unlike Eckart Schmithals accepts the whole letter as Pauline. He agrees with the latter however in arguing that 3.11-13 is what we would expect towards the end of a Pauline letter but after an examination of the conclusions to the various genuine Pauline letters, as he reconstructs them, he claims that it should be accompanied by a brief paraenetic section, and so he adds 4.1 (or 4.1-2; he does not finally decide between them). Personal notices are usually found prior to the concluding prayer and we have these in 3.1-10. Paul's letters normally open with a thanksgiving; nowhere is this so extensive as in 1 Th.; 2.13ff in effect repeats the theme of 1.2ff and is what ought to appear at the beginning of, and not partly through, a Pauline letter. Finally 4.2(?3) knits more satisfactorily to 2.12 than does 2.13. Thus 2.13-4.1(2) form an independent letter which was written after Timothy's return whereas the remainder was written earlier. The insertion of one letter bodily inside another resembles the way in which Paul's editor joined his other letters together. This solution also explains the positioning of 4.13-5.11 within our present letter, the unexpected introduction of personal references as early as 2.13-3.10, and the careful and cautious discussion of matters in Thessalonica as if Paul's information was not very reliable in letters A-C compared with what we would expect if Timothy had supplied Paul with information before he wrote them. It also explains Paul's defence of his conduct in 2.1–12 whereas in 2.13ff the news he has obtained from Timothy makes him joyful as if there was nothing wrong.

This is a much simpler solution than Eckart's and at first sight appears a strong case yet the evidence is not all on one side nor as straightforward as Schmithals suggests.

(i) The pattern which Schmithals outlines for the concluding sections of a Pauline letter (p. 94) is, by his own analysis, not followed completely in any genuine Pauline letter; the only letter of which it is true is Hebrews! In particular the alleged concluding prayer, whether doxology or intercession, is found only in Phil. 4.19f; 1 Th. 5.23f; 2 Th. 3.16. On the other hand prayers are found at other points than the conclusions: Rom. 15.5f, 13; 2 Th. 2.16; 3.5 (all of similar structure to that of 1 Th. 3.11–13). 2 Th. may not be Pauline and therefore inadmissible as evidence but Schmithals takes it to be genuine. Schmithals would however say that it is improper to use 2 Th. as evidence because it is itself composite; this in effect begs the question because it is only after Schmithals has divided the letters up that he is able to formulate properly his theory about how letters end; moreover if 2 Th. 3.5 shows the end of another letter (C) then this includes 2.16, a prayer not at the end. Prayers, though of different structure to that of 2 Th. 3.11–13, are found in Phil. 1.9–11; Col. 1.9–12, in each case at the conclusion of the thanksgiving.

(ii) Schmithals' table shows that he is justified in saying that a brief paraenetic section is also found at the conclusion of each letter (e.g. Rom. 15.30–32, assuming that Rom. 16 did not belong to every edition of the letter; Gal. 6.17; Col. 4.2–6) and that this is often introduced as in 4.1 with παρακαλεῖν (Rom. 15. 30–32; 16.17–20a; 1 Cor. 16.15f). But it must also be noted that the main paraenetic sections of letters are introduced by the same verb or an equivalent (e.g. Rom. 12.1; 1 Cor. 1.10; 2 Cor. 10.1—this may be another letter from what precedes it; Eph. 4.1–3), and so the verb at 4.1 is appropriate if 4.2ff is the main paraenetic section. Although the verb is found at 2.12 it is in participial form; a finite form of the verb is universal in the introduction to paraenetic material; moreover at 2.12 it does not relate to the situation of the letter but to Paul's original preaching; thus 2.12 cannot be the introduction to 4.2(3)ff (see C. J. Bjerkelund, *Parakalô*, Oslo, 1967, pp. 125–40 and notes on 4.1). Lastly we must note that the paraenetic material normally follows on the thanksgiving and if 1.2–3.13 represents the latter then it does so in 4.1ff (cf. 1 Cor. 1.10; J. T. Sanders, 'The Transition from Opening Epistolary Thanksgiving to Body in the Letters of the Pauline Corpus', *J.B.L.* 81 (1962) 348–62). 4.1–12 holds together as a unit; there is the threefold reference to previous teaching (4.1, 6, 11), the double reference of behaviour to God (4.1, 8) and to it as 'walking' (4.1, 12); 'to excel more and more' in 4.10 takes up the same phrase in 4.1. Finally the junction of 2.12 and 4.2(3) would be sharp (cf. Jewett, 'Enthusiastic Radicalism').

(iii) It is possible to argue that the introductory thanksgiving may run as far as 3.13. P. Schubert, *The Form and Function of the Pauline Thanksgivings* (Beihefte, *Z.N.W.* 20), Berlin, 1939, claimed that it begins at 1.2 and works up to a climax at 3.13 through the repeated reference to thanksgiving in 2.13 and 3.9; in this way it is narrowly linked to the paraenetic section (4.1ff) which normally follows it in Pauline letters. Schubert also pointed out that in 1 Cor. 1.8f; Phil. 1.11; 2 Th. 3.5 we work to a similar eschatological climax as in 1 Th. 3.13 and this can be regarded as terminating the thanksgiving. J. T. Sanders, *op. cit.*, has examined in some detail the way in which Paul moves from the opening thanksgiving to the main body of the letter and shown that the thanksgiving period ends in something like a prayer or a liturgically related statement followed by a formula of injunction normally in the first person. This is what we find at 1 Th. 3.11–13 and 4.1; 4.1 ought then to introduce the body of the epistle whereas on Schmithals' view it actually is part of the end of his letter D. It is possible that 1.9f and 2.1 while not exactly fitting the formula as devised by Sanders come near enough to it for it to be argued that we have the transition from the thanksgiving period to the body of the letter at that point. If so there would appear to be a stronger case for seeing 2.13 as the beginning of a letter. But such an analysis leads to the result that the letter consists entirely of thanksgiving, beginning at 2.13 and ending with the prayer of 3.11–13; there is no other suitable ending earlier than this and 3.9 indicates that the thanksgiving is still continuing at that point. Thus this supposed letter would have a most peculiar structure, utterly unlike any other Pauline letter. We have then to choose between a letter which contains two thanksgiving periods (our present 1 Th.) and one which consists entirely of a thanksgiving period: the latter would be much the more difficult to justify (F. O. Francis, 'The form and function of the opening and closing paragraphs of James and 1 John', *Z.N.W.* 61 (1970) 110–26, argues that two thanksgiving periods, or their equivalent, do occur in a number of letters). It is probably impossible to say why Paul decides on a second thanksgiving; presumably having left the subject he realizes he has not covered it adequately, perhaps in view of the hesitancies of 2.1–12, and so he returns wishing to leave a stronger impression of thankfulness; who in writing a letter has not returned to a point previously covered and dealt with it again from another angle?

There is a possibility not considered by Schmithals: 2.13–3.13 is the thanksgiving section of a letter the main body of which we do not possess. It is then a fragment of a letter which has been incorporated as 2 Cor. 6.14–7.1 was into 2 Cor. The latter fragment has been detected because it is a foreign body in 2 Cor. at this point; 2 Cor. 6.13 and 7.2 join easily together; the content of the intervening section is irrelevant to the total context; the evidence in the early Fathers for the existence of 2 Cor. comes from a much later period than that for 1 Cor. and it may not have been put together and published as early as 1 Cor. While there is some break in thought at 1 Th. 2.13 it does not resemble the jolt at 2 Cor. 6.13 and has not occasioned great difficulty to commentators (see notes). There is no break between 3.13 and 4.1; indeed 4.1 is exactly what we should expect to find after 3.13; the redactor, if there was one, has therefore acted in a more reasonable way than the redactor of 2 Cor.

(iv) There are no discrepancies of thought between 2.13–3.12 (or 2.13–4.2) and the remainder of the epistle which might suggest they were written in the light of different situations. All Schmithals points out is: (*a*) in 1.1–2.12; 4.1–5.28 Paul is not as precisely informed about Thessalonica as might be expected after Timothy's return; (*b*) whereas in 2.13–3.13 he appears full of joy because of the good news brought by Timothy, in 2.1–12 he is busy defending his own conduct as if there was no reason for joy. We acknowledge that at times there is a certain vagueness in 1.1–2.12; 4.1–5.28, but this can be attributed in some measure to Paul's pastoral tact (see notes throughout). Paul can write a truly joyful letter like Phil. yet show considerable worry and displeasure (Phil. 1.15–18; 2.19–30 with their fulsome praise of Timothy and

Epaphroditus imply that Paul realizes his associates may not be acceptable to the Philippians; if Phil. 3.2ff is part of this letter, our point is all the more true). Schmithals' view would be stronger here if we could agree with him on the existence and identity of Paul's opponents in Thessalonica.

(v) More positively we can argue that there are links between Schmithals' letters B and D which suggest they were always a unity. Jewett argues that the epistolary benediction of 3.11–13 takes up themes in the earlier part and cannot therefore be dissociated from it (see on 3.11–13). K. Thieme, 'Die Struktur des ersten Thessalonicher-briefes' in *Abraham Unser Vater* (Festschrift für O. Michel), Leiden and Köln, 1963, pp. 450–8, has argued that the whole letter is held together by recurring words and concepts.

(vi) Paul was both too profound a thinker and too excitable a personality to be held within the categories of a fixed pattern of letter writing. Romans shows how he could allow one section, a theological, which does not really appear in any of his other letters, to dominate the remainder of the material; Gal. shows how he could jettison the thanksgiving. It is therefore easier to assume that he permitted a second thanksgiving period in 1 Th. than to assume that two letters are here combined.

(vii) If a satisfactory exegesis can be made by treating the letter as one letter and if there are no convincing grounds for its division then it is better to regard it as a unity. The success of our exegesis therefore must be the final proof of the unity of the letter.

Before leaving this subject it would be well to note that the views of Schmithals on the structure of 1 Th. are largely independent of his views on the existence and nature of Paul's opponents; either might be accepted without the other. Jewett's views on opponents are not so far different from those of Schmithals but he holds that the letter is a unity.

G. External Testimony

The evidence for any early external attestation for 1 Th. is so slender as to be almost negligible. The Oxford Society of Historical Theology in their publication *The New Testament in the Apostolic Fathers* (Oxford, 1905) rate the evidence of knowledge by Ignatius as D?, by Hermas as D and exclude the other Fathers completely. Other writers (e.g. Askwith, *op. cit.*, pp. 40–52) have taken a brighter view. As evidence they present: (i) Ign. *Rom.* 2.1 depends on 1 Th. 2.4. Ignatius undoubtedly knew some of Paul's letters and Paul frequently uses ἀρέσκειν in them; the contrast in Ign. *Rom.* 2.1 is perfectly natural and not verbally the same as in 1 Th. 2.4. Ignatius may then be indebted here to Paul but by no means necessarily to 1 Th. (ii) The comparison of 1 Th. 5.17 (cf. 2.13) with Ign. *Eph.* 10.1 depends on the doubtful reading ἀδιαλείπτως in the latter. (iii) Hermas, *Vis.* III 9.10 repeats the phrase, 'Live at peace among yourselves', found in 1 Th. 5.13 but the phrase was part of the common catechetical tradition (see on 5.13) and therefore we cannot claim the use of 1 Th. Generally speaking where earlier scholars saw the literary dependence of later writers on the N.T. more recent scholars have seen dependence on the common stock of credal, liturgical and catechetical tradition; thus the proof of actual dependence is much more difficult.

When we move to a slightly later period we find Marcion, about the middle of the second century, including two Thessalonian letters in his Pauline canon and the yet later Muratorian Canon also lists two.

Attention has been drawn to the possibility of a literary dependence one way or the other between 1 Th. 2.16c and T. Levi 6.11; this is unlikely (see notes on 2.16c); the text of T. Levi went through many recensions and we cannot be sure what it was at the time of 1 Th.

It has been argued that some of the later N.T. writings show acquaintance with 1 Th.: (i) 1 Pet. displays similarities to 1 Th. 4.1–12; 5.1–22; these similarities are more easily explained by the use of common catechetical tradition; see notes on the passages and cf. Best, *1 Peter*, pp. 28ff. (ii) R. H. Charles, *Revelation* (I.C.C., Edinburgh, 1920) I, pp. lxxxiiiff, argues that the author of Revelation knew our letter though the only evidence he produces is the dependence of Rev. 16.15 on 1 Th. 5.2 and of Rev. 14.13 on 1 Th. 4.16; the first is traditional material (see on 5.2) and the second is too slender for any deduction to be drawn. (iii) The synoptic apocalypses share much common material with passages in both 1 & 2 Th. but we can neither maintain that these apocalypses were in existence in their present form at the time of 1 & 2 Th. nor that all in them goes back to Jesus; it is equally impossible to argue that the synoptic apocalypses depend on our letters (see notes on the passages).

2. THESSALONIANS

III. 2 THESSALONIANS

A. The Problem

As Jülicher says 'If we did not possess 1 Thessalonians we would not object to 2 Thessalonians' (*Einleitung in das Neue Testament*, 6th edn., 1906, p. 56; this sentence is not in the English translation of the 2nd edn.). By this he means that if we only possessed 2 Th. few scholars would doubt that Paul wrote it; but when 2 Th. is put alongside 1 Th. then doubts appear. There is a great similarity between the two; this is not only one of words, small phrases and concepts but extends to the total structure of the two letters which is in addition different from what is taken to be the standard Pauline form. At the same time the second letter is alleged to be less intimate and personal in tone than the first, and in some of its teaching, particularly in relation to eschatology, to conflict with that of the first. To solve this problem a number of solutions have been offered and after we have briefly looked at the evidence for the use of the letter in the early church we shall examine these in turn; in this way all the normal questions of authorship, unity, order of the letters will be covered.

B. External Testimony

This appears to be stronger than in the case of 1 Th. Marcion knew two letters. The verdict of the Oxford Society of Historical Theology (*op. cit.*, p. 95) is that Polycarp's 'use of 2 Thessalonians appears to be very probable' (on the possibility that he knew it as a letter to the Philippians, see pp. 40–2). Polycarp, *Phil.* 11.3, 4, 'for he *boasts about you in* all the *communities*' and '*do not treat* such men as *enemies*' recall phrases in 2 Th. 1.4; 3.15. Unfortunately this portion of Polycarp's letter is only extant in Latin. It is also exceptionally difficult to date because it is not clear whether at the time of writing Ignatius was or was not dead (cf. P. N. Harrison, *Polycarp's Two Epistles to the Philippians*, Cambridge, 1936; W. R. Schoedel, *The Apostolic Fathers*, ed. R. M. Grant, Vol. V, Camden, N.J., 1967). We are unable therefore to date it with any certainty earlier than A.D. 135 and its information on the date of 2 Th. is then little better than what we learn from Marcion. The only other possible evidence is Ignatius, *Rom.* 10.3 but the phrase 'in the *steadfastness* of Jesus Christ' is too slight to create a link with 2 Th. 3.5 since 'steadfastness' (ὑπομονή) occurs

37

regularly in primitive Christianity. There are good grounds for believing that Justin Martyr may have known our letter (cf. *Dial.* 32.4; 110.2 with 2 Th. 2.3f) but he is slightly later than Marcion and is therefore no help in fixing a *terminus ad quem*. Contacts have also been suspected between 2 Th. 2.3–10 and Asc. Isaiah 4.2ff; the latter passage belongs to one of the Christian portions of the book and is of uncertain date in the second century A.D.; apocalyptic imagery once adopted circulated widely and quickly and the references in Asc. Isaiah are insufficiently exact to warrant the assumption of knowledge of 2 Th. This also goes for Barnabas 2.1 (cf. 2 Th. 2.7). If the first collection of Paul's letters was made towards the end of the first century (see pp. 40f) and contained 2 Th. then it must have existed at that stage, and this is much earlier evidence than anything in the Fathers.

C. An Interpolated Letter?

Various attempts have been made to overcome the alleged differences in the eschatological teaching between 1 Th. and 2 Th. by assuming an interpolation of later material into 2 Th. (for details see Rigaux, pp. 146f; Moffatt, *Introduction*, pp. 81f). These attempts have been unsuccessful because there has been nothing singularly un-Pauline about the passages which have been suggested as interpolations; even if they were omitted there would still remain those passages in chs. 1, 3 from which is drawn the argument against authenticity from the similarity of the two letters.

D. The Recipients

A number of attempts have been made to solve the problem of literary similarity by arguing that the two Thessalonian letters were sent more or less simultaneously to two different groups. Because they were written at about the same time Paul will naturally have expressed himself with the same words and in the same form. A Harnack, 'Das Problem des zweiten Thessalonicherbriefs', *Sitzungberichte der Akademie der Wissenschaften* (Berlin), 1910, pp. 560–78 (cf. Lake, *op. cit.*, pp. 83–6), argued that the community in Thessalonica consisted mainly of Gentile Christians (cf. Acts 17.4) and 1 Th. was written to it; within it however there was a small minority of Jewish Christians and 2 Th. was addressed to them. In support of this he alleged: (i) the greater use of the O.T. in 2 Th.; (ii) the demand in 1 Th. 5.26 for the letter to be read to the whole church, implying that there was a group who worshipped apart and these could only have been Jewish Christians; (iii) the lack of specific Gentile reference in 2 Th. (contrast 1 Th. 1.9f); (iv) 2 Th. is written to the first converts (cf. 2.13f) and in every church these were Jews; (v) 3.2, 'not everyone has faith', is most easily understood of Jews.

Because the 'address' of 2 Th. 1.1f refers to the whole church Harnack supposed that the original address was changed when Paul's letters were collected. There is no textual evidence for this assumption. Apart from that the difficulties raised by Harnack are susceptible of alternative and often easier explanations (see notes on 1 Th. 5.26; 2 Th. 2.13f; 3.2).

Outside the apocalyptic passages in 2 Th. there is little which refers to the O.T. and therefore 2 Th. only seems to have more O.T. colouring because it contains a greater proportion of apocalyptic material than 1 Th. In any case Jewish apocalyptic material was obviously acceptable to Gentile audiences as Mk 13 indicates, and Lake, *op. cit.*, p. 81, n. 3, argues that the extent of Paul's use of the O.T. is determined by his subject matter and not by his recipients. Harnack's thesis implies both that the belief in the presence of the Day of the Lord has appeared within the Jewish Christian community and that the 'loafers' were of Jewish descent. But ex-Jews would have been the least likely group to accept a belief that the End had come since either in the Diaspora they were not interested in it or they would have known from their apocalyptic literature of the need for the fulfilment of particular signs, and if 1 Th. and 2 Th. were written simultaneously we might have expected some warning about the error in 1 Th. since Gentile Christians would have accepted it more easily. Former Jews, whose culture laid great emphasis on the importance of work, would be much less likely than Gentiles to abandon it. More positively, it is improbable that Paul who contested so strongly the possible split between Jewish and Gentile Christians would have so easily acquiesced in a split in Thessalonica and indeed encouraged it by writing separately to the two sections without even mentioning the need to come together. The absence of reproof about disunity is a valid and conclusive argument against any attempt to see a division in the community at Thessalonica (Dibelius viewed 1 Th. as written in a fatherly and intimate manner to the leaders of the church and 2 Th. as written to the whole community; however large sections of 1 Th. are certainly addressed to the whole community); everywhere else Paul fought fiercely against any type of division in the community (cf. 1 & 2 Cor. *passim*; Rom. 14.1-15.6; Phil. 4.2-4; passages like 1 Th. 3.12; 5.11, 15 cannot be compared to these).

If Harnack's Jewish Christian community is rejected as the recipient of 2 Th. it is difficult to see what other division there could have been and therefore other scholars who have sought to solve the problem of 2 Th. by recourse to different recipients have argued that 2 Th. was originally written to another community altogether, the name in the address being later changed. M. Goguel, *Introduction au Nouveau Testament*, Paris, 1925, IV, 1, pp. 335-7, suggested Beroea, the city in Macedonia which Paul visited after Thessalonica. Acts 17.10f tells how the Jews in Beroea welcomed Paul and carefully examined the O.T. with him; this strongly Jewish Christian church would account for the more Jewish colouring of 2 Th. Goguel supposes that at the time when the Pauline letters were collected a copy of the letter to Beroea with the initial address missing was found in the archives of the church at Thessalonica to which it had been loaned (cf. Col. 4.16); the collector of the letters assumed it had been sent to Thessalonica. There is insufficient positive evidence for such a theory and too many inherent improbabilities in it for its acceptance.

Philippi instead of Beroea has been suggested by E. Schweizer, 'Der zweite Thessalonicherbrief ein Philipperbrief?' *T.Z.* 1 (1945) 90-105; cf. the further discussion with W. Michaelis in *T.Z.* 1 (1945) 282-9; 2 (1946) 74 and W. Michaelis, *Einleitung*, pp. 236ff. Schweizer notes that Polycarp in his letter to the Philippians (11.3f) quotes 2 Th. 1.4 and 3.15 after a direct reference to Paul's letter to the Philippians and that in 3.2 he indicates his knowledge of a multiplicity of letters to the Philippians by Paul; he therefore argues that 2 Th. was originally written to the Philippians and a copy sent later to Thessalonica from which it entered the Pauline corpus, though Polycarp himself knew the letter with its original address. Various attempts have been made to amend Polycarp, *Phil.* 11.3, so that the implied reference to a Pauline letter to the Philippians containing 2 Th. 1.4; 3.15 disappears, but none is really satisfactory. Explanations of the plural references in 3.2 have been more successful, e.g. Paul's Philippians is often taken to be a composite letter (on Polycarp, *Phil.* 3.2; 11.3 see W. R.

Schoedel, *op. cit.*, *ad loc.*). In respect of 11.3 it is probably best to allow that Polycarp either was mistaken as to the source of his quotations (he would have been quoting from memory) or had Phil. 4.15f in mind and used words from 2 Th. to summarize his view; his mind appears to have been full of Paul's letters and he continually uses their words without reference to the source; he makes no special attempt to relate the words from 2 Th. to his reference to Paul's Philippian letter. Our 2 Th. would have been Polycarp's *2 Phil.* and he would have needed to distinguish it from 1 Phil., i.e. our Phil. Moreover he speaks of Paul's letter (singular) to the Philippians and since he knew our Philippians this must be it, and there can be no other Philippian letter.

Schweizer's view also encounters the same basic difficulty as Goguel's: how did the address come to be changed? If Paul wrote 2 Th. in the early fifties and if it is recognized as addressed to the Thessalonians in Marcion's canon, at what point was the change made? If the relevant portion of Polycarp's letter is as late as A.D. 135 this is hardly a possibility; some trace of the altered address would have been left in the textual evidence (cf. Ephesians). For Schweizer's theory to have any chance of being true we must assume that all of Polycarp's letter was written prior to the martyrdom of Ignatius (c. A.D. 110), and even this is late for a change in the address to have taken place in such a way that the original completely disappeared.

This raises the not irrelevant matter of the date of the collection of Paul's letters which contained 2 Th. It is not clear how and where this collection came into existence. The author of Acts does not know it, yet shortly afterwards Ignatius shows himself aware of a number of Pauline letters. The conclusion of W. G. Kümmel, *Introduction to the New Testament*, London, 1966, p. 338, seems justified, 'At least by the beginning of the second century, then, a collection of Pauline epistles was known in Asia Minor, and it is thoroughly probable that this canon already contained all of the ten epistles in Marcion's canon'. A number of scholars following Goodspeed have argued firmly that the first collection of Paul's letters must have been made shortly after the composition of Acts for this would have revived interest in Paul (cf. C. L. Mitton, *The Formation of the Pauline Corpus of Letters*, London, 1953, for a full discussion of this and other views; cf. Schmithals, *Paulus und die Gnostiker*, pp. 175–200; from a completely different angle he argues for a collection of seven letters, including 2 Th., by A.D. 90). If 2 Th. was in a collection by A.D. 100 it is most improbable that Polycarp who uses so much of the language of Paul as to imply he knew the collection would have known 2 Th. as a letter to the Philippians.

E. Order of the Letters

Another solution to the difficulties of the relationship of the two letters inverts their order. This goes back as far as Grotius; in more recent times it has been strenuously defended by J. C. West, 'The Order of 1 and 2 Thessalonians', *J.T.S.* 15 (1914) 66–74; J. Weiss, *Earliest Christianity*, New York, 1959, Vol. I, pp. 286–91; T. W. Manson, 'St. Paul in Greece', *B.J.R.L.* 35 (1952–3) 428–47; R. Gregson, 'A Solution to the Problems of the Thessalonian Epistles', *Evangelical Quarterly*, 38 (1966) 76–80. This solution, while it attempts to deal with some of the older objections to Pauline authorship (e.g. alleged differences in eschatological teaching), does nothing to answer the linguistic and structural difficulties. It must be allowed at once that the present canonical order is no evidence for the original order; Paul's letters are not arranged chronologically in the N.T.

The case for the priority of 2 Th. has been strongly argued by Manson, *art. cit.*, who gives five grounds in its favour: (1) In 2 Th. the persecutions are a present reality whereas in 1 Th. they belong to the past (2.14). (2) In 2 Th. the unwillingness of some members to work is a new development of which Paul has just been told (3.11–15) but in 1 Th. the same problem seems to be well known (5.14; cf. 4.11 where 'just as we instructed you' refers to 2 Th. 3.5ff). (3) The emphasis in 2 Th. 3.17 on the letter's genuineness is only appropriate in a first letter. (4) 1 Th. 5.1 says that there is no need of instruction about dates and times for this has already been given in 2 Th. 2.3–12. (5) In 1 Th. 4.9–5.11 Paul is replying to points raised by the Thessalonians and each of these points depends on previous discussions in 2 Th.: (*a*) 1 Th. 4.9–12 arises out of 2 Th. 3.5–15; (*b*) the question about the position of the dead at the parousia implicit in 1 Th. 4.13 arises because in 2 Th. 2.1–12 Paul has told the Thessalonians that the parousia is indefinitely postponed; (*c*) The question implicit in 1 Th. 5.1 (How long until the parousia?) arises because in 2 Th. 2.1–12 Paul has said that the parousia is 'not yet'.

Other arguments have been used. (6) Both Gregson and West
find differences in the eschatological teaching of the two letters:
(a) West holds that 2 Th. is more Jewish and 1 Th. more Gentile
in their outlook on this and that Paul's churches gradually became
more Gentile as time went by; (b) Gregson considers that in this
respect 1 Th. is 'more mature' or is 'written for more mature
Christians'. (7) Gregson holds that in everything on which 1 & 2
Th. teach 1 Th. is fuller and introduces new material. (8) The
church looks much more advanced in 1 Th. than in 2 Th. (Gregson): in 2 Th. 1.3 the love of the Thessalonians is said to be growing while in 1 Th. 4.9ff it seems to have matured; 2 Th. 3.7 says
they ought to imitate Paul while 1 Th. 1.6–10 says they have
done so. (9) There is no reference in 2 Th. to Paul's proposed
visit (1 Th. 2.17–3.5) because when he wrote 2 Th. he had not
yet had the idea of visiting Thessalonica again. (10) It would be
natural that when Timothy went to visit the Thessalonians he
would take written greetings from Paul; these written greetings
are in fact 2 Th. Both Gregson and West place 2 Th. earlier than
Paul's visit to Corinth; Gregson argues that it was written from
Athens and West from Beroea; Manson holds that both letters
were written from Corinth.

These arguments are by no means as convincing as a cursory
reading might suggest. We shall examine them in order.

(1) According to 1 Th. 3.3 (see notes) persecutions are a present
reality at the time of the writing of 1 Th.

(2) 2 Th. 3.10 refers to Paul's oral instructions on his visit;
therefore 1 Th. 4.11 does not need to refer back to 2 Th. 3.11–15
but can equally refer back to that oral instruction. The problem
existed even during Paul's mission; it had not disappeared when
Timothy visited them and so Paul alludes to it in 1 Th. 4.11;
5.14; afterwards it became much more acute and led to the more
detailed teaching in 2 Th. 3.6–15.

(3) 2 Th. 3.17 is difficult whether it belongs to the first or second
writing of Paul to the Thessalonians. None of his other letters
(and most of them are *first* letters; the fact that we do not possess
'second' letters to the Romans or the Galatians does not make the
letters we have any less 'first' letters) contains such a reference.
Paul did not then write 2 Th. 3.17 because 2 Th. is a 'first' letter
but because for some reason he feared a forged letter might exist
(see on 3.17). If 2 Th. is the earlier letter then 3.17 implies a yet

earlier possible forgery; but would a forgery to Thessalonica be a real possibility before at least one authentic letter existed?

(4) 1 Th. 5.1 can refer as readily to preceding oral instruction about dates and times as to 2 Th. 2.1–12.

(5) (a) This is very similar to (2) above; 1 Th. 4.9–12 could as easily have arisen out of the preceding oral teaching (cf. 2 Th. 3.10 for its existence) as out of 2 Th. 3.5–15. (b) The question implicit in 1 Th. 4.13 would emerge much more probably out of the actual death of a member of the community, as the reference to sorrow demonstrates, than out of theoretical speculation on the delay of the End occasioned by 2 Th. 2.1ff. (c) The question implicit in 1 Th. 5.1 would emerge perfectly naturally in any situation where people have been assured that the End is coming reasonably soon. 2 Th. 2.1ff itself only appeared because the situation in Thessalonica had changed through the erroneous teaching of 2.2. As Kümmel (*Introduction*, p. 186) points out, if Paul had been replying in 1 Th. to issues arising out of an earlier letter we could reasonably have expected some allusion in 1 Th. to that letter.

(6) (a) As we have already pointed out in relation to Harnack's theory 2 Th. is by no means so much more Jewish than 1 Th. (b) As Jewett says ('Enthusiastic Radicalism'), this is to judge Paul by modern standards. The situation of 'persecution' which evoked 2 Th. 1.5ff is different from that of 1 Th. and therefore Paul *seems* less mature (Gregson is incorrect in attributing the lack of maturity to the readers; all we can estimate is Paul's maturity). Paul would hardly have matured much in the short interval which Gregson allows between the two letters.

(7) This is not so in relation to the 'loafers'; 2 Th. 3.6–15 is much fuller.

(8) (a) In 1 Th. 3.12, i.e. in the alleged second letter, the love of the Thessalonians is not mature for Paul prays for it to grow. (b) The situation is different: 1 Th. 1.6–10 (see notes) refers to the reception of the gospel by the Thessalonians which is necessarily past, whereas 2 Th. 3.7 refers to the present situation and must therefore be imperative in form.

(9) This is a valid point. We can only say that Paul saw no reason to mention it, but we do not know why he refrained.

(10) This is a gratuitous assumption; Timothy only needed to convey Paul's greetings orally; in any case he is a co-author of 2 Th. and therefore not primarily its bearer but its sender.

We have to note also that difficulties appear if we invert the canonical order of the letters:

(1) 1 Th. 1.9–2.12 which refers to Paul's initial reception by the Thessalonians is much more appropriate in a first letter than in a second; in it Paul gives thanks for the foundation of the community, in 2 Th. 1.3ff for its growth; this is the natural order. If 2 Th. precedes 1 Th. why did Paul not say in 1 Th. that when he wrote 2 Th., as well as when he was with them, he was not soliciting contributions? Why does he not say that in his letter as well as in his presence he was gentle to them, treating them as a nursing mother her children (2.7) or as a father counselling his children (2.11f)? Since *ex hypothesi* the instruction of 2 Th. 3.6–15 ended the attitude of the loafers why is there no reference in 1 Th. to this result? 2.9 almost demands it.

(2) 2 Th. lacks any warm personal greetings (contrast 1 Th. 2.17–3.10); are they not more appropriate in a first letter?

(3) The simplest interpretation of 2 Th. 2.15 (see notes) is a reference to a previous Pauline letter to Thessalonica. If it is not our 1 Th. it has been lost. The assumption that it is our 1 Th. is the easier.

(4) An adequate interpretation of 2 Th. can be given on the assumption that it followed 1 Th., but the success of this can only be estimated as the letter is worked through. It appears that no one who has actually written a commentary on 2 Th. has maintained its priority.

F. Unity

Schmithals, 'Die Thessalonicherbriefe als Briefkompositionen' (cf. *Paulus und die Gnostiker*, pp. 138ff), has made a very different attempt to deal with the problem of 2 Th. He argues that the main objection to Pauline authorship has lain in the peculiar structure of the letter to which Wrede first drew attention (cf. pp. 50–1 *infra*); 1 Th. and 2 Th. both have similar and unusual structures (e.g. two 'thanksgivings' and parts of two 'endings') and therefore both are composite letters. If 2 Th. was an imitation of 1 Th. by a later writer why did he follow its peculiar structure (cf. pp. 50–3) for he knew other Pauline letters? There is imitation but it is not the imitation of one author by another; it is instead the redactor who put together Paul's letters for publication imitating himself or, more precisely, working to his usual pattern of omitting as little as possible and setting material together in large sections (cf. *Paulus und die Gnostiker*, pp. 175ff). Working on this assumption Schmithals divides 2 Th. into two letters: 1.1–12 + 3.6–16 and 2.13f + 2.1–12 + 2.15–3.5 + 3.17f (cf. p. 31 *supra* for the four letters Schmithals finds). 2.13 is the beginning of a thanksgiving period and 2.16f with its prayer followed by a brief paraenesis (3.1–5) the conclusion; but a letter cannot consist of thanksgiving plus conclusion alone; where is the body of the letter? 2.15 refers back to 2.2, and links better to 2.12 than to 2.14 and to 2.12 better than 2.13 links to 2.12; therefore 2.1–12 must be the central portion. 3.17 also relates to 2.2 and 2.15 and so 3.17f must belong also to this letter. Schmithals assumes that all the four letters he discovers were written on the third missionary journey (see pp. 10f) within a brief period, otherwise we cannot account for their verbal similarities. He further argues that if the letters are so arranged the problem of the order of 1 & 2 Th. disappears as irrelevant; those sections of 2 Th. which led scholars to argue for the priority of 2 Th. now indeed have temporal priority and those sections of 2 Th. which were used to argue for the priority of 1 Th. are now in fact later than the corresponding sections of 1 Th. Schmithals instances the aorist 'we instructed' (1 Th. 4.11 = B) which now refers back to the instructions of 2 Th. 3.6–16 (= A) and the more logical order in which the references to persecution now appear. The difficulty of the failure to mention Timothy's visit in a subsequent letter or letters disappears since it is only mentioned in D.

This hypothesis of Schmithals is linked to a more general hypothesis about the first collection of the Pauline letters in which he envisages an editor putting together six Corinthian letters into our two, three Philippian letters into our one, a Roman and an Ephesian (not our Ephesians but Rom. 16) into one (our Romans) and four Thessalonian letters into two; only the Galatian letter remains as one. The editor did this to produce a collection of seven. But why not issue a collection of sixteen? Schmithals points out that later collections (e.g. Ignatius, the letters of Rev. 2, 3) were in sevens; these were influenced by the Pauline collection and so it must have consisted of seven. This is hardly a reason. If it is argued that seven is a sacred number, so also is twelve. Schmithals not only fails to show why there should be only seven Pauline letters in the collection but he fails to outline the situation in which the editor was bound to edit the letters and not simply issue them as they stood. And if he did choose to have seven letters, why not reduce the six Corinthian letters to three and make the much smaller Thessalonian material into one, as he did with the Philippian material? Although Schmithals has given a convincing reason why the form of 2 Th. resembles that of 1 Th. he has not explained why the form of 1 Th. is different from that of the other Pauline letters. By his very possession of all the letters the editor knew what a Pauline letter looked like and in his editorial work on Philippians and Corinthians he maintained this form. Why did he choose another form for the two Thessalonian letters he constructed? It would be easier for Schmithals if he could argue that there was a different editor for the Thessalonian correspondence but his overall theory postulates one editor.

If we now examine letters A and C in more detail we see that while A is fairly easy to understand C is strange. Why did the editor take 2.13f away from the head of C and place it after 2.1–12? Schmithals argues that he did so to maintain the same pattern as in 1 Th. But is this the result? 2 Th. 2.1–12 is exhortation based on doctrine to meet a particular situation; this is precisely what both 1 Th. 4.13–18 and 1 Th. 5.1–11 are and what 1 Th. 2.1–12 is not. If the pattern of 1 Th. was being followed 2 Th. 2.1–12 ought to have come after and not preceded the renewed thanksgiving as it did, *ex hypothesi*, in the material lying before the redactor. There does not seem to be any reason why he should have put 2.15–3.5 before 3.6–16. The latter being paraenetic material would follow adequately after 2.13f + 2.1–12 and would be in the more normal position in a Pauline letter with 2.15–3.5 following it and introducing the end of the letter; the editor would not then have needed to separate 3.17f from 2.15–3.5. On the whole there are no great difficulties in explaining the progress of thought in 2 Th. as it stands at present (see commentary). Schmithals claims that 2.15 follows 2.1–12 better than it does 2.13f. As Jewett ('Enthusiastic Radicalism') points out the transition from 2.12 to 2.15 is abrupt and **so then** would lack any reference. In addition there is no real link between 2.14 and 2.1. The δέ at the beginning of 2.13 seems unnecessary if 2.13f originally stood at the beginning of a thanksgiving period directly after the address, though in its present position it is not difficult (see notes).

The re-arrangement of material which Schmithals has made resolves some of the difficulties that have led scholars to place 2 Th. before 1 Th. (cf. pp. 42–5). But it does not account for all of them: e.g. 2 Th. 3.17 is most easily explained if it is in the first letter; according to Schmithals' re-arrangement it would be in the third. The re-arrangement coheres with reasons (see pp. 42f) (1), (2), (5a), (7), (8a, b), (9), (10); we have seen that most of these do not stand up to examination as valid grounds for altering the order of the letters; it does not cohere with (3), (4), (5b), (5c); (6a), (6b) are indeterminate. The reasons (1), (2), (4) which we have adduced for objecting to the priority of 2 Th. still stand with the rearrangement. The re-arrangement itself moreover creates difficulties in the order of the material. In A the 'loafers' are rebuked and to some extent excluded from the community (Schmithals says they are excommunicated), yet in B (1 Th. 5.14; cf. 4.11f) they are treated as members of the community in good standing and only rebuked, i.e. their sin is now treated as less serious; the traditional order sees their failure as assuming greater seriousness through their continued obduracy. It is possible as Schmithals suggests that 1 Th. 5.5ff created the error of 2 Th. 2.2 but it is just as likely that 1 Th. 2.16 did, though neither may have; 1 Th. 2.16 falls in D, i.e. after 2 Th. 2.2. In B (1 Th. 1.5f, 9f; 2.1ff, etc.) Paul is made to refer back to his original contact with the Thessalonians without reference to the intervening letter A, and C (at 2 Th. 2.14) and D (at 1 Th. 2.13) do the same; D at 1 Th. 2.18 refers to Paul's several attempts to visit the community but never refers to the written contact (three letters, A, B, C, and perhaps replies) which has taken place.

Is Schmithals correct in his claim that 2 Th. repeats the structure of 1 Th? We have already pointed out that because 2.1–12 precedes 2.13f, 2 Th. does not follow that structure. There are other dissimilarities. 1 Th. has in fact three references to thanksgiving (1.2; 2.13; 3.9) but 2 Th. has only two (1.2; 2.13). After the thanksgiving period of 1 Th. there is catechetical instruction (4.3–12) and exhortation based on teaching (4.13–5.11) and finally more catechetical instruction (5.12–22). All that corresponds to this is 2 Th. 3.6–15, resembling most closely 1 Th. 4.3–12. Moreover as Bjerkelund, op. cit., p. 138, points out 2 Th. is different from 1 Th. in that the main section of the letter, 2.1–12, precedes the renewed thanksgiving. If, then, the structure of 2 Th. is not the same as that of 1 Th. a substantial portion of Schmithals' case falls away.

We have already argued (cf. pp. 30–5) that 1 Th. is one letter, but 2 Th. might still be composite. There is the unusual position of the second or renewed thanksgiving (2.13) and the resemblance of 2.16–3.5 to the normal sequence of material in a Pauline conclusion. Sanders, *art. cit.*, finds as in 1 Th. no objection to the renewal at 2.13 of the thanksgiving which he takes to run on to 3.5. 3.5 is then followed by a section introduced by παραγγέλλειν which may be taken as equivalent to the παρακαλεῖν clause which he and Bjerkelund argue regularly follows the thanksgiving period. Thus 3.6–15 is not unnaturally placed. This still leaves two difficulties: (i) The παραγγέλλειν clause (3.6) which follows the thanksgiving does not normally lead through paraenetic material to the conclusion. But such clauses are found near the conclusion of letters and are then followed by paraenetic material, e.g. Rom. 12.1; Eph. 4.1–3; 1 Th. 5.14. Paul, after starting on a παραγγέλλειν = παρακαλεῖν clause which is followed by paraenetic material containing a great deal of ethical teaching and forming one of the two main reasons for writing the letter, may have decided that the clause fulfils a threefold purpose, viz., makes the normal step forward from the thanksgiving, introduces a main subject, and allows the approach to the conclusion; in other words he telescopes normal literary practice; does not everyone who writes letters do this kind of thing from time to time? We have already seen that his practice in 1 Th. differs from that of some of his other letters; it also varies in Gal., where there is no thanksgiving period; may we not have another variant there? We have too few letters of Paul to draw up rigid rules about his habits. (ii) The internal arrangement of the material in 2.16–3.5 is unusual for there are two prayers (2.16f; 3.5); incidentally this abnormality remains with Schmithals' rearrangement for both fall in letter C. In 1 Th. we have two prayers, 3.11–13 and 5.23f, but they are far apart, and 5.23f corresponds in position to 2 Th. 3.16 and not to 2 Th. 3.5. In 1 Th. 3.9 we have a renewal of thanksgiving followed by one prayer (3.11–13; cf. Phil. 1.3, 9–11; Col. 1.3, 9–12); this therefore is not unusual. Neither is the presence of a request for prayer (3.1f) within a thanksgiving period (2 Cor. 1.11; cf. Phil. 1.19), nor the personal details which are obviously suggested by 3.2 (cf. Rom. 1.11–15; 1 Cor. 1.10ff; 2 Cor. 1.15ff), though we may not have the necessary information to understand them. Again there are parallels at the thanksgiving stage in other letters to 3.3 (cf. 1 Cor. 1.8f; Phil. 1.6; Col. 1.12f) and to 3.4 (2 Cor. 1.7; Phil. 1.6f). Thus only verse 5 is exceptional in being a second prayer. Justification for it can only be obtained from the context (see notes) and rejection of it can only be occasioned by assuming that Paul always followed a rigorous pattern without deviation, and this has never been proved.

We therefore assume that 2 Th. stands today in the same form as it was when originally written.

G. *Authenticity*

The most drastic solution to the problem of the relationship of the two Thessalonian letters is that which denies the Pauline authorship of the second. (Curiously no one seems to have attempted to solve the problem by denying the Pauline authorship of the first while retaining that of the second.) At least as far back as J. E. C. Schmidt (1798) Pauline authorship was attacked. (For the history of older discussions see Bornemann, pp. 498–537, and for more recent work, Rigaux, pp. 124–52.) Generally speaking the earlier attacks were made because (i) of alleged differences in eschatological teaching between 1 & 2 Th., (ii) 2 Th. 3.17 so vigorously affirmed authenticity as to arouse suspicion, (iii) the teaching of 2.3–12 appeared to pre-suppose the *Nero redivivus* legend, (iv) 2 Th. seemed less intimate and personal than Paul's other letters and than 1 Th. in particular.

A new chapter in the discussion was opened by W. Wrede, 'Die Echtheit des zweiten Thessalonicherbriefes', *T.u.U.*, 24, 1903, who developing work by H. J. Holtzmann stressed that the main argument against Pauline authorship lay in the relationship of 2 Th. to 1 Th. The structure of 2 Th. is so similar to that of 1 Th. and so dissimilar from that of the remaining Pauline letters that it could only have been devised by someone deliberately using 1 Th. as a model. For every section of 2 Th. we can find a parallel section in 1 Th., e.g. the renewed thanksgiving of 2 Th. 2.12 repeats that of 1 Th. 2.12; the use of the optative in prayers introduced by 'the Lord (God) himself . . .!' at similar points (1 Th. 3.11–13; 5.27; 2 Th. 2.16; (3.5); 3.16). There are no concrete data in respect of personalities, places, or dates in 2 Th. It draws on 1 Th. developing points in it (e.g. the parousia, the 'loafers').

And, most importantly, there are a great many verbal parallels between the two letters and these appear in the same order in the two letters. It is impossible to list these here in detail and we single out what appear to be the most significant: (*a*) 2 Th. 1.1f and 1 Th. 1.1 resemble each other more closely than any other two Pauline addresses; (*b*) **effort of faith** (2 Th. 1.11) and **achievement of faith** (1 Th. 1.3); these phrases are more nearly identical than our English suggests and do not appear elsewhere in Paul; (*c*) the collocation of **faith, love, endurance** in 2 Th. 1.3f and 1 Th. 1.3; (*d*) **who do not know God** (2 Th. 1.8 and 1 Th. 4.5); (*e*) **finally** (2 Th. 3.1) and **as our last matter** (1 Th. 4.1), which are practically identical in Greek and are rarely used elsewhere by Paul as transition phrases; (*f*) **brothers loved by** (2 Th. 2.13 and 1 Th. 1.4); (*g*) **hard labour and toil, worked, day and night, so as not to be a charge on any of you** (2 Th. 3.8 and 1 Th. 2.9). There are a great many other places where single words appear to be repeated. Such an exact similarity can only arise out of literary dependence; it is quite ridiculous to suppose, as Zahn does (*op. cit.*, I, pp. 249f, n. 6), that Paul had kept a copy of 1 Th. and consulted it before he wrote 2 Th.

Since Wrede little has been added to further the very strong case which he made out. The views of R. Scott, *op. cit.*, do not meet many of the real difficulties of 2 Th. By holding both 1 & 2 Th. to be redactional compositions of separate works by Silvanus and Timothy he accounts neither for the alleged differences in thought, e.g. in eschatology, nor for the literary similarities.

H. Braun, 'Zur nachpaulinischen Herkunft des zweiten Thessalonicherbriefes', *Gesammelte Studien zum Neuen Testament*, Tübingen, 1962, pp. 205–9 = *Z.N.W.* 44 (1952–3) 152–6, sees certain theological differences between 2 Th. and the genuine Pauline letters: (i) In 2 Th. 1.5ff judgement is related to whether a man belongs to the persecuted or to the persecutors and not to his total acceptance or rejection of God; it has thus become 'moralized', a view typical of the post-Pauline period. (ii) This same process of moralization has affected terms like 'obedience' and 'truth' and the retributive nature of God's judgement. (iii) While the thought of the parousia in the genuine letters call forth joy, in 2 Th. 2.1f it leads to anxiety; indeed 'joy' is absent from the whole letter. (iv) The replacement of 'God' by 'Lord' (= Jesus) at 2.13, 16; 3.3, 5, 16 is typical of a period later than Paul.

Masson is one of the few commentators who reject Pauline authorship. (It is curious how the vast majority of the commentators accept the letter as genuine while its rejectors are found among those who approach the letter from the aspect of 'introduction'.) For his main argument he returns to earlier views and sees the eschatological teaching of 2.1–12 as un-Pauline and in conflict with what is found in 1 Th. 5.1–11; in the latter passage the End comes suddenly and unexpectedly and the believer must live in the light so that he may not be surprised; in 2 Th. 2.1–12 there are signs of the End which ought to be looked for, and therefore the End cannot take Christians unawares. Paul when he used apocalyptic material did so to set before men the ultimate issues of life and God; he was not an apocalyptic thinker interested in signs and the date of the End, as we find the author of 2 Th. to be.

The most recent attack on Pauline authorship has come from W. Marxsen, *Introduction to the New Testament*, Oxford, 1968, pp. 37–44. (i) Like Schmithals he finds that the letter is written against Gnostic heretics because of the refutation of their claim that the Day of the Lord has already come (2.2; see notes there) and of the unwillingness of some in the community to work (3.6–15), expressive of a libertinism often found in Gnosticism; unlike Schmithals he does not find that Gnosticism is directly refuted in 1 Th. Consequently the two letters were written to different situations. (ii) Certain Pauline ideas are absent from 2 Th.; in particular there is nothing which shows that the writer believed that eschatology was a present reality, that Christians were already living in the New Age. (iii) The emphasis on apostolic authority (2.15, with its reference to Paul's letters) belongs to a post-Pauline period, and it is by this appeal to Paul's authority that gnostic aberrations are countered. In consequence of his discussion Marxsen dates the letter soon after A.D. 70.

Taken together we have here a strong case against authenticity. Are there any initial and positive reasons for its rejection? As we have seen the linguistic and stylistic evidence favours a common authorship of 1 Th. and 2 Th.—either by Paul himself or by someone in his entourage; we saw that in the case of 1 Th. the former was more probable and so the linguistic evidence would suggest Pauline authorship for 2 Th. We must therefore examine more closely the arguments set out against authenticity, provided we widen the concept of authenticity to include authorship by a companion of Paul writing at his behest (and not one of his companions or someone from a 'Pauline' school writing after his death). The arguments against Pauline authorship fall largely under two heads which at first sight seem almost contradictory, but are not really so: (1) The stylistic and linguistic similarities of 1 Th. and 2 Th.; this was Wrede's main argument and is generally recognized today to be the most serious. (2) The differences between 1 Th. and 2 Th. in matters of content and thought.

(1) (i) Wrede pointed to the structural similarities of the two Thessalonian letters. In discussing Schmithals' attempt to explain the similarity of 2 Th. to 1 Th. as the result of editorial work we saw (pp. 45–50) that this structural similarity is not as great as either he or Wrede allege. In 2 Th. the main theological discussion (2.1–12) falls before the 'second' thanksgiving period and not after it as in 1 Th. (4.13–5.11); there are two references to thanksgiving in 2 Th. (1.3; 2.13) but three in 1 Th. (1.2; 2.13; 3.9); there are three prayers in 2 Th. (2.16f; 3.5; 3.16) but only two in 1 Th. (3.11–13; 5.23). If 2 Th. was written by a post-Pauline continuator (the term 'forger' is loaded) we have to ask why he should choose to follow the structure of 1 Th., and follow it imperfectly, instead of following the structure of one of the other Pauline letters (which scholars who argue against Pauline authorship suppose he knew). If there is a general Pauline epistolary structure why did he not choose to use it? If there is not a general structure (and Gal. has no thanksgiving period) then the similarity of 2 Th. to 1 Th. is not as significant as Wrede supposed. All in all we cannot see that the argument from similarity of structure to non-Pauline authorship has been satisfactorily made. Yet the differences between the two Thessalonian letters and the other Pauline letters remain; it may be due to Paul's creative freedom as a writer or possibly to his employment of Silvanus or Timothy as an 'executive' secretary for both letters but for none of his others.

(ii) It is impossible to enter into details on the minor points of similarity to which Wrede drew attention; it is their cumulative effect which is important. But each point must first be examined individually on its merits in relation to literary dependence. When this is done we find that many of the points Wrede raised disappear and some even turn out to be evidence for the authenticity of the letter: see notes on 1.1, 3, 4, 8, 9, 11; 2.13, 16f; 3.1, 3, 5, 7f.

There are also many little changes between the two letters which do not suggest literary dependence but actually argue against it, e.g. the substitution of **endurance** in 2 Th. 1.4 for **hope** in 1 Th. 1.3, the substitution of **Lord** for **God** in the prayers, the prayer of 2 Th. 2.16f is not as eschatologically oriented as that of 1 Th. 3.11–13 though **strengthen** is used in each of them; see also the notes on 1.3, 4; 2.13; 3.5, 8. The result of this examination of detail suggests that the cumulative value of the similarities is much less than appears at first sight.

(2) (*a*) Braun pointed to various characteristics which led him to place the letter in the post-Pauline period; we shall deal with these in turn: (i) It is the total eschatological orientation of Paul's discussion with the Thessalonians (and this is true of 1 Th.) which has produced the relation between judgement and persecution; had Paul elsewhere been required to deal with eschatology and persecution at the same time he might well have used his terms as he does in 2 Th. (ii) The way in which concepts like 'obedience' and 'truth' are used is by no means so different from Paul's usage elsewhere; cf. A. Strobel, *Untersuchungen zum Eschatologischen Verzögerungsproblem* (Suppl. to N.T. 2), Leiden, 1961, pp. 194ff. In so far as a harsh retributive judgement is seen in God's judgement in 1.5ff the same is already found in 1 Th. 2.16c (see notes). (iii) There is certainly a difference between the attitude to the parousia in 2.1f from that in the other Pauline letters, but the anxiety of 2.1f is not produced by the imminence of the parousia but by the fear that it is past. (iv) The use of 'Lord' instead of 'God' in prayers is ancient; cf. 1 Cor. 16.22.

(*b*) Marxsen's views are akin to those of Braun in that he attempts to find post-Pauline ideas in 2 Th. Against him we would point to: (i) Gnosticism is not the only explanation for the ideas of 2.2 and 3.6–15 (see notes). (ii) In 2 Th. Paul has to stress the futurity of the Day of the Lord because of the false idea of 2.2 and because he is trying to encourage his readers to endure through persecution by reminding them of their future full salvation; the result is that he has little time or inclination to maintain the present nature of eschatology; but the present nature of eschatology is found in 2.13f (see Jewett, 'Enthusiastic Radicalism'). (iii) Paul exercised his authority, whether it is termed apostolic or not, in all his letters (e.g. 1 Cor. 5.3–5; 7.12; Gal. 2.11–14) and there is nothing which goes beyond what we find elsewhere in our letter; indeed, as von Dobschütz pointed out long before Marxsen, why, if the author of 2 Th. wished to emphasize apostolic authority, did he not make Paul describe himself as an apostle? The title is missing in the address of 2 Th. though it is found in all the other letters except Phil. and 1 Th. and it is used in 1 Th. 2.7.

(c) From the beginning of the modern critical period many scholars (most recently Masson) have detected a difference in eschatological thought between the two Thessalonian letters and also between 2 Th. and the other letters of Paul: 1 Th. 5.2 speaks of the parousia as coming suddenly and unexpectedly; 2 Th. 2.1ff points to signs by which its coming may be detected; 2 Th. 2.3ff is difficult to reconcile with 1 Cor. 15.23ff. The solution of Giblin that 2 Th. 2.1ff does not deal with 'signs' is unacceptable (see notes, esp. on 2.3). But the difference between 1 Th. 5.2ff and 2 Th. 2.1ff is not as great as it is sometimes made out to be. In 1 Th. 5.1 Paul uses the phrase **dates and times** in such a way as to imply it is a technical term known to the Thessalonians; if so it can only refer to **dates and times** of certain events, not one event, but a series of events; this implies that on his original visit Paul taught about a sequence of events leading up to the parousia; in 2 Th. 2.1ff he does no more than remind his readers of this sequence. Does this not then imply a conflict between 1 Th. 5.2 (the Day comes as a thief in the night) and 1 Th. 5.1? This makes the problem more acute. But let us note: (i) It removes the contradiction between the two letters. (ii) A sequence of events which are few in number, as in 2 Th. 2.1ff, is not an exact clue to date; the sequence may be fulfilled and then at some later date the End come suddenly and unexpectedly. (iii) In the synoptic apocalyptic passages we find the same alleged 'conflict' between signs and unexpectedness, sometimes in adjacent sections (Mk 13; Mt. 24; Lk. 17.24f; 21.7ff). Apparently the early church did not see the conflict between these views. (iv) We ought also to note that Paul could change his eschatological reference with changing circumstances: 1 Th. 2.16 (see notes) is at variance with Rom. 9–11. Curiously 2 Th. 1.5ff differs from Rom. 11.25ff in a very similar way because both it and 1 Th. 2.16 are much harsher in tone in relation to the ultimate fate of unbelievers. 1 Th. 4.13ff differs in part from 1 Cor. 15.51ff.

(d) It has been argued that 2 Th. is much less personal than 1 Th.; if we omit the self-defence of 1 Th. 2.1–12, which by its nature must be highly personal, this difference is no longer significant. Whatever warm personal elements are found in 1 Th. arise out of its subject matter.

(e) From time to time various other arguments have been used: (i) 3.17 by its over-emphasis is said to suggest an imitator; there are valid alternative explanations: see notes on 3.17 and also on 2.2, 15. (ii) In the nineteenth century 2.1ff was held to be dependent on the *Nero redivivus* legend, but our greater knowledge of Jewish apocalypticism renders this improbable.

(3) What concrete situation could have produced 2 Th.? This question requires an answer whether or not the letter is Pauline. Those who regard it as post-Pauline do not agree about the situation: (i) Wrede dates it around A.D. 100 saying that it was not written for Thessalonica but for another church though its writer addressed it to Thessalonica; it could not have appeared originally in Thessalonica since people there would have asked where it had been hidden all the time since Paul's death; a distant church would not have been so inquisitive, particularly if they knew that Thessalonian correspondence existed; the absence from the letter of personal data about Paul and the Thessalonians would make its acceptance easier. (ii) Masson suggests that it was written towards the end of the first century to counter the belief that the Day of the Lord had come. (iii) Marxsen places it soon after 70 A.D. and says it was written to counter Gnosticism. If the widely accepted theory that the first collection of Paul's letters was made at least by the beginning of the second century and that this contained 2 Th. is valid then a date nearer A.D. 70 rather than the end of the century is more probable.

The letter itself gives no precise data which can help us to place it in its true situation if we reject 1.1f as genuine. All we can learn is that some in the community to which it was written were unwilling to work for their living, but the typical Hellenistic attitude to labour could have produced this at almost any period. Others, probably not the same people, believed the End had come; such a belief may also be present in 1 Cor. 4.8; if its origin is gnostic or libertinistic Schmithals and Jewett are willing to date this as possible in Paul's own lifetime, but Marxsen concludes that it must have been later. This is little help in finding a date and situation. The community were aware of two figures: (i) the *Rebel*, who would not have been so termed by the end of the first century but would have been called the 'anti-Christ'; (ii) the *katechon*, whose failure to materialize in any other contemporary, or near contemporary, literature also suggests an early date. Despite this vagueness the references in 2.2 and 3.6–15 together with the very use of *Rebel* and *katechon* as semi-technical terms are sufficiently definite to imply that 2 Th. was not a general letter like Ephesians or 1 Peter but was written to a particular situation. It is easier to see how a general pseudonymous letter could be accepted than one to a particular community. 2 Th. must therefore either have been written to Thessalonica or to some other community which knew that correspondence with Thessalonica existed; and the author certainly knew both 1 Th. and the major Pauline letters as is proved by the use of Pauline language. If it was written to a community other than Thessalonica then we have to suppose a community which was eschatologically oriented like Thessalonica and which was also troubled by those who were unwilling to work. This demands too much; therefore we assume that it was written to Thessalonica. If the author knew other Pauline letters than 1 Th. then the beginnings of a Pauline collection must already have existed, and *ex hypothesi* this collection did not contain 2 Th. This conflicts with the generally accepted view that 2 Th. was part of the first collection and would imply that the date of the first collection was much earlier than usually supposed. Moreover if the author knew the other Pauline letters why did he not follow the general pattern of those letters rather than approximate his pattern to the unusual structure of 1 Th.? There must have been some reason for keeping to the latter; this can only be solved by assuming that 2 Th. was written to a congregation which knew only 1 Th. (though the writer himself may have known more letters) and therefore it must have been written to Thessalonica.

We must now look more closely at the possible date of writing. We have seen that if the letter is written against a gnostic or libertinistic group any date in or after Paul's life-time is possible depending on how the evidence is read in relation to the spread of gnosticism and 'libertinism' in the first century. We saw that Marxsen and Braun offered evidence implying a date late in the first century but examination showed that this evidence was not convincing. Is there any positive evidence which would conflict with a post-Pauline date and therefore suggest that the letter belongs to an earlier period? (i) If 2.4 refers to the temple in Jerusalem (see notes) then its existence is implied, i.e. the letter is prior to A.D. 70; this is not as strong an argument as it looks, for the apocalyptists often write as if things are still in existence when they are not (cf. Rev. 11.1ff re the Temple). (ii) 2.7 implies that the process leading to the End is already in being, i.e. the eschatological expectation is no less in 2 Th. than in 1 Th. The primitive nature of the eschatological expectation in 2 Th. has often been commented on as fitting into an early period in Paul's thought. (iii) There is no reference in 2 Th. to office-bearers (1 Th. 5.12 shows a rudimentary organization); if the letter was written towards the end of the first century it is difficult to see how the author could have avoided making some reference to them, instructing them to carry out the disciplining of the 'loafers' (3.6–15) and to enforce the teaching of 2.3ff against heresy; there is no idea of the developed orthodoxy and its defenders that we find in later literature. (iv) The method by which discipline is to be exercised (3.6–15) is obscure and implies that the concept of discipline itself was not yet even clear. (v) Tradition has obviously been given to the church (cf. 2.15; 3.10) but we are not yet in the situation where care is being taken to preserve this tradition and hand it on to those who follow (cf. the Pastorals). (vi) There were 'loafers' at the time of Paul's own visit and at the time of the first letter (1 Th. 4.11; 5.14; cf. 2 Th. 3.7–10); did this problem continue so long that a letter was necessary after Paul's death to drive home his teaching again? If the problem was so persistent in Thessalonica why do we not hear more about it from other areas of the church?

All in all it seems preferable to conclude that 2 Th. was written by the author of 1 Th. who was probably Paul but may have been Silvanus or Timothy; if so it must have been written about the time of 1 Th. because of the similarity of language and structure.

H. *Occasion, Date, Place of Writing*

The answers to these questions have been determined by the preceding discussion. If the letter is post-Pauline it will have been written shortly after A.D. 70 to the church in Thessalonica to deal with a situation created by gnostic or libertinistic elements in the community; the place of writing is indefinite but since the Thessalonian situation is known to the writer and he is seriously concerned over it it must have been written by someone living in the situation or by someone who had just paid a visit to it.

If the letter is Pauline, as we believe it to be, it will have been written shortly after 1 Th. to meet a new situation in respect of eschatology and a deteriorating situation in respect of idleness; we do not know from where Paul received his information. Paul had still the same associates with him as were present when he wrote 1 Th.; it was probably therefore written shortly after 1 Th. from Corinth. It is preferable to suppose that Paul as he wrote remembered much of 1 Th. and used the same language than to suppose that he had kept a copy of 1 Th. and re-read it. Often having formed a phrase or come to use a word writers continue to use them for a time and then gradually change to others; this characteristic may well explain both the resemblances and the subtle differences in the use of words. 2 Th. will have preceded any second visit Paul may have paid to Thessalonica. If we were to date 1 Th. on the third missionary journey (see pp. 7–11) then we would have to date 2 Th. at the same time, for 2 Th. is so bare of concrete detail that there is no means of determining its date independently of 1 Th.

ADDITIONAL NOTE, page 2. J.–B. Frey, *Corpus Inscriptionum Judaicarum*, I, p. 504, records a Jewish grave inscription (end of second century A.D.?) and B. Lifshitz and J. Schiby, 'Une synagogue samaritaine à Thessalonique', *R.B.* 75 (1968) 368–78, give information about a later fourth century Samaritan synagogue in Thessalonica (I am indebted to Dr H. Chadwick for both these references).

1 THESSALONIANS

ADDRESS AND GREETING 1.1

From Paul, Silvanus and Timothy to the Christian community of the Thessalonians in God the Father and the Lord Jesus Christ: grace and peace be with you.

Although unlike the form of a modern letter the form of this letter, as of all those by Paul, follows contemporary conventions. Letters began with the address 'A to B', invariably followed by a greeting (1.1) and sometimes also by a prayer of thanksgiving (cf. 1.2ff) or a prayer for the good health and prosperity of the recipient. Each item could be quite lengthy and Paul often does expand the simple form (cf. Rom. 1.1–7; Gal. 1.1–5); those of the Thessalonian letters are his briefest. His letters are neither private and personal communications nor public letters intended for publication to the world at large; they are directed to particular Christian communities, probably to be read aloud when they met together (cf. Col. 4.16).

In all his other letters, apart from 1 & 2 Th. and Phil., **Paul** describes himself at the beginning as an 'apostle' (cf. 2.7). In those other letters he may use it to make his apostolic authority clear at the outset in view of the advice and counsel he has to give later. Our two letters, no less than the others, bear the stamp of his apostolic authority, and it may be that in these two early letters he is not yet aware of the need to make this explicit; when he does use the title in later addresses it may be a part of the general development and growth of the address as he uses it. There may also be special reasons for its omission in Phil. 1.1 (cf. Best, 'Bishops and Deacons: Phil. 1.1', *Studia Evangelica* IV, *T.u.U.*, Vol. 103, 1968, pp. 371–6). Since he terms Timothy and Silvanus apostles at 2.7 he cannot be omitting it here because he does not wish to term them 'apostles'. (He may be making such a distinction between himself and his associates in 1 Cor. 1.1; 2 Cor. 1.1; Col. 1.1). As in other letters Paul joins his helpers' names to his own in the address (cf. 1 Cor. 1.1; Phil. 1.1; etc). **Silvanus** (on the possible share of Silvanus or Timothy in the composition of the letter see pp. 23–9) is the Silas of Acts 15.22ff; 16.19ff; the two names probably represent Latin and Greek transliterations of the same Jewish name (See Rigaux, *ad loc.*, Selwyn, *op. cit.* p. 241); just as Paul always calls himself by his Roman name and not Saul, so he always uses **Silvanus**. According to the story in Acts Silvanus was with Paul on his mission to Thessalonica (17.4) and Timothy was certainly in Macedonia (18.5) and may also have been in Thessalonica itself. (On the founding of the church in Thessalonica see pp. 2ff) Silvanus had been one of those who were sent by the Jerusalem church to the Gentile churches with the 'apostolic decrees' about the entry of Gentiles into the Church (Acts 15.22ff) and had later joined with Paul in missionary service (Acts 15.40). Whether the Silvanus (Silas) of the Pauline epistles and Acts is the same as the Silvanus of 1 Pet. 5.12 is not quite certain (see Best, *1 Peter*, pp. 55ff). **Timothy**, of mixed Jewish and Gentile parentage from Galatia (Acts 16.1), was a more junior companion; later he became a well-known figure in the early church so that either Paul wrote letters to him or, more probably, pseudepigraphical letters addressed to him appear; this would not have happened in the case of a nonentity; in view of the latter possibility we cannot be sure how much of the detail given about him reflects genuine tradition as to his religious upbringing (2 Tim. 1.5; 3.14f).

Christian community: the Greek word ἐκκλησία is normally rendered 'church', but this suggests a more formal organization than existed in this period. Originally the word denoted an assembly of people (cf. Acts 19.32, 39) but it had been used by the Greek translators of the O.T. for the people of God, whether assembled together or not, and so in the N.T. it is not a neutral concept, 'community', but has always a definite and necessary religious content (cf. Rom. 16.1, 4(!); 1 Cor. 4.17; 6.4, etc., where it is used without qualification) which is brought out here by the addition of the adjective **Christian.** It is used for the whole Christian community (1 Cor. 10.32; 12.28; Col. 1.18, 24), for the Christian community in a town (Rom. 16.1; 1 Cor. 1.2), for the Christian community in a house (Rom. 16.5; 1 Cor. 16.19; Col. 4.15) of which there may be many in the town. The use of one word for all these indicates that the whole is not regarded merely as the sum total of the units but rather that the whole appears as smaller units in particular places, the whole being the basic conception. (Cf. R. N. Flew, *Jesus and His Church*, London, 1938;

G. Johnston, *The New Testament Doctrine of the Church*, Cambridge, 1943, pp. 35–45; K. L. Schmidt, *T.D.N.T.* III, pp. 501–536.) **Thessalonians** defines the Christian community as that found in Thessalonica; it is not a community on its own but part of the whole people of God.

in God the Father and the Lord Jesus Christ: Paul is particularly fond of using **in** with the various titles and descriptions of Jesus: in Christ, in the Lord, etc. By this he means that for the believer salvation lies **in** what God accomplished by Christ's life, death and resurrection (**in** with an instrumental sense) and that the believer is made a member of the body of Christ (**in** with a spatial sense which it can have because Christ is conceived as an 'inclusive personality'). Sometimes one sense predominates and sometimes the other. Here it is the first since **in** with Christ must be used in parallel fashion to **in** with God and Paul nowhere thinks of the believer as 'in God' in the spatial sense (Acts 17.28 does not represent Paul's original words though placed on his lips by Luke). In comparison with his frequent usage of 'in Christ' Paul rarely uses 'in God'. To be a member of the Christian community is to participate in the salvation which has been achieved by God through Christ. Here then we may take the phrase to mean primarily 'the Christian community brought into being by God the Father and our Lord Jesus Christ', yet we cannot completely exclude the secondary meaning that the community stands in a special relationship to Christ, a relationship elsewhere spelt out by Paul as being Christ's body. This may be part of the reason Paul does not simply say 'by God through Christ', but Paul also regularly puts God the Father and the Lord Jesus Christ together without distinguishing their function in salvation. The phrase does much more, then, than differentiate the Christian assembly from the Jewish synagogue or any secular gathering in Thessalonica, for as we have seen in Christian usage this differentiation is already contained in ἐκκλησία. (On 'in Christ', see Best, *One Body in Christ*, London, 1955, pp. 1–33; M. Bouttier, *En Christ*, Paris, 1962; F. Neugebauer, *In Christus*, Göttingen, 1961). God is occasionally termed **Father** in the O.T. (e.g. Deut. 32.6; 2 Sam. 7.14; Isa. 63.16) and in Greek literature but never with the same frequency as we find it in the N.T. nor with the same depth of meaning. The N.T. usage goes back to Jesus himself who in applying the word to God used it himself and taught his disciples to use it in a more intimate way than it had been used previously (see J. Jeremias, *The Prayers of Jesus* (S.B.T. 2nd series, 6) London, 1967, pp. 11–65; G. Schrenk and G. Quell, *T.D.N.T.* V, pp. 945–1014). The description of God as Father alongside the reference to Christ is not an attempt to define their mutual relationship as in later Trinitarian discussion but to indicate God's relation to men, just as Lord denotes that of Christ to men. We cannot however exclude the conception of God as the Father of Christ (cf. Rom. 15.6; 2 Cor. 1.3) for the single occurrence of **in** binds the whole phrase closely together. In the phrase **Lord Jesus Christ** the personal name Jesus is defined by two seemingly more theological concepts. **Christ,** the Greek equivalent of the Hebrew *Messiah* (both mean 'anointed one'), passed fairly quickly from use as a title to being the equivalent of a personal name; because of its Jewish origin it must have been applied to Jesus from the earliest period of the Palestinian Christian community. The use of **Lord** probably also dates back to the community since a partial Aramaic equivalent for it was in use in Greek speaking congregations (1 Cor. 16.22). By the time of Paul the Greek word had a wide background of meaning because it was used in the LXX to translate the divine name and in the non-Jewish world to denote the deities of many religions and also the Emperor when he was accorded divine honours. This should not be taken to imply a deliberate equalization of Jesus with God by Paul but does suggest that in Jesus Paul saw God expressed and expressing himself. In the early church the term was widely used in worship (e.g. 1 Cor. 12.3; Rom. 10.9) where exactitude of theological definition is not to be expected. (On both terms, see O. Cullmann, *The Christology of the New Testament*, London, 1959, pp. 111–36, 195–237; L. Cerfaux, *Christ in the Theology of St. Paul*, Edinburgh and London, 1959, pp. 461–79, 480–99; W. Kramer, *Christ, Lord, Son of God* (S.B.T. 50), London, 1966, *passim*.)

Grace and peace be with you: the normal greeting in a contemporary letter in the Greek world would have been the simple word 'greetings'; **grace** comes from the same Greek root. By this alteration Paul (or some pre-Pauline Christian writer) has transformed the customary greeting into one with deep theological import. Accompanying it is the normal Jewish salutation **peace.** This 'designates the unimpairedness, the wholeness, of a relationship of communion, and so a state of harmonious equilibrium, the balancing of all claims and needs between two parties' (G. von Rad, *Old Testament Theology*, London, 1962, I, p. 130). It does not therefore signify primarily an internal condition of contentment but a relationship between God and man, and Paul's greeting is here concerned with the relationship not between himself and his readers but between them and God; he desires that they may be wholly at one with God; the entire Gospel is involved in this word (cf. G. von Rad and W. Foerster, *T.D.N.T.* II, pp. 400ff; E. M. Good and C. L. Mitton, *I.D.B.* III, pp. 704–6; L. Morris, *The Apostolic Preaching of the Cross*, London, 1955, pp. 210–17). This is true also of the other half of the greeting, **grace**, whose meaning for Paul runs back into the O.T. rather than into secular Greek usage. But Paul has made it so much part of his own vocabulary that its meaning must be found in his own usage. 'Grace has two basic strands in its make-up. There is the thought of the freeness of God's gift, and there is the thought of the power that God gives.' (L. Morris, *The Cross in the New Testament*, Exeter, 1965.) Thus like peace it implies the fullness of God's free unmerited gift of salvation and a relationship between man and God which has been created by God through the Christ-event, which does not depend on any effort by man and which enables him to live as a Christian. (On **grace**, see C. R. Smith, *The Biblical Doctrine of Grace*, London, 1956; A. Richardson, *An Introduction to the Theology of the New Testament*, London, 1958, pp. 281–4; R. Bultmann, *Theology of the New Testament*, London, 1952–5, pp. 288–92.)

THANKSGIVING FOR THE THESSALONIANS
1.2–10

(2) We are always thanking God for you all, constantly mentioning you whenever we pray, (3) remembering your achievement of faith, costly labour of love and endurance of hope directed towards our Lord Jesus Christ before our God and Father (4) since, brothers loved by God, we know your election: (5) that our Gospel did not come to you with words only but with power and with the Holy Spirit and with much conviction, as you know the kind of people we were among you for your own sakes; (6) and you for your

part became imitators of us and of the Lord, in receiving the word in much tribulation with joy of the Holy Spirit, (7) so that you became an example to all the believers in Macedonia and Achaia. (8) For the word of the Lord has sounded out from you not only into Macedonia and Achaia but your faith, a faith in God, has come into every place, so that we have no need to say anything (about you); (9) for these report about us the kind of an entrance we had to you and that you turned to God from idols, to serve the living and real God, (10) and to wait for his Son out of heaven, whom he raised from the dead, Jesus who delivers us from the approaching anger.

1.2–10 is one long untidily constructed sentence which it is difficult to punctuate and in which it is difficult to place each adverbial phrase accurately. It forms part of the 'thanksgiving' which follows the 'address' and 'greeting' in every letter of Paul (except Galatians where he was in no mood to thank God for the behaviour of the recipients). The 'thanksgiving', though occurring sometimes, was not a regular part of contemporary letters and Paul would therefore appear to have largely evolved a new form for himself, one which was later abandoned by Christian writers. The 'thanksgiving' in our letter appears to be much longer (1.2–3.13) than in Paul's other letters (cf. pp. 31–4), though if Paul is evolving a new form and this is an early letter we need not expect consistency with the later letters.

In 1.2–10 Paul thanks God for the way in which the Thessalonians have expressed their faith (v. 3) and for its ultimate ground in God's choice of them as Christians (v. 4), which was made clear in the successful mission by Paul to Thessalonica (v. 5) and in their response, despite tribulation (v. 6), for they became an example to others (v. 7) and a spur to evangelical activity (v. 8) by their complete acceptance of the faith, whose content is expressed in a credal form (v. 9f).

We are always thanking God: Paul takes to heart his own 2 admonition of 5.18. He likes the word εὐχαριστεῖν **(thanking)** and uses it especially at the beginning of his letters (Rom. 1.8) 1 Cor. 1.4; etc.). Elsewhere it is associated with the Lord's Supper (1 Cor. 11.24; Mk. 14.23; Mt. 26.27; Lk. 22.17) and probably under the influence of the latter is used in the feeding

65

miracles (Mk. 8.6; Mt. 15.36; Jn. 6.11, 23; Acts 27.35?), eventually giving the name Eucharist to the sacrament. Paul's usage is not so restricted and here as almost always with him the word has a wider significance. He does not make clear when this thanksgiving actually takes place, whether in prayers offered in public worship or in the prayers which he, Silvanus and Timothy offered individually or together in private. The plural form of the verb (contrast Rom. 1.8; 1 Cor. 1.4; etc.) suggests that Silvanus and Timothy had some share in thanksgiving (on the use of the first person plural see pp. 26–9). Paul's prayers are normally addressed to **God,** though this was not the invariable practice of the primitive church if, as probably, 1 Cor. 16.22, 'Lord, come' is a prayer addressed to Christ (cf. 3.11). The present thanksgiving is comprehensive both temporally **(always)** and personally **(you all)**, but this does not imply that there was any division or schism in the Thessalonian community. By this use of **you all** rather than of a corporate term like 'church' Paul shows his interest in them as individuals within the whole community. Rom. 16 (whether this chapter was written to Rome or not) evidences Paul's interest in the individual members of his churches; but he never refers to particular individuals in his thanksgivings because this would be invidious; it is what has happened through all of them that draws out his praise. Thanksgiving is always a part of Paul's prayers: **whenever we pray,** *lit.* 'at the time ($\dot{\epsilon}\pi\dot{\iota}$ not here in its more normal local sense but in its secondary temporal sense, cf. Moulton–Turner, p. 271) of our prayers'. The plural 'prayers' suggests a number of acts of prayer. **constantly** can be taken as qualifying either **mentioning** or **remembering** (v. 3); there is nothing in Pauline usage to determine which. If the word is taken literally it is difficult either way, but we may suppose that Paul uses it hyperbolically; he does not spend all his time praying about them (cf. 5.17 where the word is again used). The rhythmic structure of the sentence appears to favour its connection with **mentioning** (so Rigaux); we then have three participles, **mentioning, remembering, knowing** (v. 4), each dependent on **are thanking,** each standing at the head of its clause and each introducing a new facet of Paul's thought about the Thessalonians. But with whichever verb we associate the adverb the thought remains the same, emphasizing the **always** of the first clause: the Thessalonians are never far from the prayers and thoughts of Paul and his companions.

In order to give thanks and pray intelligently it is necessary to know something of those who are prayed for and Paul reveals this knowledge in **remembering your achievement of faith** and in **we know your election** (v. 4). Though he is aware they have faults (3.10) he thinks first of the great worth of their new lives as Christians, and this forms the basis of his prayer of thanksgiving. He expresses this worth in three parallel phrases: **achieve-** 3 **ment of faith, labour of love, endurance of hope.** Here we encounter, though in a different order, the triad **faith, love, hope** known from 1 Cor. 13.13. This triad appears surprisingly often in the N.T. and early Christian literature: Rom. 5.1–5; Gal.5.5f; 1 Th. 5.8; Col. 1.4f; Eph. 4.2–5; Heb. 6.10–12; 10.22–24; 1 Pet. 1.3–8; 1.21f; Barnabas 1.4; 9.8; Polycarp, *ad Phil.* 3.2f; A. M. Hunter (*op. cit.*, pp. 33–5) claims 'that the triad in Paul is not his own creation, but something common and apostolic, perhaps a sort of compendium of the Christian life current in the early apostolic church'. Since all the non-Pauline references to the triad are clearly later than Paul it is possible that Paul himself is its creator. On a possible extra-Christian origin to the formula see Lietzmann–Kümmel, *An die Korinther* (4th edn.), Tübingen, 1949, *ad* 1 Cor. 13.13 and for criticism, see C. K. Barrett, *1 Corinthians*; E. B. Allo, *1 Corinthians*, also at 13.13. In the present passage each of the triad is qualified by a word which suggests activity; the triad thus does not consist of three virtues to be contemplated but three to be expressed. **your** is placed emphatically at the head of the three phrases and should be taken with each; it probably governs each of the six main words, though adhering more closely to the second in each phrase, i.e. 'your achievement of your faith'; certainly not 'your achievement of the faith', but possibly 'the achievement of your faith'. **achievement . . . labour . . . endurance . . . :** each of the triad is qualified by a result flowing from it and is a genitive of the subject (cf. Moulton–Turner, p. 211); this gives to the triad, around which the whole is constructed, its primary importance. To take them as 'the achievement belonging to, characterized by, faith, etc.' places the emphasis at the wrong point.

your achievement of faith might be objected to at first sight on the ground that Paul normally opposes works to faith. Against this we may argue: (i) when he does so he uses the plural 'works' and not the singular 'work' ($\ἔργον$ = 'achievement') as here;

(ii) At times he does use the singular in a good sense, cf. Rom. 2.7; 13.3; 14.20; 1 Cor. 3.14. (iii) The contrast of faith and works relates to the attainment of salvation and not to salvation as it works itself out in daily life as in our context. Thus the present phrase is not at odds with Paul's fundamental objection to 'works of the law'. Indeed in Gal. 5.6 Paul does stress the activity which results from faith—faith works itself out in acts of love. For Paul **faith** is the total response of man to the goodness of God seen in the death and resurrection of Christ through which man is redeemed; such a total response includes man's obedience to God and must therefore result in activity **(achievement)** on the part of man. Paul does not specify here what he takes that activity to be, whether direct missionary work in the preaching of the Gospel or acts of goodness and kindness towards others or loyalty to Christ; the latter seems most appropriate here since **faith** sometimes passes into the sense 'faithfulness' and 1.6 refers to the tribulations the Thessalonians have experienced on becoming Christians. It is possible that in view of the accompanying reference to hope and love, faith may be slightly limited here and the **achievement of faith** relate to the kind of result suggested in 1 Cor. 13.2; 12.9, i.e. acts of healing, etc.; the implication in 1 Cor. 13 that this faith may be inadequate is removed in our context by the reference to love; this would then be the faith that makes the impossible possible (Schürmann).

labour of love: labour (κόπος) is similar to **achievement** in referring to effort but goes beyond it in emphasizing either the fatiguing nature of what is done or the magnitude of the exertion required; the latter is intended here since the one who loves as a Christian is never wearied by his love. The Thessalonians have given themselves with great zeal in their love (note that at 4.9 Paul says he has nothing to teach them about love). Paul frequently uses **labour** and the cognate verb of his own missionary work (1 Cor. 15.10; Gal. 4.11; Phil. 2.16; 1 Th. 3.5) and of that of others (1 Cor. 15.58; 16.16; 3.8; 2 Cor. 10.15). He also uses them of the manual efforts by which he supported himself in this work (1 Cor. 4.12; cf. 2 Th. 3.8). It is used here in the former sense of direct Christian activity rather than of its financial support (cf. F. Hauck, *T.D.N.T.* III, 827-30). This costly exertion is inspired by **love**. This word has a wide range of meaning in English: sexual activity, family affection, friendliness. When the Christians began to express their idea of love in Greek they chose a word (ἀγάπη) which had not been greatly used and was therefore, so to speak, uncommitted in any particular direction; this allowed them to set their own meaning into it. *Agape* and its cognates are used widely by Paul and denote principally God's, and Christ's, love for men and the Christian's love for his fellows. God's love for men is seen in his sending his son to men who do not deserve that God should be good to them, and their love is seen in imitation of his when they seek the complete good of all others including those who appear to be outside the ordinary range of love. This love is neither a mere warmth of heart towards others, for many have to be loved who have nothing about them which would arouse affection, nor is it devoid of warmth, for then it would become a burden. Only very occasionally does Paul use the term for the Christian's love of God (Rom. 8.28; 1 Cor. 8.3; 2.9, in a quotation); it is used relatively much more frequently in this way by John (e.g. Jn. 8.42; 14.15, 21; 1 Jn. 4.20f). We leave the question towards whom the love in our text is directed until after our discussion of the next phrase.

endurance of hope: The N.T. constantly uses ὑπομονή (endurance) for the trials which face Christians (Rom. 12.12; Lk. 21.19; Heb. 10.32; 1 Pet. 2.20), especially in an eschatological context (Mk. 13.13; Rom. 8.25; 2 Cor. 1.6; 2 Tim. 2.12). Paul links it to **hope** also in Rom. 5.3f; 8.24f; 1 Cor. 13.7. It denotes steadfast perseverance in affliction, and the affliction comes not through the ordinary strains and chances of anyone's life but through the persistent and constant trials that affect the Christian because he lives a Christian life and seeks to extend his faith. The **hope** by which this perseverance is inspired is not a 'mere hope', a slender chance that things will turn out all right in the end, but a confident hope that rests on what God has done in Christ (Rom. 5.1–5; 1 Cor. 15.19f), and looks forward expectantly to a complete and final salvation (Rom. 8.18ff; Phil. 1.20), and is thus appropriate to the strongly eschatological tone of our letter. It is this certainty in **hope** that produces **endurance** in trial. (On **hope**, cf. C. F. D. Moule, *The Meaning of Hope*, London, 1953; R. Bultmann and K. H. Rengstorf, *T.D.N.T.* II, pp. 517–35). Paul may have some particular phase of the life of the Thessalonian church in mind when he made this reference, but if so it is lost to us.

Hope always has an object; it is here defined as **our Lord Jesus Christ,** for all certainty rests on the God who has made his nature known through Jesus Christ. Is **our Lord Jesus Christ** also the object of **faith** and **love**? The object of **faith** for Paul is often Christ (Rom. 3.22, 26; Gal. 2.16) but, following the usage of the primitive church, he rarely connects the title **Lord** of the combined formula **Lord Jesus Christ** to faith (cf. Kramer, *op. cit.*, § 3); when we remember also that he rarely uses God or Christ as the object of love it would appear better to take **our Lord Jesus Christ** only with **endurance of hope**. It is possible that **our Lord** . . . should not be taken as a genitive of the object but of the subject: Christ creates faith, hope and love. It is however difficult to have one genitive of the subject following another (endurance has its source in hope which has its source in Christ) and we reject this possibility. This is not to say that the source of faith, hope, love is not divine (cf. Gal. 5.22f); that is assumed here, though not expressed.

Where now is the phrase **before our God and Father** to be attached? It can go either in accordance with its position at the end of the clause with **hope directed . . . Christ** or be referred to **remembering** and govern the whole clause. The former makes a somewhat clumsy expression, though it is not unlike the way in which Paul can pile one qualifying phrase on another; it is thus simpler to take it here with **remembering**; it then rounds off the clause as **constantly** did in v. 2. We are thus reminded that not only are Paul's prayers offered to God (v. 2) but that his thoughts **(remembering)** are always directed to him; he 'thinks' before God as much as he acts before him; his whole life is continually held in the presence of God. That his thoughts are 'before God' is a guarantee that his estimate of the Thessalonians as expressed in this verse is not the result of prejudice or partiality (cf. Plummer).

4   Paul continues his expression of thanks **(we know)** referring now to what God has done in selecting the Thessalonians. This 'selection' and their behaviour (v. 3) are two aspects of the same reality: God chooses and man responds. The latter may be logically the result of the former and testify to it but Paul has recalled it first because it is what can be seen; human knowledge of election rests on it and on knowledge of the way God works. Frame correctly says that **know . . . election** gives the ultimate cause for thanksgiving: without God's antecedent activity there would be no faith, love or hope for which to return thanks; so Paul

does not thank the Thessalonians for their faith, love and hope but thanks God.

Brothers is the ordinary word used in family relationships but prior to Christianity this meaning had been extended both in Greek secular and religious contexts and in Jewish where Jews regarded fellow-Jews as brothers (Jer. 22.18; 1 QS 6.10, 22; CD 6.20f; cf. Josephus, *B.J.* 2.122). While its appearance in a religious context would not then have surprised a Greek its introduction into Christianity goes back at least to the Palestinian period of the church and beyond that to Jesus himself. He gave it a new foundation by the clear way in which he taught his disciples to regard God as their Father; it is explicit in sayings like Mk. 3.31ff; 10.30; Mt. 25.40, for the concept of brotherhood is essential to their content; in passages like Mt. 5.22 'brother' is probably original but may be due to Christian modification of a saying from which it was originally absent. Within the early church the term was widely used of fellow-Christians; it is found in every N.T. writing except 2 John and Jude; the Christian community knew itself as 'the brotherhood' (1 Pet. 2.17; 5.9; 1 Clem. 2.4). The close link between the relationship of Christians to one another and their relationship to God is brought out by the words **loved by God**; it is because both Paul and the Thessalonians know each other to be loved by God and to have responded to that love that they can accept one another as brothers. Though Paul loves the Thessalonians God's love for them is primary and is the sole basis of his approach to them. Paul expresses **loved** here with the perfect participle (cf. 2 Th. 2.13; Col. 3.12, indicating that God's love began in the past and continues steadily) of the verb from the same root as **love** in 1.3, though the normal N.T. word is the verbal adjective ἀγαπητός. On brotherhood in the early church cf. A. Harnack, *The Expansion of Christianity in the First Three Centuries*, London, 1905, pp. 9f, 31f.

God has chosen (**election**) the Thessalonians to be in his church. This idea, offensive to modern (and ancient) ears because it appears to exclude the possibility of man's freedom to choose or reject his religion, was a strong element in early Christianity generally as well as in Paul (cf. Jn. 15.16; 1 Pet. 1.1f; 2.8f). It has often been true that those who believed that their adherence to Christ did not rest ultimately on their own determination, which could vary too easily, have been enabled by their belief in their election to endure unshaken all types of suffering, persecution and even death. Rom. 9–11 shows that Paul was aware of the tension between God's election and human free will for in the midst of a detailed discussion of God's election he makes clear (9.30–10.21) that those who are not chosen have themselves rejected God, but it cannot be said that he has a solution to offer to the tension itself. Election by God harmonizes with Paul's teaching on justification by faith; no one can be a Christian through his own achievement but only because a gracious God enables him through the death and resurrection of Christ. In this sense election is one aspect of the grace of God. Conflict however arises when it is argued that the election of some implies the rejection of others; it is doubtful if Paul ever taught the latter (see also on 5.9), though it is found in the N.T. (1 Pet. 2.8; Jude 4; Rev. 13.8; 17.8; 20.15). The N.T., as the O.T., is largely preserved from this view because it generally regards election as election to the service of God (2 Th. 2.13 is an exception), so much so that even Judas is 'elected' to betray (John 6.70f; 13.11, 18f), and it is also preserved from suggesting the self-satisfaction of the elect because the primary emphasis does not lie on the election of individuals but on that of the church, as of Israel in the O.T. (cf. Rom. 9–11, where it is never a question of the choice of individuals for eternal destiny but always of peoples and nations for historical service). Elements of individual election are present in the N.T. (e.g. Acts 9.15; Gal. 1.15; Rom. 1.1) and came to be stressed much more in some later theology. Since the emphasis in the N.T. lies on election to service we cannot conclude that the elect are necessarily saved eternally; eternal salvation is rarely related to election. Election is something more than a choice by God of men at the time they respond to the Gospel; it implies an antecedent choice by God and this must therefore be non-historical or pre-historical; it does not lie in the historical situation. Its antecedent nature is seen in Rom. 9.11 where Jacob and Esau are selected for different services before they are born; similar ideas operate in Rom. 8.29f; Gal. 1.15 contains the same in relation to Paul himself; in Eph. 1.4ff, which if not by Paul does seem here to interpret his views correctly, this election is described as taking place before the foundation of the world. While there is no temporal reference in 1 Th. 1.4 it is difficult to view Paul as limiting his words to a choice by God of the Thessalonian Christians from the population of the city at the moment of the foundation of their church; this was when their election became effective or when they became aware of it. Election is not explicitly referred here to God but at no place in the O.T. or the N.T. is there any suggestion that anyone other than God elects; certainly the Thessalonians do not elect themselves to be Christians; v. 5 goes on to speak of God's power as active among them, not of their power to choose him. We should note finally the close connection of love **(loved by God)** and election; popular misrepresentation of election depicts God as an arbitrary tyrant playing with the lives of men; God acts because he loves men (cf. Rom. 11.28; Col. 1.13) and elects some to serve him that he may save all (Rom. 11.25ff). On **election** see H. H. Rowley, *The Biblical Doctrine of Election*, London, 1950; A. Richardson, *op. cit.*, pp. 271–81; G. Quell and G. Schrenk, *T.D.N.T.*, IV, pp. 144–92).

We have taken this verse to be explanatory of v. 4 (or of all 5 vv. 2–4) but it might be regarded as giving the ground for it; is ὅτι epexegetical or causal? If it is the former then 1.5 gives the historical occasion and manner of their election; if it is the latter 1.5 gives the grounds on which Paul infers their election, i.e., because the Spirit was at work both in preacher and hearers, or else it gives the ultimate grounds for Paul's thanks to God. Either interpretation suits the context, but when ὅτι appears in the construction εἰδέναι τι ὅτι (Rom. 13.11; 1 Cor. 16.15; 2 Cor. 12.3f; 1 Th. 2.1) it never seems to be causal but always epexegetical (cf. Lightfoot). If it is objected that this requires 'election' to have the meaning 'the manner of your election' a similar qualification must be made in respect of the nouns following εἰδέναι in the examples just listed. Rom. 5.4f; 8.28f are not true parallels because in them we have two ὅτι clauses, the first meaning 'that' and the second 'because'. 1 Cor. 1.26 is a clear parallel to our verse. We therefore take ὅτι as epexegetical and the clause as explanatory (so Rigaux, Milligan, etc). Wohlenberg's suggestion that we should link it directly to **we are always thanking** (v. 2) is excluded by its distance from it.

Paul sometimes speaks of the **gospel** as the gospel of God (Rom. 1.1; 15.16; 2 Cor. 11.7; 1 Th. 2.2), sometimes as the gospel of Christ (Rom. 15.19; 1 Cor. 9.12; 2 Cor. 2.12; 1 Th. 3.2), sometimes as 'my gospel' (Rom. 2.16), sometimes, as here, as **our gospel** (2 Cor. 4.3; 2 Th. 2.14), but more frequently he uses the word absolutely. The gospel originates with God, is about Christ, and is presented by Paul and his associates. Thus Paul does not represent himself here as the author of the Gospel or as its object but as its mediator and **our** indicates he is referring to the historical occasion on which he offered it to the Thessalonians. **Gospel** can denote either the activity of preaching (2 Cor. 8.18; Phil. 4.3, 15) or its content (Rom. 1.16; 2.16; 1 Cor. 9.14; 15.1); the two meanings are closely related and are probably both present here. The activity is the speaking of words but only because the words are what they are is there a result in power and the Holy Spirit. Paul does not allude to the actual nature of the content since he knows his readers will remember it. In the early church the gospel appeared under different forms which may be detected as more primitive elements in the epistles and are set in relation to (*a*) sin and redemption (1 Cor. 15.3–5; Rom. 3.24f; 4.24f), (*b*) the conquest of evil powers (Phil 2.6–11; 1 Tim. 3.16), (*c*) idolatory (1 Th. 1.9f). Eventually it came to be expressed in the Gospel according to Mark in terms of the history of Jesus (Mk. 1.1). (On **gospel**, see G. Friedrich, *T.D.N.T.* II, pp. 707ff; O.A. Piper, *I.D.B.* II, pp. 442ff). Although Paul writes of **our gospel** he does not say that he and his companions brought the gospel to Thessalonica; he uses an impersonal expression **(come to you)** because they were the messengers of God in bringing the gospel. It was not given 'to' the Thessalonians (simple dative) but 'directed' (εἰς ὑμᾶς) at them (for γίνεσθαι with a sense of movement cf. Acts 26.6; Gal. 3.14).

The **gospel** must be expressed in human words but it is never **words only**, for what God speaks are always words effective in accomplishing their intent (cf. Gen. 1.3; Ps. 33.6, 9; Isa. 55.10f). There is probably no parallel here to 1 Cor. 1.17; 2.4; 4.19 where rhetorically 'wise' words are contrasted with God's power and dismissed; words are not dismissed here; they are necessary but they are not enough; the statements of 1 Cor. arise out of the Corinthian situation. 1 Th. 2.1–6 shows how easily the same thought can be taken up and extended in a slightly different way once the basic contrast of word and deed is introduced. The gospel which does not come with **words only** does come **with** (ἐν is probably instrumental) **power and with the Holy Spirit.** The association of power and Spirit is natural because in the O.T. the Spirit is manifested powerfully (men are empowered to perform mighty deeds), and in the N.T. we find the phrase 'in the power of the

Spirit'(Lk. 4.14; Rom. 15.13, 19; cf. Rom. 1.4); but the paralleling of power and the Spirit is only found elsewhere in 1 Cor. 2.4. **Power** is God's power (Rom. 1.16; 1 Cor. 1.18, 24, etc.); it can be seen in miracles for which the plural of our word (δύναμις) is sometimes used, but this is not the meaning here where we have the singular. The gospel can be described as the power of God (Rom. 1.16; cf. 1 Cor. 4.20), as can the cross (1 Cor. 1.18); it is God's power because it effects what it proclaims—the redemption of men and their freedom from idolatry, sin and evil supernatural beings. **Power** and **Spirit** might then be taken as identical but in the N.T. the Spirit is much more than a Spirit of power; he is also the Spirit of love and goodness; Gal. 5.22f does not even mention power among the fruit of the Spirit. Thus Paul is not writing tautologically when he conjoins power and Spirit, for the latter is much the wider term. Perhaps **power** contrasts more vividly with **word** than would **Spirit** and prepares the way for **Spirit**. Among the Thessalonians the gospel was present not as mere words but as utterance empowered by God and as speech made wise and effective through the Holy Spirit (cf. the association of wisdom and Spirit in the case of Stephen, Acts 6.3). **Holy Spirit** lacks the article in the Greek here and thus probably means no more than 'a divine spirit inspiring man' (Moulton–Turner, p. 175); we ought not to interpret it in terms of a developed Trinitarian doctrine. On **Spirit**, see E. Schweizer *et. al.*, *T.D.N.T.* VI, pp. 332ff.

The gospel is said to have come, thirdly, **with** (with B א 33 sah ἐν should probably not be read here) **much conviction**: πληροφορία (**conviction**, assurance) is difficult. Our rendering is suitable in all the N.T. occurrences (1 Th. 1.5; Col. 2.2; Heb. 6.11; 10.22; cf. 1 Clem. 42.3), and also in most of those of the cognate verb; otherwise the verb means 'fill, fulfil'. It is possible to give the noun the meaning 'fulness' at Col. 2.2; Heb. 6.11; 10.22; 1 Clem. 42.3 (cf. Bauer) but this neither fits the context here nor is it easy to add to it the adjective **much** since 'fulness' is an absolute and it is impossible to have more or less of it. Rigaux argues strongly for this sense taking it to refer to the objective result of the **power** and **the Holy Spirit** among the Thessalonians and points out that **conviction** implies that the third term in this sequence changes from objective realities (power, Spirit) to a subjective assurance on the part of Paul and his companions. Yet such a change prepares for the last clause of the verse which does refer to human judgement. Moreover Rigaux's rendering leaves it doubtful in what the fulness consists: the full harvest of the Thessalonian elect? the fulness of their dedication to Christ? their being fully filled with the Holy Spirit? Taken all in all **conviction** is more appropriate in the context. It, of course, results from the work of the Spirit in Paul and his companions and is in that sense not purely subjective but objective and is an assurance both about their message and about themselves as its messengers. (It is just possible that the **conviction** is that of the Thessalonians—in knowing their election; cf. Masson.) The Thessalonians were well aware of the great assurance of Paul and his fellows when they preached the gospel among them at the first, an assurance produced by the Holy Spirit, and which called forth in them behaviour corresponding to the gospel they preached: they knew **the kind of people we were among** (read ἐν with B D G; its omission is probably due to haplography) **you.** Paul did not apparently regard himself as someone likely to attract attention through his appearance or personality but when he took up the work of the gospel he became a new, powerful and exciting person (cf. 2 Cor. 4.7ff; 11.6; 13.4b). Perhaps we have already an indication here that Paul will defend his ministry among them (2.1ff).

6   **and you for your part:** the Thessalonians know the kind of people (v. 5) Paul and his associates were and became the same by imitating them. Verse 6 depends on v. 4 and further explains Paul's knowledge of their election; it also continues the reasons for which Paul is returning thanks (v. 2).

Paul and his companions set themselves with the Lord before the Thessalonians so that they became their **imitators.** Paul writes frequently about imitation of himself (1 Cor. 4.16; 11.1; Gal. 4.12; Phil. 3.17; 1 Th. 1.6; 2 Th. 3.7, 9; cf. 1 Th. 3.12), of Christ (1 Th. 1.6; 1 Cor. 11.1), and of God (Eph. 5.1, if this letter is by Paul; 5.2 suggests that imitation of God is to be understood in terms of imitation of Christ); he also writes of the Thessalonians as imitating the churches of Judea (1 Th. 2.14) and of themselves being imitated by the churches in Macedonia and Achaia (1 Th. 1.7). The conception of imitation goes back to the O.T. (Lev. 19.2) and appears in this and in other forms in the N.T. (Mt. 5.48; Lk. 6.36; 1 Pet. 1.16). Jesus called men to follow him in suffering (Mk. 8.34; Mt. 10.38f; Lk. 14.27) and in 1 Pet. 2.21 slaves are

exhorted to follow him in that way. In what respect does Paul call
for imitation of himself and the Lord? **in receiving** (probably in
the sense, 'receive willingly, gladly') **the word** (i.e. the gospel
which comes from God and is about Christ as preached to men;
word is used frequently in this sense in the N.T. with and without
the addition 'of the Lord'; cf. Mk. 2.1f; 4.14ff; Acts 4.29, 31; 8.25;
1 Th. 1.8; 2.13) or **in receiving the word in much tribulation?**
Grammatically the aorist ἐγενήθητε (**became**: it is possible to
take this as in v. 5 passively 'were made' and understand God as
the logical subject; following Jewish usage passives are often so
used in the N.T.; whatever **became** was not a matter of chance but
was directly under God's control) suggests imitation at one point,
i.e. at the time they became Christians and the aorist participle
δεξάμενοι will then be an aorist of 'identical action', 'in that you
received the word'. They will certainly have known that Paul
received the word in tribulation (in 2.14 they are assumed to know
of the persecution of the church in Judea), and vv. 4f relate to their
conversion. However Paul does not elsewhere confine imitation of
himself to the period of initial Christian decision (cf. 1 Cor. 11.1;
Phil. 3.17; Gal. 4.12; 2 Th. 3.7, 9; 1 Cor. 4.16 might be taken in
that sense since it speaks of Paul as their father); in 1 Th. 2.14;
3.3, he implies that 'tribulation' may continue right through
Christian existence. Thus it is more natural to think of Paul as a
continual example to them, as they to the other churches of Greece
(v. 7; but they could still be an example to those who were later
converted); in that case we ought to have had the perfect tense of
γίνεσθαι (**became**) and the imitation would refer only to their
suffering, **receiving the word** ('after you had received the word')
being a parenthetical clause. However **in much tribulation** is
more easily taken with **receiving the word** and the earlier
explanation is therefore preferable. This means that the emphasis
in imitation must be placed on the way in which they received the
word, i.e. with much tribulation, rather than on the fact of reception. No matter which way it is taken the phrase **and of the Lord**
still remains difficult. We would expect the use of 'Jesus' rather
than of **Lord** if the historical example of his suffering and death
were in mind (in the parallel passage, 1 Cor. 11.1, Paul speaks of
the imitation of Christ). But **Lord** may be used to concentrate
attention on the central features of the Christ event; it is to these
rather than to the daily life of Jesus that Paul directs attention when

he sets out Jesus as an example (2 Cor. 8.9; Phil. 2.5ff). If then the use of **Lord** is discounted the difficulty still remains that Christ did not receive the word; we are then forced to emphasize **in much tribulation**, which certainly was his lot. The word always calls to obedience and Christ was obedient (Phil. 2.8). Dibelius (cf. W. Michaelis, *T.D.N.T.* IV, p. 670) suggests that **and of the Lord** may be a self-correction of Paul after elevating himself as example to the Thessalonians, and the position of the phrase in the sentence may be said to support this. R. C. Tannehill, *Dying and Rising with Christ* (Beiheft, *Z.N.W.* 32), Berlin, 1967, pp. 100–4, argues that since suffering is not something in which conscious imitation is possible because it is inflicted at the whim of others, we ought to see the imitation of the Thessalonians as 'the result of the power of the Gospel working itself out in the lives of the believers so that a certain pattern results' (p. 103). He considers the best parallel to 1 Th. 1.6 (and 2.13) to be 2 Cor. 4.7–12 where suffering and joy are related to the death and life of Christ and this therefore accounts for Paul's introduction of **and of the Lord;** but since this is only a minor element in the general argument Paul does not expand it. 'This explains why the reference to being "Imitators" of the Lord comes in the second place in 1.6 and then is dropped. The significant thing is that Paul brings in the thought that this pattern goes back to the Lord even though this is not the point which concerns him at the moment' (p. 104). But, in any case, does not Paul pass beyond the bounds of humility when he sets himself up as an example to Christians? D. M. Stanley, 'Become imitators of me . . .', *Bib.* 40 (1959) 859–77, points out that it is only to the churches which he has founded that he writes in these terms. He stands to them in a unique relationship (cf. 1 Cor. 4.15). Their knowledge of Christian behaviour is not something that can be learnt through a code of rules, and Paul never sets it out in this way, but in the first instance it proceeds from a new attitude to God, or Christ, and to the world; those who have been justified have become new men and must express in action their new life. Yet just as some principles of behaviour may be a guide to them, so even more can the example of a Christian life. Paul points more often to himself as example than he does to Christ, for his own example is more readily available. (It is doubtful if in the early period of the church Christ was regarded much as an example to Christians; he was Saviour rather than moral pattern.) The spirit of the Christian life is seen embodied better in a Christian life than in a code of instruction.

θλῖψις **(tribulation)** is rare in classical Greek but is more frequent in the LXX, especially in relation to the ills that befall the people of God. Paul takes it up in this way in the N.T. and the suffering of tribulation becomes almost the normal condition of the Christian (cf. Rom. 5.3; 12.12; Phil. 4.14). Often an eschatological note attaches to it (e.g. 2 Cor. 1.4, where it may denote the Messianic woes which introduce the return of Christ) and this may be the reason for the comparative frequency of its appearance in our letters (1 Th. 1.6; 3.3, 7; 2 Th. 1.4, 6; cf. 1 Th. 3.4; 2 Th. 1.6f for the verbal form). We are not told here the nature of the tribulation; the description is too strong to be a reference to Acts 17.5–9 alone. In the early church persecution was endemic, ranging from verbal taunts to riots with physical damage to the lives and property of Christians. The reference is certainly to outward trials and not to the inward anxieties which might accompany them. Indeed inward anxieties are actually absent, for the outward tribulations are received **with joy of the Holy Spirit**, i.e. with divinely inspired joy. The seeming paradox of suffering accompanied by joy ran right through the experience of the early church, e.g. Acts 5.41; 16.25; 2 Cor. 7.4; 8.1f; Phil. 2.17; Col. 1.24; 1 Pet. 4.13. This joy is not a human joy which may come from the sense of a duty, even a hard duty meeting opposition, carried to fruition, but a joy which originates in God and is mediated by his Spirit to those who suffer, not a joy which comes at the end of suffering as its reward but a joy which accompanies the suffering itself and upholds the sufferer in his suffering.

If Paul and his associates had been an example to the Thessalo- 7 nians they themselves had become **an example** (Paul uses the singular because he thinks of the church as a whole as an example) to others. Paul associates imitation and example again in 2 Th. 3.7–9; Phil. 3.17; he is consequently not giving himself a unique place, e.g. as apostle, as if he alone could serve as a pattern (cf. 2.14, where the Thessalonians are said to have imitated the churches of Judea). **Macedonia** and **Achaia** were the two provinces comprising Greece. At the time when Paul wrote there were churches in Philippi, Beroea, Athens and Corinth as well as in Thessalonica. There was also a Christian community in Cenchreae, one of the sea ports serving Corinth (cf. Rom. 16.1), if not at that time, then shortly afterwards; probably Christianity was spreading from each main centre into the surrounding towns and villages. It is therefore natural for Paul to describe the area to which the Thessalonians were examples by naming provinces than the much larger number of cities and towns (Dibelius and Rigaux remark that it is Paul's general practice to refer to provinces rather than to cities, cf. Gal. 1.21). The tribulation which fell on the Thessalonians as they accepted Christianity and the accompanying joy encourage **believers** in other areas and also encourage outsiders to become believers.

8   This is a difficult sentence; we would expect it to continue after **Achaia**, 'But also has come into . . .' The introduction of a fresh subject **your faith** and the omission (it is grammatically possible, cf. Bl.–Deb. § 448.1) of 'also' ($\varkappa\alpha\iota$) have led some commentators (e.g. Wohlenberg) to punctuate with a semi-colon after **from you** and to render the remainder 'your faith in God has come not only into Macedonia and Achaia but also into every place'. However this makes an awkward break and is clumsy since so much of the sentence precedes the subject and verb. It is thus easier to take it as it stands; it is 'another example of St. Paul's impetuous style' (Milligan; cf. the detailed discussion by Henneken, pp. 59–61). Paul has attempted to combine two ideas into one sentence, viz., the evangelical activity of the Thessalonians in Greece and their example everywhere. **The word of the Lord** and **your faith** are of course not unrelated concepts for Paul.

Verse 8 **(For)** gives the basis for v. 7. In the Greek **from you** is placed emphatically at the beginning of the sentence: the Thessalonians have been a centre from which **the word (the word of the Lord** in the N.T. is often a synonym for the gospel; cf. G. Kittel, *T.D.N.T.* IV, pp. 114ff) of God has been proclaimed. They themselves received it (v. 6) despite difficulty and persecution and either by their deliberate action or possibly through their example in tribulation the word has again spread in the provinces of Greece. Those who gladly receive the word can never keep it to themselves; it always spreads out from them. The metaphor behind the word **(sounded out)** which describes this spread is not clear; the Greek word is linked to sound but not necessarily to any particular sound or musical instrument; Lightfoot suggested the idea of thundering out, Chrysostom that of a trumpet blast. In any case the idea is twofold: a sound is made and it is heard spreading out from a centre over an area. **but . . . into every place** ought to take up **not only** but instead introduces an extension of the thought. **Faith** (picking up **believers** in v. 7; they come from the same Greek root) has a fairly wide range of meaning in Paul. Here it does not have its principal meaning, a personal relationship to God through Christ, but is more objective, i.e. what is known is either the fact of this faith relationship or their faithfulness. The object **(God)** of faith is emphasized in the Greek, perhaps in preparation for the reference to the idolatry which they have left (v. 9). **in every place** is a pardonable exaggeration by which Paul shows his pleasure with them; he exaggerates similarly in Rom. 1.8; 16.19; 1 Cor. 1.2. It is probable that their faith would be known beyond the boundaries of their immediate neighbourhood since Thessalonica lay on a major Roman road (cf. pp. 1f), and since Christians seem to have moved freely from one centre to another (Rom. 16.1f; 1 Cor. 1.11; 16.10, 17). Because this news has spread Paul has not needed to tell of them, but doubtless he did talk of them to others and hold them up as an example (cf. 2 Cor. 8.1f; 9.2).

Paul now goes on to give the reason why he has no need to tell 9 of his mission in Thessalonica and of the faith of the Thessalonians: **for these**, the people of Macedonia, Achaia and everywhere, **report** the story of the **entrance** of Paul and his associates into Thessalonica; it is not made clear to whom they **report**. In Greek as in English **entrance** has the double meaning, 'act of entering' and 'place of entering'; in view of the repetition of the word in 2.1 where it has the former meaning it will have the same here, and this suits the context. The appearance of Paul and his companions led to the conversion of the Thessalonians even though they suffered greatly in becoming Christians. Some MSS (B 81 Thdrt) read 'about you' instead of **about us**; the essential meaning is not really affected for it concerns ultimately not what Paul did but the result of what he did, i.e. the conversion of the Thessalonians. The reading 'you' makes this a little more consistent and we ought therefore to read **us** as *lectio difficilior*.

The remainder of v. 9 with v. 10 is drawn, as we shall see, from a traditional credal formula which is now used to describe their conversion. **that** ($\pi\tilde{\omega}\varsigma$) can be rendered 'how' and describe the manner rather than the fact of their conversion, but the word began to take the meaning **that** in Hellenistic Greek (Moulton–Turner,

81

p. 137) and it is all the context requires; it is the fact of the conversion of the Thessalonians which is reported far and wide. If the element of 'manner' is allowed to enter then it will refer to their conversion in tribulation (v. 6). They **turned** from **idols**, i.e. they were converted; Paul only uses the word elsewhere in 2 Cor. 3.16, an O.T. citation, and Gal. 4.9 where the context is similar to here. It is a suitable word to express the change from one faith to another. In this way it is used more often in Acts (3.19; 9.35; 11.21; 14.15 etc.) and is possibly dependent on Isa. 6.9f. Paul tends to describe entrance into the Christian faith as the moment of belief using the aorist of πιστεύειν (cf. Rom. 13.11; I Cor. 3.5; 15.2, 11; Gal. 2.16) or he speaks of receiving the word (1 Th. 1.6; 2.13); these lay greater stress on the essential nature of the Christian position whereas **turn** brings out the extent of the rupture from pagan ways (cf. Masson). The break made, the Thessalonians now **serve the living and real God.** Obviously the Thessalonians were Gentiles before they became Christians for Jews would not have been described as turning from idolatry. There were, of course, Gentiles, as the Stoics, who attacked idolatry but never in the consistent way in which the O.T., followed by Judaism, inveighs against it. Idols are vain things, non-entities; as such they are really dead. In the LXX **idol** means both the image and the god to which it is related and as such it is spoken of as false and as non-existent (cf. F. Büchsel, *T.D.N.T.* II, pp. 375–8). There is a certain latent ambiguity here in that what is non-existent can hardly be termed false and this ambiguity appears even in the N.T.; cf. 1 Cor. 10.19 (cf. 8.5) where the objects of the idolatrous worship of the heathen are regarded as demons; this idea is probably not present in our passage. In contradistinction to false and non-existent idols, God is described as **real** and **living.** The use of **real** (ἀληθινός) in relation to God goes back to the LXX (Exod. 34.6; 2 Chron. 15.3; Ps. 86.15; Isa. 65.16), is continued in Hellenistic Judaism and is found quite frequently in John (1.9; 7.28; 15.1; 17.3). This is its only appearance in Paul. Similarly **living** is a description of the God of the O.T. and of Judaism (Num. 14.21, 28; Deut. 32.40; Ps. 41(42).2; 83(84).3 etc.); it is taken up in almost every strand of the N.T. (Mt. 16.16; Acts 14.15; 2 Cor. 3.3; 1 Tim. 3.15; Heb. 3.12; 1 Pet. 1.23; Rev. 1.18); the living God is not merely one who is alive but one who gives life, both the life of creation and the new life of redemption (cf. Rom. 4.17; 1 Tim. 6.13; Jn. 5.21). Such a God, in contrast to false, non-existent idols, can be served, and ought to be served, and the Thessalonians have turned to **serve** him (**serve** is not to be restricted to worship but means service in every aspect of life). Elsewhere Paul writes of serving the Lord, i.e. Christ, in contrast to the service of sin (Rom. 6.16–20; 7.25) or the law (Rom. 7.6); in Gal. 4.3, 8, 9 it is contrasted with the service of demonic powers which Paul may have linked to idolatry.

Converted from idolatry and serving God the Thessalonians **wait** expectantly **for** their full deliverance. The belief that Jesus would return again from heaven to which he had gone after his resurrection was common to primitive Christianity and is particularly emphasized in our epistles. There is nothing here to say how soon this expectancy will be fulfilled but its very mention suggests that it cannot be far off (see further on 2.19). Nowhere else in the Thessalonian epistles is Jesus termed God's **Son** (for the title cf. W. Kramer, *op. cit.*, §§ 24–29, 53–57; O. Cullmann, *op. cit.*, pp. 270–305; F. Hahn, *The Titles of Jesus in Christology*, London, 1969, pp. 279ff), but the title is used frequently in Paul's other letters and elsewhere in the N.T., though its association here with the Parousia is unique (cf. Kramer, *op. cit.*, § 28a–c). It implies a close relationship between God and Christ and may be occasioned here by the implication of the following words that Christ has been with God since his resurrection. In association with the Parousia we would expect Jesus to be called 'Lord' or 'Son of Man', the latter being the more probable if the text originated in Palestinian Christianity (cf. Mk. 13.32 where Son (of God) may represent an original Son of Man; R. H. Fuller, *The Foundations of New Testament Christology*, London, 1965, p. 165).

The Son will come **out of heaven. Heaven** is a plural form in the original; plural and singular forms are both found in the N.T., apparently used indiscriminately, the plural arising either because the Hebrew word is plural in form or out of the Jewish conception of a plurality of heavens (cf. 2 Cor. 12.2). However where Paul elsewhere uses the preposition ἐκ **(out of)** he always has the singular. God's Son will come back out of heaven from God to earth to **deliver** men **from the approaching anger.** As **Son** so also the use of **Jesus** is peculiar. Rigaux suggests that it protects the risen Jesus from degenerating into a spiritual being since it maintains the connection between the historical and the exalted Lord. It may however go back to the most primitive formulation of belief in the resurrection: Jesus is risen (cf. Kramer, *op. cit.*, § 8e); this does not of course clash with Rigaux's explanation. This Jesus **delivers** (ῥύεσθαι is much less frequent in the N.T. than σῴζειν and appears to emphasize the negative aspect of deliverance *from* rather than salvation *to*; it is used here as a present participle implying that the deliverance is taking place even now before the return of Jesus). Deliverance is **from the approaching anger**, i.e. the anger of God on the day of Judgement. How quickly this anger approaches is not said but if it were regarded as infinitely remote it would hardly be described as **approaching** (emphatic by position in the Greek). The Thessalonians may be enduring tribulation now but when the day of the Lord comes because of their present (the present tense **delivers** is thus not inappropriate, cf. Jn. 3.18f) service to the living and real God they will escape his judgement, unlike those who now cause them tribulation (cf. 2 Th. 1.5ff)

How are we to think of **the anger**? It occurs here without any explicit reference to God and many scholars consider that it ought to be taken in an impersonal manner: God has constructed the world in such a way that punishment, i.e. anger or wrath, inevitably follows on sin as effect after cause (cf. C. H. Dodd, *Romans* on 1.18; A. T. Hanson, *The Wrath of the Lamb*, London, 1957). The argument runs briefly: (i) Paul never uses the verb 'to be angry' with God as subject. (ii) He uses 'the anger' impersonally, e.g. 1 Th. 1.10; Rom. 2.5; 9.22. (iii) The conception of God as angry is repugnant to a proper understanding of his love. These arguments do not stand up to full investigation though it must be allowed that punishment can follow inevitably and impersonally on sin, e.g. the neglect of elementary precautions can lead to natural disaster as when waste products of manufacture are disposed of carelessly. Generally speaking Paul and the O.T. regard God's wrath as personal (cf. L. Morris, *The Apostolic Preaching of the Cross*, London, 1955, pp. 161ff; H. Kleinknecht, O. Proksch, J. Fichtner, E. Sjöberg, G. Stählin, *T.D.N.T.* V, pp. 382–447). (i) The O.T. position is well summed up by E. Jacob: 'The Israelite really believed in the wrath of Jahweh and did not project it upon God from the testings and punishments which he himself had passed through . . . wrath is primarily an action: God pours it out (Ez. 20.33; Lam. 4.11), he makes it rise up (2 Chron. 36.16), he sends it out (Job 20.23; Ps. 78.49), he performs it (1 Sam. 28.18; Hos. 11.9).

Wrath is so much part of the figure of God in the Old Testament that the ancient Israelites saw no problem in it, but they accepted this reality as being a normal part of the irrational and mysterious in God' (*Theology of the Old Testament*, London, 1958, p. 114). (ii) In Rom. 1.18 there is a strong parallelism between the wrath of God and the righteousness of God; both are said to be revealed and righteousness is certainly conceived as 'personal'; wrath comes 'from heaven' (a circumlocution for God); in Rom. 1.24, 26, 28 **God** is said to give men up to sin which is punishment. (iii) When we compare Rom. 2.5 with 2.6 we find the personal pronoun (for God) used in a parallel statement. (iv) Though 'anger' is not mentioned in 2 Th. 1.6–9 the idea is present and closely related to God. (v) In our present text the **approaching anger** is not an impersonal law of cause and effect in this world but refers to an eschatological event standing outside world history and entirely caused by God. But if we take the 'anger' as God's personal anger we ought not to think of it as emotional passion; it is no more so than his love. Rom. 1.18ff, the most famous passage in Paul about the anger of God, is preceded by 1.16f and succeeded by 3.21ff both of which tell of God's redeeming action. It is always within the context of God's love that we have to understand his anger. It may be that the conception of God's wrath causes difficulty for a true understanding of his love; it does not appear to have done so for Paul, i.e., Paul, even if the twentieth century theologian cannot, could hold the two concepts of love and anger together, though in tension.

A number of times in the notes on vv. 9b, 10 we have pointed out that Paul has employed words he does not normally use, or employed those he does use in unusual ways, e.g. **turned, real, to serve** in relation to God rather than Jesus, **out of heavens.** To these we may add: a different word for **wait** (ἀναμένειν; elsewhere he uses compounds of δέχεσθαι); in the formula **raised from the dead** (cf. Gal. 1.1; Rom. 4.24; 10.9; Acts 3.15; 4.10; 1 Pet. 1.21; etc.) he uses the article (the evidence for its omission, A C K *al*, is hardly sufficient) whereas elsewhere he omits it; he never uses the word **deliver** elsewhere in an eschatological context (he uses σῴζειν). The only particularly favourite Pauline word is **idol** (7 times in Paul against 11 times in the N.T.). Moreover when Paul states the content of the Christian faith he makes the cross central (not in place of the resurrection but alongside it) and defines it as 'for us' (Rom. 5.6, 8; 14.15; 1 Cor. 1.13; 8.11; 2 Cor. 5.14; Gal. 2.20); yet there is no reference here even to the death of Jesus. Taken together these facts indicate that we have a pre-Pauline statement of the Church's faith; others have been identified; in 1 Cor. 15.3–5 Paul clearly states that he is using one. The evidence in our present case is reinforced when we observe that 1.9b, 10 can be set out in two three-line stanzas:

> You turned to God from idols
>   to serve the living and real God
>   (and) to wait for his Son out of heaven
> Whom he raised from the dead
>   Jesus who delivers us
>   from the approaching anger.

In each stanza the first line refers to the past, the second to the present and the third to the future. If this is a pre-Pauline fragment, where did it originate? Several things suggest that its provenance was Jewish-Christian rather than Gentile-Christian: the contrast of idols and the living and real God, the plural 'heavens', the use of the name Jesus in relation to the resurrection, the possibility, if the original was in Hebrew or Aramaic, of a pun on the name Jesus (= deliverer, cf. Mt. 1.21) and the verb **deliver**, the absence of reference to the pre-existence or exalted condition of Jesus as in Hellenistic formulae (cf. Phil. 2.6–11; 1 Tim. 3.16). These indications of Jewish origin also imply that it is a statement emerging from a situation in which Gentiles were becoming Christians and not a confession of the Jewish-Christian church itself. It would thus have been a summary of the preaching of (Hellenistic?) Jewish Christians to heathen. We do not need to conclude that the entire statement appeared first in the early Gentile mission: obviously the clauses about the resurrection and the Parousia may come from an earlier period when the Church was exclusively Jewish Christian. It may well also go back to Jewish preaching to heathen; Jews would have to turn Gentiles away from their idols to the real and living God (a monotheistic preaching for which evidence exists) and might well include a warning of the coming judgement. In the early years of the Jewish-Christian preaching a reference to Christ would be added. Paul may indeed have used it at times as an initial approach though he would quickly have brought his hearers on to an understanding of Jesus' death

(4.14; 5.10 show that he also used formulae with this as content). J. Munck, 'I Thess. i. 9–10 and the Missionary Preaching of Paul. Textual Exegesis and Hermeneutic Reflexions', *N.T.S.* 9 (1962–3) 95–110, denies that Paul would have used this as a formula since the cross is not central to it; he argues that the verses must be explained from the remainder of the letter. His explanation is hesitant, he fails to discuss the unique character of the vocabulary and he does not account satisfactorily for the references to the initial mission (**entrance**) in 1.9 and 2.1 which form the context. Rejecting Munck's argument we note more generally that Paul could use traditional formulae which are not wholly in agreement with his own theology: Rom. 1.3f implies a designation of Jesus as Son of God because he was raised from the dead and contains no reference to his cross or his death for sin; Phil. 2.5–11 has no reference to his resurrection. Paul was aware of many tentative formulations of the faith; that of our verses, while not his own, is suitable to the Thessalonian situation where the readers are greatly exercised over the Parousia. He will have used it in his original mission because of its relevance to idolatry but will also have used other formulations (4.14; 5.10) which introduce the death of Christ. It is indeed in 1 Th. that we learn more about Paul's initial visit to a city than in any of his other letters and 1.9f probably does therefore represent a factor in his preaching. Finally we note that there are traces of similar formulae in Acts 14.15–17; 17.21ff. and of similarly based catechetical instruction in Heb. 6.1–2 which has no mention of Christ but has eschatological emphasis. On the pre-Pauline formula see G. Friedrich, 'Ein Tauflied hellenistischer Judenchristen, 1 Thess. 1.9f,' *T.Z.* 21 (1965) 502–16; P.-É. Langevin, *Jésus Seigneur et l'Eschatologie*, Brussels/Paris, 1967, pp. 43–106; G. Schneider, 'Urchristliche Gottesverkündigung in hellenistischer Umwelt', *B.Z.* 13 (1969) 59–75; P. Stuhlmacher, *Das Paulinische Evangelium, I Vorgeschichte* (F.R.L.A.N.T. 95) pp. 258–66; U. Wilckens, *op. cit.*, pp. 81–91.

For you on your part, brothers, know that our entrance to you has not proved fruitless (2) but, although, as you know, we had earlier suffered and been abused in Philippi, we were courageous in our God to speak to you God's gospel amidst great conflict. (3) For our appeal does not spring from error or impurity nor does it work through deception (4) but even as we have been approved by God to be entrusted with his gospel so we speak, not as pleasing men but God who scrutinizes our hearts. (5) For we never behaved with flattering speech, as you know, nor with a veiled desire to exploit—God is my witness—(6) nor as seeking after honour from men, neither you nor others, (7) although as Christ's apostles we were able to have a position of importance, but we were gentle when we were among you; as a nursing mother cherishes her children, (8) so in our great care for you we gladly determined to share with you not only the gospel of God but also our own being because you had become beloved to us. (9) And you remember, brothers, our hard labour and toil; it was while we worked day and night so as not to be a charge on any of you, that we preached to you the gospel of God. (10) You yourselves are witnesses, and so is God, how we behaved in a holy, just and faultless way towards you who believe; (11) as you know we counselled each one of you as a father his children (12) exhorting, encouraging, and insisting that you should walk worthily of God who calls you to his kingdom and glory.

As in 1.2–10 there is a movement of thought in 2.1–17 from the activity of the missionaries (2.1–12, cf. 1.3–5) to the response of the Thessalonians (2.13–17, cf. 1.6–10). Paul affirms the spirit of love in which they came to Thessalonica; negatively he denies that they had been wrongly motivated (2.3–6, 10); positively he asserts their care for the Thessalonians whom they had cherished as a nursing mother her baby (2.7f), as a father instructing his children

(2.11f) and on whom they had laid no burden of expense for their maintenance (2.9). He continually appeals to the Thessalonians' own knowledge of his mission among them and behind this appeal lies his belief, which emerges more clearly in Galatians and 2 Corinthians, that his message and his personal integrity cannot be separated. On the question of the possible opponents with whom Paul may be dealing see pp. 16–22.

For you on your part (αὐτοί is emphatic): Paul turns to their own knowledge of what had happened when he with Silas and Timothy had first come to them from Philippi. **For** implies some connection with chapter 1 but it is not entirely clear what it is. It cannot relate back to 1.9b, 10 which is a statement of the content of the gospel. It may to 1.9a in view of the common use of **entrance**, 1.9b, 10 being a parenthesis; but **for** suggests that we should find in 2.1ff either an explanation of, or a basis for, what precedes; the knowledge of the Thessalonians about the original mission can hardly be either a basis for, or an explanation of, what people report about that mission. Moreover if Paul was making a direct link to 1.9a, setting the knowledge of the Thessalonians alongside the report of Christians elsewhere, he would almost certainly have written, '*And* you on your part.' Probably therefore **For** must link 2.1ff to the whole of 1.2–10 with special reference to 1.5 where the entrance of Paul was discussed, though in different language; 1.5 is still in Paul's mind though he does not specifically allude to it now (cf. Rigaux, Wohlenberg, Lightfoot, etc.; **for** can be used of an unexpressed thought, cf. L & S, Bauer). The arrival of Paul and his companions in Thessalonica had been 'with power, and with the Holy Spirit, and with much conviction,' and the Thessalonians themselves had therefore been able to see that it had not been powerless or without effect. κενός, **fruitless**, has a fairly wide range of metaphorical meaning derived from the basic physical sense 'empty'. It can mean 'false' (i.e. empty of truth, Eph. 5.6; Col. 2.8; in 1 Cor. 15.14a perhaps 'without power') or 'fruitless' (i.e. empty of effect or result, 1 Cor. 15.10, 58; 2 Cor. 6.1; Gal. 2.2; 1 Th. 3.5). 'False' is hardly possible here since there is no reference in the context to truth but 'without power' might be in the light of 1.5 (cf. Findlay, Bornemann; but if given this sense it relates not to the word but to Paul's entrance, *pace* Schmithals, p. 99). However 'fruitless' appears more satisfactory; this is the normal meaning in Paul when applied to the activity of himself or other Christians.

It can hardly mean 'empty-handed' (so Frame) since its reference is not directly to Paul, Silas and Timothy, but to their coming to Thessalonica. A.–M. Denis, 'L'Apôtre Paul, prophète "messianique" des Gentils: Étude thématique de 1 Thess. 2.1–6,' *Eph. T.L.* 33 (1957) 245–318, sees in the use of this word a reference to Isa. 49.4 and goes on to argue that many of the terms of 2.1–6 recall the servant of the Lord, Jeremiah and the righteous man of Wisdom (cf. especially Wisd. 4.10–5.14) and that Paul sees himself as standing in the tradition represented by these concepts, exercising a prophetic and messianic function no longer in Israel but among the Gentiles. Denis's evidence is overstretched and fails to validate his view; e.g. in Isa. 49.4 the work of the servant was fruitless whereas Paul says his was not. The perfect tense of the verb **has proved** (γέγονεν) implies that the visit of Paul and the others was not only fruitful but that the fruit then produced still continues. The church came into being then and still exists. The fruit was produced by the preaching of the gospel (see v. 2) and the response of the Thessalonians in faith (1.6–8).

2   According to Acts 16.19ff Paul and Silas had been flogged and fastened in the stocks in the jail at Philippi; Paul as a Roman citizen claimed that such treatment without a trial was contrary to Roman law. Presumably he refers to this now when he says they had **suffered and been abused** (πρό, in the first verb, is normally temporal in Paul and probably carries over to **abused** also; cf. Lightfoot and 1 Cor. 16.16). **Suffered** might then relate to their physical sufferings and **abused** to the illegal treatment of a Roman citizen. But the Greek word (ὑβρίζειν) as our English **abused** can mean both physical and verbal outrage (cf. Mt. 22.6; Acts 14.5; cf. L & S, Bauer); it is the insolent and outrageous nature of the action which is emphasized. Would Paul have taken it a personal insult when he was imprisoned without trial? Surely it was Roman citizenship which was outraged? If Paul was so proudly conscious of his Roman citizenship as to use such a strong word here we would expect to find this pride elsewhere, but we do not. We cannot, in any case, be sure of all the details in the Lukan accounts of Paul's visits to different cities. Probably therefore the word expresses the wanton nature of the treatment he and Silas received—despite which they preached in Thessalonica and that courageously.

There is again an appeal, **as you know**, to the knowledge of the Thessalonians, an appeal which is much emphasized in this passage, cf. vv. 1, 2, 5, 9 (remember), 10 (witness), 11; if accusations or complaints have been made in Thessalonica about Paul's conduct then the readers are in the best of all positions to make a sound judgement from their personal experience of Paul's visit among them. For the remainder of the passage Paul recalls his behaviour, and that of his associates, on that visit. Here the phrase refers to the Thessalonians' knowledge of the condition in which they arrived in Thessalonica, with their backs still marked (de Boor). After what had happened in Philippi they might well have been expected to draw in their horns or lie low for a little, instead they boldly and frankly proclaimed the gospel. παρρησιάζειν (**were courageous**, still governed by **know that** of v. 1) is often used in relation to preaching and stresses the confident, free and outspoken manner in which the Christian mission was carried out, e.g. Acts 9.28; 13.46; 19.8 (cf. the use of the noun at Eph. 6.19; Phil. 1.20; Acts 2.29; 4.13, etc.; cf. Wisd. 5.1; cf. W. C. van Unnik 'The Christian's Freedom of Speech in the New Testament', *B.J.R.L.* 44(1961–2) 466–88). Paul traces the source of this courage to God. We have again the somewhat unusual phrase **in (our) God** as in 1.1; it may have been verbally influenced here by the LXX text (11.6) of Ps. 12.5, though there it is God who is 'courageous'. It is unnecessary to think of a God-mysticism in Paul; ἐν **(in)** had a wide range of meanings in Biblical Greek and is probably used here instrumentally. Without God, and the gospel of which he is the author (note the explicit and almost redundant reference to God in **God's gospel**), Paul would have been weak and useless in mission work (cf. 2 Cor. 1.4). The God who makes Paul courageous to preach the gospel is the God who supplies the gospel, the creator of the good news who in a real sense is for that reason the good news himself, both its author and its object (the genitive **of God** is primarily a genitive of the subject).

The proclamation of the gospel in Thessalonica for Paul and his companions had not been easy; there had been **conflict.** This (ἀγών) has been taken in different ways: (*a*) anxiety within the minds of Paul and others (Rigaux); (*b*) intense effort on their part (Dibelius; de Boor, effort in prayer; cf. Rom. 15.30; Col. 4.12); (*c*) conflict created by opposition to the gospel (Masson, Milligan). (*a*) is supported by an apparent contrast with what happened in Philippi, by the absence of any record in Acts 17.1ff of actual suffering on Paul's part, and by an easier junction to v. 3 where

Paul goes on to speak of his conduct. Against it we note: preaching can only be described as **courageous** if there is external opposition, 1.6; 2.14ff imply there was physical persecution of the Thessalonians who became Christians, it is not clear of what nature Paul's anxiety was (inward anxiety and outward courage are in strange contrast), and Acts 17.5–9 does imply opposition at Thessalonica (we have no need to assume that Acts tells us all that happened and that therefore because no persecution of Paul is mentioned there was no opposition to his preaching). (*b*) has little to support it; it hardly agrees any better with the context than does (*a*), and when Paul refers to struggle in prayer he makes this clear as his meaning. (*c*) accords with Paul's normal use of the word (Phil. 1.30; Col. 2.1; for the cognate verb cf. 1 Cor. 9.25; Col. 1.29; 4.12); it therefore implies hostility to Paul's preaching, absence of which would have been surprising in the light of what we know of his missionary activity elsewhere. The metaphor is basically that of an athletic contest and was widely used by the contemporary Greek moral philosophers of the struggle for moral virtue; in Hellenistic Judaism it began to be associated with the sufferings of the martyrs in the struggle for the faith (4 Macc. 11.20ff; 16.16; 17.11–16). Paul extended this, dissociating the word from the moral struggle and applying it to his apostolic mission, and employing it as a description of the Christian life (cf. V. C. Pfitzner, *Paul and the Agon Motif*, Supplements to N.T. Vol. xvi, Leiden, 1967). It is not of course used here in relation to any opponents Paul may have had in Thessalonica.

3   Paul now explains the methods and motives which govern his work as a missionary, setting it out as he likes to do (cf. 1.5; 2.1f) first negatively (v. 3) and then positively (v. 4); at this stage he writes generally of all his mission work; it is at v. 5 that he begins to deal with Thessalonica in particular. **For:** Paul would never have preached in Thessalonica or anywhere else if he had not been entrusted by God with the gospel and known himself responsible to God. His preaching is an **appeal** (παράκλησις—see on 4.1; in 2.3 the word refers to Paul's original preaching, cf. 2 Cor. 5.20; 6.1, and the **appeal** is that of the gospel. This usage is, however, hardly the same as the 'consolation' of Isa. 49.10 etc., *pace* Denis, *op. cit.*) to men to respond to Jesus Christ who is the content of the gospel he proclaims. This **appeal** is no neutral presentation of the facts about Jesus but an exhortation to accept what is presented: to

turn from idols to God and to accept Jesus as deliverer. The term takes up **speak** (v. 2) and points forward to **speak** in v. 4; the emphasis therefore lies on the activity of preaching rather than on its content.

Paul's **appeal** is defined negatively with three nouns, **error, impurity, deception;** the first two are governed by ἐκ, i.e. the source of his appeal is not **error** or **impurity**, the third by ἐν which is to be taken instrumentally or modally. Paul's preaching cannot **spring from error** because its source is God—it is the **gospel** of **God,** that is, the gospel which originates in God (cf. v. 2). Schmithals (pp. 103f) prefers to give the word **error** what he acknowledges to be its much less usual sense, viz., 'deception, fraud', and links it with the accusation that Paul had appropriated to himself some of the collection (see on 2.5) for the saints in Jerusalem, which accusation, he argues, is also reflected in 2 Cor. 12.16. Behind this he sees on the part of Paul's opponents, though not on his part, the use of πλάνη as a gnostic term (note its relation to 'magicians' in 2 Tim. 3.13); they regarded him as a satanic deceiver (Rev. 12.9—Satan is a deceiver). If πλάνη is given the sense he suggests then it is difficult to distinguish it from δόλος **(deception).** (For the possible gnostic background see pp. 17ff, and for the accusation of theft see on 2.5.) Denis, *op. cit.*, relates it to the last times (cf. Mk. 13.5f; Rev. 13.14; 18.23) when the devil and the false prophets will attempt to deceive, notes that our letter is eschatologically oriented and compares the way in which the servant of the Lord (Isa. 53.6) and the righteous man (Wisd. 5.6) were persecuted by false prophets. But Isa. 53.6 and Wisd. 5.6 do not apply the word to the servant of the Lord or the righteous man but to those who see what happens to them. There is little reason then for seeing a parallel here between Paul and the messianic prophet. As Paul's preaching does not spring from **error** neither does it from **impurity** (ἀκαθαρσία) because its source, God, is alone wholly pure. What conception of purity is intended? —physical, moral, ritual? It cannot be the first or third (cf. Mt. 23.27) but is the second. Often in the N.T. **impurity** denotes sexual impurity (Rom. 1.24; 2 Cor. 12.21; Gal. 5.19; etc.) yet it is certainly understood more generally in Rom. 6.19 and perhaps in Eph. 4.19; 5.3. In its Jewish background it is linked primarily to ritual impurity but in the later parts of the O.T. and in Hellenistic Judaism it obtains an ethical connotation; in Prov. 3.32 (LXX) the transgressor is described as impure (cf. 16.5) and in 20.10 incorrect weights are termed impure (cf. F. Hauck, *T.D.N.T.* III, pp. 427-9). In view of this wide range of meaning it is incorrect, as some commentators do (e.g. Frame, Morris, Lightfoot, Rigaux), to restrict impurity in 1 Th. 2.3 to sexual impurity. While the relationship between religion and morality was never close in the ancient world, and sexual excesses—prostitution becoming a part of the ritual—were found in many religions with which Paul would have had contact, he is nowhere else accused of sexual misbehaviour and a defence against it fits rather oddly between **error** and **deception**. **Impurity** is one of those words (cf. 'immorality' in English) which can be used in quite a general way but in certain contexts must be given a restricted sexual connotation, and where this should be done is usually obvious; the existence of this restricted meaning indicates powerfully where a culture finds its chief transgression. If it is argued that **impurity** is too general a word to carry meaning in 2.3 then the same must be said of **error** and **deception**: we are not told from what errors Paul defends himself nor what deceits he may have practised. It is wrong to particularize **impurity** and connect it with avarice because this may be mentioned in v. 5. It is more general and means that Paul does not preach from any impure motive, e.g. ambition, pride, greed, popularity (cf. Hauck, *op. cit.*, Masson). Finally, Paul's appeal does not **work through deception**. The precise connotation is again obscure; presumably Paul means that he does not deceive men into becoming Christians by promises of what they may receive ('rice Christians') nor does he use improper methods in his preaching (he was no 'spell-binder', cf. 1 Cor. 2.1-4; 2 Cor. 10.10) as did many of the wandering philosopher-preachers, exponents of strange faiths, advocates of the mystery religions and practisers of magic; there were many of all these in the contemporary world, indeed all three refutations may have them in mind since initially Paul and his companions may have been confused with such. A. J. Malherbe, 'Gentle as a Nurse', *N.T.* 12 (1970) 203-17, has taken up this suggestion and shown that almost all the terms which Paul uses in 2.1-12 were used by Dio Chrysostom (see especially *Or.* xxxii, 8ff) in relation to Cynic philosophers. The majority of these he rebukes, accusing them of 'error', 'impurity', 'deception' (v. 3), of using flattery (v. 5) and of seeking honour and money (v. 6). The good philosopher is however 'gentle as a nurse' (v. 7). This then is probably the background of the language which Paul uses in vv. 1–12. **Deception** is one of the accusations against which Paul defends himself in the Corinthian correspondence (2 Cor. 12.16; 4.2); indeed he accuses his opponents of the same fault (2 Cor. 11.13). Paul however speaks to please God and not men (v. 4).

The underlying problem with which Paul deals is never absent where deviant forms of Christianity and non-Christian systems of thought and life compete with Christianity. What proof is there that God's message is God's message? The problem arises in another guise when the message has to be cast in new thought forms because the forms in which it originated or has previously been expressed are no longer operative in a particular culture or society; if it is translated into new forms how is their validity in respect of truth and relevance to be evaluated? This is the crux of attempts to restate Christian truth in our day. Differing formulations are offered; how are they to be judged? In our passage Paul in effect answers that the sincerity, courage, work and loving care of the preachers affirm its truth. Is such an answer sufficient? Probably not, for sincerity, courage and energetic work, if not loving care, can go with error. Paul also affirms that God has approved him (v. 4); but the self-certainty of being God's messenger is not itself, as history shows, a guarantee that God's message is being presented. There is no final logical answer; though it is easy to say that truth is self-affirmatory, many people miss it.

Paul does not directly refute the implied charges of v. 3 but going 4 back to fundamentals shows that they cannot be true for he preaches (**speak** is a present tense: Paul refers to his continuous practice and not just to his mission in Thessalonica) the gospel only as one commissioned by God whose sole aim is to serve God: God has approved of him and sent ('apostle', v. 7, means one who is sent) him; therefore his work is genuine. Paul did not just become interested in the gospel nor decide that the cause of Christianity was one behind which he should put his weight; the gospel, and that includes both its preaching and its content, has been **entrusted** to him (cf. 1 Cor. 9.17; Gal. 2.7), and though he does not say so explicitly he implies that it is God who has entrusted it to him; he was always very conscious that this apostolic duty was laid on him by God (Rom. 1.1, 5; 1 Cor. 9.16; Gal. 1.1, 10–15). God did this because he **approved** of Paul. **approved**

95

and **scrutinizes** are different parts of the same verb, δοκιμάζειν; it is very unlikely that it means 'approve' at its second appearance. The basic sense is 'test, try, examine', but since tests and examinations are only carried out so that whatever passes them may be used the word comes to mean 'tested thoroughly and therefore fit for the purpose designed' and so **approved**. Does this mean that God examined Paul and found him worthy to be entrusted with the gospel? Did Paul think that God looked round for a suitable preacher and chose him because of his capabilities? Was he not always too conscious that God chose him despite what he was (Gal. 1.23; 1 Cor. 15.9) and chose him before he had even shown of what he was capable (Gal. 1.15)? This is true, but just as Paul believed that the other side to God's election or rejection of men was their free decision (see on 1.4) so he could believe that while God chose him as preacher yet he was also fit for the task for which God had chosen him. He speaks of Apelles as 'approved in Christ' (Rom. 16.10) and of the 'approved' being known through their behaviour at the Corinthian celebration of the eucharist (1 Cor. 11.19). In a long passage in 2 Cor. 13.5ff he emphasizes the need for both his Corinthian opponents and himself to be approved. All true approval is before God, even though a man ought always to 'prove' himself (1 Cor. 11.28). 'Approvedness' is thus closely linked to God's judgement, and Paul always served God hoping that he would not in the end be 'unapproved' (1 Cor. 9.27). There is no reason then to doubt that when Paul speaks of himself here as **approved** (perfect tense representing a past action which has resulted in a settled fact or state) for the task of the gospel he means more or less than he says; either more if **approved** is made to carry the nuance of election (Rigaux) or less if it implies a denial of his election. But he does not tie down God's approval to some specific period in his life, e.g. the years between his conversion and his mission with Barnabas. **approved** can hardly be reduced to the primary meaning 'test' in the first part of the verse; if Paul is entrusted with the gospel after 'test' it goes without saying that he has been approved.

If Paul has been **approved** and **entrusted** by God with the gospel this does not mean that God takes no further interest in Paul and leaves him to get on with his preaching; God continually **scrutinizes** (present participle) Paul's life and conduct and Paul could lose God's approval (1 Cor. 9.27). Knowing this he therefore serves men in the cause of the gospel not as pleasing them but as **pleasing God** (cf. Gal. 1.10). The unusual negative οὐ which Paul uses here with the participle **pleasing** means that he affirms not just his intention ('seeking to please') but the actual fact that it is being accomplished—and accomplished because he does not act out of error or impurity or deceitfully (v. 3). This may appear an arrogant claim on Paul's part: it would be easier to say 'seeking to please', but if there is no certainty about what he is doing the message itself will sound uncertain; the claim is no greater than that of v. 3, viz., that his motives were pure. He might deceive men but he cannot deceive God who knows what goes on in his **heart**; Paul's language is influenced here by Jeremiah (e.g. 11.20; 12.3) as it is also in Gal. 1.12, 15, 16; Paul often speaks of himself in language drawn from the prophets, e.g. 2 Cor. 12.1–12, as if he regarded himself as in their succession. Henneken, pp. 98ff, suggests that he saw himself as the prophet of the End which is shortly to break in; in Galatians and 2 Corinthians Paul writes in the first singular but here in the plural; either then he says the same here of Timothy and Silas as of himself or else he forgets that he is writing in the joint name or at this earlier stage of his theology he may have been ready to say of others what he later restricted to himself. **Heart** is not used metaphorically as in English of the centre of emotion; Paul's usage derives ultimately from the O.T. where the heart is the seat of the mind and will and can stand simply for the whole person (cf. 3.13). Here it is Paul's inner life in its totality of thought and intention which God **scrutinizes** (on **heart** see W. D. Stacey, *The Pauline View of Man*, London, 1956, pp. 194–7; J. Behm, *T.D.N.T.* III, pp. 611–13); what goes on may escape the eye of the human beholder but God sees where men cannot see (cf. 1 Sam. 16.7). What Paul has been saying of **5** his mission in general (vv. 3f) he now applies (vv. 5–12) directly to his mission to Thessalonica, and as in 2.1 and 2.3 he begins with the negative aspect and moves to the positive. Even though he now moves to the particular situation of the Thessalonians we should not take the three negative statements (vv. 5,6) as parallel to and explanatory of the three negative phrases of v. 3; only the general ideas are similar.

The Thessalonians had heard Paul and his companions and therefore could **know** (when Paul was speaking generally in vv. 3f he made no such appeal) whether they spoke flatteringly or not. If the gospel were presented with **flattering speech** (literally 'speech of flattery', meaning either 'motivated' or 'characterized by flattery') its whole cutting edge would be blunted: the truth of God must be expressed in true words. It has always been one of the great temptations of speakers to gain their ends by flattery, though of course words which the speaker only intends in a friendly manner are often taken by those already disposed to criticism as 'flattery'. In our passage the idea goes even further in that the orator is not merely depicted as attempting to cajole his hearers by skilful flattery to accept what he believes to be true, and which may well indeed be true, but he is depicted as using **flattering speech** to gain some selfish purpose for himself. Schmithals is a little far-fetched in comparing Paul's plain words with the ecstatically convicting speech of his opponents (pp. 106f).

From the outward behaviour which the Thessalonians could judge **(as you know)** Paul turns to the inward motive which God alone can know. Frequently Paul calls in **God** as **witness** to the sincerity of his behaviour in matters which his readers could know nothing about themselves (Rom. 1.9; 2 Cor. 1.23; 1 Th. 2.10; cf. Ps. 9.1, etc.; the usage is a development from the O.T., e.g. Job 16.19; Ps. 88(89).37; Wisd. 1.6).

With a veiled desire to exploit is literally 'in (by) a pretext (πρόφασις) of avarice'. πρόφασις can be 'cause' or 'reason' and morally neutral, producing the meaning, 'by reason of avarice', i.e. avarice was the real motive. But it regularly has a bad sense (e.g. Phil. 1.18; Mt. 23.13), 'pretext', pretence', and so means here 'in a false outward attitude inspired by avarice'. If ἐν is read (with ℵ* A D) the latter is more likely; if it is omitted (with B ℵᶜ 33), the former. In either case the meaning is quite clear: Paul and his companions did not come to Thessalonica to exploit the Thessalonians. 'Avarice' (πλεονεξία) is wider than a mere desire for money, though that is part of it (cf. v. 9; by the time of 1 Pet. 5.2 money was a temptation to church leaders, cf. 1 Tim. 3.3; Tit. 1.7); in the N.T. it and its cognates are often associated with impurity, but this seems accidental, rather than imparting a special N.T. flavour to the word. Lightfoot, discussing Col. 3.5, aptly defines it as an 'entire disregard for the rights of others'. In this wider sense it goes quite naturally with the other two members of the triad.

6, 7a   The third rebuttal of Paul runs into verse 7; the verse division in most printed Greek texts is wrongly placed and would be better after ἀπόστολοι, where in fact most translations make the division.

If Paul and his companions in their preaching did not use the wrong weapons of flattery nor set out for their own selfish ends to exploit their hearers, neither did they desire **honour from** (ἐκ and ἀπό are synonymous; cf. Moulton–Turner, p. 259) **men** (**you**, the Thessalonian Christians; **others**, either Christians in general or men in general; it is not clear which) so that everyone would look up to them and praise them and satisfy their vanity and pride. Paul, of course, is not indifferent to the success of his mission and God's praise which goes with it (cf. 2.19f). If the second member of the triad referred to material gain this is no longer in view and Paul is dealing with a greater peril—spiritual pride. It may seem almost laughable that Paul who endured so much and appears to us so sincere should seek so strenuously to defend the purity of his missionary activity but the ancient world was full of wandering philosophers, prophets of new religions, magicians, 'divine men', about whom secular writers warn as to their sincerity (cf. Lucian, *De Morte Peregrini* 13; *Dialogi Mortuorum* 10.8; Dibelius, *ad loc.*, gives a long selection of evidence; cf. Georgi, *op. cit.*, pp. 234ff). The *Didache* warns about wandering Christian prophets who try to impose themselves on a community by settling down in it and living on it (11.3ff). Paul is quite obviously also aware of the motives that move men and of the depth of evil in the human heart so that what seems to be a wholly good action is performed from baser reasons; no one who is fully honest with himself when he writes or speaks can be unaware of the subtle temptations of which Paul writes; someone of Paul's vigorous leadership may have been above all conscious of the possibility that he might act for 'glory' rather than to serve God. Though Paul does not seek honour from men perhaps the unspoken contrast is to be accepted that he does seek it from God (Rigaux). Denis (*op. cit.*) notes that while Paul is describing his own position he uses O.T. language but when he turns to his missionary activity in vv. 5, 6 he uses words either drawn from the Hellenistic world (**flattery, exploit**) or words common to both used with a non-Biblical but good Hellenistic sense (**honour**).

But as **Christ's apostles** might not Paul and his companions have been expected to receive **honour**? In other letters Paul emphasizes his apostolic position (e.g. Gal. 1.1, 15-17; Rom. 1.1) and the authority which he exercised (2 Cor. 10.8; 13.10; 2 Th. 3.4; 1 Cor. 5.3) and yet also his 'weakness' (1 Cor. 4.9ff; 2 Cor. 3.4ff; 4.7ff, 17; 6.4ff; 12.9). How far is this to be understood of his companions? Paul never elsewhere explicitly names Silvanus and Timothy as apostles though he does send them on missions; yet he does not restrict **apostle** to himself and the Twelve (cf. Rom. 16.7; 1 Cor. 4.9; Phil. 2.25) though he also uses the term of himself in a way comparable to the way it was used of the Twelve but not of Apollos, Junias, etc. At this stage on the second journey he may not have formulated fully his own position as an apostle as he did later in 1 Cor. 9.1; 15.5ff; 2 Cor. 10.13, and therefore may have been able to consider Silvanus and Timothy as apostles alongside himself. The way in which he exercises his apostleship is outlined here in vv. 7b-12; love, not authority, is the mainspring of his apostolic actions. However whatever responsibility the church ought to have towards an apostle he envisages this as here including Silvanus and Timothy. (On **apostle** see the articles by A. M. Farrer and G. Dix in *The Apostolic Ministry* (ed. K. E. Kirk), London, 1946, pp. 113-303; K. H. Rengstorf, *T.D.N.T.* I, pp. 407-47; T. W. Manson, *The Church's Ministry*, London, 1948, pp. 31-52; V. Taylor, *The Gospel According to St. Mark*, London, 1952, pp. 619-27.) But what was that responsibility? The word rendered **importance** could be rendered 'burden', and mean a material burden, the church being responsible for the financial upkeep of the three missioners. Elsewhere Paul indicates that the church was so responsible, though as here he did not himself always expect to be looked after (cf. 1 Cor. 9.3-18; 2 Cor. 11.7-11; 12.14-18; 2 Th. 3.8). 'Burden' accords with this and is in harmony also with the references in v. 5 to exploitation and in v. 9 to Paul's refusal to be a charge on them. On the other hand this clause is more closely linked to v. 6 which deals with dignity, authority and importance **(honour)** than to **exploit** in v. 5; the same Greek word is found in 2 Cor. 4.17 associated with **honour** and we would expect an explicit reference 'to you' as in v. 9 but it is lacking. We therefore take **importance** to be the primary significance (cf. Henneken, pp. 14-17) but Paul may well have been aware of the word's ambiguity and intended a secondary allusion to his upkeep (for a Jew 'burden' and 'honour' are closely related in the root *kbd*); if so the secondary meaning comes to the surface in v. 9. Findlay suggests 'we might have sat heavily upon you' as a rendering combining both meanings.

but we were gentle: now comes the antithesis as in v. 2 and 7b v. 4. There is an important variant here: ἤπιοι A K 33 81 **(gentle)**; νήπιοι P⁶⁵ ℵ B D* G ('infants'). The MSS evidence favours the latter, we should expect a noun to balance 'apostles' and it is a bold image of the type not uncommon in Paul, suggesting that he accommodated himself to the level of his hearers as children in the faith (cf. 1 Cor. 3.1). However 'infants' requires a sudden inversion of metaphor in the next clause and though Paul can change his metaphors rapidly (2 Cor. 3.13-16; Rom. 7.1ff) this is no argument that he would have done so here; **gentle** fits in appropriately with the defence Paul puts up in vv. 5, 6, contrasting vividly with 'exploit'; it leads on easily to the image of mother-love in the next clause; and at 1 Cor. 3.1 where Paul uses νήπιοι of his converts he uses it derogatively, and this is his general usage: Rom. 2.20; 1 Cor. 13.11; Gal. 4.1, 3; Eph. 4.14(?); at 1 Cor. 4.14 he uses a different word. In the copying of the manuscripts either reading could have come from the other through dittography or haplography since the preceding word ends in *v*. (For a fuller discussion see B. M. Metzger, *The Text of the New Testament*, Oxford, 1964, pp. 230-3.) In using his legitimate apostolic authority and asserting his importance Paul treated the Thessalonians gently.

Commentators are divided whether the last clause of v. 7 goes with what precedes it or what follows. We take it with what follows (cf. Dibelius) because the **as . . . so . . .** seems to hold it together, and vv. 7c, 8, and not 7c alone, appear to expound the conception of 'gentleness'.

Paul pictures himself as a **nursing-mother** (for the image, cf. 1 QH 7.20-2; 9.29-32 where the relationship of the teacher of righteousness and the community may be set under the metaphor of a nursing-father; cf. H. D. Betz, *N.T.S.* 3 (1957) 320-2; W. Grundmann, *N.T.S.* 5 (1959) 198-200. But the parallel is not very exact and it is probably better to see the image as derived from the cynics where the good philosopher is pictured as a gentle nurse; cf. Malherbe, *op. cit.*). This word is used of a 'wet-nurse' but often also of the mother herself for the period until the child is weaned; a nurse could hardly be expected to show as much care for the children in her charge as their mother and Paul can regard his converts as his children, usually from the point of view of a father (1 Cor. 4.14; 1 Th. 2.11). In the very early days after their conversion the Thessalonians were like unweaned children and Paul as their spiritual parent has to **cherish** and love them with great gentleness. We have a somewhat unusual picture of ministerial care, even more tender than that of the pastor-shepherd. The same word **cherish** is used in Eph. 5.29 of Christ's care for the church. 'A mother in nursing her child makes no show of authority and does not stand on any dignity . . . (and) reveals a wonderful and extraordinary love, because she spares no trouble or effort, avoids no care, is not wearied by their coming and going, and gladly even gives her own life blood to be drained' (Calvin, *ad loc.*). Schmithals (p. 108) compares 2 Cor. 12.14 and argues that the same image is used there of 'upkeep': but the comparison is not as exact as he supposes and the words are very different; v. 8 which continues the metaphor here goes far beyond the financial idea.

8   This verse, closely joined to v. 7c, continues to express Paul's deep love of the Thessalonians. The derivation of ὁμείρεσθαι **(great care)** is uncertain but though it is very rare its meaning is broadly clear: it expresses desire and affection as its use in Job 3.21 (LXX) and the explanations of the Church Fathers testify (cf. Rigaux for discussion and bibliography). **to share with you . . . being:** the one verb **share** governs both parts of the clause. But perhaps we ought to discern a zeugma (cf. Lightfoot), i.e. the second part should have another, perhaps related, verb and be translated 'but also to give our lives for you'. This can be supported by arguing that Paul's willingness to die for the Thessalonians is a full proof of his love for them and that ψυχάς is better rendered 'lives' than 'being'. While a zeugma is possible it is more reasonable to attempt to explain the clause as it stands and only if this fails to have recourse to it. ψυχή (cf. W. D. Stacey, *op. cit.*, pp. 121–7) means much more than the physical life; it is the personality, the real person. The translation **we gladly determined** (imperfect tense as the context shows despite the absence of augment; cf. Bl.–Deb. § 67; Moulton–Howard, p. 191f) **to share** (μεταδοῦναι; if the word referred to the risking of life we would expect παρδοῦναι or θεῖναι) . . . **our own being:** Paul not only gives what he has, the gospel, but what he is, himself (cf. von Dobschütz). The true missionary is not someone specialized in the delivery of the message but someone whose whole being,

completely committed to a message which demands all, is communicated to his hearers; it is because of this total involvement that Paul could write earlier of their imitation of himself (1.6; cf. 2 Cor. 7.3; 12.15). The being of the preacher and his message are not unrelated and he gives himself not only to God but also to his hearers. But no one can give where he does not love and so Paul explains his communication of himself in terms of love: when he began to preach the Thessalonians became as dear **(beloved)** to him as the child to a nursing mother; it is only God who can create such love in a man's heart. (On vv. 7f see C. Spicq, 'ἐπιποθεῖν: Désirer ou Chérir?' *R.B.*, 64 (1957) 184–95.)

This verse does not give the reason (**And** = γάρ, which, as 9 often, has here a weakened sense) for the statements of v. 8 or any earlier verse, but Paul continues to drive home his care for the Thessalonians by reminding them that even while he preached to them he was not dependent on them for his upkeep (cf. v. 7). The accusation that they were in it for the money has been thrown up against so many successful evangelists that we ought not to be surprised to find Paul accused of it (cf. the accusations made against some Cynic philosophers). **hard labour and toil** represents two words which Paul employs (2 Th. 3.8; 2 Cor. 11.27) as a unit to express the fatigue and hardship of work; they are in any case difficult to distinguish from one another. In 2 Th. 3.8 the phrase refers to the work which Paul does for his upkeep; here it could refer both to this and to his preaching, but it is hardly likely that Paul would apply such terms to his preaching. The extent of Paul's labour to support himself is brought out further by **day and night;** it was time-consuming. In the Greek the phrase runs 'night and day' which is the regular order for the joint phrase in Greek, Latin and Hebrew; no significance therefore attaches to it here (i.e. that Paul worked by night and preached by day); English requires the reverse sequence. Unlike the Greeks and Romans the Jews did not look down on working with the hands and every Jew was expected to teach his son a trade; in particular a Rabbi was required to learn a trade if he was not financially independent. Rabbi Gamaliel III said 'Excellent is study of the Law together with worldly occupation, for toil in them both puts sin out of mind. But all study of the Law without (worldly) labour comes to naught at the last and brings sin in its train' (M. Aboth 2.2; cf. 4.5; translation as in Danby, *The Mishnah*, Oxford, 1933;

contrast Sir. 38.24–39.11). Yet seemingly Paul did not always abide
by this principle and in 1 Cor. 9.3ff he argues that the missionary
has the right to maintenance by the church and elsewhere in
Phil. 4.16 (cf. 2 Cor. 11.8) he acknowledges that he received help
from the Philippians for his work in Thessalonica. In Phil. 4.16
καὶ ἅπαξ καὶ δίς probably means 'both (when I was in Thessalonica)
and more than once (in other places) you sent . . .' (L. Morris,
'ΚΑΙ ΑΠΑΞ ΚΑΙ ΔΙΣ', N.T. 1 (1956) 205–8); it does not therefore mean that he received help a number of times from Philippi
when in Thessalonica. It may be that though Paul worked hard in
Thessalonica and elsewhere (cf. 1 Cor. 4.12) the wages were not
sufficient to allow him the necessary time off to preach; gifts from
other churches would have given him this freedom. Presumably
Paul worked at 'tent-making' (Acts 18.3; the precise significance
of the word is doubtful). Such manual labour would lead many
Greeks to despise him and his continuance at it is a measure of his
love for those to whom he preached. The way in which he emphasizes the time it took up and the degree of hardship implies a stay of
some duration in Thessalonica. He further pleads that he had not
wished **to be a charge on** them; this may take up part of the
meaning of vv. 5f; had Paul wished to exploit them he would never
have worked so hard (see also on 2 Th. 3.7–9). **preached:** this
word is related to the noun 'herald' (cf. G. Friedrich, *T.D.N.T.*
III, 683ff; C. H. Dodd, *The Apostolic Preaching* (London 1944),
pp. 7ff). As a messenger Paul brings the Gospel of God: it does
not originate with him and it is not his to adapt or change;
naturally it must be presented in a form and language that its
hearers (**to you** could be taken of movement; Paul presented himself as a herald; but probably it is equivalent to a simple dative;
so Moule, p. 69, cf. Mk. 13.10; Lk. 24.47) can understand and
accept and so though Paul uses the terms and conceptions of the
contemporary world he would have denied that he created the
gospel.

10   In vv. 10–12 while Paul continues to affirm the goodness of his
behaviour and that of his associates the stress lies not so much
now on their initial evangelism of the Thessalonians as on their
pastoral care. Again, as in v. 5, he summons God and the Thessalonians as **witnesses.** The Thessalonians are named first and
emphasized, but since even the most watchful of men can be
deceived, and part of the case of any opponents Paul may have had

must have been that the Thessalonians were deceived, he also calls on God as witness to their sincerity. Three words **holy, just, faultless** (adverbs in the original) describe their behaviour; the first two are positive in emphasis and the third negative; not only can no omission be found in their conduct (for **faultless** see Phil. 3.6) but it fulfilled the highest ideals of goodness. It is difficult to distinguish precisely between **holy** and **just. holy** here renders ὁσίως, though English **holy** in the Bible is usually the rendering of ἅγιος; but our word is found in both Jewish and Greek religious usage corresponding roughly to our 'pious' and describing an inner attitude towards God without the additional sense of 'consecrated' which is present in ἅγιος. **just** (δικαίως) does not possess here the root's profound Pauline theological sense (righteousness, justify, etc.) but has the simpler and more Greek meaning of conformity to right standards of behaviour. Lightfoot goes too far in arguing from Greek classical usage that **holy** refers to man's duty towards God and **just** to his duty towards men; to a Jew like Paul it would have been impossible to make such a rigid distinction. The two words together represent the whole gamut of man's behaviour towards God and men, **holy** stressing the inner attitude and **just** the fulfilment of God's requirements (cf. Rigaux). **towards you who believe** (a participle, cf. 1.7) is a simple dative which may be taken in a number of ways among which it is difficult to choose with any certainty: 'among you believers' (Rigaux), 'towards, to the benefit of you believers' (Lightfoot), 'in the eyes of you believers' (Wohlenberg), or taking **behaved** in another sense, 'we devoted ourselves to you believers' (Findlay). The first would have been expressed much more easily with a preposition, the third coming after **witnesses** seems superfluous, the fourth is very little different in meaning from the second, which itself would be much easier if the adverbs had been adjectives (cf. Moulton–Turner, p. 239) but is slightly preferable. There is no implicit contrast here between those who believe and those who do not as if Paul's conduct varied towards different groups; he is merely directing attention to his behaviour as they knew it as members of the Christian community.

Paul completes his defence by introducing a new metaphor, that 11– of **father** and **children**; this is more appropriate to the continued 12 pastoral situation than that of the nursing mother which relates to birth, i.e. to evangelism and mission. The mother cares for the child in its first few months but as it grows it has to be treated as a morally responsible being and advised how to live; this was the function of the father in the ancient world. (For the use of the metaphor see references to Qumran given at v. 7.) As at vv. 6, 7 there is considerable variation here as to the point at which v. 12 begins; we have followed the convention accepted by the majority of Greek printed texts though it is at variance with many English translations. There is also considerable difficulty in the construction, though not in the meaning. **exhorting, encouraging, insisting** are participles; they may be taken as representing indicatives (so Frame; cf. 2 Cor. 7.5) but this is unsatisfactory since v. 11 is then left without any verb (we have supplied **we counselled**; it is not in the Greek). It is therefore better to take the participles as dependent on **behaved** in v. 10 (so Wohlenberg, Masson) though this, as Lightfoot says, is harsh since it gives two objects to the participles (**each one of you** and **you**) which is very clumsy and the participles are distant from the verb, or, preferably, to take vv. 11f as an anacoluthon (so Lightfoot, Rigaux); Paul in his dictation becomes involved in a long sentence and omits a finite verb (see Gal. 2.4; Rom. 8.3; 2 Cor. 7.5b; cf. 1 Th. 2.19; 3.6; 2 Th. 2.3f) which we have supplied with **counselled**. The first two participles, **exhorting, encouraging,** are very similar in meaning; the first is used more frequently by Paul than the second and he never uses the second in any of its verbal or substantival forms except alongside the first (5.14; 1 Cor. 14.3; Phil. 2.1); it is therefore probably better to see them as supporting one another rather than to take the first, because **you** follows it directly, as explained by the second and third. In Paul's letters the first has a technical function (see on 4.1) which is not present here since he is referring to his oral pastoral advice, encouragement and admonition of the Thessalonians when he was with them (at 5.14 the technical meaning is present but **encourage** is used as here). However when Paul spoke as a pastor to his people in this way he believed that he spoke in God's name and with God's authority (2 Cor. 1.3–4; cf. O. Schmitz and G. Stählin, *T.D.N.T.* V, pp. 773–99). Paul never took his pastoral work lightly as if he were merely issuing good advice; he counselled his churches whether individually or collectively (**each one of you** shows how important he took the individual to be as if he were remembering their separate needs and difficulties; cf. 5.14) with what he believed to be the word of

God (cf. 1 Cor. 7ff for the way he dealt authoritatively with particular matters) as seriously as when he first preached the gospel to them (cf. 2.3 where **appeal** comes from the same root as **exhort** here). Both **exhort** and **encourage** contain the meanings 'admonish' and 'console', but these two meanings are not as far apart as it may appear: 'In the N.T., however, admonition becomes genuine comfort and *vice versa* . . . The unity of admonition and consolation is rooted in the Gospel itself, which is both gift and task.' (Stählin, *op. cit.*, p. 820.) The third participle, **insisting**, introduces a slightly different conception: with God's authority behind him Paul's admonitions and consolations are not mere entreaties and requests but demands for God's way to be followed. These demands are summed up in the metaphor **walk**, one of Paul's favourite words to describe the Christian life which he derived from his Jewish background where it was very common: the metaphor is also found in non-Biblical Greek and would have been easily understood by his readers. In Acts Christianity is known as 'the way' (19.9, 23; 22.4; 24.14); primitive Christianity looked on discipleship as 'movement', 'pilgrimage' (Mk. 8.34). Since **walk** is a neutral concept and can denote good or bad behaviour Paul qualifies it here with the adverb **worthily**, which does not give a detailed prescription of commandments but sets conduct directly in relationship to God and his character. Its use (cf. Phil. 1.27; Col. 1.10) might suggest that Paul expected men to be worthy of God before they reached his **kingdom and glory** but he is saying no more than he does in any of his letters where his statement of the Christian's new being and new relationship to God must be expressed in terms of a way of life, a way of love which imitates the love of God who has created the new being and relationship. There is no implied threat here that their attainment of God's kingdom and glory depends on the worthiness of their walk, though the eschatological reference implies that a 'worthy walk' is the kind of conduct appropriate to God's kingdom and glory, the kind of conduct which those who inherit the kingdom will demonstrate in the kingdom. The whole purpose of his counselling, his pastoral work, is that they should live obediently to God's will. He does not abandon them to others once they have become Christians through his mission.

Though Paul preaches it is God **who calls**: there is a variant reading here of an aorist tense, 'who called' (ℵ A syr^{p,h} cop); the support for the present tense (B D G 33 81) is slightly stronger. Elsewhere Paul normally uses the aorist (4.7; 2 Th. 2.14; Gal. 1.6, etc.) relating God's call of the Christian to the beginning of the Christian life but he occasionally uses the present (5.24; Gal. 5.8) and our variant is probably due to the assimilation of an original present tense to his normal procedure. The present (a participle) may either be taken as a substantive, 'God is the one who calls' (i.e., a description of his character, 'the caller', who keeps on calling new members into his people) or more probably, since it accords with the future reference of **kingdom and glory**, denotes the continuous and effective call of God (for Paul God's call is effective, Rom. 8.30; 1 Cor. 1.9; 1 Th. 5.24) which can reassure his readers that they will attain to the kingdom and glory even though their walk is not always worthy of God. But also if God continually calls man must continually answer in faith.

Men are called to God's **kingdom;** this concept formed an important part of the teaching of Jesus for whom the kingdom did not primarily denote a place but the active rule of God and as such was both present in his own activity and was to be realized fully in the near future. Paul uses the term more rarely and for him it is sometimes a present reality (Rom. 14.17; 1 Cor. 4.20; Col. 1.13) but more often something which men will inherit in the future (1 Cor. 6.9f; Gal. 5.21; 2 Th. 1.5) after they have been given a wholly new nature (1 Cor. 15.50). It is this eschatological sense which is present here and, unlike Jesus, Paul thinks rather of it as a place than as God's active rule, though of course God will rule in the 'place'; those whom God has called will inherit his kingdom (cf. K. L. Schmidt, *T.D.N.T.* I, pp. 579ff; R. H. Fuller, *The Mission and Achievement of Jesus* (S.B.T. 12), London, 1954; W. G. Kümmel, *Promise and Fulfilment* (S.B.T. 23), London, 1957; H. M. Shires, *The Eschatology of Paul*, Philadelphia, Penn., 1966, pp. 60–3). The Thessalonians are also called to God's **glory;** this term has an extensive O.T. and Jewish background. Glory belongs essentially to God who confers it on objects and people associated with him; in the N.T. this glory is seen above all in the life, death and resurrection of Jesus (2 Cor. 4.4–6). Because glory comes from God men ascribe it to him (Rom. 4.20; 11.36; 2 Cor. 1.20) and because God will manifest himself fully in the end glory obtains an eschatological significance (Mk. 13.26; Mt. 25.31; 1 Pet. 4.13; etc.); men will share in this glory (Rom. 5.2; 8.18;

etc.) when they are raised in glory (1 Cor. 15.43) and for this they are already being prepared (2 Cor. 3.18); it is this eschatological significance which is present in our passage and because **kingdom** and **glory** are joined (cf. their association at Mk. 8.38 and 9.1) with only one article we might well translate 'glorious kingdom' (cf. Morris). (On **glory** see G. von Rad and G. Kittel, *T.D.N.T.* II, pp. 233ff; A. M. Ramsey, *The Glory of God and the Transfiguration of Christ*, London, 1949).

RENEWED THANKSGIVING 2.13-16

And because of (all) this we for our part unceasingly thank God that when you received from us the word of the message of God you accepted not a word of men but, what it really is, a word of God, which works in you who believe. (14) For you, brothers, became imitators of the Christian communities of God which are in Judea in Christ Jesus because you endured the same afflictions from your fellow-countrymen as they endured from the Jews (15) who killed both the Lord (i.e. Jesus) and the prophets, who persecuted us, who are not pleasing to God and who are opposed to everyone, (16) hindering us from preaching to the Gentiles that they may be saved, so as always to fill to the full their sins; and the anger has caught up with them finally.

Paul continues his exposition of 2.1, that the word had not been fruitless among them, and renews his thanksgiving. It is here that Schmithals believes the fourth letter (his D) began, written in a mood of rejoicing after Timothy's return (cf. pp. 31ff). 2.13f take up 1.6-8, whose key themes (the word, imitation, affliction) recur here, with the movement from the presentation of the gospel (2.1-12) to its reception (2.13f); this reception is seen in the way in which the Thessalonians have endured persecution. The reference to persecution leads Paul to a violent outburst against the Jews and to a declaration that God has finally judged them (2.15f).

And: the argument is advanced from the manner and fact of 13 the preaching of Paul and his companions to the way in which the Thessalonians received it. It is not **because** he dealt lovingly with them (2.10-12) but **because** the gospel was not delivered in vain (2.1; cf. 1.5–7) that he now makes it clear that he is still giving thanks (cf. 1.2; 3.9). He did not **thank God that** (ὅτι could be causal but more probably gives the content of the thanksgiving) he was sincere in this mission but he does thank him that the Thessalonians responded to it. In the Greek **we** is preceded by καί, 'and, even, also'; 'and' is an impossible meaning here; καί might go with **thanks** in the sense 'we give thanks again' (i.e. after 1.2) but its position suggests it qualifies **we**. It could thus mean 'we also'; but 'also' implies others are giving thanks; who would these be? There is no clue here; the only possibility is the Thessalonians; but when did they do so and would they not also have given thanks at 1.2? R. Harris has used this to argue that the Thessalonians had written to Paul and that he is answering their letter; there is little positive evidence for such a letter (cf. pp. 14–16). It is better with Rigaux (cf. Lightfoot, Masson, etc.) to take καί in a weakened sense as emphasizing **we**, 'we for our part' (cf. the whole phrase διὰ τοῦτο καί + a personal pronoun at Eph. 1.15; Col. 1.9; 1 Th. 3.5).

In **when you received** Paul employs a verb (παραλαμβάνειν) which he uses regularly for the transmission of material in more or less fixed form: 1 Cor. 11.23, of the Eucharist; 1 Cor. 15.1, 3, of an early confessional statement; 1 Th. 4.1, of catechetical material; 2 Th. 3.6, of ethical 'tradition'; Gal. 1.9, 12, of the gospel which he originally preached in Galatia (Col. 2.6 is akin to this if 'Jesus Christ' is the content of the gospel); in Phil. 4.9; Col. 4.17 the word is used differently. Here the verb follows Paul's normal usage since it refers to the gospel which he originally handed over to the Thessalonians; it is suggestive of the action of a Rabbi transmitting material to a pupil, and of course Paul was accustomed to this before he became a Christian. (Cf. W. D. Davies, *Paul and Rabbinic Judaism*, London, 1948, pp. 247–50; O. Cullman, *The Early Church*, London, 1956, pp. 59–99; G. F. Moore, *Judaism*, Cambridge, Mass., 1927–30, I, pp. 251–62; B. Gerhardsson, *Memory and Manuscript: Oral and Written Transmission in Rabbinic Judaism and Early Christianity*, Uppsala, 1961; K. Wegenast, *Das Verständnis der Tradition bei Paulus und in den Deuteropaulinen*, Neukirchen, 1962, pp. 9–23, 49f; see also notes on 2 Th. 2.15.) The Greek word was already in use for the instruction which a philosopher gave to his pupils and in the mystery religions for the handing on of secrets to new initiates. If Paul took over the Greek word for a process somewhat akin to one to which he was accustomed in Judaism, the emphasis lies much more on the transmission of existing material than on its creation through speculative thought in philosophy, and the public nature of its transmission distinguishes it from the mystery religions. Paul does not regard himself as the creator of the gospel but its transmitter; he hands on what he has received from God; 'from the Lord' in 1 Cor. 11.23 cannot mean 'by direct revelation' since what he hands on is partly an account of a historical event; it is 'from the Lord' because he is the ultimate source as its initiator.

The gospel or **word** which he transmitted to the Thessalonians has been equally initiated by God (cf. G. Delling, *T.D.N.T.* IV, pp. 11–14). Part of this is expressed in the compact phrase **from us the word of the message of God**: what they heard **(the message)** was **the word** (see on 1.6) **of God** received through **(from)** his apostles. **Message** (lit. 'report') probably entered the Christian vocabulary from Isa. 53.1 and became equivalent to 'gospel', 'preaching' (cf. Rom. 10.16f; Gal. 3.2, 5), but since it comes from the word 'to hear' it may also contain the idea of obedience which to the Jew was implied in true hearing; there was then 'obedient hearing' among the Thessalonians (cf. Henneken, pp. 47–52). The Thessalonians **accepted** (ἐδέξασθε, practically synonymous with **received** but perhaps lays more stress on the action of the hearers than the latter which emphasizes rather the transmission of the message; **accept** is used regularly for the acceptance of the gospel, e.g. 1.6; Acts 8.14; 11.1; 2 Cor. 6.1; 11.4) **not a word of men** (plural: Paul, Silvanus and Timothy) **but . . . word of God.** Certainly the Thessalonians accepted human words, those of the apostles, but since these were the proclamation of the gospel they were **really** the word of God. The divine word sounding in the human words could be so easily missed and the words taken as merely human words. Paul makes here the daring claim which identifies his words with God's word. Whoever accepts his words believingly (this is the significance of **you who believe** and of **message** = 'hearing') accepts what those words really are, viz., 'the word of God', the divine message. This is not an identification of Paul's words, word by word, with God's word as if he were an infallible and verbally inspired channel, but a statement that the gospel which Paul preached (and for Paul there was no other gospel; Gal. 1.6–9) was God's good news. Of this Paul never had any doubt. What he said 'he did not submit to men as a theme for discussion . . . he published it . . ., as the word of God, for the obedience of faith' (Denney). When the word is believingly accepted in this way then it transforms those who accept it because it **works** in them. With Lightfoot we have taken ἐνεργεῖται as middle; if it is passive, as J. A. Robinson, *Ephesians*, pp. 243ff, argues, then God is the virtual subject, 'which is worked in you by God'; the meaning is in either case the same since the word is the word of God (cf. G. Bertram, *T.D.N.T.* II, pp. 652–4; K. W. Clark, 'The Meaning of ἐνεργέω and κατεργέω in the N.T.', *J.B.L.* 54 (1935) 93–101; and notes on 2 Th. 2.7). Faith means a new relationship; when one person trusts another this reflects back on his own conduct and changes it; when man trusts God he is by that very fact being changed. Consequently **who believe** is not a verbose addition to the verse but essential to its thought; a simple **you** would be inadequate to carry the first part of the verse. Verse 14 provides the evidence that the word worked in the Thessalonians. That the **word** of God is powerful is seen both in creation (Gen. 1.3; Ps. 33.6) and in the redemptive history of Israel (Jer. 23.29); by it men are reborn (1 Pet. 1.23–5) and sanctified (John 17.17). It possesses this power because it is the word coming from God who himself makes it effective.

14 **For:** the Thessalonians have clearly shown their acceptance of the Word of God by the persecution they have endured. As in 1.6 imitation is linked to suffering; this also is the motif in Jesus' own call to his disciples (Mk. 8.34). In v.14 however the emphasis does not lie so much on the individual imitation by Christians of other Christians as on the imitation by the Christian community in Thessalonica of **communities in Judea.** There may have been individual failures in any of these communities but taken as a whole the Thessalonians have followed worthily in the footsteps of their Judean fellows. Why did Paul pick on the relatively remote Judean churches and not on some community which he had himself evangelized? If we argue the parallel that the church in Thessalonica was persecuted by its fellow-countrymen incited by Jews and that the Jews in Judea had persecuted the churches there then we should not forget that most of the churches founded by Paul suffered persecution at the hands of their fellow-countrymen incited by Jews, and this parallel is closer. Moreover since

Paul could use the example of one of his churches to others (e.g. 2 Cor. 8.1ff; 9.2ff) why did he not do so here? Did Paul select the Judean churches: (a) because of their prestige as the area where Christianity was born; (b) because their endurance was widely known; (c) because they had stood up to their persecutions more stoutly than others; (d) because he himself had been involved in persecution in Judea both as persecutor (though Gal. 1.22 may go against this) and as persecuted (in v. 15 he refers to his own persecution); (e) because the history of the primitive community was included in the Pauline kerygma (so D. M. Stanley, op. cit.; there is no real evidence that it was)? We simply do not know sufficient of the circumstances to be able to answer with any certainty. Elsewhere Paul compares the sufferings of others with his own (Phil. 1.29f; 2 Cor. 1.6; cf. 1 Pet. 5.9). It is interesting that Paul can assume knowledge in Thessalonica of what the Judean Christians endured and refer to it when he refers so rarely to the life of Jesus (perhaps his own personal involvement accounts for it) and that (cf. Lightfoot, Lünemann) he cannot have been at such odds with the Judean churches as the Tübingen hypothesis proposes if he chose them as examples (Baur was led to reject vv. 14–16 as a gloss). We do not know to what persecutions Paul refers; he writes as if they were past (**endured** is an aorist); this would be so if they were those in which he himself had been involved. Bo Reicke, 'Der geschichtliche Hintergrund des Apostelkonzils und der Antiochia-Episode, Gal. 2.1–14' in *Studia Paulina* (Haarlem, 1953), pp. 172–87, thinks that Paul is referring to contemporary persecution of Christians by Zealots. This is more doubtful. The Judean churches appear to have remained a well-organized body throughout this period (cf. D. R. A. Hare, *The Theme of Jewish Persecution of Christians in the Gospel according to St. Matthew* (S.N.T.S. Monograph Series No. 6), Cambridge, 1967, pp. 62–4) and the phrase 'endure affliction' (πάσχειν) is general; physical persecution may not have been the main element in their sufferings. It is unlikely that the Thessalonians will have been conscious **imitators** (see on 1.6 for the idea) of the Judean churches; rather 'the power of the gospel' 'has worked itself out in the lives of the believers so that a certain pattern results' (Tannehill, *op. cit.*, p. 103); this is confirmed by the fact that persecution cannot be self-induced but is the result of others' action.

Christian communities: see on 1.1. Although there was only one in Thessalonica, divided perhaps into a number of house-meetings, there would be many in Judea, one in each town. **Judea** itself is not the restricted area of Roman Judea but includes Samaria and Galilee, what we normally term Palestine (cf. Luke 1.5; 23.5; Acts 10.37; Josephus, *Ant.* 1.160; Tacitus, *Hist.* 5.9). The **communities** are defined as **of God**: this clearly distinguishes the word for 'Christian community' from its secular usage of any assembly; it is derived from the LXX where it frequently qualifies ἐκκλησία. Cerfaux, *La Théologie de l'Église suivant saint Paul* (Paris, 1948), pp. 80ff, argues cogently that Paul always adds **of God** when he is referring to the churches of Judea (cf. 2 Th. 1.4; Gal. 1.13, 22; 1 Cor. 11.16) and that this represents their primitive pre-Pauline title; if so the addition has really no special significance in our context. The further qualification **in Christ Jesus** (see on 1.1) has been taken (cf. Frame) as distinguishing the Christian church from the Jewish since the Jews would have understood it to refer to themselves in the LXX; more probably Paul uses it here after the plural to denote the unity of the Judean Christian communities and also, perhaps more importantly, to stress the unity between them and the Christians of Thessalonica; whereas the mention of Judea distinguishes the Thessalonians from the Judeans, **in Christ Jesus** unites them. All are one in Christ and all owe their salvation to the redemption which took place in Christ. With **fellow-countrymen** Paul refers primarily to the Gentile fellow-citizens of the Thessalonians but Jews may also be included. In Acts 17.1ff, as often in Acts, the Jews incite the Gentiles against the young church in Thessalonica and the indefinite nature of the word would cover this. Ἰουδαῖοι **(Jews)** which Paul uses of them is not the word which they themselves would normally choose to describe themselves (it would be 'Israel'), but it was in common use in the Gentile world for them both as a race and as those who practised a particular religion. Paul means those who are Jews both by race and religion; there were many like himself who were Jews by race but Christian by religion.

15   Quite suddenly and seemingly without provocation Paul bursts out in vv. 15f into a violent accusation of the Jews; that vv. 15f are subordinate to v. 14 only makes the problem more acute. Nowhere else does Paul write quite like this; sometimes he eloquently praises the Jews (Rom. 3.1f; 9.4f), but this is really

praise of Israel as God's people rather than of their actual behaviour: he eagerly longs for their salvation (Rom. 9.2f; 10.1);
here in contrast he condemns them outright. There does not appear
to be anything in the situation of the Thessalonians, even if the
Jews were the cause of their suffering, to explain adequately the
vehemence of Paul's language; we are left to surmise an unknown
persecution in Paul's situation as he writes from Corinth. Elsewhere he tells us how he suffered greatly at the hands of the Jews
(2 Cor. 11.24, 26; cf. Acts 9.23; 13. 45, 50, etc.) **who killed the
Lord.** The N.T. employs the word **kill** ($\dot{a}\pi o \varkappa \tau \varepsilon \acute{\iota} v \varepsilon \iota v$) for the
death of Jesus elsewhere only occasionally; the normal word is
'crucify'; the present choice may be dictated by 1 Kings 19.10
where the LXX uses it (Paul quotes 1 Kings 19.10 at Rom. 11.3).
That the Jews killed Jesus is not historically accurate; he was
crucified by the Romans but the Jews plotted his death; this again
may have influenced Paul to choose the neutral **kill** rather than
the specific 'crucify' since the Jews did not actually crucify Jesus.
In the early church we find an increasing tendency for apologetic
reasons to blame the Jews for the death of Jesus and to play down
the part of the Romans; here Paul appears to be motivated by a
mixture of theological and sociological reasons; he has endured
Jewish persecution and he has seen God's elect people turn
against God's elect Messiah. **The Lord (i.e. Jesus):** Paul separates these two words, not with the intention of emphasizing one
over against the other, but of stressing their identity: the Jews
may argue that they have only plotted to kill **Jesus** but in fact
they killed the **Lord** (see on 1.1 for the title). But long before the
Jews had plotted against him they had revealed their rebellious
nature in killing God's messengers, **the prophets,** i.e. the O.T.
prophets and not the prophets of the early church (the variant
reading $\dot{\iota} \delta \acute{\iota} o v \varsigma$ was intended to make this clear). That the Jews
killed God's prophets was a persistent strain in the anti-Jewish
apologetic of the early church (Lk. 13.34; Mt. 23.31, 35, 37;
Acts 7.52; Rom. 11.3) and material for the accusation was drawn
from the O.T. (Rom. 11.3 quotes 1 Kings 19.10; cf. Jer. 2.30)
and from Jewish legends which recounted the murder of many of
the prophets of whose death Scripture said nothing (cf. *Martyrdom
of Isaiah*).

The rebellious strain in Judaism which came to a climax in
the death of Jesus did not cease then but continued with the

persecution which Christians experienced—at least that is Paul's view. The **us** who are **persecuted** are probably Paul and his companions, if the first plural is to be taken consistently in the epistle. Curiously the verb is in the past (aorist) tense as if the persecutions were over; some grammarians explain this by attraction, i.e. the past tense **killed** draws what ought to be a present tense 'persecute' into the past; but the verbs following are in the present; why were they not also attracted, or, more correctly, why did they not hold **persecuted** in the present tense? An alternative and grammatically possible translation, 'who killed the Lord, i.e. Jesus, and persecuted the prophets and us', avoids this difficulty; here the past tense of **persecuted** is quite natural in referring to the prophets; this rendering also avoids what appears to be an anti-climax in moving from the killing of the Lord to the killing of his prophets; its association of Christians and O.T. prophets in persecution is paralleled in Mt. 5.12. On the other hand Christ and the prophets are associated in suffering in Acts 7.52 and in the Christian understanding of Mk. 12.1-9, and if Paul is here dependent on 1 Kings 19.10, as Rom. 11.3 suggests, then **prophets** must go with **killed.** This is the more natural translation (cf. 1.6; 2.10). We then take **persecuted** as a real past tense referring to the persecutions Paul and his companions (and perhaps the Thessalonians also) suffered on their visit to Thessalonica and which were instigated by Jews (Acts 17.1ff). **Persecuted** (ἐκ—διώκειν) itself may have the translation 'drove out' if the prefixed preposition is given a strong sense; this would also preserve the full value of the aorist tense because expulsion by the Jews in Thessalonica would have been one definite act; the reference would be to this actual expulsion for there is no evidence that at this time Christians as a whole had been formally excommunicated from Judaism or even that Paul had been. However in the Greek of this period prepositions had lost much of their value when attached to verbs and served only to intensify their meaning; hence our rendering **persecuted.** In any case the precise application of 'drove out' is difficult; certainly the prophets could not then be included and the context (v. 14) suggests that persecution rather than expulsion from Judaism is in mind.

In the following three clauses **(pleasing, are opposed, hindering)** the verbs are in the present tense indicating a constant attitude of the Jews whose fundamental disposition became particularly observable in the crucifixion of Jesus, the death of the prophets and the persecution of Christians. **not pleasing to God** sounds weak but **pleasing to God** is one of Paul's favourite expressions for true behaviour (Rom. 8.8; 1 Cor. 7.32–4; Gal. 1.10; 1 Th. 2.4, 15; 4.1; cf. 2 Cor. 5.9); he uses it even of Jesus himself (Rom. 15.3). The opposite of pleasing God may be the direct negative as here or may be expressed as pleasing oneself or men (Rom. 15.1; Gal. 1.10; 1 Cor. 7.32–4; 1 Th. 2.4), though in Rom. 15.2 to please men for their good and not one's own is the ideal of neighbourly conduct. The Jews simply do not please God, i.e. they act directly contrary to his will, and in correlation with this they **are opposed to everyone.** Many writers of the ancient world (e.g. Tacitus, *Hist.*, 5.5, 'toward every other people they feel only hate and enmity'; Philostratus, *Life of Apollonius*, 5.33, 'The Jews have long been in revolt, not only against the Romans, but against humanity' (translations as in Loeb); Dibelius has collected a full selection of quotations in an appendix to his commentary) complain about the behaviour of the Jews and comment on the way they have earned hatred, but this is hardly Paul's attitude; he is not commenting on their cultural superiority, let alone their pride as God's people, but on their rejection of God's will seen now (v. 16) in their attempts to hinder the spread of the gospel. If that means Paul is anti-Semitic it is not because he fears Jewish hegemony over life but because he sees those whom God chose to be his people now opposing the extension of that people in the way God wants (in v. 14 he has already shown himself aware that the Gentiles oppose God's way also). Elsewhere Paul expresses his personal love of the Jewish people (e.g. Rom. 9.1–3).

hindering us ... is parallel to the preceding four clauses but is **16** not linked to them by 'and' (unexpressed in the translation) as they are to one another; it therefore explains the last clause. The Jews are opposed to all men in that they hinder Paul **from preaching** ($\lambda \alpha \lambda \epsilon \tilde{\imath} \nu$ is used of 'speaking the word' in Acts 4.29, 31; 8.25; Mk. 2.2; 4.33; cf. 14.9) **to the Gentiles** (**everyone** in v. 15 may be equivalent to **Gentiles** by a pardonable exaggeration or it may mean that by their opposition the Jews are opposed not only to the interests of the Gentiles but to their own true interests, as the rest of v. 16 demonstrates). Jewish opposition to the preaching of the gospel to the Gentiles will have been much more vehement than to its preaching to themselves for it necessarily involves the denial of their continued privileged place as the people of God. **that they may be saved** may be either final or consecutive or both; Moule, p. 142, comments 'that the Semitic mind was notoriously unwilling to draw a sharp dividing-line between purpose and consequence'. The purpose of Paul's preaching was the salvation of the Gentiles and this was also its result. The Jews would have objected to both purpose and result. **saved** is a general term expressive of redemption but not qualified here in any way in relation either to that from which the Gentiles are delivered or to that to which they are brought; it embodies everything which God has done in Christ for men; since in 1.10; 5.9 the idea is coupled with the **anger** of God the primary conception here may be deliverance from this anger.

The next clause, **so as** ($\varepsilon\iota\varsigma$ $\tau\delta$) **always to fill to the full their sins,** does not depend on **saved** but on the whole of vv. 15, 16a, or possibly on v. 16a if one of the conditions of the End is the conversion of the Gentiles (cf. Mk. 13.10), for their attempt to hinder this may be a more serious sin of the Jews than their killing of Jesus. Like the preceding clause this may be final or consecutive or both; in so far as it denotes purpose it will refer to that intended by God and not by the Jews. In Paul $\varepsilon\iota\varsigma$ $\tau\delta$ almost always denotes purpose (Moulton–Turner, p. 143) and the thought here would then be akin to what is expressed by the same phrase in Rom. 1.20 and by the general thought of Rom. 8.28–30 and chaps 9–11; the main objection to this view is the use of **always** since it is easier to envisage a continuous result than a purpose continuously achieved. In **fill to the full their sins** (the aorist infinitive with **always** is difficult; Frame suggests that the whole phrase 'while logically progressive, is regarded by the aorist collectively, a series of $\dot\alpha\nu\alpha\pi\lambda\eta\varrho\tilde\omega\sigma\alpha\iota$ being taken as one') Paul is using words drawn from Gen. 15.16 (cf. Dan. 8.23; 2 Macc. 6.14) where they refer to the sins of the Amorites against Abraham the father of the Jews; he turns them against the Jews themselves. It suggests a definite measure of sins which when completed will be followed by God's judgement (v. 16a); cf. Col. 1.24 and the filling up of a measure of sufferings. It is the implication of vv. 15f that this measure is nearly filled up—Jesus and the prophets have been killed, Paul and his fellow Christian missionaries have been persecuted, and the preaching to the Gentiles is being hindered. There has been a terrifying consistency about the conduct of the Jews throughout their history; now it has reached its climax.

The final clause of the verse has been taken in a number of different ways because its component parts are subject to varying interpretation. **the anger** can be taken either as an anger which will be disclosed at the End (cf. 1.10) or as an anger working itself out in the present to punish men (Rom. 1.18); it is doubtful if Rom. 1.18 can be wholly cleared of eschatological overtones and although 2.16 unlike 1.10 has no deliberate eschatological qualification yet because (*a*) 1.10 does precede it, (*b*) the definite article picks it out as a known phrase, (*c*) the whole tone of the letter is eschatological, and (*d*) v. 16b suggests the fulfilment of a measure, a limit, we are compelled to take it in the former sense. If it was to be understood as in Rom. 1.18ff as working out in the lives of the Jews we should expect some reference to this, e.g. to their spiritual hardening. The verb φθάνειν **(caught up with)** has been examined in great detail because of its importance for Jesus' teaching about the kingdom of God (cf. Matt. 12.28 = Lk. 11.20); it is certain that it can mean 'precede, anticipate' as in 4.15 and possibly in 2 Cor. 10.14 but it can hardly have this meaning here; it also means 'arrive, reach' and discussion has centred on whether it only means 'arrival at' without participation in whatever experience lies at the destination (see K. W. Clark, 'Realised Eschatology', *J.B.L.* 59 (1940) 367–83) or also includes participation (see W. G. Kümmel, *Promise and Fulfilment*, pp. 106f). In our verse these two meanings might be expressed as 'anger hangs over them and is just about to fall upon them' and 'anger has fallen on them and they now experience it'. The aorist tense of the verb is also difficult. To the first meaning we can compare Dan. Th. 4.24 where God's judgement has been pronounced and in that sense is in being but has not yet taken effect in the life of Nebuchadnezzar, though it is just about to do so. With the second meaning judgement has actually fallen and the aorist tense implies that it can be seen in a concrete act, or series of acts regarded as one; this does not imply that the End is in full being since it may be regarded as appearing in stages, one stage being God's judgement of the Jews (cf. E. Bammel, *op. cit.*). However this interpretation raises the question of the concrete act or series of acts which embody God's anger against the Jews. Various suggestions have been offered; the most likely appears to be Claudius's expulsion of the Jews from Rome (49 B.C.; Acts 18.2) a year or so prior to the writing of the letter (cf. also the death of Agrippa, A.D. 44; the insurrection of Theudas, Acts 5.36, c. A.D. 46; the famine of A.D. 46-7, Acts 11.27-30); but some event unknown to us may have been in mind; the history of apocalyptically oriented sects shows again and again how, given such orientation, a seemingly unimportant event can bring the conviction that God is acting, or about to act, finally. Yet, whatever it was, the event must have been well-known to his readers or they would not have appreciated Paul's casual reference here, and none of the events suggested meets this criterion. For this reason and because it fits the more general usage of the verb we prefer to take the first interpretation: judgement is about to overtake the Jews. (A related interpretation is given if we take the aorist as 'prophetic' or 'proleptic'; what is going to happen is viewed as having happened; cf. R. H. Fuller, *Mission and Achievement of Jesus*, p. 26; but this does not tie the event down to the immediate future as the general thought of 1 Thess. requires.) Paul is led to this conclusion not by some historical event but by the inner logic of what he has written about the sins of the Jews combined with his belief, apparent elsewhere in the epistle, that the End is only a short time away. It is like a condenser charged with their sins which is ready suddenly and completely to discharge itself in a destructive flash. We do not need to specify how Paul envisaged God's anger falling on the Jews; certainly there is no implication that he has the fall of Jerusalem in A.D. 70 in mind (J. B. Orchard, 'Thessalonians and the Synoptic Gospels', *Bib.* 19 (1938) 19-42, believes that Paul is dependent here on Mt. 23.29-38; 24.2b taken as actual words of Jesus and referring to the fall of Jerusalem; cf. E. Cothenet, 'La deuxième Épître aux Thessaloniciens et l'Apocalypse synoptique', *Rech. de Sc. rel.* 42 (1954) 5-39). Either interpretation of the verb accords with v. 16b; when the filling up of sins is complete, as it apparently is, judgement falls. The explanation of A. T. Hanson, *The Wrath of the Lamb*, pp. 69ff, 'the wrath has come upon them to the uttermost. The fact that the Jews were outwardly prosperous when he wrote makes no difference to the fact. To be under, or in, the wrath is primarily a spiritual condition or process' (p. 70), requires the verb to be a perfect or the use of a more straightforward 'is'; it is true that the perfect appears as a variant (B D* 330 2127 256) but this is quite obviously an attempt to remove the harshness of the verse.

The clause, whatever way we understand it, represents a complete reversal of values in Paul; the sufferings of Israel, the so-called Messianic woes, were the herald of the End and God's anger would fall on their oppressors; now the Jews are not persecuted but persecutors, not those expecting God's wrath to fall on others, but its recipients; the very people who were the objects of God's grace (Rom. 9.4f) are now the objects of his anger.

Finally: of the four possible meanings suggested for this phrase (εἰς τέλος) by Bauer the second ('to the end, until the end'; cf. Mt. 10.22; 24.13; Mk. 13.13) can be dismissed since it carries the nuance of something which happens for a period and then ceases and the eschatological tenor of the present context implies a finality about what takes place. The fourth meaning ('decisively, extremely, fully, altogether') carries that connotation but lacks any temporal reference; if as is likely v. 16c and v. 16b are parallel then our phrase which occupies the same place in the order of words as **always** should also be taken temporally (that it appears by word order to qualify **the anger** rather than the verb is true also of **always** in its clause and may not therefore be significant); but this meaning cannot be completely excluded. The third meaning ('forever, through all eternity') with the connotation of continuity is frequent in the LXX and certainly is appropriate here but with our interpretation of the verb is perhaps not as suitable as the first ('in the end, finally'); the measure of the sins of the Jews is filled up and so 'finally' the anger of God has caught up with them and is about to break on them.

It has been suggested that as in 1.9f Paul is here using traditional material similar to Mt. 23.29–38 (cf. R. Schippers, 'The pre-synoptic tradition in I Thessalonians ii 13–16', *N.T.* 8 (1966) 223–34; Orchard, *op. cit.*, Cothenet, *op. cit.*). In the Matthean passage we find that the Jews are held accountable for the death of the prophets (23.30f, 37), the persecution of the church (note the future tense in v. 34) and the completion of a measure of sins (v. 32, conceived here apparently as the death of Jesus), and there is a visitation of divine judgement (vv. 33, 36, 38). Mt. 23, an amalgam created by the evangelist, is directed against the Pharisees, but the address 'Jerusalem' in v. 37 shows that it contains material with an originally wider ambit, and while it has the fall of Jerusalem in mind, this is natural if it belongs to the period after A.D. 70 but need not have been so earlier. We have already noted Paul's unusual use of 'kill' instead of 'crucify' in v. 15; it is also used in Mt. 23.37; and **persecuted** (ἐκδιώκειν) and **opposed** (ἐναντίος) are not found elsewhere in Paul. It is therefore probable that Paul and Matthew are using the same piece of tradition, though neither is dependent on the other, and each will have worked it over (cf. Paul's favourite **please**). If this is so it to some extent lessens the contradiction between our passage and Rom. 9.3; 10.1; 11.2, 14, 26, 31, where Paul sees that while for a time the Jews may be displaced or rejected yet they will finally be saved (though it is not certain that Paul implies that every Jew will be saved). This can hardly be so here where the Jews are subject not to God's temporary displeasure but to his eschatological wrath. However Paul, using traditional material here, and perhaps suffering from some Jewish source an outrage unknown to us, may have gone beyond the solution which he worked out later and more systematically in Rom. 9–11 and 2 Cor. 3.16. Similar conceptions to that of 1 Th. 2.16c are found in parts of Mark (e.g. 11.12–25; 15.38). It must be allowed that 1 Th. 2.16c shows Paul holding an unacceptable anti-Semitic position.

The difference between the eschatological judgement of v. 16c and Rom. 9–11 has led some scholars to suggest that v. 16c is a post-Pauline addition to the letter after the fall of Jerusalem (cf. J. Moffatt, *Introduction*, pp. 72f). In some MSS of the Greek text of T. Levi 6.11 similar words are found and it is suggested that v. 16c was either derived from T. Levi or from the tradition on which it drew. The origin of the *Testaments of the XII Patriarchs* has been much disputed; the discovery of fragments of T. Levi at Qumran makes it very probable that the *Testaments* went through many editions and that T. Levi is one of the older sections, though not in its present form (cf. D. S. Russell, *The Meaning and Message of Jewish Apocalyptic*, London, 1964, pp. 55–7; O. Eissfeld, *The Old Testament: An Introduction*, Oxford 1965, pp. 631–6; M. Smith, *I.D.B.* IV, pp. 575–9). This does not answer the question of the priority of T. Levi 6.11 or 1 Th. 2.16c but we note that the saying is lacking in some MSS of T. Levi and that where it is found it is applied to the enemies of the Jews and not to themselves. It was therefore probably a piece of apocalyptic tradition which was taken up both by T. Levi in one of its editions and by the primitive church but applied in very different ways. Verses 15f as a whole have also been challenged as un-Pauline and recently Eckart, *op. cit.*, has argued this of vv. 13–16, alleging that none of it is the prose writing we would expect in a letter, that it contains no concrete material referring to actual events, that in particular there is no reference to Acts 17.1–10, that we can move easily from v. 12 to v. 17, and that the appearance of a second thanksgiving section at 2.13 is unusual. Over against this we must say: it is very difficult to resolve vv. 13f into parallel structure or see it as anything other than prose; the liturgical or credal structure of vv. 15f is clear; v. 14 has concrete data within it and these are not unsuitable for what we know of the Thessalonian situation; v. 17 admittedly does not fit well after v. 16 but it fits no better after v. 12; it is not however inappropriate after vv. 13f, recollecting that vv. 15f break the connection through the use of traditional material; there are favourite Pauline expressions (ἀκοή, ἀρέσκειν, ἀδιαλείπτως, ἐνεργεῖν, the idea of imitation) as well as traditional material. There is no need therefore to reject this entire section as un-Pauline (cf. Kümmel, *Neotestamentica et Patristica*, pp. 213–27).

PAUL'S RELATIONSHIP WITH THE THESSALONIANS AFTER HIS DEPARTURE
2.17–3.13

Continuing the thanksgiving Paul relates what has happened since the foundation of the church; after his hurried flight from Thessalonica he desired deeply to return (2.17–20) but being unable sent Timothy who reported back on the faithfulness of the Thessalonians (3.1–10); Paul ends with a prayer (3.11–13).

(a) PAUL'S DESIRE TO VISIT THESSALONICA FRUSTRATED
2.17–20

Now, brothers, when we were made orphans, physically but not spiritually, from you for a short period, we endeavoured all the more to see you face to face with great desire, (18) for we resolved to come to you, I, Paul, indeed and that several times, but Satan prevented us. (19) For

who is our hope and joy and crown of boasting—is it not you, with others—before our Lord Jesus in his Parousia? (20) Yes, indeed you are our glory and joy.

Paul's separation from the newly founded church in Thessalonica had been sudden but, though physically distant, he still felt himself linked to them and wishing to see them he made several attempts to return; frustrated each time he saw Satan's hand behind it. His great interest in and respect for the Thessalonians is evident in the language he applies to them; they are and will be everything to him.

17   **Now:** Paul moves on to a new stage in the development of his thanksgiving. It would be possible to make some contrast between **now we** and either the Jews (vv. 14–16) or the Thessalonians (v. 14) but it is difficult to define what it is and it is therefore better to take **now** (δέ) as a mere transition particle (cf. 3.6, 11; 2 Th. 2.1; etc). **brothers** also suggests a transition but by resuming the preceding address (2.1, 9, 14) serves in addition to bring out the continuity of Paul's thought. He chooses a vivid metaphor to express his sense of separation from the Thessalonians: **made orphans.** Previously he had described himself as a nursing mother (v. 7) and a father (v. 11) to them, now as a child deprived of parents. ἀπορφανίζειν has a wider sense than English **orphan** and applies also to parents deprived of children; since Paul has spoken of himself as a parent this has been taken to be the thought here; the case for it would be strengthened if Paul had written νήπιοι, 'babes', in 2.7. But Paul can switch his metaphors rapidly (cf. 'nursing-mother' to 'father') and the more vivid conception 'orphan' should be accepted. No one is orphaned voluntarily; Paul was forcibly separated from the Thessalonians (Acts 17.10). The aorist tense of **made orphans** implies a single action and not a continued state, and suggests that the **short period** (a combination of two phrases πρὸς καιρόν, cf. 1 Cor. 7.5; Lk. 8.13, and πρὸς ὥραν, cf. 2 Cor. 7.8; Gal. 2.5; Philm. 15) is over. Paul, however, has not yet been back and the aorist may refer to the period after the separation when it was felt most acutely or up to the period when Timothy returned with reassuring information (3.6). Von Dobschütz suggests that the aorist represents Paul's confidence that the separation could not be final and contains the promise that he will return to them (if the participle had

been a perfect it might have been taken as causal rather than temporal). The separation was **physical** and not **spiritual** (lit. 'in face and not heart'; a similar phrase is used at 2 Cor. 5.12; cf. 1 Cor. 5.3; Col. 2.5); **spiritual** is therefore to be understood in its modern loose usage with no reference to the Spirit of God. Paul says no more here than in 1.2f; the Thessalonians are never out of his mind though he cannot see or visit them. For Paul as for the Jew, the 'heart' is the centre of life where the mind and will are found (see on 2.4). So though Paul was aware of his spiritual unity with the Thessalonians he was not satisfied and he **endeavoured** to renew physical contact, for man is a unity of soul and body and neither can be ignored (cf. de Boor). As the reference to insuperable difficulties in v. 18 shows, Paul was not just sighing for the end of the separation but making positive efforts to bridge it and see them **face to face. all the more** ($\pi\varepsilon\varrho\iota\sigma\sigma\sigma\tau\acute{\varepsilon}\varrho\omega\varsigma$) seems to suggest a comparison and has been taken in a number of different ways: either, as often in the contemporary Greek, as equivalent to a superlative, or elatively (e.g. 'excessively', so Frame), or as a true comparative with attempts made to say where the comparison lies. Paul does not normally use it elatively but comparatively, though often without any clear indication of the comparison (cf. 2 Cor. 2.4; 7.15; 12.15) but as signifying an intensification which approaches the elative usage, here of the idea contained in **endeavoured;** English **all the more** has the necessary vagueness which lies in the word. It is difficult in our present text to find any precise comparison between Paul's greater efforts to see the Thessalonians than other Christians or the Thessalonians at other times, nor is he implying that absence itself had caused him to make greater efforts to return or that he desired to see the Thessalonians more because they were being persecuted (persecution was the normal condition of Christians, cf. 3.1-5). All that Paul intends is that he has made more than ordinary efforts to see them again (cf. Findlay). This is again intensified through the phrase **with great desire;** the urge to return drove him to make every effort. Paul's love for his converts is a fulfilment of the promise of Mk 10.29f; he had separated himself from his own race and found in his converts a new family for whom he longed and cared most deeply (cf. Denney).

Paul now explains, as it were expanding **with great desire** 18 (v. 17; $\delta\iota\acute{o}\tau\iota$ gives a reason for v. 17 and is subordinate to it), the reason for his endeavours to travel to Thessalonica: he **resolved** (an aorist like the other verbs in the passage; see on **made orphans) to come to** them; he reiterates with different words what he has just said without adding any new thought; it serves to emphasize his longing to be with them. Suddenly he narrows attention on himself **(I, Paul).** Although a contrast normally lies in *μέν* **(indeed)** it need not do so and it would be inappropriate here, for Paul has used the first plural throughout to include Silvanus and Timothy with himself and he would need to make much clearer any conception that either or both of them had not wished to return to Thessalonica as much or as often as himself or had not been hindered by Satan as he was. There is no point at which we can isolate his activity in relation to the Thessalonians in this period from that of either of his companions. The first singular represents rather a boiling up of his own personal feeling and he cannot forbear to bring it in as he writes (did he seize the pen from the hand of the scribe to whom he is dictating?). It is not clear whether **several times** goes with **I, Paul** or with **we endeavoured.** The phrase itself (lit. 'both once and twice') is idiomatic for a number of times (cf. Phil. 4.16, and in the LXX Deut. 9.13; 1 Kgdms. 17.39; Neh. 13.20; 1 Macc. 3.30); 'twice' would be too weak a rendering and 'repeatedly' too strong (cf. L. Morris, *art. cit.;* see on 2.9). We do not know when Paul made these **several** attempts to revisit Thessalonica, nor how many they were nor why they failed. Various suggestions in relation to his failure have been made: sickness (cf. Gal. 4.13; 2 Cor. 12.7), but this would not have prevented his companions (Paul is writing in the first plural); restraint by the civic authorities in Thessalonica, but this would be a continuous ban rather than the frustration of individual efforts. Paul does not need to specify the reasons for they would have been known to the Thessalonians through Timothy's visit; instead he removes them from the sphere of history into that of meta-history: **Satan prevented us.** Behind the human and physical causes lies a supernatural. Just as Paul sees his life determined by God who called and appointed him an apostle (Gal. 1.1, 15) so he sees an opposite force working to thwart God's plans. This opposite force, **Satan,** is given one of the Jewish names for the devil. Satan appears in the O.T. though he does not occupy an important position there; it is only in its latest sections that he is set out as God's adversary. In inter-testamental Judaism he increasingly became this, though always as one whose power was not unrestrained: God had created him and would completely annul his power at the End. To the contemporary world he was not just personified evil but an evil personal being. In the N.T. Satan becomes the opponent of Jesus tempting or testing him in the desert, whose lesser allies, the demons, Jesus exorcises, and who is ultimately held responsible for the crucifixion (Lk. 22.3; Jn. 13.27). Defeated in the cross he still continues to attack, tempt and frustrate men, being utterly hostile to the ways of God and always endeavouring to thwart his plans (2 Cor. 2.11; 11.3, 13–15; 12.7). At the End he will be completely vanquished. The O.T. managed for the most part to do without Satan and explained evil in other ways; it is questionable if his entrance into Jewish thought (probably under Iranian influence) really advanced theological clarity; often what is the fault of men themselves has been traced to this superhuman power and the actual causes of evil have not been fully explored and conquered. (On **Satan** see T. Ling, *The Significance of Satan*, London, 1961; E. Langton, *Essentials of Demonology*, London, 1949; T. H. Gaster, *I.D.B.* IV, pp. 224–8; Russell, *op. cit.*, pp. 235–40, 254–7.)

We do not know whether Paul ever did succeed in revisiting Thessalonica. Nor do we know how he perceived it was Satan who prevented him and not God's Spirit guiding him into other ways (Acts 16.6–10; Rom. 1.13, where the passive form of the verb probably indicates that God is the agent): we can only assume that as time went by he saw God's plans being hindered here whereas elsewhere he saw them advanced.

In words whose broken structure shows his depth of feeling 19 Paul explains in yet another image his desire to see them: they are his **hope and joy and crown of boasting** ($\mathring{\eta}$ . . . $\mathring{\eta}$ . . . can be copulative as well as disjunctive; cf. Moulton-Turner, p. 334; Bl.-Deb. § 446); there is no verb and we have supplied **is**; it might be thought that 'will be' would be more appropriate to the future reference of the Parousia but v. 20 repeats the thought and there Paul uses the present tense; moreover the contrast between **is** and 'will be' is not great if the Parousia is expected at any moment and does not belong to the indefinite future. What then does Paul mean by describing the Thessalonians in these terms? The use of **hope** seems peculiar; we expect Paul to say, 'You are our hope of joy and of the crown'. It must have here the meaning 'confidence'. In 1 Tim. 1.1 Christ is proclaimed as 'hope' (cf. Jer. 17.7 LXX; Col. 1.27) and this is a natural attribution, but we do not expect to find Paul saying that men are the basis of hope or confidence (cf. Jer. 17.5). Here however he is expressing his confidence in the Thessalonian Christians, not in men but in men of faith, and is not merely saying that because of them he hopes to be saved in the End; he is writing instead about the reward, if it can be put that way for it is not a reward for service, that lies there and which he expresses more clearly in **joy and crown** of boasting. The idea is that of the mother who says of her child, 'he is my joy'. In Phil. 4.1 he describes the Philippians as his joy and crown without any overt eschatological reference, though it is present in 3.20f if this is not part of another letter; the two ideas are linked with eschatological overtones in 1QS 4.7. The Thessalonians and the Philippians are the object of Paul's joy and he is happy to see their faith; but more than this, if indeed there is joy before God because he has been served, then Paul has served him in Thessalonica and has joy (a different aspect of **joy** appears in 3.9). The phrase **crown of boasting** comes from the O.T. (Prov. 16.31; Ezek. 16.12; 23.42) but the connections there hardly shed much light on Paul's usage. The crown in ancient times symbolized many things, among them royalty, victory (e.g. in athletic contests and in war) and priesthood. It is almost certainly the second which is relevant here. In the N.T. there is the crown of the martyr (Rev. 2.10; 2 Tim. 4.8), of the Christian who endures through trial (Jas. 1.12; Rev. 3.11) and of the faithful minister (1 Pet. 5.4); it is this note of faithfulness unto victory which lies in 1 Th. 2.19 and Phil. 4.1; the faith of the Thessalonians represents the victory of Paul. The crown is that of **boasting**. For Paul boasting is utterly wrong if undertaken in any way which suggests a man's confidence in himself. Man may only boast in God's activity; God's activity is seen in an apostle's work and in the faith of Christians; so his converts are Paul's boast before God (Phil. 2.16; 2 Cor. 1.14; cf. R. Bultmann, *T.D.N.T.* III, pp. 645ff); thus Paul can legitimately boast of a victory, won through him by God, and represented by his converts. (The rendering 'crowning glory' of Morris is incorrect since **crown** does not have in Greek the sense 'chief' as it does in English.) The Thessalonian community exists now and so Paul's boast exists now also; it is not just a fact which will come true at the End. Why then does Paul refer to the End (**Parousia**: see Appendix, pp. 349–54)? Because then what is true now, though it may not appear to be so, will be apparent as true to all (cf. 1 Cor. 3.13; 2 Cor. 5.10; Rom. 2.5). Paul cannot wait to give a formal answer to his rhetorical question and breaks into his sentence with another—**is it not you, with others?** Whatever he says about the Thessalonians he must say about others (cf. Phil. 4.1); they are no special case.

The formal answer only comes now: **Yes, indeed** (for γάρ as 20 introducing a question see Bl.–Deb. §452) they **are** his **glory and joy.** This hardly needs to be said except that Paul wishes to drive it home and therefore emphasizes **you: you** as well as others. **Joy** is repeated from v. 19; **glory** (see on 2.12) has a somewhat similar connotation to **crown** when it is used eschatologically as here (not that Paul is 'in glory'; they are his glory). Already what will be manifest at the End exists now for there can be no doubt of the reality of the Thessalonians' faith nor of their ability to endure to the End; Paul's doubts have been removed by the return of Timothy and his news (3.1–10). Neither here nor in v. 19 is there any idea that Paul is thinking in terms of service and reward; he does not say that there will be hope for him at the appearance of Jesus nor that he will receive joy, glory or a crown. The Thessalonians will be his hope, joy, glory and crown, and it is because he is thinking in such terms that he can say they are such now. Everything that a man might hold as important for himself Paul says that these Christians are and will be.

(b) TIMOTHY IS SENT 3.1–5

And so because we were no longer able to endure it we willingly resolved to remain behind alone in Athens (2) and we sent Timothy, our brother and God's fellow-worker in the gospel of Christ, to strengthen you and encourage you in respect of your faith (3) so that no one may be disturbed by these tribulations; for you yourselves know that we are destined for this; (4) for indeed when we were with you, we foretold you that we were to experience tribulation, as even it happened and as you know; (5) so, because I for my part was no longer able to endure, I sent Timothy to

129

learn about your faith, fearing that in some way the Tempter had tempted you and our labour might have been fruitless.

Hindered from going himself (2.17–20) Paul does the next best thing and sends one of his associates, Timothy, to encourage the Thessalonians against persecution which in eschatological times is a normal part of Christian life, and to learn how in fact they were faring.

1   **And so:** the stage came when Paul's anxiety about the Thessalonians became unbearable and even though it meant that he would himself be isolated he sent Timothy to Thessalonica to encourage the Thessalonians and bring back news of their progress. In this Paul displayed a true love for those in his care and a carelessness about himself. What Paul was not **able to endure** (the basic sense of the word is 'cover' which passes into the meaning 'contain', as a roof contains water from entering a building or a top to a vessel contains the liquid in it, and so passes again to the metaphorical senses 'ward off' and 'endure, bear'; the latter accords with the two other places where Paul uses the word, 1 Cor. 9.12; 13.7, and in any case it is difficult to see what Paul might be 'warding off') is not specified, but must be gathered from the context: it might be separation (2.17f) or, more probably, the inability because of the separation to strengthen the Thessalonians (v. 2), or the lack of news about what was happening to them (3.6f).

The final words, **we willingly resolved to remain behind alone,** sound almost tragic but we are unable adequately to grasp their meaning (cf. the similar phrase in the LXX of Gen. 42.38; Isa. 3.26; 49.21; 1 Macc. 13.4); Paul is making some kind of sacrifice in sending Timothy away. What was it that made Paul feel particularly **alone** (stressed by its position in the Greek **alone** almost carries the connotation 'forsaken') **in Athens?** We do not know and cannot even begin to guess. Acts 17.16ff suggests that Paul was mocked by the philosophers of Athens, did not have much success in preaching and stayed only a short time, i.e. he could not have been long alone in Athens. Perhaps its alien culture gave him a sense of isolation; cf. Bicknell, 'Athens was particularly uncongenial to St. Paul's temperament'; this however both assumes the accuracy of the account in Acts and also reads more

into it than is necessarily there. But was Paul alone in Athens?
Verses 1–4 are in the first plural and elsewhere in the letter this
seems to be a genuine plural, i.e. Paul associates Silvanus and
Timothy with him. If then the three of them were together in
Athens and Timothy was sent away Silvanus was still with Paul
and Paul's words seem too strong. Lightfoot therefore supposes
that Paul sent Silvanus on another mission (Beroea?), but we have
no actual knowledge of this; such an explanation requires that
the plural be epistolary. Support for an epistolary plural can be
found in v. 5 where the thought and words of v. 1a are repeated
in the first singular. But since this interpretation would involve
taking the first plural as epistolary only in this short passage it is
better to reject it and regard it as a genuine first plural; in addition
as Moule (p. 119) argues μόνοι almost definitely implies more than
one person. Of course Timothy may have been very dear to Paul
and Silvanus enriching their fellowship and doing many things for
them that would have left them freer to preach. Another possibility is to take the **we** of this verse as a genuine plural but with an
extent different from that of the other first plurals, i.e. by it Paul
may mean 'we in Athens', viz., himself, but not Silvanus, but
including the very few who had become Christians in Athens; it is
easy to pass from one type of first person plural to another as
v. 4 shows. It is also possible that Paul may have cast the experience of all in terms of his own experience. Whatever we decide
in relation to the plural the account in Acts raises further difficulties. Paul, Silvanus and Timothy went from Thessalonica to
Beroea (Acts 17.10); Jewish pressure forced Paul to leave but the
other two remained (Acts 17.15). Going on to Athens Paul sent
back word for them to rejoin him as quickly as possible (17.15)
but his mission was finished in Athens and he had gone on to
Corinth before they caught up with him (Acts 18.5). If Timothy
was not with Paul in Athens how did Paul send him from there to
Thessalonica? If it is argued (cf. von Dobschütz) that he sent word
to Timothy in Beroea to go this deprives his willing determination
to remain behind alone in Athens of meaning. The information
on which the author of Acts depended cannot have been complete;
apart from the difficulty of reconciling Paul's and Timothy's
movements with what we learn in 1 Th. Acts contains no hint
of a special mission of Timothy to Thessalonica. Further, if the
plurals of this verse are true plurals and include Silvanus, then

Acts is unaware of his return to Paul in Athens, setting it instead in Corinth.

2   **and we sent Timothy:** see v. 1 for discussion of Timothy's movements. If Timothy is **sent** this suggests that Paul, if not also Silvanus, occupied some position of authority over him. This was not the only time Paul sent Timothy on missions (1 Cor. 4.17; Phil. 2.19, 23), and he had other followers whom he could send (Epaphroditus, Phil. 2.25; certain unnamed Christians, 2 Cor. 8.22; 12.18; 8.18f); but there were those also whom he asks to go rather than sends (Apollos, 1 Cor. 16.12, who declined to go; Titus, 2 Cor. 8.6; 12.18). Yet it is not possible to distinguish between the activities of Timothy on the one hand and Apollos and Titus on the other; all three appear to do what Paul would have done if he himself had gone. Unfortunately there is nothing in the Pauline letters to determine his relationship to Silvanus. Timothy may thus be regarded as coming under Paul's authority in the church's mission; he was a most suitable person for the present mission because he had been in Thessalonica and was known to the Christians there.

Paul describes Timothy as **our brother** and **God's fellow-worker.** The first title is one used of all Christians (cf. 1.4; 2.1, 9, 14, 17, etc.) but Paul also often uses it of particular Christians engaged on the church's mission (1 Cor. 1.1; 16.12; 2 Cor. 1.1; 2.13; etc.); in this way he is probably only indicating his special affection for these fellow-workers and we are not to take it as a title; elsewhere he calls Timothy his 'child' (1 Cor. 4.17; cf. Phil. 2.19–22). **God's fellow-worker** (συνεργόν D* 33) may not be the correct reading here; when conflate readings are eliminated there remain two other strong contestants, viz. 'fellow-worker' (B 1692) and 'minister (διάκονον) of God' (ℵ A 81). It may be argued that **God's fellow-worker,** which has the weakest textual support, was a difficult theological concept and was changed in different textual traditions to the other readings, in the one case by the omission of **of God** and in the other by the alteration of **fellow-worker** to 'minister' (one of Paul's favourite terms) which, lacking the prefix σύν, contains no idea of fellow-work with God. Yet in 1 Cor. 3.9 **God's fellow-worker** has been allowed to stand and must therefore have been theologically acceptable, though there it could be possibly understood as 'workers together for God', to which no objection is possible. If the original reading

was 'minister of God' we have to suppose that at some stage
fellow-worker (which Paul uses regularly without the addition
of God) was substituted for 'minister' and that later **of God** was
omitted as theologically objectionable; such a two stage alteration
is more complex than that which assumes **God's fellow-worker**
as original. The third possibility, that the original reading was
'fellow-worker', implies that at some stage **of God** was added but
it is difficult to see the reason, for Paul usually puts a personal
pronoun with it and **of God** creates theological difficulties; later
fellow-worker was changed to 'minister' because of these difficulties. It is simpler to suppose that the original reading was **God's
fellow-worker** (for a full discussion see Metzger, *op. cit.*, pp.
240-2). Is this, however, really theologically unacceptable? We
have already noticed the parallel in 1 Cor. 3.9. More generally
Paul is aware that God works through men (Rom. 10.14f; 2 Cor.
5.20-6.1); while the expression may be loosely framed, suggesting
that men put themselves alongside God, yet within the general
context of Paul's thought, remembering that 1 Thess. is one of
his earliest extant writings, it is not an impossible statement; moreover it is qualified by **in the gospel of Christ** indicating that the
work is God's and that Timothy and God are not equal partners
in it though of course the gospel cannot be proclaimed without
men (cf. Henneken, pp. 19-27; G. Bertram, *T.W.N.T.* VII,
pp. 869ff). If 'fellow-worker' is read then this means 'fellow-
worker' with Paul and Silvanus, and Paul is reminding the
Thessalonians of Timothy's real position though he may only
seem to be a messenger. If 'minister of God' is read this has to be
understood against a whole background of service; the term originally denoted humble service, e.g. that of a waiter, and is used in
Mk. 10.45 of the service of Jesus for men; it would imply that the
service of Timothy was like that of his Lord. Whatever the reading
Paul is attempting to honour his assistant and upgrade his mission
rather than to indicate the depth of his own loss at his departure;
on the original visit Timothy may have played a very minor part
and seem now an unimportant messenger. But he goes as Paul's
representative, does what Paul himself would have done in
strengthening and encouraging the converts. But before Paul
speaks of this he writes of his past work **in the gospel of Christ**
thereby reminding the Thessalonians of Timothy's work when he
first came with Paul to Thessalonica. It is often asked whether

of Christ is a subjective or objective genitive, i.e. is Christ the author or the content of the gospel? Surely on many occasions Paul will never have been intending one to the exclusion of the other and it would be wrong to try and distinguish them here and pin Paul down to one of them.

strengthen and **encourage** are technical terms of the pastoral work of the early church (found together again in 2 Th. 2.17; cf. Acts 14.22; 15.32; Rom. 1.11; and also frequently used separately). It is difficult to isolate the special meaning of each; together they represent what a good pastor does to build up his people in the face of persecution, trouble, lack of resolution and imperfect knowledge of the Christian way. Sometimes it is said that God **strengthens** men (Rom. 16.25; 1 Th. 3.13; 1 Pet. 5.10) and sometimes that men do it (Lk. 22.32; 1 Th. 3.2; Jas. 5.8)—another illustration, perhaps, that men are **God's fellow-workers**. Those strengthened are able to stand firm and the word often contains this element of making others steady, especially in the face of persecution (1 Pet. 5.10; Lk. 22.32; cf. Acts 14.22), though also at times it is related to strengthening in moral and spiritual activity (2 Th. 2.17; 3.3; 2 Pet. 1.12; Rev. 3.2; cf. G. Harder, *T.W.N.T.* VII, pp. 653ff). For **encourage** see on 4.1. In our context the strengthening and encouragement are related to **faith**. This is not 'the Faith', i.e. the Christian Faith, nor is it the trustful response of the believer to what God has done; it is instead the moral and spiritual virtue of faithfulness, though not in the sense of steadfastness but rather in that of being full of the works of faith, i.e. the activity which flows from the relationship of faith (trust) to God (cf. 1.3). **in respect of** may be a little weak here as a rendering of ὑπέρ (often used for περί in the N.T.; cf. 2 Th. 2.1) and it may carry the additional connotation 'for the benefit of'; the strengthening and encouragement will result in an increase of faith.

3   It might seem sufficient for Paul simply to write of Timothy as strengthening and encouraging the Thessalonians in respect of their faith but, conscious that the building up of their faith takes place against the background of difficulty and persecution, he goes on to refer directly to this in **so that** (final, cf. Moule, p. 140, rather than a simple infinitive, the object of **encourage**, as Moulton-Turner p. 141; there is no need to presuppose a hypothetical verb of fearing as Bl.-Deb. § 399.3) **no one may be disturbed**

by these tribulations. The meaning of σαίνεσθαι **(be disturbed)** has been much contested and textual emendations have been suggested to clarify it. The root meaning is of a dog wagging its tail, which gives the more general sense, 'cringe, fawn upon, beguile', and hence in the passive 'be beguiled, flattered, allured'; the clause would then mean, 'so that no one may be enticed (drawn aside) in these tribulations'. This does not quite fit the sequence of the argument since not until v. 5 is there any reference to enticement. The patristic commentators and the ancient versions give a meaning similar to 'disturb' and though there is little evidence of contemporary use in this way it fits the flow of thought so much better that it should probably be adopted (cf. H. Chadwick, '1 Thess. 3.3, σαίνεσθαι', *J.T.S.* 1 (1950) 156–8 and F. Lang, *T.W.N.T.* VII, pp. 54–6). It may refer either to a disturbance coming from outside, e.g. persecution, insult, outrage, or, more probably, to an inner disturbance of spirit which would be more suitable to the context and the usage of the word. Paul refers primarily to the **tribulations** of the Thessalonians but also includes his own as the first plural of the rest of the verse shows. The thought may be even more general: Paul may intend the tribulations which belong to the period before the end, the so-called Messianic woes or birthpangs which herald the return of the Messiah and which would fall on his people, or the tribulations which pertain to the mere fact of being a Christian (Mk. 8.34). The afflictions can hardly be regarded however as chance or occasional for Christians **are destined** for them. Paul is not thinking of a period of persecution which will pass and the church return to normality; normality is persecution (cf. Acts 14.22). This sense of 'destiny' makes the idea much stronger than the belief that it is a tragic fact of Christian existence that suffering accompanies goodness or that the imitation of Jesus will lead to persecution. These **tribulations** have been appointed (see Lk. 2.34 for a similar use of **destined;** cf. Mt. 3.10 = Lk. 3.9; Phil. 1.16) to the Christian by God, and not by blind fate or mischance, and the Christian is involved in them through his union with Christ who suffered and by his place in the last days when tribulation is allotted to the people of God before the Messiah will come (cf. H. Schlier, *T.D.N.T.* III, pp. 139–48; D. S. Russell, *op. cit.* pp. 272ff; Dibelius, *ad loc.*). In the first plural **we** Paul includes the Thessalonians with himself and his companions (otherwise ἡμεῖς or even ἀπόστολοι would be expected): not missionaries nor apostles only but all Christians since all are united to Christ and all await the End as people of God. Schmithals argues that **tribulation** does not refer to persecution here but to trials through heretics and says (p. 129f) that it can mean this elsewhere; but persecution goes better with the idea contained in **destined.**

4   The Thessalonians themselves **know** this because earlier Paul had taught them about it during his visit. Then he had **foretold** (an imperfect tense implying that he had warned them on a number of occasions) **that we were to experience tribulation** (the same word as in v. 3 but now in verbal form). **We were to** (cf. Rom. 4.24; 8.13) is more than a round-about way of writing a future; it involves necessity, as in v. 3b. This affliction has been experienced by the Thessalonians themselves **(it happened)** and so they **know** all about it, not now as prophecy but as part of their own experience. The use of the first plural is a little puzzling. It might be taken as a direct reference to Paul and his associates right through the verse relating to their tribulations in Thessalonica and Beroea; certainly Paul was well aware of the tribulations that would come in his own life but these were always part of the general tribulations of the people of God (v. 3b) though they would take different forms in the lives of different Christians. If however he intended this direct reference to the apostles themselves then the first **you know** ought to be more specific. It is therefore easier to read the verse: 'when we (Paul, Silvanus and Timothy) were with you, we (Paul etc.) foretold that we (the people of God) were to experience tribulation'; 1.6; 2.14 make it quite clear that the Thessalonians did suffer in this way. But if this tribulation has already **happened** can it bear any relation to the tribulations of the End and must it not just be a general reference that those who follow Christ must experience what he experienced? If however we realize that Paul expects the End shortly and that there is nothing to suggest that he sees these tribulations as completed then it is probable that he has in mind here as in v. 3b the sufferings which belong to the End as well as those which come through union with Christ.

5   **So:** Paul resumes the thought of v. 1 but also that of vv. 3, 4, the existence of tribulation which the Thessalonians have certainly had to endure. He uses the same words he used in v. 1 but now puts them in the singular: **because I for my part was no longer**

able to endure it. We have already seen that the first plural in
v. 1 is difficult but is to be accepted as a genuine plural. The first
person singular (κἀγώ, cf. 2.13) is stressed here; it has been explained in different ways: the verse refers to the sending of a second
messenger, not Timothy (no name is given in the Greek; we have
supplied **Timothy** from vv. 1, 6), by Paul alone (so Hofmann),
but in v. 6 only the return of Timothy is reported; it implies that
Paul had been picked on by the Jews in Thessalonica and he
especially needs to send to Thessalonica for news (so Frame) but
this gives too prominent a place to Jewish opposition. More probably as at 2.18 Paul's personal anxiety boils up and he cannot
avoid stressing himself; probably he was in actual fact the initiator
of the action; at 3.1 Silvanus (if the plural includes him) has only
been brought in by way of courtesy; Paul was the directing force
in the mission work. No subject is expressed for **learn;** the same
was true of **strengthen** and **encourage** in v. 2; there the subject
might be Timothy or Paul and Silvanus with Timothy as their
agent. Here the absence of Timothy's name after **sent** suggests
that the subjects of **learn** and **sent** are the same, i.e. Paul. Paul's
knowledge will, of course, come through Timothy. He wishes to
learn about their **faith;** it would come more naturally to us to say,
'to learn about the life and success of the church'. As elsewhere
faith is a many-sided and complex conception. Paul obviously
wishes to know about their ability to be faithful or steadfast in
persecution but this itself depends on their faith relationship to
God through Christ and involves an understanding of the Faith
and issues in obedience to God (cf. 1.3). All these ideas are inter-
locked in the use of the word here. **fearing** is not in the Greek
but Paul frequently introduces clauses expressing apprehension
with μή πως as here (cf. Gal. 2.2 and see Bl.–Deb. § 370.2) and it
is easier to take it in this way than as an indirect question. Paul
fears the activity of the Tempter, i.e. Satan (cf. 2.18). **Tempter**
and **tempted** (aorist; cf. Moulton–Turner, p. 99) come from the
same root πειράζειν which has the wider meaning 'test, prove' but
perhaps should be taken here in its narrower sense 'tempt'; it is
quite obviously used pejoratively, and can be so without implying
temptation (cf. Mt. 6.13; Lk. 11.4); there is no idea of testing
in order to approve of the one tested (contrast the use of δοκιμάζειν
at 2.4). Satan (see on 2.18) as **Tempter** is hardly known in the
O.T. but emerges with this function during the inter-testamental

period and retains it in the N.T. (1 Cor. 7.5; Mt. 4.1; Lk. 4.2; it is by no means certain that Satan 'tempts' in Mk. 1.12f). Gradually he came to play a more active role in temptation (in Lk. 22.3; Jn. 13.27, unlike Mark, the betrayal by Judas is attributed to him) until he is eventually held to be responsible for it all; but this is not true throughout the N.T. (Jas. 1.14; cf. Best, *The Temptation and the Passion: the Marcan Soteriology* (S.N.T.S. Monograph Series No. 2, Cambridge, 1965), pp. 44–60 for a discussion of the role of Satan in temptation). The emergence of Satan into this position is part of the world-view of a war between God and the powers of evil whose leader attacks the followers of God. We might then render it 'the Assailant . . . assailed'. Had Satan (from his point of view) successfully assailed the Thessalonians so that under persecution they failed to maintain their faith then Paul's **labour might have been fruitless** (aorist subjunctive from the point of view of the time Paul sent Timothy when there was doubt as to the issue of temptation though none as to its fact; **tempted** is an aorist indicative) even though it had not been fruitless when he first preached to them (2.1). Paul, as he writes, knows that it was not the Thessalonians who failed but Satan. Kümmel ('Das literarische und geschichtliche Problem des ersten Thessalonicher-briefes') goes too far when he suggests that Paul was worried lest the church might no longer exist; he would hardly have expected it to die within the first few months of its foundation. Paul always exaggerates in his statements about his congregations (cf. 1.8 and notes there); he probably only feared that some might have lapsed through persecution or, as Schmithals would probably argue, through the work of heretics.

(c) TIMOTHY'S GOOD NEWS 3.6–10

However when Timothy returned just now to us from you and told us the good news of your faith and love and that you always remember us affectionately, for you wish to see us,—just as we also wish to see you—(7) for that reason we were encouraged, brothers, because of you in all our affliction and tribulation through your faith (8) because we now live if you stand firm in the Lord. (9) What thanksgiving, then, are we able to return to God for you in all the joy with which we rejoice on your account before

**our God (10) as we pray day and night with deep earnestness
so that we may see you in the flesh and make good the
deficiencies of your faith?**

Timothy returns with good news which not merely removes
Paul's fears about the Thessalonians but enables him to stand firm
in his own trials as one who lives as a Christian. Thanksgiving to
God, joy at their success and prayer for their needs mingle
together in his response to what he is told.

Timothy came back only a short time before this letter (**just 6
now;** it is better to take this with **returned,** to which it is nearer,
than with **encouraged,** v. 7, the main thought of the section, because of the broken structure of the sentence; see on v. 7) bringing
good news. If Acts 18.5 correctly refers to this then Paul was at
Corinth at that time and our letter would almost certainly have
been written from there. Acts 18.5 implies a joint return of Silvanus and Timothy, though not necessarily from Thessalonica
but rather from Beroea (cf. 17.5). The first plural of v. 6 suggests
Silvanus was with Paul when Timothy returned and conflicts with
Acts 18.5; the first plural may however just possibly represent
the Christian community in Corinth. Luke's information was very
probably defective. Within vv. 6–10 the personal pronouns are
frequent and emphatic; we have 'we, our, us' expressed explicitly
seven times in addition to first plural verbs; 'you, your' comes ten
times; this drives home the wealth of personal feeling and affection
between Paul and the Thessalonians.

Timothy **told us the good news** (lit. 'gospellized'): 'preached
the Gospel'. This is the only place in the N.T. where the verb
($εὐαγγελίζεσθαι$) is used without a full and direct reference to
the gospel which is Jesus Christ (Heb. 4.2, 6 equates the gospel
with the O.T. promises). Outside Biblical Greek (the N.T. usage
comes from the LXX) the verb is used in the general sense
'announce, proclaim', often with the implication that what is
announced will be welcome to the hearers, i.e. good news. Paul
uses it here at least in this sense. But does he imply more? Is there
a proclamation of the gospel in the news about the Thessalonians?
This is obviously excluded if we restrict the verb to missionary
preaching, i.e. the initial offering of salvation to men. But Paul
frequently relates the gospel to his continued work in a community
(1 Cor. 9.14; 2 Cor. 11.7; Gal. 2.14; Phil. 1.27); most interestingly

in the context of Rom. 1.15 he speaks of a mutual encouragement (1.12) which he and the Roman Christians will enjoy together. May not then the **news** which he receives from Thessalonica be a preaching of the gospel to himself? From it results **encouragement, life, joy** (vv. 7, 8, 9); all these are normal products of the gospel's preaching. If the establishment and maintenance of a congregation is God's activity, it is a preaching of the gospel to be told of this as much as it is to be told of his activity in the O.T. (Heb. 4.2, 6). What then is the **good news** from Thessalonica? (1) Their **faith** and **love** (cf. Col. 1.4; Philm. 5 for this association). It is wrong to distinguish these terms too rigidly. Calvin is often quoted, 'In these two words he (Paul) states concisely the sum total of godliness', but this suggests that Paul here considers **faith** and **love** as the two main virtues. Their relationship is better expressed by Gal. 5.6, 'faith working through love'. Their faith represents their attitude to God rather than their faithfulness, and love is its result.

Obviously then **love** will not be love for God (Paul rarely writes of men loving God; see on 1.3) but for men; though many commentators assume on the basis of 4.9 that this means the love of the Thessalonians for one another this is not certain; for when Paul sets out love as that which denotes the Christian life as the fulfilment of God's purpose it is love to all men and not to fellow-Christians alone which he intends; cf. Rom. 13.9f; Gal. 5.14; 1 Cor. 13. Love, unqualified as here, ought then to be given its widest meaning. Such love is, of course, manifested in their remembrance of Paul. It is unnecessary to see 'hope' as deliberately omitted (cf. 1.3) because Paul treats this in 4.13ff as one of the deficiencies of their faith, for 4.1ff goes on to show deficiencies in faith and love also. (2) They **always remember** Paul and his associates **affectionately.** If Paul had feared that his hurried departure from Thessalonica or his inability to return had been wrongly interpreted or that some Jewish enemies had spread tales about him or that some Gnostics (cf. Schmithals) had worked successfully contrary to his teaching, he is now reassured: they bear no ill-will against him, rather the opposite. The proof of the sincerity of their feelings lies in their **wish (always** might come here rather than with **remember) to see** him again, a desire which as we already know (2.17f) Paul reciprocates and which he restates here.

for that reason (διὰ τοῦτο) is a transitional phrase taking up 7
what precedes (here the whole of v. 6); elsewhere Paul invariably
puts it at the beginning of a sentence. It appears then that v. 7
is a fresh sentence and that that of v. 6 is never completed (cf.
2 Th. 2.3, 4). Perhaps Paul intended to move directly to thanks to
God (v. 9), but he stops to tell how he has been **encouraged**
(for the word see on 4.1) **because of** (ἐπί after a verb of feeling
often has a causal sense, cf. Bl.–Deb. § 235.2) the good news
from Thessalonica. Paul not only encourages his converts but
frequently tells how he has been encouraged by them (Rom. 1.12;
2 Cor. 7.4, 13; Philm. 7; cf. 2 Cor. 7.7). This encouragement has
come **through** their **faith** (used here as in v. 2): Paul by means of
Timothy had encouraged (v. 2) them about their faith and is now
himself **encouraged** through that faith, i.e. through what he
learns of their whole Christian existence. **Faith** by itself is almost
equivalent here to faith and love in vv. 6, 10; it is not merely steadfastness under persecution but relates to the whole of Christian
existence as a response to God from which steadfastness will
necessarily issue. This encouragement comes to Paul and Silvanus
while they are in the midst of **affliction and tribulation;** the
reference here is not purely temporal, i.e. 'we were encouraged
in a time of affliction', but because of the **all** it implies that the
encouragement was in relation to the affliction. The two words
affliction and **tribulation** are difficult to distinguish; both refer
to external evil rather than to disquiet of mind and both carry
eschatological overtones. For **tribulation** see on 1.6; 3.3; for
affliction see Lk. 21.23; 1 Cor. 7.26. The two words are found
together again in 2 Cor. 6.4; Ps. 24.17 (LXX; 25.17 EVV);
118.143 (LXX; 119.143 EVV); Job 15.24; Zeph. 1.15 and probably formed a word-pair denoting the persecutions, sufferings and
distresses of the End. We do not have the information to identify
them fully here and it is useless to speculate whether Paul refers
to what happened in Beroea (Acts 17.13f), Athens (17.32) or
Corinth (18.6, 9f, 12ff); in none of these does Acts suggest that
Paul suffered physical persecution; Paul however was constantly
in such peril (2 Cor. 4.8–12; 6.4ff; 11.23ff). If the ultimate reference is eschatological then the sufferings which Paul endured and
those which the Thessalonians endured are the same and in them
they give each other mutual comfort (3.2f; 3.7). **All** relates to
the intensity of their afflictions rather than to their variety or

completeness, for in essence it is all one affliction, that of the End.

8   Paul spells out the encouragement received from the Thessalonians: they, i.e. Paul and his companions, **live (now** can either be temporal, a contrast between the period before and after Timothy's return with his good news, or logical, 'this being so'; the two are not really distinct here). When Paul says that they **live** he refers to more than ordinary physical life for there is an implied contrast to an earlier period of what was in comparison non-life and which cannot have been physical death. He means their Christian existence, lived in fullness and power, a life given a new sense of strength and joy, a life renewed in vigour, not just in physical vigour but in moral and spiritual power and this because of Timothy's good news. So in Rom. 15.32 Paul writes of his hopes to visit the Roman Christian community and be refreshed; cf. 1 Cor. 16.18; 2 Cor. 7.13; Philm. 7, 20. There Paul uses words from the root ἀναπαύειν; here he uses ζάω, which can mean physical life in all its aspects, but is also without qualification the root for eternal life. Is Paul thinking of this here? There are two similar passages: writing of his persecutions and sufferings he says that 'death works in us, but life in you' (2 Cor. 4.12; cf. 13.9), i.e. his affliction brings life to the Corinthians, life moving in the other direction than our text; again in 2 Cor. 7.3 he says that the Corinthians and himself die together and live together in his heart. Paul is not saying that eternal life comes to his converts while he is persecuted and seems to die, i.e. that the blood of the martyrs is the seed of the church, but is writing of a communication of life within the Christian community. He speaks many times of Christians dying and living with Christ, eternal life being communicated within the Body of Christ from Christ to his followers. In our passages he thinks of a communication of life at the horizontal level between one member and another. At 2 Cor. 4.12 this is specifically linked in v. 11 to the life of Christ; it is linked here in v. 8 in a more veiled way in the words **you stand firm in the Lord** (cf. Phil. 4.1), which are parallel to **through your faith** (v. 7) but are not the same. Paul does not say, 'you stand firm in the faith', as in 1 Cor. 16.13, meaning either that they stand firm in persecution or hold the faith firmly. While the context of persecution might suggest this we have already seen it is not the meaning of **through your faith,** nor is it the meaning of the

phrase in Phil. 4.1. It is unlikely that **stand firm in the Lord** is intended to answer **no one may be disturbed** (3.3) but, if it is, it probably refers to an inner stability. If Paul does not say 'stand firm in (your) faith' but **stand firm in the Lord** how do these differ and how does the latter differ from **through your faith** (v. 7)? The change from 'faith' (1 Cor. 16.13) to **in the Lord** represents a personalizing of the description of the nature of Christian existence in terms of a relationship to Christ. Believers are said to 'trust, labour, hope, etc. in the Lord' (Phil. 2.24; 1 Cor. 15.58; Phil. 2.19; etc.) which means a great deal more than saying that they trust, labour, hope, etc. because of the Lord or that they trust, labour, hope as Christians. They trust, labour, hope because of what the Lord has done for them (in his death, etc.) and because their response to this has brought them into a relationship with him. They **stand firm** in a relationship to the Lord. Others stand in this relationship with them also (cf. the use of **in the Lord** in 1 Cor. 7.39; 11.11; 4.17; Phil. 1.14; 1 Th. 5.12; Philm. 16); so this phrase links together the first and second halves of the verse. Both Paul and the Thessalonians are **in the Lord** and there is an interchange of life between them. Their Christian life is communicated to Paul (**stand firm** is in the indicative mood indicating the reality of their stance; it is actually taking place; **if** means, 'if, as indeed you do'). Such communication of life is 'gospel' (v. 6); its proclamation, viz. that the Thessalonians stand in the Lord, has brought life as it always does. There is thus a coherent thought running through this passage and it is carried on into vv. 9, 10.

The 'gospel' he has received leads Paul to thank God (cf. 9 Rom. 1.8; 1 Cor. 1.4; Phil. 1.3; 1 Th. 1.2; 2.13; 2 Th. 1.3) though the fact that he frames it as a question shows his realization that any thanksgiving he can offer is inadequate. He does not offer his **thanksgiving** to the Thessalonians but to God, for what the Thessalonians are, they are by the grace of God. If the Thessalonians **stand firm in the Lord** (v. 8) it is only because God sent the Lord into the world and gave him to the death of the cross. Their Christian condition comes from God's action: they were chosen by him (1.4) and this was made effective in them by his power and Spirit (1.5). On the movement from the proclamation of the Thessalonians' faith to Paul's thanksgiving cf. Rom. 1.8, and to **thanksgiving** as a response to the gospel cf. Rom. 7.25; 2 Cor.

4.15. (**then:** γάϱ in an interrogative can mean **then**; cf. Mt. 27.33; Bl.-Deb. § 452.1.) **in all the joy** seems to be a deliberate and careful balancing of **in all our affliction and tribulation** in v. 7; in both cases **all** is used of intensity rather than variety or completeness. Just as Paul wrote in 1.6 at the same time both of the joy and affliction of the Thessalonians so he does the same now of his own and of his companions'. **joy . . . before God** properly accompanies **thanksgiving to God** and is present in affliction because while they were afflicted they were encouraged with the good news. This **joy** is not a secular joy but a joy **before our God;** the eye of the unbiassed observer might not observe it for it has its seat not in the human but in the divine sphere. Their lives are as much before God now (1.3; 3.9) as they will be at the return of Jesus (2.19; 3.13). Paul frequently refers to the way in which his churches bring him **joy** (2 Cor. 2.2f; 7.4; Col. 2.5). When he says **our** God he does not mean the God of Silvanus, Timothy and himself alone but the God in whose presence both he and the Thessalonians live their lives and rejoice.

10   While **joy** can lead to forgetfulness of others in self-pleasure this is not so here where rejoicing is accompanied by prayer (cf. Phil. 1.4; Rom. 12.12; 15.32; Col. 1.11), for in God's presence it is only natural to talk about those who are the occasion of joy; so Paul **prays** regularly (**day and night;** see on 2.9; morning and evening prayers are not meant!) for the Thessalonians **with deep earnestness** (ὑπεϱεκπεϱισσοῦ: Paul loves to build up Greek compounds with ὑπέϱ, e.g. 2 Th. 1.3; 2 Cor. 9.14; Rom. 8.26; 1 Th. 5.13; the present word means literally 'super-abundantly' and since **day and night** refers to the frequency of his prayers this probably refers to their intensity). The object of Paul's prayers is his return to them; Satan has prevented this until now (2.18) but prayer may open up the way. Even though Timothy has returned with good news Paul has not given up his desire to **see** the Thessalonians **in the flesh** (lit. 'see your face'; cf. 2.17); yet his prayer is not just to **see** them but to see them so that he can help them by making **good the deficiencies of** their **faith.** ϰαταϱτίζειν and ὑστεϱήματα (**make good** and **deficiencies**) have each a wide range of meaning, the first through 'put in order, restore, repair, equip', and the second through 'shortcoming, need, absence (of a person)'; the latter can, though not necessarily, imply a moral or religious shortcoming (cf. Hermas, *Vis.* III,

2.2; 1 Clem. 2.6). Our rendering (cf. Frame, Milligan) seems to combine the words satisfactorily but it leaves undecided the meaning of **deficiencies;** is Paul blaming them for a failure on their part or merely saying that he would now do something which he ought to have done for them while he was with them but was unable to do because he had to leave so hurriedly? Presumably, though not certainly, the remainder of the letter (from 4.1ff) is taken up with an attempt to meet these deficiencies in so far as this can be done by letter. If so Paul reminds them of the instructions he had previously given them in relation to sexual impurity (4.1–8), tells them that they already know how to love and ought to go further in the same direction (4.9–12), instructs them in more detail about the parousia of Christ and their behaviour in relation to its nearness (4.13–5.11) and gives them sundry brief catechetical admonitions (5.12–22). In this we may detect material additional to what was already given during his visit and a recall to what he had told them then, implying that their deficiencies were in part failures on their side (i.e. moral failures) and in part inadequacies through the brevity of his stay. **faith** here cannot be restricted either to their understanding of the Faith, though faith has always an intellectual element, or to their faithfulness to the faith, equally an element; it is the response of the whole being to God though not thought here in terms of the personal trust of justifying faith but of the response which comes in obedience. Paul uses **faith** elsewhere in this way as something which ought not to be but is inadequate (cf. Rom. 14.1; 2 Cor. 10.15). Thus he prays that what is lacking in their Christian existence may be made good. On **faith** see R. Bultmann, *Theology of the N.T.* I, pp. 314ff; A. Weiser and R. Bultmann, *T.D.N.T.* VI, pp. 174ff; D. E. H. Whiteley, *The Theology of St. Paul*, Oxford, 1964, pp. 161ff.

(d) PRAYER 3.11–13

Now may our God and Father himself and our Lord Jesus direct our path to you; (12) and as for you may the Lord make you to abound and overflow richly with love for one another and for all men, as we do for you, (13) so that he may strengthen your hearts to be blameless in holiness before our God and Father at the parousia of our Lord Jesus with all his holy ones.

145

This prayer picks up **as we pray** (v. 10) and forms the end of the first main section of the letter (1.2–3.13; Schmithals regards it as almost at the end of his letter D; see pp. 31–5). There are two main interlocking petitions: that Paul may visit them and that the deficiencies of their faith may be made up so that they will be blameless at the time of judgement.

11 δέ **(Now)** is regularly used with an adversative sense but it is difficult to see what this could be here; it cannot be that after making various unsuccessful attempts to visit the Thessalonians Paul now turns to prayer to achieve this, for the reference to prayer was already present in v. 10, nor can it be a contrast between God and Satan for we have to travel too far back to find this (2.18). δέ instead is used here to indicate a break in the passage; it introduces each of Paul's prayers in these letters (5.23; 2 Th. 2.16; 3.5, 16; cf. Rom. 15.5, 13). Apart from 2 Th. 3.5 each of these prayers is also characterized by an introductory reflexive pronoun **himself.** Including 3.5 (and Rom. 15.5, 13) the optative mood is used in each of them; this, while earlier a perfectly normal usage in prayers and wishes, was dropping out of use in Hellenistic Greek (cf. Moulton–Turner, pp. 118–33; Burton §§ 174–9). In some of his other letters Paul's intercessions are more closely interwoven into the texture of what he is saying (Phil. 1.9–11; Col. 1.9–12; 2 Th. 1.11f) and use indirect speech; his doxologies have, of course, a form of their own. **himself,** actually the first word of the sentence (though it has no special emphasis, *pace* Moulton–Turner, p. 41), is perhaps an adaptation of an original vocative 'you' ('Do you, O God . . . direct . . .') deriving from the time when the prayer was used directly in worship (so Masson) and is retained now to indicate the change of subject; Paul has been writing to the Thessalonians and now addresses God. R. Jewett, 'The Form and Function of the Homiletic Benediction', *Anglican Theological Review*, 51 (1969) 18–34, suggests that the original setting of these prayers was the sermon. Flexible in content they summarize preceding material and open up the way for what follows. While the petition of v. 11 clearly links with 2.17–3.10 and **holiness** and **parousia** (v. 13) may point forward, the reference to **holiness** is so general and its importance so obvious and that to **parousia** hardly unexpected after 2.19 that it is difficult to prove any real connection with 4.1ff other than with v. 3. Verse 12 is also so general that it could

relate to practically anything. The singular verb **direct** (it is impossible to distinguish properly between the singular and plural in English) is surprising. The phrase runs literally, 'May himself our God and Father and our Lord Jesus direct'; in 2 Th. 2.16 we find the same with the order of the subjects reversed. Because of this reversal and the singular verb it is difficult to view **himself** as adhering strongly to **our God and Father** alone. Paul constantly places God and Jesus alongside one another (cf. 1.1, 2; Rom. 1.7; 1 Cor. 1.3; etc.) and the singular may be used in Greek where two subjects are regularly thought of as together; cf. Mt. 24.35; 1 Cor. 15.50 (see on 1.1 for the meanings of **Father** and **Lord**). The introduction of the **Lord Jesus** is not just an after-thought to a formula relating basically to God the Father alone for in vv. 12f the prayer is addressed to the Lord Jesus alone; either God the Father or the Lord Jesus may be the recipient of prayer but this does not imply Paul held a Trinitarian or Binitarian theology. So far as certain of their activities go Father or Son or both may act and their action be so closely related that a singular verb is used as here and in 2 Th. 2.16f, but in other activities Paul sees a primacy lying in one or other (Jesus dies, the Father sends him). As in 1.1 the titles **Father** and **Lord** relate their bearers to believers and not to one another.

The content of Paul's prayer concerns his hoped for visit to Thessalonica. **Direct** can be taken in one or other of two ways: either that God will guide (direct his journey) Paul to Thessalonica (cf. Rom. 1.10) or that he will prepare the way for him by smoothing out the difficulties that lie in it. Whichever it is, it was some considerable time (according to our information) before Paul returned there: Acts 19.21; 20.1 (cf. 1 Cor. 16.5; 2 Cor. 2.13) route him through Macedonia and although the city is not named we can assume that the prayer was then fulfilled. In 2.17 Paul spoke of his own efforts to visit them; now he appears to leave the matter to God. This does not mean that Paul was now despairing of what he could do himself and was leaving all to God but Paul's efforts and God's directions are the two sides of the one coin. He neither sits and waits for God to transport him nor does he believe that his journeys are his own planning and achievement alone.

When Paul thinks of his visit he automatically thinks of its pur- 12 pose, to 'make good the deficiencies' of their faith (v. 10), and so

he prays now **(and as for you)** for this, going right to its heart—
love. (Many commentators point out that we find the idea, if not
the name, of the third member of the triad, 'hope', in v. 13;
'faith' was in v. 10; but there is no formal linking of the three
here; love develops naturally out of faith as in Gal. 5.6.) Paul's
prayer is now addressed to the **Lord;** this is Jesus and not the
Father; some MSS have indeed added Jesus and although this
is not the original reading it correctly interprets Paul because of
the explicit reference to Jesus in vv. 11, 13. Paul directs prayers
to Jesus at 2 Th. 3.5, 16; 2 Cor. 12.8; 1 Cor. 16.22 (cf. 2 Tim.
1.16, 18; Acts 7.59f) and 2 Th. 2.16f has a combined address as
v. 11 here. Paul has already acknowledged that the Thessalonians
do **love** (1.3) and will do so again (4.9f) but **love** (see on 1.3) can
never stand still; if it is not growing it is dying; therefore Paul
must pray for its growth in them and this he does in no uncertain
terms. He uses two synonymous verbs (both are normally in-
transitive but can be used transitively as here) whose basic meaning
is 'to be more (than enough)'; taken together they are stronger
than either by itself; the addition of one to the other is more easily
rendered in English by two non-synonymous words **(abound,
overflow)** and an adverb **(richly)** which together imply a super-
abundance beyond all imagining. In Phil. 1.9 Paul creates the
same effect using one of these verbs with an adverbial phrase,
'superabound more and more'. The overflowing quality of love is
spelt out most clearly in 1 Cor. 13 though any attempt to reduce
it to words tames its extraordinary nature (Chrysostom writes of
'the unrestrained madness of love'). This love is never a mere
feeling or emotion but is loving activity directed towards men;
this direction is expressed by εἰς **(for)**; the noun ἀγάπη is usually
followed by this preposition with the accusative (1 Pet. 4.8;
2 Th. 1.3; 2 Cor. 2.4; Col. 1.4; Rom. 5.8) but we sometimes find
ἐν with the dative (Jn. 13.35; 2 Cor. 8.7); in 'the love of God' we
have the genitive but it is often unclear whether it is an objective or
subjective genitive. The verb ἀγαπᾶν normally takes the object
with the simple accusative. The frequent occurrence of εἰς
instead of the expected simple dative suggests a primitive formula;
it is in any case probably erroneous to link the εἰς here to the
verbs. Love is directed towards **one another,** i.e. their fellow
Thessalonian Christians rather than all Christians, **and all men,**
i.e. not all Christians but all men.

The command to love is found in the N.T. in a double form: either as a command to love fellow-Christians (Jn. 13.34f; Rom. 13.8; 1 Th. 4.9; 1 Pet. 1.22; 1 Jn. 3.11, 23) or as a command to love all men, though this appears normally in the form 'love your neighbour' (Rom. 13.10; Gal. 5.14) going back through Jesus' interpretation (Lk. 10.25–37), which makes all men any man's neighbours, to Lev. 19.18. Paul has combined the two forms here by making the second conform to the first (cf. also 5.15 and Gal. 6.10 where he has done the same by speaking of goodness rather than love). It is surprising that in the N.T. epistles there are so many references to the mutual love of the brotherhood (see also the use of the word φιλαδελφία, Rom. 12.10; 1 Th. 4.9; Heb. 13.1; 1 Pet. 1.22; 2 Pet. 1.7) and so few to the love of all men, since Jesus taught the latter so clearly (Lk. 10.25–37; Mt. 5.43–7 = Lk. 6.32–6). Probably the ghetto existence of Christians together with their strong feeling that they were a family promoted the interest in love for one another leading eventually to the 'new command' (love one another) in the Johannine literature. It is easier to love those who love us and loving within the Christian community may then be a school for learning to love those outside. In our present passage (cf. 5.15; Gal. 6.10) Paul corrects this inward-looking formula and makes it outward-looking. He thus shows himself aware of the radical nature of the teaching of Jesus which, while foreshadowed in Judaism, is put by him far more pointedly. Paul must be indebted here to more than his Jewish upbringing (cf. 5.15). In the final clause he might have been expected to write 'and us for you', i.e. a prayer that his love and that of his associates might grow for the Thessalonians. Instead he prays that the love of the Thessalonians might grow to the standard of his own **(as we do for you).** The sentence lacks a verb and the **do** which we have supplied stands for **abound and overflow richly.** At first sight this is an astonishing claim but it is no greater in reality than that implied in those passages where Paul asks his readers to imitate him (see on 1.6). He can be their example of love.

Paul's prayer goes on to state the purpose (as in 2.16; 3.2 εἰς τό is   13 final; this is not then a second and parallel request to v. 12) of growth in love: their full acceptance by God when he judges. This on the one hand sets love within the wider context of God and men (Jesus joined love to God with love to men as commandments of equal value), but on the other hand it appears to subordinate the good of the men who are loved (they are not loved for their own sake) to the eternal reward of those who love. There is a tension here which runs through the whole of the N.T., for the Christian must always be aware of his standing before God, and yet if he attempts to establish that position alone ('whoever would save his life will lose it') he fails in the attempt; but if he ignores his position before God the perspective in which he loves others is so narrowed that the love itself becomes restricted. The self-corrective to these extremes lies in the very nature of love; if men are loved so that the one who loves may be saved or rewarded, they are not loved; the pattern for man's love is God's love and God never loves in order to achieve some good for himself but to bring good to those whom he loves; love involves the forgetting and giving of self. Paul, as we have seen (v. 12), has on the one hand widened the apparently traditional catechetical Christian duty 'love one another' into the more radical 'love all men', but now on the other hand it is as if he has perhaps overplayed the desire to please God by suggesting that love may serve this purpose. He has not, we note, said it of himself, but of his converts; his desire that they should be blameless at the judgement has led him to it. Yet he frames it in such a way that we see the essence of the Christian life not in terms of obedience to a law or moral ideal, or as observance of ritual or ceremony, or as knowledge of the divine nature, or as philosophical penetration of mind, all of which can more easily lead to the 'reward' aspect, but as love for all men. In another way also Paul avoids the pitfall, 'behave and you will be rewarded', for he does not simply say, 'love in order to be blameless', but 'love in order that the Lord may strengthen (**the Lord** must be carried on from v. 12 as the subject of this verb) you to be blameless.' The strengthening does not come directly from the loving: rather loving creates the kind of person whom the Lord can strengthen and so is set again within the context of God as well as of man. Man's love by itself would not strengthen his heart but his love creates the condition in which the Lord strengthens it and thus makes it blameless; ultimately man cannot make himself blameless before God, only God can.

The phrase **strengthen** the **heart** probably comes from the O.T. where it is used in a variety of ways (of food as sustaining the body, Judg. 19.5, 8; Ps. 104(103).15; in relation to the mind,

Sir. 6.37; 22.16; in relation to courage Ps. 112(111).8; in the N.T.
cf. Jas. 5.8) because of the broad manner in which physiological
terms were used in Hebrew for psychological purposes. In view of
the association of the verb with the personal pronoun in 3.2 **heart**
probably stands here for the whole person (see on 2.4) and **your
hearts** could be replaced by 'you'. When a man loves, his intellect,
volition and feeling, i.e. the whole man, are all involved and so
through love it is the whole person who is strengthened. (We do
not need to look here then for a contrast between the inward and
outward as if Paul was thinking of the building up of the spirit
regardless of outer behaviour or of the spirit's fortification against
temptation.) When the person is so strengthened he becomes
blameless before God. **Blameless** (= 'faultless' at 2.10) is used
in the N.T. of man's behaviour in relation to God (Lk. 1.6;
1 Th. 5.23; Phil. 3.6, where the law implies judgement by God)
but as a negative term it only attains a content from its context.
Here it is set in relation to **holiness;** this comes from the same
root as 'sanctified' in 4.3 but denotes the state of holiness rather
than the process of its attainment as there; **holiness** is also somewhat vague; through its O.T. usage (see on 4.3 for literature) it
denotes that in God which marks him off from men and then that
which he desires in men (Lev. 19.2). Christians are holy because
of the Christ-event and their response to it; Paul regularly calls
them 'the holy ones' (= saints) in the addresses of his letters.
But they have also continually to seek holiness (this is implicit in
our verse). In so far as holiness is negative, i.e. the absence of sin
(for God does not sin), it already contains the concept **blameless;**
in so far as it is positive, i.e. the right conduct of which God
approves, it is equivalent to love which is the fulfilling of God's
will (Gal. 5.14; Rom. 13.8–10). Thus **love** and **holiness** are not
in our context two virtues among other virtues but are umbrella
words for the whole of Christian activity. The latter, unlike the
former, contains a negative element whose over-emphasis easily
leads to a form of Christianity in which personal sinlessness is
valued more highly than active love for others. Paul holds the two
in tension; in reference to men total behaviour is characterized as
love, in reference to God as holiness. So it is **before our God and
Father** that men need to be holy. While many commentators
speak of the confidence the believer may have because **our Father**
is judge, **our Father** is found so often associated with **God** in

solemn, almost liturgical, phrases in the N.T., as here, that it goes too far to read into its use a deliberate softening of the concept of God as judge. What in fact it does do is to place the relationship of man to God on another plane from that of criminal to judge; this however is inherent in all the thought of the N.T. and not especially prominent here. Similarly we should not make anything special of the reference to **our Lord Jesus**. Christians stand in a new relation to God through Christ and it is this which is decisive at the **parousia** (see Appendix, pp. 349–54); Paul does not introduce the name Jesus to assure his converts that their judge will be easier than one who is a stern accountant of good and bad deeds. But why does Paul wish them to be **blameless** at the **parousia?** Since his prayer relates to their growth in love he is not praying that they may become or remain Christians; nor is there any suggestion as in 2.19 that their blamelessness will redound to his glory. It is better therefore to think along the lines of 1 Cor. 3.10–15 where Paul sees Christians receiving different rewards in God's judgement because of their behaviour; there as here he desires them to be without fault. The **parousia** has been introduced by Paul because he associates it with God's judgement, an association which must have been known to the Thessalonians otherwise he would have had to explain it; elsewhere Paul does refer to judgement without mentioning the parousia (Rom. 2.5; 1 Cor. 2.10–15). He clearly associates judgement not only with God but also with Christ (2 Cor. 5.10; 1 Cor. 4.4f; 11.32; 1 Th. 4.6).

In **all his holy ones** (ἅγιοι) is Paul referring to angels or Christian saints as present with Christ at the parousia? Elsewhere he invariably, and frequently, uses the word of Christians but never in the context of the parousia except for 2 Th. 1.10 and there they are not regarded as accompanying Jesus; in our epistle Christians, the dead and living saints, meet Jesus at the parousia (4.16f; 5.10) and are with him thereafter. Paul is probably quoting from Zech. 14.5, 'the Lord, my God, will come and all his holy ones with him' which refers clearly to angels; in the early Christian tradition from Did. 16.7 onwards 'holy ones' is often taken to mean 'saints'; but if, as is probable, Mt. 25.31 (cf. Jude 14) is also quoting this verse then it understands 'holy ones' as angels, and so the alternative interpretation was also in existence; and there appears to be some relationship between the apocalyptic tradition contained in Mt. 24, 25 and the Thessalonian letters (cf. J. B. Orchard, *op. cit.*; however there is no need to see a dependence of Paul on an apocalypse going back to Jesus). When we also recall that **holy ones** is a regular term in the O.T. and inter-testamental Judaism for angels and that angels are associated with judgement both in the O.T. and the N.T. (Dan. 7.18ff; Mk. 8.38; 13.27) there are good grounds for regarding our text as an exception to Paul's general usage; all the more so if we are dealing with a liturgical or credal phrase. Paul cannot but have known and been accustomed to the meaning 'angels' and therefore could easily have made an exception here; in 2 Th. 1.7 he does associate angels with the judgement. All this is confirmed when we take 4.13–18 into consideration; there Paul deals with the doubt of the Thessalonians that their dead may have no share in the parousia; if he had already taught them that at that time Christ comes with the dead saints this doubt need never have arisen, and even if it had Paul could have answered it by saying that he had already taught them that Christ would come with his saints; in fact his answer is quite different, viz., that at Christ's coming the dead are raised and ascend to meet the descending Christ. Thus we conclude that the **holy ones** are angels (for 'angels' see notes on 4.16) but the argument is evenly balanced and 'saints' is a real alternative; there is almost nothing to be said for the view that both are intended.

Many MSS add 'amen'; such liturgical additions tend to appear and though there is good early evidence (ℵ* A D* 81, etc.) it is probably better to omit it.

PARAENESIS 4.1–5.22

(a) INTRODUCTION 4.1–2

As our last matter, then, brothers we ask and request you in the Lord Jesus that—just as you received from us how you ought to progress and so please God, just as indeed you are progressing—that you excel more and more. (2) For you know what instructions we gave you through our Lord Jesus.

Paul in 4.1–5.22 amplifies instruction he gave while with the Thessalonians in the light of information he has had from Timothy and of questions on which they have apparently sought his counsel. Thus he passes from a discussion of his own relation with them to a consideration of their life and faith. The present two verses serve to set the stage for the details of this and prepare particularly for vv. 3–12.

1 Paul is not at the end of his letter though λοιπόν (**As our last matter**) which he uses here does tend to come near the end of letters (2 Cor. 13.11; 2 Tim. 4.8; Phil. 4.8, and possibly Phil. 3.1 if two letters are joined at that point; here and in 2 Th. 3.1 Schmithals also takes it as a sign that two letters have been united; apart from these three instances its meaning is usually undisputed; cf. Moule, p. 161). Paul employs it here because he is moving to his final point, or series of points; though these are somewhat lengthy, there is definitely a change both in the type of material and in the subject matter and he may be using it to indicate this. In Hellenistic Greek it can have the sense 'therefore', which could be its meaning here were it not that it is followed by οὖν (= therefore, then); if it does have this sense it cannot refer back to 3.11–13 but rather (cf. Rom. 12.1) bases the paraenesis on the gospel as a whole. This is true in any case and 4.1ff must be linked to the whole sweep of Paul's thought implicit in the preceding chapters and not to 3.11–13 in particular.

So Paul **asks and requests.** The two words are often used in contemporary Greek as synonyms and are so here; Lünemann's distinction in which **ask** refers to the approach of one friend to another and **request** refers to apostolic authority is untenable. Paul employs the second (παρακαλεῖν) much more regularly than the first. It has a wide range of meanings: 'to call to, to beseech, to exhort, to comfort'; of these the last is only found outside the N.T. with any degree of frequency in the LXX (cf. O. Schmitz and G. Stählin, *T.D.N.T.* V, pp. 773–99). In the Pauline letters it appears at a number of important turning points in the argument, especially, though not exclusively, where Paul, as here, is moving into paraenetic material, e.g. Rom. 12.1; 15.30; 1 Cor. 1.10; 1 Th. 4.10b. C. J. Bjerkelund, *op. cit.*, has isolated in Hellenistic Greek a formula: the verb in the first person + address (e.g. 'brothers') + (sometimes) a prepositional phrase + a request or command usually introduced either by ἵνα or appearing as an infinitive. He finds this formula in

Paul at Rom. 12.1f; 15.30–2; 16.17; 1 Cor. 1.10; 4.16; 16.15f; 2 Cor. 10.1f; 1 Th. 4.10b–12; 5.14. Synonyms for **request** in the formula are often found, among them ἐρωτᾶν (= **ask**) and sometimes compounds of ὁρκίζειν (5.27). The formula though often used by Jewish writers is of Hellenistic origin. In private letters a request is made between two people of similar status and well-known to each other; the prepositional phrase is then usually lacking (except where ὁρκίζειν is used). The formula also appears in more official documents (extant in inscriptions and the historians) which detail the relations between rulers and partially subject peoples, e.g. cities which come within the sphere of power of a king and yet which have a certain measure of independence; on diplomatic grounds these are not simply ordered to take some particular action but a more friendly approach is made with the παρακαλεῖν formula. In these, unlike the personal letters, we nearly always meet the prepositional phrase. The inscriptions and documents which employ the formula approximate to the form and tone of letters rather than of decrees and laws. Curiously the formula also appears in requests made by cities to their overlords. The Pauline usage conforms to the ruler-people form; between Paul and his churches there exists a definite bond; diplomatically he does not command but **requests**; 'παρακαλεῖν in the "formula" has neither the character of an order (as ἐπιτάσσω) nor of a supplication (as δέομαι)' (Bjerkelund, p. 188). The only letter in which Paul does not use the formula is Galatians and it is in this letter that he is least diplomatic. Paul's **request** must thus be considered as more than a mere 'request'; it derives from his authority as the founder of churches, from his position as an apostle or prophet; it is difficult to tie this down precisely for in Galatians he does not use it where he is asserting his apostolic authority, and in 1 Cor. 14 it is used extensively of prophetic activity; Paul probably never analysed the exact 'office' to which his authority belonged; it was sufficient to exercise it. Bjerkelund shows also that in letters and inscriptions the formula frequently follows a section of thanksgiving; this is true also in the Pauline letters (cf. 1 Cor. 1.10; Philm. 9–12); 2.13–3.13 has been such a section here. In our verse the 'address' is **brothers,** the 'prepositional phrase' **in the Lord Jesus,** and the 'request' is introduced by ἵνα **(that).** The formula thus forms a recognized method of passing from thanksgiving material to the moral teaching Paul is about to give about sexual sin and brotherly love, but it is not itself part of this exhortation.

in the Lord Jesus (see on 1.1; 2.14) goes with both verbs but is it to be attached more specifically to their subject **we** or their object **you**? This is an unreal question. Had Paul been writing to non-Christians he would not have used the phrase; it connects writers and readers; both are related to Christ; both are within the church; it is only because of this that Paul can ask and request them and that they will accept his instruction. The phrase is thus neither a sign of Paul's authority nor is it an appeal to them to respond to the indwelling Christ. As Bjerkelund shows of the prepositional phrase in the formula it emphasizes the urgency of the request.

At this point the grammar goes astray; Paul is about to state the object of his request **that** . . . but as soon as he begins he realizes that he wants to refer them back to their initial instruction and to acknowledge the way in which they kept it; having done this in a parenthesis **(just as . . . progressing)** he resumes with another **that** which is strictly unnecessary but serves to pick up his thought; and now, because he has already in the parenthesis given the content of his exhortation, his final clause **(you excel more and more)** is very general.

In the parenthesis Paul reminds them again of what happened while he was with them; they had **received** instruction from him in behaviour. **Received,** as we saw on 2.13, is one of the technical words for the transmission of tradition (cf. 1 Cor. 11.23; 15.3; 2 Th. 2.15), especially of moral instruction (Eckart, *op. cit.*, denies this; but see 2 Th. 3.6; Col. 2.6; cf. 1 Cor. 11.2; Rom. 6.17). Jewish Christians took over from their Jewish background regular instruction in ethical behaviour and continued it with extra emphasis when Gentiles began to enter the church since pagan standards were generally very low by comparison with Jewish. (The Stoic ethic will not have had much grip on the majority of those who became Christians.) Fixed areas of instruction, with partly fixed forms (e.g. *Haustafeln*, the 'Two Ways', catalogues of vices and virtues) came into use. In vv. 3-12 Paul takes up and repeats instruction from the areas of 'sex' and 'neighbourly love' though his wording does not appear to be drawn from a fixed code or catechism. The Christian is to **progress** (see on 2.12 where the same word is rendered 'walk') in such a way (καί is consecutive,

and so, cf. Bl.–Deb. § 442.2) as to **please** (see on 2.4) **God;** he is not left to do as he himself pleases; his aim must be to please God. When Paul argues that man is not saved by works he does not draw the conclusion that behaviour is unimportant; on the very basis that he is saved the Christian must aim to please God. For this some guiding rules are necessary, especially for those entering Christianity from paganism; when Paul was with them he had to supply these. This is not to re-introduce a system of rigid laws but to offer guidance by which in concrete situations the believer may do what pleases God. In the case of the Thessalonians Paul is not displeased with the progress they have made and so he tactfully softens his exhortation with a reminder of this: **just as indeed you are progressing.** His request proper comes in the last few words in general terms: **that you excel** (the word literally means 'abound'; the phrase is Pauline, cf. 2 Cor. 3.9; Phil. 1.9; 1 Th. 4.10) **more and more.** They are already moving in the right direction; let them continue and increase their speed. No limit can be set to possible attainment for though a level may seem reasonable by human standards it is never so by divine. Since Paul has left **excel** without an object (though he normally supplies one, cf. 3.12) its meaning is as wide as possible in relation to behaviour.

This verse is parallel in thought to v. 1 in recalling them **(you 2 know:** this phrase has echoed again and again in the letter; cf. 1.5; 2.1, 5, 11; 3.3, 4) to Paul's earlier oral teaching. This he terms **instructions** (παραγγελίας), a word (cf. 4.11; 2 Th. 3.4, 6, 10, 12) originally drawn from the military sphere and denoting a command; Paul's use of it is a little more complex than English 'command, order' since it also involves the content of the 'order' as taught to them; it cannot however be softened into 'advice, teaching, principle', for Paul speaks from a position of authority. When with them he had already imparted to them their directions for the Christian way and in what follows (4.3–5.12) he is generally returning to this, amplifying it and driving it home. The precise significance of **through our Lord Jesus** (cf. Rom. 15.30) is not clear. It certainly does not mean that the Lord Jesus has been an intermediary through whom the **instructions** have been transmitted by Paul to the Thessalonians. Nor does it appear to be the exact equivalent of **in the Lord Jesus** (v. 1); these phrases are normally not synonymous though there are a few places where they may be (cf. 1 Cor. 1.10 with 2 Th. 3.6 and Col. 3.17 with Eph.

5.20). Possibly the words may denote the origin (i.e. the instruction as based on the *verba Christi*) or inspiration of the instruction; the former is unlikely since elsewhere Paul rarely attaches the name or authority of Jesus to teaching he gives; the latter (cf. Lightfoot, 'prompted by the Lord Jesus') would be expressed more easily in other ways. In view of the difficulties of any explanation the ideas of W. Thüsing, *Per Christum in Deum*, Münster, 1969, pp. 164–237, are worth consideration. He argues that Paul uses διά with Christ in a 'mystical' sense somewhat similarly to 'in Christ' though they are not synonyms. Basically Paul envisages the Christ in the phrase as the living active Lord of the present and not just as the Christ who suffered and rose in the past and so it means 'through the activity of Christ in whom we are'. The preposition is sometimes causal when Christ is considered as the source of the new life and sometimes instrumental when he is considered as the mediator who accomplishes God's will. In v. 2 when Paul instructs the Thessalonians it is the exalted Lord who is active in these instructions; our passage is then a kind of reverse of Rom. 15.18; 2 Cor. 5.20. Whatever the precise meaning of the phrase the instructions have been firmly tied in to the Lord Jesus; they are Christian instructions arising in the Christ-event and intended for the followers of Christ. But Paul has not yet given us their content and this he now proceeds to do.

(b) SEX 4.3–8

For this is the will of God, that you sanctify yourselves: that is to abstain from sexual sin, (4) each one of you to know how to keep his wife in sanctification and honour, (5) not in lustful passion as even the pagans do who do not know God, (6) (and) in this matter (none of you) is to injure or exploit his brother. (This is to be done) because the Lord is an avenger in all these things as indeed we told you earlier and strongly testified; (7) for God did not call us because of our impurity but so that we might exist in santification. (8) Consequently he who spurns spurns not man but God, the very one who sets his Holy Spirit within you.

We move now from the general to the first of the particular issues Paul takes up with his readers, viz., sexual sins; he indicates in detail what these are (vv. 3b–6a) and gives three reasons (v. 6b, v. 7, v. 8) why his instruction should be followed. Verses 3–8 are all one sentence in Greek and the first part is difficult because some of the words can be given different meanings and its clauses construed in differing relationships to one another. No solution can be claimed as wholly satisfactory and new evidence on the use of words could easily tilt the balance in another direction.

For this resumes **how** (v. 1) and **what** (v. 2); it is still general 3a but is about to be particularized. As a Jew Paul had been brought up to view **the will of God** as the ultimate guide to, and motivation for, behaviour. This **will** might be broken down into a series of regulations and when attention was directed to them the danger came of an attempt to please God by obedience to them as such ('justification by works', Gal. 2.16); this was the peril to which Phariseeism lay open and into which Paul had fallen in his pre-Christian days; it led him afterwards to speak harshly at times of the Jewish Law. But true Judaism was never just obedience to particular laws but a relationship to God which on man's side could be defined as obedience to God's will; in this sense Paul can speak well of the Law, e.g. Rom. 7.12, 14. Thus despite his animadversions against the Jewish Law Paul never loses hold on the necessity to obey God. Just as Paul's preaching is God's message so his paraenesis is God's will (cf. von Dobschütz). He now explains what that will is in relation to sexual behaviour. God's will is not of course to be restricted to this area of life for in the Greek **will** lacks the article, indicating that Paul is not giving the total extent of that will but its relevance to one sphere of conduct.

He begins with a general instruction, **that you sanctify yourselves** (lit. 'your sanctification'). In many languages there is a tendency to associate morality with sexual chastity (e.g. 'immorality' often describes sexual immorality alone) and this may possibly occasion Paul's choice of the word here. But **sanctify** has a much wider meaning. In the O.T. it was applied primarily to God and therefore to those things which are associated with him, cultic objects and people (holy place, holy people), and to that type of conduct which pleases him; God is holy and man must therefore be holy (Lev. 11.44f; 19.2; 20.7; 1 Pet. 1.16); the original sense of 'separation' is often still present later as it is here where Paul's demands are seen in part as a separation from pagan ways (see also notes on 3.13 and O. Proksch and K. G. Kuhn, *T.D.N.T.* I, pp. 88ff; N. Snaith, *The Distinctive Ideas of the Old Testament*, London, 1944, pp. 21–50; E. Jacob, *op. cit.*, pp. 86–93). The form of the word (ἁγιασμός; contrast 3.13) lays emphasis on the process of sanctification, the activity associated with it, rather than on sanctification as a completed state; Christians are 'the holy ones' (the saints) and for this reason and this reason only are they able to seek holiness. ἁγιασμός can be taken either passively, 'that you may be sanctified (sc. by God)', or reflexively, 'that you may sanctify yourselves'; since the emphasis in the following verses lies on what they are to do the latter is preferable, though it must be realized that Paul would never think of the believer as able to consecrate himself apart from God's action (4.8; 5.23; 2 Th. 2.13; 1 Cor. 1.2, 30; Rom. 15.16).

3b   We now move to the particular area of conduct with which Paul is going to deal first, viz., sex. **abstain** may have been a technical word in the catechetical instruction of the primitive Christian community indicating separation from the morals of the contemporary culture (cf. Acts 15.20, 29; 1 Th. 5.22; 1 Pet. 2.11; see E. G. Selwyn, *op. cit.*, 372ff). πορνεία (= **sexual sin**) can be used in the restricted sense, fornication, but often, as here, it has a much wider connotation and covers sexual sin of all types. To the Jew the pagan world displayed its decadence in the presence of such sin (cf. Rom. 1.24ff) and sex was often linked to pagan religious practice so that those entering Christianity would need a particular warning. Because Gentile standards were so much lower, and seaports are notorious in this respect (e.g. Corinth), Paul's converts were in danger of a relapse. 'As in the mission-field today, when the initial fervour was over, it was only too easy for converts to slip back into the low standards of pagan living. A few months of Christianity could not be trusted to undo the habits of a lifetime' (Bicknell). Probably Timothy has told Paul of some of this; that he praises them in 1.3 cannot exclude his knowledge of it for the praise is couched in very general terms and the Corinthians are similarly praised in 1 Cor. 1.4–9 yet grave sexual perversion was found among them (5.1–5; 6.12–20). Many of the relapses into sexual sin in the early church will not of course have been accompanied by an abandonment of Christianity. Paul demands a total rejection of pagan practices in the matter.

4   It is at this point that problems arise. Including **to abstain**

there are five infinitives; the last two, **to injure** and **to exploit** (v. 6) are obviously coordinate but do they continue the theme of sexual sin of the second **(to know how to)** or are they dependent on v. 3 and parallel either to **sanctify yourselves** or to **abstain** and introduce another theme, viz., business morality? Is the third, **to keep** parallel to, or dependent on, the second, **to know how to**? In addition the meaning of **wife** is not certain and to it are closely linked the meanings of **know how to** and **keep**.

From the beginning of interpretation commentators have been divided over the meaning of σκεῦος (lit. 'vessel, tool, utensil') which we have translated **wife** (cf. C. Maurer, *T.W.N.T.* VII, pp. 359–68). Theodore of Mopsuestia and Augustine took it in this sense but Tertullian and Chrysostom preferred 'body'. In either case the word is used metaphorically. Paul's usage elsewhere is not of much assistance; in Rom. 9.22f he is influenced by the potter imagery of the O.T. (Isa. 29.16; 45.9; etc.) where the vessels are vessels of God (or in later Judaism, of the devil) and in 2 Cor. 4.7 the same idea is present though to a lesser degree; it is not present here. The meaning 'body', influenced by Greek ideas of the body as the dwelling-place of the soul, was coming into general use about the first century A.D. It depends on a basic dualism of body and soul which though it was beginning to penetrate Judaism in this period (4 Ezra 8.6; Philo, *Quod Det. Pot. Ins.* 170; *Migr. Abr.* 193) is foreign to Paul; the distinction which we so easily make between 'human being' and 'body' was by no means so clear-cut for him and if the word means 'body' here it must do so in the sense of the whole being viewed as the person engaging in activity. When Paul uses 'body' and associates a pronoun with it, it is practically the same as if he had used the personal pronoun (e.g. Rom. 12.1; 1 Cor. 9.27; Phil. 1.20). If 'vessel' then means 'body' here, 1 Cor. 6.18 provides a good parallel to its use in the sexual context. Thus there is nothing which directly forbids the meaning 'body' and a good deal which encourages it. Difficulties arise however when we relate it to **keep**, for κτᾶσθαι in the present tense as here normally means 'gain, acquire'. No one can be said to 'gain his body'. The verb does have the sense 'keep' in the perfect and there is also some slight evidence in the papyri for this in the present (cf. M.–M. *ad verbum*).

The alternative rendering **wife** appears repulsive to modern thought, but this should not deter us if on other grounds it is the

161

better meaning, for it would not have been so abhorrent to the ancient world with its very different view of women; Paul moreover is arguing here for sexual abstinence on the part of the man as over against the prevalent two-standard morality which allows the man sexual freedom but refuses it to the woman. There is some Rabbinic evidence that the Hebrew equivalent to vessel, כלי, was used of women in sexual contexts (Dibelius denied this but Maurer appears to have successfuly refuted him). We can combine this easily with the meaning 'gain, acquire' for κτᾶσθαι in the sense 'marry'—'each one of you to know how to marry his wife . . .'; but we should then expect his to be a dative and not a genitive, i.e. acquire a wife for himself (the verb is used in the sense 'marry', cf. Sir. 36.24; Ruth 4.10; Xenophon, Conviv. 2.10). The difficulty of the genitive case would again be overcome if we could take the verb in the durative sense keep rather than in that of 'gain': if so taken it would mean that a man should 'have' his wife in order to avoid sexual sin (cf. 1 Cor. 7.2ff). There is more support for the durative sense in the case of the translation wife because, as Maurer has shown, the verb and noun together probably reproduce a Hebrew idiom בָּעַל אִשָּׁה which can be used both of entrance into marriage (Deut. 21.13; 24.1) and of its continuance (Isa. 54.1), in each case with reference to sexual relations. Its meaning would then be 'to possess a woman sexually' passing into the sense 'to live with a woman' where 'live' would have sexual overtones. Combined with the personal pronoun this gives our translation. It has a parallel in 1 Cor. 7.2 where the reference may be to entrance into, rather than continuance in, the state of marriage. If these verses offend us by appearing to regard woman as a possession we need to remember that they would not have sounded so harsh to first century ears and in 1 Cor. 7.3f Paul ameliorates such a view. If it is objected (so Rigaux) that the translation wife is unduly restrictive in that Paul will therefore only be writing to married men whereas the sentence (each one of you) appears much more general and ought to include the unmarried it can be answered that in the social codes (Haustafeln) of Col. 3.18ff; Eph. 5.21ff; 1 Pet. 2.13ff no instruction is given to single men; Paul in 1 Th. 4 is probably acting on information received through Timothy and may know that the vast majority of the Thessalonians were married.

The meaning would then be that husbands are to restrict their sexual activity to their own wives and to enter on this with them in

sanctification and honour. Paul deals with extra-marital relations
and with marriage in much greater detail in 1 Cor. 6.12–7.40. If
the meaning 'body' is chosen the reference will still be to honour-
able behaviour in sexual relationships though not now as
restricted to married men; for single men it will be manifested in
the total absence of such relationships. The contrast would then
probably lie with much Greek thought for which the body was
unimportant: Paul tells the Christian that the preservation of the
holiness of the body is of first importance (cf. 1 Cor. 6.19f). There
is also evidence that κτᾶσθαι can have the meaning 'win someone
for oneself' in the sense of making him favourably inclined to
oneself (see W. Vogel, 'Εἰδέναι τὸ ἑαυτοῦ σκεῦος κτᾶσθαι. Zur
Deutung von 1 Thess 4.3ff in Zusammenhang der paulinischen
Eheauffassung', *Theologische Blätter* 13 (1934) 83–5; cf. Xenophon,
Cyrop. VIII, 2, 10; Plutarch, *Pomp.* 25.4; 44.2). Paul often uses a
circumlocution for sexual intercourse (1 Cor. 7.3, 4, 5). Thus the
phrase may mean: 'to make his own wife favourably inclined towards
him for sexual intercourse'. This is to be done in **sanctification
and honour** and not in the passionate licentious manner of the
pagan who used his wife to produce children and enjoyed himself
with other women. Lust is not to rule the sexual relationships of
husbands and wives (1 Cor. 7.2–6).

We return now to **know how to** (εἰδέναι) for which other
meanings have been suggested. It might seem as if **wife** could be
its direct object and not that of **keep** but although the context is
sexual the word used for **know** here is not the one used to render
the Hebrew word for **know** when it is used sexually ('to know a
woman'). The meaning 'respect' (cf. 5.12) would result in 'each
one of you to respect his own wife (body)'; this is possible but it is
such an unusual meaning for the verb that, unless there were
positive evidence suggesting it, it ought not to be extended to the
present context; it also breaks the relationship of **keep** and **know
how to.** The rendering **know how to** which we have chosen is
suitable whether we decide on **wife** or 'body'.

H. Baltensweiler, 'Erwägungen zu 1 Thess 4.3–8', *T.Z.* 19
(1963) 1–13, suggests a completely different solution which has
the advantage of uniting v. 6 to the earlier verses. Choosing the
rendering **wife** he follows Maurer in regarding κτᾶσθαι σκεῦος as
Paul's translation of a Hebrew idiom (see above). He argues that
a particular question has been referred to Paul: is the Greek law

on the inheritance of a daughter to be observed by Christians? This law which operated when no legal male issue existed involved the marriage of the daughter with someone of near kin in order to continue the family by providing a 'son' and might be incestuous according to Jewish law as within the forbidden degrees (cf. Lev. 18.6–26; 20.10–21). It would then be sexual sin ('fornication') according to the Jews; it is probably marriage within the forbidden degrees which is prohibited in the apostolic decrees (Acts 15; cf. Haenchen, *ad loc.*). The decision as to whom the daughter should marry would lead to legal disputes (as 'wills' often do today) and v. 6 refers to legal actions in the matter. The Christian is consequently to avoid incestuous union by taking a wife in honour and sanctification and not in licentious desire like the pagans, and he is not to argue out in court his right to marry a particular heiress. There are difficulties to this theory: (1) There is a lack of specific reference to the law of inheritance; **in this matter** (v. 6) is too general to be made to carry it. (2) 4.9ff; 4.13ff; 5.1ff are all introduced by the same phrase (περὶ δέ) which leads us to believe that Paul is answering questions in them, but this phrase is not found here and so he is not answering a question. (3) Would the members of the church often have been the type of people involved in disputes about inheritance? Admittedly 1 Cor. 5 shows they did sometimes go to law with one another, but there Paul makes clear the reference. The question of the law of inheritance would only have arisen occasionally and Paul's words are too general for this; how many actual instances could there have been in the short time since the church was founded? (4) Verses 4, 5 are a little weak to bear all this and are much more general than a backward reference from v. 6 would require. (5) In v. 2 Paul says he is referring back to previous instruction; if he had given this in respect of daughter-inheritance he could have been much briefer here. (6) Verse 2 does not govern vv. 13ff where he is giving new material but vv. 3ff; therefore vv. 3ff do not contain new material, i.e. they are not an answer to a question.

The man is to take his wife sexually **in sanctification and honour** (this phrase is adverbial; cf. Moule, p. 78); he is not to look on her as a tool to satisfy his lusts but to appreciate her as a being who with himself is part of God's holy people (1 Cor. 7.2–6). What Paul means by **honour** can best be understood from Rom. 1.24 where sexual perversion is a dishonouring of men; in true

marriage the other partner is honoured (cf. 1 Pet. 3.7 where σκεῦος
is also used of the wife; on the place of 'love' in marriage see Eph.
5.22ff). These two terms in v. 4 are not 'humanitarian' words but
'religious'. If there is to be a true marriage then it must be carried
through in Christian faith; **sanctification** is not something for
worship alone but for every act of life. Later in the church men
and women were united in marriage by a church official and
presumably therefore in a religious ceremony (Ign. *Polyc.* 5.2; cf.
Acts Thomas 10ff).

The attitude of the Christian is now contrasted with that of the 5
pagan, which had been his own only a few months before and which
he could not be expected to forget completely on becoming a
Christian. In Rom. 1.18ff Paul's attack on the sins of the pagan world
begins from its failure to know God though he is knowable; in
1 Th. 4.5 he does not deal with the nature of pagan ignorance but
assumes it using a phrase, **who do not know God,** drawn from
the O.T. (Jer. 10.25; Ps. 79(78).6); he employs it also in Gal. 4.8;
2 Th. 1.8; cf. 1 Cor. 1.21. If the Jew is characterized by the fact
that God has made himself known to him, the pagan is characterised
by his failure to know God—and the inevitable result is sin, here
particularized as **lustful passion.** Morality for Paul is always
firmly tied to belief in God. Pagan marriage is motivated by lust,
Christian marriage ought to be by faith.

It has been strongly urged by some commentators, and most 6a
recently by R. Beauvery, '*Πλεονεκτεῖν* in 1 Thess. 4.6a', *Verbum
Domini*, 33 (1955) 78–85, that Paul introduces a new subject here
and that we should render the first part of the verse 'not to injure
or defraud his brother in commerce' (thus making this clause
parallel to that beginning **that is to abstain . . .** (v. 3)) because:
(*a*) it is difficult to understand the verbs with any other connotation
than a commercial; (*b*) Paul precedes the infinitives here, unlike
the others in vv. 3–5, with an article so suggesting a change of
subject; (*c*) it is hard to see the precise reference in sexual matters
to the injury of a brother since the earlier emphasis lay on the
nature of the sexual act within marriage rather than on the rejection of sexual intercourse outside it; (*d*) there were probably many
petty traders in the Christian community of a commercial city like
Thessalonica who would need to have their business practice
brought into line with Christian concepts. On the other hand:
(*a*) the article before the infinitives may imply that these are not

governed by **know how to** (v. 4) as was **keep** (v. 4) but are in apposition to it and represent a further explanation of **to abstain from sexual sin** (v. 3); (*b*) if so, v. 6a is not directly dependent on vv. 4, 5, but takes up a new point out of v. 3b, viz., sexual sin in relation to others, not just the marriage partner; (*c*) the remainder of vv. 6b–8 appears to deal with sexual sin, and if 6a dealt with commerce this would break the chain of thought; (*d*) πρᾶγμα **(matter)** does mean 'commerce, business' in the plural but never in the singular which is used here. What does it mean here? As we have seen Baltensweiler takes it in the sense 'legal proceedings', and this is a possible rendering, but on more general grounds we have rejected his solution. The word is probably a euphemism for 'sex' (cf. L. & S.; C. Maurer, *T.D.N.T.* VI, pp. 639f; S. Grill, 'In das Gewerbe seines Nächsten eingreifen', *B.Z.*, 11 (1967) 118; cf. use of English 'affair'): do not defraud or injure your brother in matters of sex. Sexual sin (v. 3) may either be seen in a sexual act within marriage based on lust, in the use for sex of another's wife, possibly in the idea that if a man uses another woman he defrauds the brother who will later marry her, or, even possibly, since sexual impurity corrupts the whole of society, in the defrauding of all the brothers (cf. Plummer). When Paul says **brother** is he envisaging a sin against a member of the community through fornication with his wife, or does he use **brother** to mean anyone? It is hard to see him using it in the latter sense and so we take the primary reference to be to sexual sin within the community; this is not to suggest that Paul would have been unworried by its manifestation with someone outside (cf. 1 Cor. 6.12–20) but that at this moment he is looking at the community and its internal good order. He thinks first of those who are nearest to the Christian who might sin, and of the effect on them; similarly at v. 9 he restricts himself to 'brotherly love'. It is just possible that he may be referring to homosexuality in which the brother might be considered to be exploited; homosexuality was widely prevalent in the ancient world and in Rom. 1.24f is clearly associated with not knowing God. It should be noted that the problem about the reference in **brother** remains even if the general context is commerce and not sex.

6b   The **Lord** is Jesus and not God, otherwise the explicit introduction of God in v. 7 would be unnecessary. While Paul does not equate Jesus and God he attributes to Jesus many of the functions of God (so also in 2 Th. 1.7f; 2 Cor. 5.10), here that of judge, the judge being one who not merely pronounces a sentence but himself inflicts it. Because it is a frequent O.T. conception that God takes vengeance on evil-doers or avenges evil deeds (Deut. 32.35; Ps. 99.8; Mic. 5.15; Nah. 1.2) it is probably unnecessary to view Paul as directly quoting Ps. 94.1 although there are certain verbal similarities. It is not clear whether he is referring to the present judgement of God on these wrongdoers (cf. 1 Cor. 11.30–2; Rom. 1.18ff; 13.4) or to the future final judgement; he uses both aspects of God's judgement as sanctions for moral conduct. Here(contrast 1 Cor. 11.30–2) he gives no instances of believers enduring judgement, perhaps because he is still dealing only in possibilities. **all these things** is somewhat vague but presumably refers to the various forms of sexual sin to which Paul has been referring in vv. 4–6a, or to the injury of the commercial interests of others if that is the meaning of v. 6a (cf. Heb. 13.4 for God's judgement in sexual matters). It should not surprise them that God avenges sin for Paul had **told** them this on his first visit when his instruction had included teaching on 'the approaching anger' (1.10). Now he fears that they may have forgotten this sanction to which he had **solemnly testified,** but it is no light matter to be shrugged off. Some commentators take **told earlier** (προείπαμεν) in the sense 'prophesy, predict'; if Paul had in fact been alluding to a prediction we would have expected him to mention actual instances of its fulfilment as in 1 Cor. 11.30–2; moreover 'predict' is hardly the word Paul would have used for the inevitability of the divine wrath towards sin; this would be a proposition to be asserted and not a prediction to be offered.

Paul now gives his second reason (**for** goes back to vv. 3–6a rather 7 than to v. 6b alone, but perhaps carries the implication that should they not be impressed by the reason of v. 6b then here is another and better) why they ought to keep God's will in these sexual matters: it rests on the fact that their Christian state goes back ultimately not to their own response to his preaching but to God's call to them expressed in that preaching. God's **call** (see on 2.12) is not to a particular position within the Christian community (Paul believed himself called to be an apostle, Rom. 1.1; 1 Cor. 1.1) but the call to be a Christian (2.12; 5.24; 2 Th. 2.14; Eph. 4.4; Col. 3.15). It is noticeable that Paul says here that God calls **us**: writers, readers, and all Christians are joined together and put in a new category distinguishable from mankind in general; it is on this that Paul grounds his appeal. Sometimes Paul uses a different preposition (εἰς) and we learn the purpose of God's call (cf. 2.12; 1 Cor. 1.9; 2 Th. 2.14). Here he tells us first (using ἐπί) that God's call was not **because of** (or possibly, 'with a view to') their **impurity** (cf. Masson), an impurity which characterized pagan life and was seen especially in a debased sexual morality. God's call, of course, does not depend on the degree of man's goodness. (If v. 6a refers to business morality then we must take **impurity** more widely; it has the limited sexual sense in 2 Cor. 12.21.) They were called secondly **so that** they might exist **in** (ἐν) **sanctification** (cf. Lightfoot; **in** describes their condition as Christians, cf. 1 Cor. 7.15). If **impurity** characterized their pre-Christian existence, their Christian existence ought to be characterized by **sanctification.** It indeed is, for they are 'the saints', the sanctified, they belong to the domain of God. The word **sanctification** runs through our passage (vv. 3, 4, 7; cf. 'holy' Spirit, v. 8); earlier the stress lay on their self-sanctification (v. 3); now it lies on God's sanctification of them (by his call they were made 'saints'). If God is working in them in this way they ought not to fall back into the old ways, and the realization that God is so working should itself be a motive leading to their self-sanctification. The slave called to be a Christian remains a slave, though now he is free in Christ; the free man called to be a Christian remains a free man, though now he is the slave of Christ (1 Cor. 7.20–3), but the impure man called to be a Christian cannot remain impure but must seek sanctification.

8 Paul's third reason for obedience to God in sexual matters is introduced by an unusual and fairly strong connecting particle, **consequently** (τοιγαροῦν). If those who have been called to sanctification live on in impurity this is to **spurn God,** for he has given them the **Holy Spirit** for their sanctification. The discussion is now entirely general with no word suggesting sexual matters, and so it is also the final answer in this context to the man who does not seek to please God and do his will (vv. 1–3a). There is a saying which appears in different forms in the Gospels to the effect that the man who receives Christ's disciple receives Christ, and in turn receives God (Mk. 9.37 and *par.*; Mt. 10.40; Lk. 10.16; Jn. 12.44, 48; 13.20). Our phrase is its negation, being closest in that respect to Lk. 10.16 (cf. Jn. 12.48). It may be that Paul has been influenced by

some form of the logion with which he could have been acquainted
in the oral tradition, but he may depend directly on the Jewish
shaliach principle which he would have known from his Jewish
upbringing; this principle is that a man's *shaliach* (ambassador,
representative) is as himself, and that therefore to receive the
shaliach is to receive the man. The principle may itself have been
the origin of the Gospel logion, whether it goes back to Jesus or not.
(For a discussion of the principle see T. W. Manson, *The Church's
Ministry*, pp. 35–52; K. H. Rengstorf, *T.D.N.T.* I, pp. 413–20;
the actual wording may be due to the LXX text of Isa. 21.2; cf.
1 Sam. 8.7). Paul's words are strong: the rejection of God's will
is the rejection of God. There is no object to the first **spurns;**
if one is to be sought it must come from the preceding context
and will be the good ways indicated therein, i.e., the spurning is
seen in the failure to abstain from sexual sin and not in a verbal
denunciation of God. More probably the phrase **he who spurns**
is really the equivalent of a noun (a participle with the article is often
so used in Greek), 'the spurner', and the implicit object comes with
the second **spurns. Not man but God:** Paul has no particular
man in view, neither himself, because he has handed on God's
commands to them (Schmithals, p. 114f, thinks that Paul is
defending himself against an attack on his apostolic authority;
this reads too much into a simple phrase; elsewhere Paul makes his
rejection of such attacks absolutely clear), nor the injured brother
of v. 6a; the contrast is rather that between man as weak creature
(**man** lacks the article) and God who creates and redeems him.
(For the human/divine contrast in Paul cf. 2.13; Gal. 1.10, and
in the O.T., Exod. 16.8; 1 Sam. 8.7; Isa. 7.13.) If a man by his
conduct rejects what Paul has said in vv. 3b–6a he is rejecting, not
human decrees or a human appeal, but God. The God who may
be rejected is further defined as the giver of the **Holy Spirit.** The
very fact that he gives the Spirit makes his rejection worse, for,
apart from his goodness in the gift itself, the Spirit is the Spirit
of sanctification (**Holy** and **sanctification** come from the same
Greek root). The particular and unusual way (the nearest parallels
are Ps. 142.10 (LXX); Isa. 63.10; Eph. 4.30) in which Paul refers
to the Spirit (lit. 'his Spirit, the holy') emphasizes both that it is
God's Spirit and that it is holy, the remainder of the phrase shows
that it has been not merely offered to them but **set within them**
(an expression probably derived from the O.T.; cf. Ezek. 36.27;

37.14; it may not be a direct citation since Paul knows the O.T. imagery so well). Some MSS (A C K Clem.) read an aorist, 'God has set . . .', and not a present participle (B ℵ* D G). This variant accords with Paul's usual practice (cf. Rom. 5.5; Gal. 4.6) when referring to the giving of the Spirit and probably therefore appeared under the influence of the aorist 'called' (v. 7); the present is non-temporal and describes the character of God rather than suggesting a continuous giving. For the Jews generally the Spirit had been a gift to be expected in the Age to come; the Qumran community saw it as already active among their members; the first Christians, convinced that they were in the New Age, believed that God had indeed already set the Spirit within them so that they were new men and new women enabled to perform his will. The Spirit both dwelt in them as a community (1 Cor. 3.16) and within each one of them. If God has acted in this way for their sanctification to fall into impurity is to spurn him and to ignore the very means he has given them to carry out his will. There is a similar connection between the presence of God's Spirit in the believer and an appeal against sexual sin in 1 Cor. 6.17, 19, 20.

(c) BROTHERLY LOVE 4.9–12

Now on the subject of brotherly love you have no need (for us) to write to you, for you yourselves are taught by God to love one another. (10) For you even do this to all the brothers in the whole of Macedonia. But we request you, brothers, to excel more and more (11) and to be ambitious to live unobtrusively and mind your own affairs and work with your hands, just as we instructed you, (12) so that you may walk becomingly in the judgement of outsiders and require no man's help.

The subject changes. In English we have one word for 'love' and it might appear as if Paul having spoken of impure love in vv. 3–8 now goes on to speak of true love, but Greek has several words and there is no necessary connection of thought in this way, though of course both sections are part of the paraenesis. Paul's first words **Now on the subject of** (cf. 4.13; 5.1) indicate the change of subject. In 1 Cor. 7.1, 25; 8.1; etc., the same words (περὶ δέ) appear at the beginning of new sections in which Paul answers questions raised by the Corinthians in a letter they had sent him (cf. also P. Lond., 1912, a letter of the Emperor Claudius to the people of Alexandria, lines 52f, 66, etc., cited in H. I. Bell, *Jews and Christians in Egypt*, London, 1924, pp. 1–37). There is no need to envisage an equivalent letter here; there may have been a letter (cf. pp. 14–16) but the phrase here and in 4.13; 5.1 only indicates a new subject, not necessarily an answer to a written question; Paul has a number of subjects he wishes to raise; his information probably comes from Timothy's verbal report.

If vv. 9–12 are not directly related to vv. 3–8, are vv. 9–10a and vv. 10b–12 directly related to one another or is there another change of subject at 10b? The general structure of the paraenesis seems to consist of a section on impurity (4.3–8) followed by three sections each of which deals with a particular subject (4.9–12; 4.13–18; 5.1–11; brotherly love, dead Christians, times and seasons, respectively) and each of which is picked out by the use of περὶ δέ **(on the subject of)**. Yet it must be acknowledged that at 10b there is some kind of a break. It is present in other places where Paul has the combination **request ... brothers** (Rom. 15.30; 16.17; 1 Cor. 1.10; 16.15; and there is some break at 1 Th. 5.14). Here the break must be Paul's movement from a general statement on brotherly love to the nature of that love in a particular situation. Verses 9–10a are so general by themselves that it is unlikely that Paul would have left them without particular application since he says that he has no need to write to them on the principle of brotherly love (v. 9); the principle is known; it is its application to different situations which is hard to comprehend and work out. There is a similar movement of thought in Rom. 13.8–10 where Paul deals with brotherly love and then after an eschatological interlude moves on in 14.1–15.13 to deal with two particular problems (vegetarianism and sabbath observance) in which brotherly love needs to be shown; there is no direct connection but an underlying current of thought. The same is true here.

In vv. 9–12 Paul may well have in mind one particular section of the church as disorderly but it is more likely that he knows of individuals who are living in a disorderly way; they are hardly to be glorified as a 'party' with its own particular line of thought and action and there are no good grounds to connect them (cf. Masson) with those who may be supposed in 5.12 to be rejecting their leaders. Whoever they are Paul begins with general praise of the community (note how often Paul pays tribute to their achievements; 1.3; 3.6 in respect of their love) for their **brotherly love** (φιλαδελφία, a different word for 'love' than in 1.3; 3.12). This word was used in the Greek world only for the love of actual brothers for one another and so also in Jewish Greek (4 Macc. 13.23, 25; 14.1; the one possible exception is 2 Macc. 15.14); its metaphorical application to non-literal brothers may well then be Christian in origin (Rom. 12.10; Heb. 13.1; 1 Pet. 1.22). This transference from physical to spiritual brotherhood will have come from the strong Christian feeling of the community as a family (cf. Mk. 3.34f; 10.29f; see also on 1.4). To the Christian, **brother** is not merely a metaphor but a reality; since the natural ties of kinship had often been broken at conversion they appreciated more firmly the ties of spiritual kinship. The outside world observed with wonder the mutual love of Christians, something difficult for Western Christians to understand today but still a reality in many areas where Christianity is young. Why does Paul restrict his attention here to brotherly love and not demand love for all men? Probably vv. 10b–12 lead to this restriction because there he is concerned with the inner state of the community which is disturbed when some members are restless and interfere with the legitimate interests of others. True brotherly love is seen when men live peacefully together as in a family (cf. 5.14f); it is not just a pleasant feeling but an active concern for others.

About this brotherly love Paul does not need to write again **for they (you yourselves**—emphatic and antithetical (see on 2 Th. 1.4) for they have not only been taught by Paul but they have been taught by God as much as 'we', i.e. Paul, etc., have been) **are taught by God to love;** the whole phrase is unusual; we would expect 'you yourselves know how to love.' Paul can hardly be contrasting himself here with God for in so far as they do know the commandment of love it is only because Paul in his first visit instructed them in it. It seems unlikely also that he means they know it from the O.T. which itself is due to God, for it will then again have been Paul himself who first drew their attention to Lev. 19.18; and if he had taught it to them from the O.T. he would almost certainly have referred to it as taught in Scripture or as written in Scripture and not as taught by God. In any case it is much more likely that Paul would have brought this commandment to their attention as part of the common Christian tradition, whether he explicitly traced it to words of Jesus or not (it is surprising how rarely Paul uses Jesus' name even when he is quoting his sayings); had he been referring it to Jesus (e.g. Jn. 13.34, assuming this correctly reproduces a dominical saying) he would again have been much more likely to say 'taught by the Lord' than 'taught by God' for there is no other point where Paul explicitly identifies Jesus and God; the same would probably be true if Paul conceived of it as taught to them as a word of an inspired prophet quoting the exalted Lord. There is no evidence anywhere that the primitive Christian catechetical tradition was regarded as the direct teaching of God. Faced with these difficulties many commentators have suggested some kind of internal teaching and pointed to Jer. 31.33f; God has spoken within the heart. However when Paul writes of internal testimony he thinks of the Spirit (e.g. Rom. 8.15f; 1 Cor. 2.13; Gal. 4.6). We note the use of the present tense; God's teaching is a fact of the present and is not to be tied down to Paul's visit in the past. The phrase itself may come from Isa. 54.13 where the LXX reads 'taught by God' though it uses our present compound word ($\theta\epsilon o\delta i\delta\alpha\varkappa\tau o\iota$) as two separate words. The idea recurs in John 6.45 which is indebted to Isa. 54.13. Perhaps nothing very deep is intended, only that the command to brotherly love is divine in origin; the idea that men are taught by God without indication how this takes place is common in the O.T. Cf. C. Spicq, 'La Charité fraternelle selon 1 Th. 4, 9' in *Mélanges Bibliques* (rédigés en l'honneur de André Robert), Paris, n.d., pp. 507-11. Whatever the precise meaning the phrase certainly says that their instruction in the commandment of love is not of human origin but comes from God **(God** is to be contrasted with 'man' in the phrase). The purpose of this teaching, or its result, is that they should **love one another,** and this they have done.

They indeed have not only loved one another but also Christians 10a everywhere throughout their province. Taught the commandment of love they practise it towards all their **brothers.** We are not told how they did this outside their own community. Paul while among them had received financial aid from Philippi (Phil. 4.16); perhaps they in turn had given financial aid to assist the spread of the gospel. More probably, since 'brotherly love' and not the mission of the church is the main subject, we must think of acts of kindness shown to Christians from other communities who came to their town. As a commercial centre and seaport many Christians would pass through it and they may have been offered hospitality (cf. Rom. 16.1f; 1 Pet. 4.9); this was very necessary in an age when inns and hotels were few. Christians going to another Christian home in a strange town could expect to find, and did find, a brotherly welcome; they were made part of the family. **To all the brothers in the whole of Macedonia** (reading τούς with B אᶜ K L, etc.) sounds an exaggeration but is not un-Pauline (cf. 2 Th. 1.3; 2 Cor. 1.1 and see notes on 1.8); there cannot have been many other Christian communities as yet in the province; certainly Philippi and Beroea; a few other towns may have been evangelized from them.

10b   In what does Paul **request** (see on 4.1) them to **excel more and more?** If we dissociate vv. 10b–12 from vv. 9–10a then it will be what is spelt out in vv. 11f where the initial **and** will have to be taken epexegetically. But if we are correct in linking vv. 9–10a to vv. 10b–12 it will refer back to **brotherly love** (v. 9): they will **excel** in this if they follow what Paul says in vv. 11f. As at 4.1 the reference of the phrase **excel more and more** is in the first instance backward; they are to excel in walking and pleasing God; what this means is then spelt out in detail in the following verses, 3–8; probably this is the way also to take the phrase here. There is no limit to the ways in which the command to love ought to be interpreted—as many ways as there are situations in life—and there is no limit to the extent **(more and more)** to which love may be exercised.

11   They are now told how to excel in love. φιλοτιμεῖσθαι (= **be ambitious**) has another recognized meaning, 'strive eagerly'; it is difficult to decide between the two. Paul uses it elsewhere only at Rom. 15.20 and 2 Cor. 5.9; our rendering suits Rom. 15.20 better; there is little to help us in 2 Cor. 5.9 or here to decide which to choose. Neither meaning would be wrong. Whichever we choose there is an oxymoron: 'be ambitious to be ambitionless' or 'strive eagerly to not-strive (with others)'! The general sense is not in doubt. To strive for the wrong ambition was not unknown in the early church; in 1 Cor. 12–14 Paul rebukes those who were ambitious to speak with tongues and bids them seek superior gifts of the Spirit.

Three closely linked phrases follow and it is impossible to explain them separately. It is first necessary to eliminate a possible false understanding (cf. von Dobschütz). **mind your own affairs** might be contrasted with 'mind civic affairs' and the first two taken together have been given the sense 'retire from public life' (cf. Plato, *Rep.* vi, 496D). Although linguistically possible this is unlikely in our context for all we know of the first Christians shows us they were not those who were occupied with public affairs but unimportant people; **work with your hands** confirms this here.

If Paul is not warning them against a preoccupation with public life he is warning them against some disruptive influence which might mar the peace of the community. Since there is nothing to suggest otherwise we assume it comes from within the community. What is it? If we take the three phrases together it is contrasted with minding their own affairs and carrying on with their daily work. We have no further clue here but in 2 Th. 3.6–15 we find some in the community rebuked because they are idle, not working to support themselves and not living quietly, and we note that there (3.10) as here **(just as we instructed you)** Paul refers to his previous teaching. Why should some of the Thessalonians always have been in danger of neglecting their work? It is customary to answer that they had been stirred up by the ferment of eschatological expectation occasioned by Paul's preaching of the nearness of the return of Christ and such a phenomenon has often been observed in Christian communities seized by the belief that the End was near. Work is neglected for the future can be ignored, and the peril in which others are believed to stand leads to excessive missionary activity towards them; much time is spent in prayer and the pursuit of personal holiness so that the community may be fit to greet the coming Saviour. Paul's original preaching did feature the return of Christ (1.9f) and this therefore seems the most satisfactory solution. The allusions to previous instruction suggest that the beginnings of the error had appeared during Paul's initial visit, and the longer treatment in 2 Th. that the danger to the life of the community grew, not having been allayed by what Paul writes now. We have argued that vv. 9–12 are a unit and that vv. 10b–12 spell out the nature of brotherly love in the Thessalonian situation; eschatological excitement could turn the attention of Christians from this so that the harmony of the community would be disturbed, with those who were themselves excited attempting to run it along their own lines and other members hindered from earning their living; but vv. 10b–12 are not explicitly linked to brotherly love in the sense that a Christian should not become a burden to others through not caring for his own needs nor that he should help to bear the burdens of those who so neglect their own needs (cf. Gal. 6.2, 5). It probably goes beyond the evidence to find a direct connection between our passage and 5.12f; there may have been those with an excessive eschatological orientation who did not welcome the rule of the church's leaders but this is quite a general tendency in men and cannot be restricted to eschatological enthusiasts. The subject may be taken up again in 5.14 (so Frame), but it is unlikely that workers in the community mistrusted the charismatics of 5.19–22. Schmithals (pp. 114–16) attributes the unrest to a false over-excitement through the Spirit, as found later in heretical gnostic circles, and parallels with our passage 1 Tim. 5.13, 15 as the first clear example. It is interesting that for his parallel he here deserts the Corinthian, Galatian and Philippian correspondence which he uses at other points to explain the opposition Paul encountered in Thessalonica. There is however very little about the Spirit in 1 & 2 Th. and where Paul deals with wrong views he does so much more extensively (1 Cor. 12–14); the Spirit was of such importance to the early Christians that vague allusions to wrongful use of its powers would not have assisted the Thessalonians.

Work with your hands gives a revealing insight into the life of the early church and is to be understood literally. Today **hands** might be taken metaphorically, 'let each get on with his own work', but Greek culture regarded manual labour as degrading and would not have used such an image. The phrase therefore implies that the great majority of the Thessalonian Christians were manual workers, whether skilled or unskilled; this is in line with all we learn elsewhere about the early Christian community (1 Cor. 1.26; Eph. 4.28). Paul while among them had worked with his hands (2.9; 1 Cor. 4.12; 2 Th. 3.8). Manual work (see on 2.9) was not considered demeaning in any way by Jews and it would have come perfectly naturally to Paul to instruct his Christians to **work with** their **hands.** He does not contrast work with prayer, telling those who are eschatologically excited to turn away from religious acts, nor does he set down a philosophy of work as good for the soul as in the Puritan ethic. If the community is to remain in existence work is necessary (see further on 2 Th. 3.6–15).

It is not clear whether **just as we instructed** (the same root as in 4.2) **you** refers to all of v. 11 or only to **work with your hands.**

If the latter then originally this instruction will have been given in the light of the Greek rejection of manual labour; if, as is much more probable, the former then it will mean Paul had already encountered eschatological enthusiasm on his initial visit and warned against it.

Paul now gives two reasons for his exhortation (v. 10b). It is 12 better to take the verse in this way than as the content of the 'instructions' of v. 11 which would make too big a break in the flow of thought before **just as we instructed you;** it would also imply that there had been no previous reference by Paul to the demands of v. 11 and instead he would be made to refer to those of v. 12 as given previously. His first reason relates directly to the impression made by Christians through their behaviour on those who were not Christians, whether Jews or Gentiles. It is based on the same metaphor **(walk)** for behaviour which he used at 2.12; there true behaviour meant being worthy of the Lord while here it means to be becoming to **outsiders** (οἱ ἔξω). This phrase was a standard designation in the early Church for those who were not in its membership (Mk. 4.11; 1 Cor. 5.12f; Col. 4.5; cf. 1 Tim. 3.7; Tit. 2.8). It implies a certain contrast and distinctness between those within and those without; it does not imply that those outside should be despised. It probably arose out of the closely knit nature of the Christian fellowship and the great cleavage between Christians and non-Christians because of the former's new attitudes in so many matters. The Christians were very conscious of the impression they made on others (Mt. 5.16; Col. 4.5; 1 Tim. 3.7; 1 Pet. 2.12; cf. Acts 2.47; 1 Cor. 10.32f) and of its importance for their faith; so they were to walk **becomingly** (cf. Rom. 13.13 for the association of the two words). Behaviour must be related both to the Lord (2.12) and to the non-Christian, as here, and the second ought to flow from the first. It does not mean that the behaviour of Christians will always please non-Christians; in the present context it implies that the behaviour of Christians will be such as to lead to no conflict with certain ideals which even the non-Christian would accept, e.g. the orderliness of society, non-interference with the rights of others, attention by a man to his own job so that he be able to support himself and his dependants. Non-Christians will recognize such conduct as good and will not therefore be put off by the wrong 'scandal' in Christianity.

Paul's second reason is related more directly to the community itself (**no man** refers in the first instance to the fellow-Christian, but is not restricted solely to him; cf. Rom. 13.8). The man who because of eschatological excitement gives up his work will become, or his family will, a burden on the community; they will require to be fed and clothed; the community in its fellowship will undertake this; much worse if it is left to **outsiders.** Stoic philosophy pictured the good man as one who was self-sufficient, independent of others, able to endure by himself whatever fate brought to him. Paul's thought is akin (cf. also Rom. 13.8) but is differentiated in two ways: (i) The Christian's self-sufficiency always comes from his dependence on God, as he clearly indicates in his own case (Phil. 4.10–14). (ii) The Christian is a member of a community which lives and works together and which neglects none of its members, so that no Christian can ever be all on his own. The whole thought here is illuminated by Gal. 6.2, 5: the believer never lets himself be a burden to others; he always seeks to help others with their burdens.

Selwyn (*1 Peter*, pp. 369–75) argues that 1 Th. 4.1–12 and 1 Peter depend on an early baptismal holiness code (see his table of similarities, pp. 370f) probably related to the apostolic decrees of Acts 15.20, 29; he also argues that Silvanus participated in the writing of 1 Thess. and 1 Pet. and draws some of his evidence for this from our passage. These conclusions would appear to conflict. If the similarities are accounted for by use of the same primitive code there is no need to presuppose a common secretary; if they can be accounted for by a common secretary there is no need to presuppose a common code. More positively, there is one consideration which militates against a common secretary (it is assumed by Selwyn that the secretary was not just a shorthand expert but actually drafted the letter), viz., similar ideas are expressed with different words: (*a*) Selwyn parallels περιπατεῖν (1 Th. 4.1) and ἀναστροφή (1 Pet. 1.15); the former is a favourite Pauline expression and the latter a favourite in 1 Pet. (1.15, 18; 2.12; 3.1, 2, 16). (*b*) Selwyn parallels μὴ εἰδότα τὸν θεόν (1 Th. 4.5) and τῇ ἀγνοίᾳ (1 Pet. 1.14); the former is derived from the O.T. (*c*) Selwyn parallels πρὸς τοὺς ἔξω (1 Th. 4.12) with ἐν τοῖς ἔθνεσιν (1 Pet. 2.12). (*d*) Even the theme of the code is stated differently, in 1 Th. 4.3 as 'your holiness' and in 1 Pet. 1.16 as 'Be holy as I am holy'. (*e*) καλός (1 Pet. 2.12) and εὐσχημόνως

(1 Th. 4.12). Some of these differences can be accounted for if we drop the idea of common secretaryship and assume a primitive code originally in another language, Aramaic or Hebrew, and translated into Greek by different Christian leaders. There are good *a priori* grounds for accepting the idea of the presence in the early church of moral exhortation based on 'holiness' as a central concept and derived ultimately from the O.T. holiness code, and there is a good case for the apostolic decrees as derived from Lev. 17, 18 which is part of that code (see Haenchen, *Acts, ad loc.*). A resemblance between the apostolic decrees and 1 Th. 4.1–12 can be argued on the grounds that both deal with sexual sin and both use the word ἀπέχεσθαι, and a resemblance to 1 Peter on the ground of the latter's use of this verb and its explicit reference to holiness. However the absence from 1 Th. of the other sins with which the apostolic decrees deal and the probable difference in meaning between 'fornication' there (marriage within the forbidden degrees) and here renders this unlikely; the use of the same verb is natural enough. There are better grounds for associating 1 Th. and 1 Pet. in the use of a common holiness code. But the code itself may not have been extensive. 1 Th. relates it directly to 'fornication' but in 1 Pet. it is much more general (fornication is never mentioned) in relation to 'desires' (ἐπιθυμίαι 1.14) which may be assumed to be evil. Moreover 1 Th. takes up 'brotherly love' in 4.9–12; this is found in 1 Pet. 1.22; but 'brotherly love' is not appropriate to a code whose emphasis is on abstinence from sin; the phrases about brotherly love in both letters probably go back originally to Jesus' reference to the love of neighbour; both letters are in fact using tradition here but not a tradition necessarily belonging to the holiness code since it is frequently found out with this code. Some of the parallels Selwyn finds cannot be sustained, e.g. the connection of καλεῖν and ἅγιος is quite different in 1 Pet. 1.15 and 1 Th. 4.7, as is the connection of ἁγιασμός in 1 Pet. 1.2 and 1 Th. 4.4. The holiness code will originally have been brief: a demand for holiness as God's will and a departure from sin, this being expanded in particular situations to make it relevant.

(d) THE DEAD AND THE PAROUSIA 4.13–18

We do not wish you to be ignorant, brothers, on the subject of those who are sleeping, so that you do not sorrow even as

the rest of men who do not have hope. (14) For if we believe, as we do, that Jesus died and rose, so also God will bring with him those who have fallen asleep through Jesus. (15) For we say this to you in a word of the Lord that we who are living, who survive to the parousia of the Lord, will certainly not have any temporal advantage over those who fell asleep, (16) because the Lord himself, accompanied by a command, the cry of an archangel and the trumpet of God, will descend from heaven, and the dead in Christ will rise first, (17) then we, who are living, who survive, will be snatched up simultaneously with them in the clouds to a meeting with the Lord in the air; and so we shall be with the Lord for ever. (18) So then encourage one another with these arguments.

The subject changes here apparently somewhat abruptly to eschatological topics (4.13–5.11) though there is an eschatological atmosphere in the whole letter. Two issues emerge; the first here, the relation of the dead to the parousia, and the second in 5.1–11. It has been argued that Paul is led to these new subjects through internal links with 4.9–12, i.e. the love of Christians for one another and the need for stability in the face of the impending return of Christ, but this requires us to read too much into the existence of these passages side by side, and it is easier to suppose that Paul has consciously moved to a new topic because of what he has heard about the Thessalonians, probably through Timothy, but possibly through a letter from them (see pp. 14–16). He is in any case continuing to make good the deficiencies in their instruction (3.10).

Some of the Thessalonian Christians have died and their friends and relations are worried about their position when Christ returns: will their death place them at a disadvantage compared with those who are still alive? Paul's primary purpose in writing is not to enunciate doctrine but to reassure them in respect of this; to do so he has however to tell them something more about the parousia: there is no need to worry for when Jesus comes he will have the dead with him (vv. 13f); he confirms this with a saying of the Lord which includes a description of the parousia (vv. 15–17). The main theme is the anxiety of the Thessalonians and Paul writes as a pastor rather than as a theologian, but all good pastoral counselling is based on, and contains, theological teaching and is not mere

consolation. Before we examine the passage in detail it is important to realize what Paul will have told the Thessalonians on his
first visit, what the questions are which are answered in this
passage and what those are which are not.

Paul must have told them about the resurrection of Christ (it is
stated as something they believe in v. 14) and it is natural to assume
that he also told them of the resurrection of believers. As a Pharisee
he will already have accepted this belief before his conversion;
when he became a Christian his faith was given a firmer basis in
the resurrection of Christ on which is grounded that of believers
(1 Cor. 15.20ff; Rom. 6.3ff). Some of his readers will have been
God-fearers and already aware of the idea of resurrection. In other
letters Paul writes as if the resurrection was generally known and
accepted (Rom. 6.8; 8.11; Phil. 3.10f). He had been a missionary
for fifteen or more years and would by now have reached definite
views about it and have realized the dangers of not making them
clear. Within our own letter 5.10 and 4.17, 'with the Lord' (see
notes there), are most easily understood if the resurrection of
believers is assumed to underly them. In the context of the present
passage it is hardly possible that Paul could have taught that when
Christ appears dead Christians will be with him without assuming
their resurrection, and if he had not previously taught this to the
Thessalonians he would have been bound to make it explicit now;
the one reference 'the dead will rise' (v. 16) is surely insufficient
as a first introduction. W. Marxsen, 'Auslegung von 1 Thess. 4,
13–18', *Z.T.K.* 66 (1969) 22–37, argues however that Paul added
this phrase for this purpose to a saying which was originally about
rapture; but if Paul had added the phrase he would have used
ἐγείρειν and not ἀνίστημι (see on v. 14). The conclusion that
Paul was not now introducing the resurrection for the first time
is confirmed by his reference to the 'hope' of believers (v. 13); if
not of the resurrection what is this hope? The fact of resurrection
does not appear to have been doubted by the Thessalonians, still
less opposed (as in Corinth), otherwise Paul would have reassured
them and given fuller teaching. What apparently he did not do
was to give a chronological position to the resurrection in relation
to the parousia and so the Thessalonians believed the dead were
going to miss the latter; perhaps they thought of the resurrection
as coming at the end of the Messianic kingdom (cf. P. Hoffmann,
Die Toten in Christus, Münster, 1966, pp. 206–38, esp. p. 232)

which would accord with some Jewish teaching (4 Ezra 5.41; 2 Bar. 30.2; 50.1-4). There would have been little need for detailed teaching on the resurrection if the parousia was expected soon. P. Nepper-Christensen, 'Das verborgene Herrenwort', *St. Th.* 19 (1965) 136-54, goes too far when he argues that because of this nearness Paul never preached the resurrection of believers. Surely before this in his mission work Paul would have already encountered the problem of those who died before the parousia? Schmithals therefore suggests (pp. 117-19) that heretics had come in and upset his teaching; he takes these heretics to have been gnostically inclined; M. L. Peel, 'Gnostic Eschatology and the New Testament', *N.T.* 12 (1970) 141-65, has shown that gnostic teaching on the resurrection is more complex than Schmithals assumes and that some gnostics believed in a 'body resurrection' after death; we cannot therefore conclude that if the Thessalonians were upset on this point by heretics the latter's teaching was necessarily gnostic. Again, if heretics had taught contrary to Paul's views on the resurrection he would surely have reacted much more strongly. U. Luz, *Das Geschichtsverständnis des Paulus*, Münich, 1968, pp. 318ff, argues that in Paul's thought the parousia lay within the paraenetic complex whereas the resurrection was part of the Christ-event complex and related to doctrine and that it was in 1 Cor. 15 that Paul himself first systematically married these concepts; if Paul himself was not clear of their relationship at the time he wrote our letter the Thessalonians would not have been clear and this may have led to their question. Whatever the solution, if we accept the assumption that Paul did teach the Thessalonians about the resurrection of believers, we must not go too far and attempt to draw conclusions from this passage about the state of the dead between their death and the parousia, nor about the temporal relationship of the resurrection to the parousia (e.g. that the resurrection follows after a millenial reign of Christ on earth; cf. G. Vos, *The Pauline Eschatology*, Grand Rapids, Mich., 1953, pp. 246ff; A. Schweitzer, *The Mysticism of Paul the Apostle*, London, 1931, pp. 90ff); equally there is nothing which describes the nature of the resurrection body (cf. 1 Cor. 15.35ff) or even says that at the parousia those who are alive will be transformed (cf. 1 Cor. 15.51-7). Least of all is there any discussion of what happens to non-Christians who die nor of their position at the parousia: Paul deals only with believers.

A second assumption is that Paul had taught the Thessalonians something about the condition of the living at the parousia for they do not inquire about it but only about the Christian dead. What would his teaching have been? He does not introduce his 'with the Lord' (vv. 14, 17) as something new (see on vv. 15–17 where we argue that v. 17c is not part of the logion he quotes); so he must have said that they would be 'with the Lord'. Some Jewish apocalyptic expectation looked for a kingdom on earth before the resurrection; if Paul had this in mind it would have been easy for him to have phrased v. 17c in some such way as 'we shall be with the Lord in his kingdom' instead of using 'for ever' ('for ever' clashes with any idea of a millenial or temporally limited kingdom).

A third assumption of the passage is the nearness of the parousia. That Paul preached this is evident throughout the whole letter (1.10; 3.13; 5.1–11, 23) and it was not only to the Thessalonians that he did so (Rom. 13.11; 1 Cor. 7.26, 29; 10.11; 15.51f; 16.22; Phil. 4.5); without such a presupposition the question of the Thessalonians would have been merely theoretical. That they expect the parousia so soon is also obvious from the way in which their question is phrased; they are not worried about what will happen to themselves if they die, as they surely would be if the parousia were far off, but about what will happen to their friends who have died; those who have asked the question expect to be alive. Surely Paul would have encountered this question earlier? Believers must have died in other places after Paul had taught about the nearness of the End. That we do not find this mentioned in other letters is irrelevant; experience ought to have prepared him for the question and led him to instruct the Thessalonians for it in advance. He does not say here, as he often does in his letters, that his readers already know the answer and that he is only reminding them of it, but he treats it as something new to them. But we need to note also that his stay in Thessalonica was brief, none of the Thessalonians may have died during this period, and he may have forgotten to prepare them for the shock which would come when this did happen. It is also possible that this was the kind of question that none of his other churches ever realized existed since they saw its solution as so obvious on the basis of the resurrection that they never needed to ask and Paul would have expected the Thessalonians to reach the solution by themselves. Paul's eschatological orientation was essentially Jewish and very foreign to Gentiles; points which would be obvious to him may not have seemed so to them. Whatever the reason for the failure of Paul to prepare the Thessalonians for the death of their friends there is no hesitancy about his answer now that he squares up to it.

A fourth assumption of the passage is the physical way in which the parousia is envisaged. If the parousia is spiritualized and no longer regarded as a real historical event the problem disappears. The Thessalonians do not appear to have been in any danger of spiritualizing the parousia. But allied to this is the possibility that from their background they may have regarded life after death as the survival of an immortal soul and not, as Paul taught, the resurrection of a transformed body (1 Cor. 15.35ff; cf. M. E. Dahl, *The Resurrection of the Body* (S.B.T. 36), London, 1962). A disembodied soul would have no place in a physical event. Yet Paul does not argue here for the resurrection body over against the immortality of the soul.

The problem already existed in Jewish apocalyptic where a great period of suffering, the Messianic woes or birthpangs (see on 3.3f), was expected before the Day of the Lord would be established. This would be a hard time for those who were alive and it would perhaps be better to have lived earlier (4 Ezra 13.16–24; 2 Baruch 48.41; 10.6, 7; 11.6, 7) and escaped this period. But since the Day of the Lord will itself be joy for the faithful it can also be regarded as a blessing to be alive then (without anything being said about the condition of the dead): Ps. Sol. 18.7; 17.44. Originally the eschatological hope of Israel was national: God's victory for the people of God. With the acceptance of individual survival in the resurrection of the dead questions would begin to arise about the place of the individual in that Day. Christianity with its greater acceptance of individual resurrection accentuated the problem and in our letter we see it surface.

13   Paul uses this introductory phrase, **We do not wish you to be ignorant, brothers,** either to emphasize what he is saying (Rom. 1.13; 2 Cor. 1.8; cf. 1 Cor. 11.3; Col. 2.1) or when introducing a new topic (Rom. 11.25; 1 Cor. 10.1; 12.1); since **brothers** is always a part of the phrase it can have no special significance here. We may note a certain contrast with v. 9 where Paul tactfully introduces his discussion of brotherly love with a reference to its existence among the Thessalonians; here obviously he is instructing them for the first time.

His new topic (for **on the subject of,** see on 4.9) concerns **those who are sleeping,** i.e. the dead. 'Sleep' is a widespread metaphor for death; it was well known in the ancient world both to pagans and Jews (e.g. Isa. 43.17 LXX; 1 Kings 2.10; 11.43; in 1 Kings 22.40 it is even used of an evil king like Ahab; cf. A. Oepke, *T.D.N.T.* III, pp. 431ff; H. A. A. Kennedy, *St. Paul's Conception of the Last Things,* London, 1904, pp. 267f; R. E. Bailey, 'Is "Sleep" the proper biblical term for the Intermediate State?' *Z.N.W.* 55 (1964) 161–7). Since it is used even where there is no belief of any kind in an after-life it does not arise from the idea of a body left behind when the soul goes off to continued life elsewhere or from the idea that the "sleeping" person will afterwards wake up to a new life, and certainly Paul does not deduce these ideas from the metaphor; we should not therefore think here of the awakening at the parousia of those who sleep as implicit in the term (such ideas can be drawn however from passages like Dan. 12.2; 1 En. 100.5; 2 Baruch 21.24; 4 Ezra 7.32 and may underlie Mk. 5.39 and par.; Jn. 11.11). Although Paul does not explicitly say it the whole context shows that he has in mind dead Christians for the Thessalonians are worried over the fate of dead members of their community. Paul uses the image of 'sleep' regularly (1 Cor. 7.39; 11.30; 15.6, 18, 20, 51; 1 Th. 5.10) but only in 1 Cor. 11.30 and here is the verb in the present tense; his main emphasis does not then lie on the present state of the believer, i.e. it is not intended to describe an intermediate state though it is adaptable to that concept; the intermediate state is better stated with the phrases 'in Christ', 'with Christ' (so Bailey, *op. cit.*). The idea of a soul away from the body would of course be foreign to Pauline thought.

As distinct from the pagan world around them, though Paul may also have the Jews in mind, Christians **have hope** (cf. 1 Pet. 1.3f, 21). This can be expressed in different ways: they will be raised as Christ has already been raised (1 Cor. 15.20ff; 15.51ff); after death they will live with Christ (Phil. 1.21–3). It is wrong to say that **the rest of men** had no hope whatsoever. Many philosophers had taught that the soul was immortal, though other philosophers disagreed; but philosophic teaching had hardly penetrated to the common people. The mystery religions did say something about an after-life. But those who accepted these ideas were at best only a part of the ancient world, and nowhere among the Greeks was the resurrection of the body accepted; life after death was proclaimed with much less certainty than among the early Christians; much of ancient literature and many grave inscriptions testify that death was regularly accepted as the complete end (cf. W. K. C. Guthrie, *The Greeks and their Gods*, London, 1950, pp. 174ff, 179ff, 260ff, 290ff, 368ff; E. Rohde, *Psyche*, London, 1925, *passim*). Paul has overdrawn the picture of the pagan world as he does in Rom. 1.18–32. Yet what hope there was of an after-life was not similar to Paul's idea of an enlarged life 'with Christ' (vv. 14, 17; cf. Phil. 1.21–3), for this rather than continued existence is the nature of the Christian **hope**.

Because they have **hope** the Thessalonian Christians should not **sorrow** as unbelievers do. The contrast does not lie in the degree or nature of sorrow, i.e. as if Christians could sorrow but not as much as unbelievers, but lies between Christian hope and pagan sorrow. Christians may sorrow when they lose someone they love (Rom. 12.15; 1 Cor. 12.26), but this is not the issue here; rather here they do not sorrow in so far as the parousia is concerned, for those whom they have loved will not be excluded from its joy. And their sorrow is not for themselves, brought on through fear that they may die, but for their dead friends, since 4.13 refers to the dead and not to the dying, let alone those about to die.

Whereas the pagan was characterized in 4.5 as **not knowing God** he is characterized here as not having **hope**. The two are not unrelated: in so far as the pagan has gods they are unable to give him the hope that is given to the Christian by his God through the resurrection of Jesus.

14   Why a Christian should not worry about the fate of the Christian dead at the parousia, already hinted at in the reference to 'hope' (v. 13), is now made more explicit: all depends on the death and resurrection of Jesus. It might seem easier if the sentence ran, 'Since Jesus died and rose, God will therefore bring . . .', for the reference to belief appears to suggest that the appearance of the dead at the parousia rests on the conviction of Christians about Jesus' death and resurrection, and if this conviction were not firm it might be concluded that the chance of their appearance at the parousia would be imperilled. This would be a wholly wrong conclusion. Paul depends on a primitive creed here. There are two possible verbs to use of the resurrection and the one appearing here (ἀνίστημι) is never used elsewhere by Paul except in citations (Rom. 15.12; 1 Cor. 10.7 are from the O.T.; Eph. 5.14, if Pauline,

is from an early hymn) and in 1 Th. 4.16 where it is either influenced by our present verse or much more probably is part of the
'word of the Lord' which Paul quotes. But other N.T. writers
employ the verb regularly of the resurrection (e.g. Mk. 9.9f;
Lk. 24.46; Acts 2.24, 32; Jn. 20.9). Paul uses the verb ἐγείρειν
almost 40 times and normally in the passive with the sense 'Christ
was raised by God'. In our present text we also find the simple
name Jesus which Paul uses comparatively rarely (e.g. 2 Cor. 4.14;
Rom. 8.11; 1 Th. 1.10, of which the last, as we have seen, formed
part of a creed). Thus the words **Jesus died and rose** are credal
and reflect formulation in a period when Jesus was more customary
than Christ, Lord, Son of God for identification purposes, i.e. the
primitive Palestinian community before Christology began to
develop (the second Jesus in the verse probably appears under the
influence of the first). Rom. 10.9 is similar in structure to our verse,
viz., 'believe that', followed by a credal affirmation 'God raised him
from the dead'. In Rom. 10.9 there is added 'in your heart' because
the speaker there is making an affirmation on which his own salvation rests; 1 Th. 4.14 lacks this reference because it is not an
existential statement. Its first plural is not that of personal conviction but of the testimony of the church to its essential belief.
(There is nothing hypothetical about **if**; it is a fact that the church
believes that Jesus died and rose.) As we said the sentence might
have been put 'Jesus died and rose; God will therefore bring . . .',
but the word 'believe' draws in the Thessalonians so that they see
it applies to their situation. The first plural also includes the
Thessalonian dead; if they had not believed that Jesus died and
rose they would not appear at the parousia. **believe . . . that**
might be wrongly construed as implying that belief in historical
facts (death and resurrection of Jesus) or in a theological proposition (that these facts are meaningful for salvation) ensures appearance with Christ at the parousia. Paul writes much more frequently
of 'belief' using a personal object, God or Christ, and the term then
takes on the tone of personal trust. But such personal trust cannot
be dissociated from the person in whom the trust is placed and so
occasionally, as here, it is stated in terms of the activity of that
person; he is shown to be a person who can be trusted. Faith
must always have an object and the object must be able to be
expressed with historical and intellectual content otherwise it
becomes self-faith and eventually disappears. Hence the credal

statements of the N.T. always possess this historical and intellectual content.

There is a second point at which the logical development of v. 14 seems broken: 'raise with him' would appear the proper sequel to **Jesus . . . rose** rather than **bring with him**. The former idea is however an unexpressed inner connection for Paul holds that believers die and rise with Christ. He elaborates this in Rom. 6.3ff where, using a number of words compounded with the preposition **with** (σύν as here), he argues that in baptism the believer died with Christ and begins to live with him. This concept is expressed widely in Paul's writings and in different ways (e.g. Rom. 7.4; 2 Cor. 4.10f; 5.14–17; Gal. 2.19f; Col. 2.12–3.5; cf. E. Best, *One Body in Christ*, pp. 46ff; R. C. Tannahill, *op. cit.*, pp. 132–4, who argues that Paul's 'for if . . . so also . . .' implies that Paul intended to speak of dying and rising but changed to the phrase of v. 14b because of its greater appropriateness to the context). Because of the inner connection of thought Paul uses the credal statement of v. 14a which immediately suggests the death and resurrection of the believer; if he is alive through the resurrection of Christ then he will be at the parousia with the risen Christ. Having used the creed which spoke of the death of Jesus Paul now makes **God** the subject of the main clause—thus returning to his normal mode of expression ('God raises Jesus' and not 'Jesus rises')—and implies that even in v. 14a God is the real subject. It is primitive Christian testimony that the parousia is God's act and its time lies in God's hands (Mk 13.32).

There has been considerable discussion whether **through Jesus** should be connected to **bring** or **have fallen asleep**. Two such similar predicates as **with him** and **through Jesus** are clumsy with one verb and their separation creates a parallelism in the verse:

'Jesus died—those who have fallen asleep through Jesus and rose—he will bring with him.'

But there is considerable difficulty in finding a meaning for **through Jesus** when attached to **have fallen asleep**. If linked to **bring** (cf. Masson) its meaning is clear and follows normal Pauline usage: Jesus is the means by which God achieves man's salvation. If we associate it with the other verb there are a number of possible explanations. (1) It may refer to martyrs (cf. Stephen, Acts 7.60;

see Nepper-Christensen, *op. cit.*), but there is no evidence that our passage refers to martyrs and not to the dead in general, though there may have been some martyrs in Thessalonica (cf. 2.14f) since there were in most Christian communities. (2) It may be taken as equivalent to 'in Christ' (cf. 1 Cor. 15.18) and imply they were Christian, but it seems rather late in the passage to identify the dead as the Christian dead; if this was at all necessary we would have expected it at the first use of **sleep** in v. 13. (3) The phrase 'through Christ' might be taken as equivalent to 'in Christ', Paul's favourite expression to denote the relationship of believers to Christ, implying that they were those who fell asleep while in a relationship to him, and that having done so the relationship continues to exist (cf. von Dobschütz, Moule, p. 57). (4) It might be taken as equivalent to 'with Christ' (cf. Moulton–Turner, p. 267) with practically the same meaning, viz., they have fallen asleep with Jesus who himself fell asleep and they are still with him, so they can appear with him. (5) The preposition might be given a causal sense (Rigaux); because of Jesus their death is one which is full of hope and not just a mere death. None of these meanings is really satisfactory and in the end it is perhaps better to take **through Jesus** with **will bring.** This association fits Paul's general usage of 'with Christ'; it relates to the creation of salvation by God through Christ and to the activity of the exalted Lord; here the reference would be to the exalted Lord's activity in the parousia. The ultimate meaning of v. 14 is not really greatly affected whichever verb we link the phrase with. But it is all-important that the Christian dead will be brought back to appear **with** Jesus at the time of his parousia together with the Christian living. This is why the Thessalonians need not sorrow; this is why Paul can comfort them (v. 18). Paul expands this and clarifies its meaning in vv. 15–18.

15–17 Paul now reassures the Thessalonians on the authority of a saying of Jesus, **a word of the Lord,** which they had not known earlier, that what he has affirmed in v. 14 is certainly true. There are three inter-related questions: (i) From where does Paul derive this logion? (ii) What is its extent? (iii) Can we reconstruct its original form?

(i) There are a number of possibilities: (*a*) Paul may have had access to a collection (probably oral) of sayings of the earthly Jesus from which he has selected this; (*b*) he may be using a saying of the exalted Jesus given to the church through one of its prophets (including himself); (c) he may have felt that he lived so close to his Lord that he could say what the Lord would have said if faced with the problem of those who had died before the parousia; (d) he may have drawn the saying from a Jewish, or early Christian, apocalyptic writing not now extant. It might seem a better procedure to determine the answers to (ii) and (iii) first in order to seek a parallel in the Gospels to the saying but modern defenders of this view (above all J. Jeremias, *Unknown Sayings of Jesus*, London, 1964, pp. 80–3) generally admit that there is no satisfactory parallel in our gospels to any portion of vv. 15–17. Although in the past Mt. 24.30 and Jn. 6.39f have been regularly suggested neither really deals with the problem at issue. The saying may then be an 'agraphon', i.e. a saying of Jesus preserved outside our gospels (for examples see Jeremias, *op. cit.*, *passim;* Acts 20.35 is clearly such). There is nothing in the phrase **a word of the Lord** which would forbid such an interpretation; it indeed suggests a definite saying, as over against (c). Is it possible to find for such a saying a suitable setting in the life of Jesus? If this can be done two views are foreclosed: (i) that Jesus expected the End almost directly after his death; (ii) that Jesus foresaw a long future for the church; rather the saying would assume he expected the end within a generation or so. Perhaps Mk. 9.1 which envisages that some will have died before the parousia while others will not (there was also speculation in Judaism about the matter, 4 Ezra 5.41f; 2 Bar. 30.2; 50.1–4) would have led Jesus to speak of the issue. But is Mk. 9.1 a genuine logion of Jesus and, if so, is it in its original form? If these questions can be answered affirmatively then our logion would be an answer to the question, 'What will be the position of those who have died before the coming of the Kingdom of God in power?' But why should this reply ever have become dissociated from Mk. 9.1, for once the point has been seen and the question asked its importance is obvious and the need for an answer continues to exist. If Mk. 9.1 is not in its original form (an original 'those standing here' might have been replaced by 'some of those standing here') or is a community formulation then it could still have produced the question about the position of the dead, though now as a question directed not to the earthly Jesus but to the community; a prophetic word (cf. (b)) might well have answered it; but Paul might not have recognized it as such and assumed it was a word of the earthly Jesus. The dissociation from Mk. 9.1 would still require explanation. Whether it was a logion of Jesus or not, did Paul think it was? Is this the way he would have introduced such a logion? There are probably only two places where Paul may be thought definitely to quote a saying of Jesus (1 Cor. 7.10, alluding to Mk 10.11f, and 1 Cor. 9.14, alluding to Mt. 10.10; Lk. 10.7) though there are also places where he shows awareness of Jesus' teaching. (This may seem remarkable to us but Paul does not appear to regard Jesus as a source of moral or doctrinal authority.) In 1 Cor. 7.10; 9.14 he refers as here to Jesus as 'the Lord' which implies that this title in v. 15 cannot of itself exclude a reference to the earthly Jesus. Otherwise the introductory formulae are very different, which is in part natural because the Corinthian passages relate to ethical instruction and ours to doctrinal comfort. Yet in the former the Lord is made the subject of the sentence (the Lord instructs, commands) rather than introduced obliquely as in v. 15, by **a word of the Lord.**

A possible variation of this view is to argue that Paul is summing up what he takes to be the teaching of the Lord on this subject without making an actual quotation but is alluding to a saying or sayings of Jesus; this is apparently what he does in Rom. 14.14 (alluding to Mk 7.15). This view is supported by the form of the saying he gives for it has been adapted to its context, see on (ii) and (iii). But Rom. 14.14 is not specifically acknowledged by Paul as an allusion let alone a citation, whereas v. 15 has a definite reference to a word of the Lord. Cerfaux, *Christ in the Theology of St. Paul*, pp. 37f argues that Paul sums up the spirit of the gospel because 'word of the Lord' is a term for the gospel (cf. 1.8; 2 Th. 3.1), but then it is *the* word of the Lord and not *a* as here.

(b) There were many prophets among the early Christians (Acts 11.27f; 13.1; 15.32; 21.9ff; 1 Cor. 12.10, 28; 14.29); the Revelation of John terms itself a prophecy (1.3; 22.7, 10, 18f). Prophets foretell the future (Acts 11.27f; 21.11) and instruct and console believers (1 Cor. 14.31), which is the function of our saying (v. 18). Consequently the association of an apocalyptic saying with a Christian prophet would not be exceptional. Such prophets may have passed on sayings of the exalted Lord to his church, and the church have made little or no distinction between these sayings and those of the earthly Jesus; confirmation of this may be seen in the ascription by Paul of sayings of Jesus to the Lord (1 Cor. 7.10; 9.14), or, rather, the distinction which we make between the two was less clear to the first Christians who saw them as identical in origin. The O.T. prophets believed that they gave the word of the Lord to God's people (Ezek. 34.1; 35.1; Hos. 1.1; Amos 5.1; Joel 1.1? etc.; the precise phrase **in a word of the Lord** is found in 3 Kgdms. 13.2, 5, 9; 21.35; 2 Chron. 30.12; Sir. 48.3; cf. Henneken, pp. 92–5). The Pauline **word of the Lord** would then be a logion of the exalted Lord spoken through a prophet. It is no objection to this view that the logion uses traditional apocalyptic imagery, for a prophet would employ the images people knew and indeed would think in such terms himself; all the 'prophecies' of Rev. are cast in traditional imagery. If then this is the origin of the saying was Paul himself the medium of its transmission or did it come through some other prophet? This is unanswerable but it is likely that had Paul been the prophet he would have alluded to this (**we say** is plural; see also notes on 2 Th. 2.15). Acts 15.32 describes Silas as a prophet; if he had been the prophet surely Paul would have mentioned this since he was known to the Thessalonians (cf. J. G. Davies, 'The Genesis of Belief in an Imminent Parousia', *J.T.S.* 14 (1963) 104–7).

(c) (This is really a variant of (b) when Paul is assumed as the prophet.) Paul lived close to his Lord and both in Acts (16.6, 9; 18.9f; 22.17ff; 23.11; 27.23) and in his own letters (2 Cor. 12.1ff; Gal. 2.2) we see him as one who had spiritual experiences through which he received guidance for his work and life; yet in none of these experiences does he receive general 'words of the Lord' with which he might instruct or console others. Nearer to this category are: Gal. 1.12, which probably refers to the Damascus Road experience and must be viewed in its context that his gospel is not human but divine; 2 Cor. 13.3, where he claims that Christ is speaking to the Corinthians through him but the reference is again to a special situation and not to a general truth as in 1 Th. 4.15; 1 Cor. 7.25–40, but here he clearly distinguishes what he says from any command of the Lord and from inspiration by the Spirit; and 1 Cor. 2.16, but this relates to much more general matters than consolation and teaching on precise points. The most interesting parallel is 1 Cor. 15.51 (cf. Masson) where Paul describes what he says about the resurrection (at the parousia?) as a 'mystery', i.e. something which has been secret but is now revealed (cf. Rom. 11.25); this passage and ours both deal with the position of the dead and the living at the End. It may well be that by his use of 'mystery' Paul implies that he has had a personal revelation, yet since in 1 Cor. 7 he so clearly distinguishes between what he himself says and the Lord's speech we cannot allow that it is an adequate parallel. Perhaps 1 Cor. 15.51f represents the same saying as ours which Paul has mulled over in his mind and now gives with additional explanations 'in the Spirit' (cf. Nepper–Christensen, *op. cit.*). For somewhat similar reasons we reject the suggestion of von Dobschütz that Paul prayed about the problem of the Thessalonians, received an answer and then set this out as **a word of the Lord.** The phrase suggests a concrete objective statement independent of Paul's present experience (cf. Henneken, pp. 84f).

(*d*) This can be only a remote possibility. There is one other place where Paul may be quoting from an apocalyptic writing, 1 Cor. 2.9. Here he uses the same introductory formula, 'as it is written', as he uses regularly with O.T. citations, suggesting that the writing from which he took the saying had for him the authority of Scripture. If he was settling the problem of the Thessalonians with an appeal to an authoritative writing ('Lord' implies authority) we would expect him to have employed one of his normal introductory phrases.

Of the views outlined above, (*b*) is by far the most probable, but whatever view is accepted Paul is affirming divine authority, not human or even apostolic authority, for what he says.

(ii) and (iii) The logion may be either v. 15b, vv. 16–17 in part or in whole, or vv. 15b–17 in part or in whole. The last of these is rarely maintained and may be safely ignored because v. 15b and vv. 16–17 to a large extent cover the same ground in the essential matter of the dead. The logion may therefore be either v. 15b which Paul expands in vv. 16f with apocalyptic images, or v. 15b is a preliminary summary of the logion which appears in vv. 16–17. Whichever is chosen the original saying will probably have been in the second or third person plural and not in the first plural as here; this must be so if it is a word of the earthly or exalted Jesus, but possibly not so if it is of origin (*c*) or (*d*). Paul has therefore adapted the saying to the extent of changing the person. Verse 15b is very much in Paul's epistolary style; if it is the logion it will probably have begun, 'Those who survive'. It ends with the metaphor

fell asleep; in a saying we might have expected the simpler 'the dead'; the metaphor has been almost certainly suggested by its use in vv. 13f. It appears where Paul is writing freely (vv. 13, 14, 15 but not vv. 16, 17); v. 15b is thus an initial statement of Paul in which he answers precisely, and no more, the question of the Thessalonians: the living have no advantage over the dead. How much of vv. 16f is then to be taken as the logion? **who survive** in v. 17, since it is also in v. 15a, must be Paul's contribution; so will be also the first person plurals of v. 17. v. 17c, **and so ...** is strictly unnecessary to the problem; it links itself to the 'with him' of v. 14; in it Paul goes far beyond an answer to the original problem; it is therefore probably better to eliminate it as Pauline. It is the final clause of v. 16 together with v. 17a **(then ... air)** which really answers the problem of the Thessalonians. Probably Paul has replaced a phrase like 'the living', 'the survivors' with his own longer phrase drawn from v. 15. Marxsen (*op. cit.*) would also omit v. 16c because it refers to the resurrection; but if Paul had inserted this he would have used his normal verb (ἐγείρειν) and not ἀνίστημι which we have here (see on 4.14). It is possible that Paul may have added **first** and **then** in order to sharpen the saying; v. 16 and v. 17 may have originally been joined by a simple 'and'. Paul probably also added **in Christ** (v. 16c), a favourite phrase, for it upsets the simple balance 'the living ... the dead'. So far we have assumed the logion was formulated by a prophet but if it came from Jesus at least one further modification is necessary: **the Lord himself** would hardly have been said by Jesus; Jeremias holds that the saying would have been in terms of the Son of Man (*op. cit.*). Assuming it came through a prophet we take the original form of the logion to have been:

> The Lord himself, accompanied by a command, the cry of an archangel and the trumpet of God, will descend from heaven, and the dead (in Christ) will rise and the living will be snatched up simultaneously with them in the clouds to a meeting with the Lord in the air.

15 Does Paul believe that he himself will **survive** to the parousia, which the first person plural with the temporal limitation certainly suggests? (εἰς τὴν παρουσίαν goes with περιλειπόμενοι which requires it and to which it supplies a temporal limit rather than with φθάσωμεν; construing it with the latter would certainly

remove the imminence of the parousia—but this imminence is clear anyway—and would rob the apposition of ζῶντες and περιλειπόμενοι of much of its meaning.) Judaism already had attached some importance to being in the generation of the End (Dan. 12.12f; 4 Ezra 13.24; Ps.Sol. 17.50). Many attempts have been made to evade what appears to be the plain meaning of the phrase. We have to reject outright any attempt to allegorize the words (cf. Origen), or to weaken their meaning (cf. Calvin) by arguing that Paul only includes himself so as to keep the Thessalonians alert (cf. A. L. Moore, *The Parousia in the New Testament*, Suppl. to N.T. XIII, Leiden, 1966, pp. 108–10). Chrysostom argued that Paul uses the first person of the faithful without necessarily intending to include himself, but it is very difficult to isolate any parallel instance of such a usage in Paul; why should Paul prefer to identify himself with the survivors and not with the dead? The participles cannot be taken as future, 'we who will chance to be living, who will chance to survive', nor as conditional, 'if we are alive, if we survive', for neither meaning is suitable in v. 17 where the phrases recur. It is not likely that Paul without agreeing with it takes up an idea of the Thessalonians that the parousia is near and that they will be alive when it comes, for there is ample evidence (1 Cor. 10.11; 16.22; Rom. 13.11; etc.) that he in common with all primitive Christianity believed it was near and he must have reckoned with the possibility that he would survive to it. It is also inadequate to say that Paul is only expressing a hope on the grounds that since Jesus did not know the date of the parousia (Mk. 13.32) he, Paul, could not think of the parousia as far distant (cf. G. R. Beasley-Murray, *Jesus and the Future*, London, 1954, pp. 183ff) and that in any case Paul does not state a date for the parousia. If Paul believed when he wrote 1 Thess. that he would survive to the parousia then he later changed his mind (Phil. 1.21–4; 2.17; 2 Cor. 1.8f; 5.8) and realized he might die before it. There is a parallel to our verse in 1 Cor. 15.51 where his belief in his continued existence until the parousia is expressed just as clearly; yet in the very same epistle he envisages his resurrection (6.14; cf. Denney), and this does not refer to a general or second resurrection dissociated from the parousia. He may therefore always have had both possibilities before him and this would appear to be so at 1 Th. 5.10; he did not know the date of the parousia but expected it soon and therefore had to reckon both with what would happen if he died prior to it and if he lived to it. The fact that in the later epistles he does not refer to survival to the parousia may be either a matter of chance (because he had no occasion to refer to this) or may have come from a realization that his death might be nearer, or the parousia a little further off, than he at first thought.

16   The logion is introduced both to reassure the Thessalonians and to give them a description of what will happen. As a description it is brief and the exact connotation of its various constituents is imprecise to us, for though the images are common in apocalyptic thought they are used in many varying ways. What we now have will have stood earlier within a wider cultural and eschatological tradition, perhaps within that of a particular Christian community, and our inability to recover this tradition in more than vague outline leads to the imprecision of its imagery for us. Imagery is necessary; given the in-breaking of the divine into the human sphere we cannot do other than express it in mythological terms, but the N.T. mythology may not be our mythology (cf. pp. 359ff). The central idea is contained in **the Lord himself . . . will descend.** The early Christians believed that Jesus was exalted at God's right hand in heaven (Rom. 8.34; Acts 2.33; Eph. 1.20; Col. 3.1; 1 Pet. 3.22; etc.). The story of Acts 1.9–11 (again necessarily in mythological form, though the first century would have realized this as little as we realize the myths in which we think) tells how he went there from earth. Thus the main myth in 4.16f is of a journey of ascent and descent whose meaning is reasonably clear, but it is accompanied by lesser mythological images and the uncertainty lies in these; but whatever they mean they serve to emphasize the grandeur and finality of the parousia.

The Lord **himself** (emphatic, perhaps as over against Jewish pictures of the End in many of which the Messiah played no part) comes and with him there is a **command, the cry of an archangel,** and the sounding of a **trumpet.** Who speaks the **command** and to whom is it addressed? Is it the command of God to Jesus to descend and begin the parousia? More probably ($\dot{\epsilon}\nu$ of attendant circumstances, cf. Moule, p. 78) it is a command addressed to **the dead in Christ** and spoken either by God or Jesus. As we saw in v. 14 God is the real author of the parousia and it is therefore difficult to distinguish the parts played by him and by the Lord at this point. This uncertainty is increased because the logion has been taken from a wider context in which it would have been automatically clear who issued the command. The command is probably to be regarded as issued through **the cry of** the **archangel** and the call of the **trumpet**. In inter-testamental Judaism, with the exception of the Sadducees, angels had come to occupy a most important place and gradually a hierarchy had developed among them, whose beginnings may be seen in Daniel (e.g. 12.1). **Archangel** was a term for those of the uppermost rank (Jude 9, the only Biblical occurrence; 4 Ezra 4.36) of whom there were a number, but it is idle to speculate whether Paul has a particular archangel in mind. (On angels see E. Langton, *The Angel Teaching of the New Testament*, London, n.d.; Russell, *op. cit.*, pp. 240ff.) Angels are regularly associated with the End (e.g. Mk. 8.38; 13.27; Mt. 24.31, where the trumpet is also mentioned; 2 Th. 1.7). The **trumpet** was used by the Jews in their festivals and was also associated with theophanies (Exod. 19.13, 16, 19; 20.18) and with the End (Zeph. 1.14–16; Isa. 27.13; Mt. 24.31); in 1 Cor. 15.52 it is again linked as here with the resurrection of the dead and the End (cf. G. Friedrich, *T.W.N.T.*, VII, pp. 71–88). The addition **of God** does not mean that God blows the trumpet but defines the sphere to which it belongs.

The summons is addressed to **the dead in Christ** for in this passage Paul is concerned only with the Christian dead and not with what happens to the wicked. **in Christ** does not refer to their existence when dead; if it did the phrase would more properly be οἱ νεκροὶ οἱ ἐν Χριστῷ; it implies instead that they were Christians in life and died as Christians. There is thus no information here about an 'intermediate' state for the dead (*contra* Hoffmann, *op. cit.*, pp. 234–8). As Christian dead they will **rise** when they hear the summons. Nothing is said of the resurrection body nor of the transformation that is to take place in those who are alive at the parousia as in 1 Cor. 15 and Phil. 3.21, but it would be wrong to conclude that Paul at this stage had not thought out his position in regard to the resurrection body; he may not have done so or it may be that the logion simply contained no reference to it.

then does not have a strong temporal sense but serves to dis- 17 tinguish another act in the drama of the parousia; the first was the descent of the Lord, the second the resurrection of the Christian dead, now in the third the risen and those **who survive** (Paul repeats the full phrase of v. 15 without the temporal limitation which is now unnecessary since the parousia is in being) are **snatched**

up to meet the Lord. There is a union of three parties: the Lord, the dead, the survivors. The risen do not go directly to meet the Lord; instead, once risen, they are again on earth and then **simultaneously with** (ἅμα σύν is not a compound preposition: ἅμα is an adverb with the meaning 'simultaneously'; cf. Bl.–Deb. § 194.3; Moule, p. 81f) the survivors are raptured. It is difficult to say what light this has to throw on the condition of the dead prior to their resurrection. There would certainly appear to be some distinction between this and their togetherness with the Lord after the parousia otherwise Paul would have said, 'They are now with the Lord; we who survive will join them at the parousia; we have no advantage over them'. (On the 'intermediate' state cf. H. A. A. Kennedy, *op. cit.*, pp. 70ff; 266ff; Hoffmann, *op. cit.*, 234ff; G. Vos, *op. cit.*, pp. 142ff; O. Cullmann, *Immortality of the Soul or Resurrection of the Dead?*, London, 1958; Shires, *op. cit.*, pp. 85ff.) It may even be that Paul did not conceive of them as having any real life because he had never thought about the problem.

The risen and the survivors are **snatched up:** the verb ἁρπάζειν contains the ideas both of suddenness and power; God (the logical subject, cf. v. 14) brings them violently and immediately to meet their Lord. Paul uses the word also at 2 Cor. 12.2, 4 referring to a temporary spiritual experience which he finds difficult to express in physical terms (he does not know whether his body was involved or not); in Acts 8.39 it is used for a material and irreversible event; the present usage lies somewhere between these. The risen and the survivors are taken out of the earthly sphere in some event which Paul conceives as taking place publicly, yet they are not disembodied (cf. Rev. 12.2; Wisd. 4.11); unfortunately Paul, or the logion, does not tell us anything about the form of their bodies.

The Christians are carried up **in the clouds** (ἐν νεφέλαις: the tradition behind Mk. 13.26 may be the origin of the use of the phrase here; cf. Lk. 21.27; Rev. 11.12. ἐν is not the equivalent of εἰς here as if they disappeared into the clouds). **Clouds** are regularly mentioned in apocalyptic events and also in the O.T. in relation to theophanies (e.g. Exod. 19.16–25; Ps. 97.2; cf. Mk. 9.7); they indicate the presence of God. Here they are related to men and not God and therefore are not regarded as supplying a veil for his majesty; they are the vehicle by which men are raptured. They are a vehicle for God in Ps. 104.3; Isa. 19.1; and for the Son of man in Mt. 26.64 (in dependence on the LXX of Dan. 7.13); 24.30; Mk 13.26; this probably forms the basis for the present usage (cf. also Rev. 11.12). Borne up by the clouds they come to **a meeting with the Lord.** Like the word parousia (cf. Appendix, pp. 349ff) **meeting** had a technical meaning in the Hellenistic world in relation to the visits of dignitaries to cities (the two words appear together in Josephus, *Ant.* 11. 327f); the visitor would be formally met by the citizens, or a deputation of them, who had gone out from the city for this purpose and would then be ceremonially escorted back into the city (cf. E. Peterson, 'Die Einholung des Kyrios', *Zeitschrift für syst. Theol.* 7 (1930), 682–702). Paul and his readers will have known this (it is picked up by Greek writers like Chrysostom), but it is difficult to say how operative it was in the original choice of the word by the prophet through whom the logion came. Unlike the citizens who go out to meet their visitor the Christians are **snatched up** by the God who sends the visitor. We cannot entirely dismiss this association as easily as J. Dupont, *ΣΥΝ ΧΡΙΣΤΩΙ L'Union avec le Christ suivant Saint Paul*, Bruges, 1952, pp. 64–73, who argues that the word, in compound or simple form, is used sufficiently often in the LXX to account for its present choice and points in particular to Exod. 19.10–18 where **clouds, trumpet** and the 'descent' of the Lord also appear; but in this passage the **clouds** are not a vehicle but a covering, the word for 'meet' (at 19.17) is not the simple form as in Paul but a compound, the people 'ascend' and are not **snatched up,** and in Paul there is nothing comparable to the giving of the Ten Commandments to which Exod. 19.16–25 serves as an introduction; in addition clouds and trumpets are common apocalyptic images. It is better to assume that though the word may not have been originally chosen for its Hellenistic ceremonial associations, overtones of them will have clung to it and that its use therefore assists in building up the atmosphere already created in v. 16.

The meeting with the Lord takes place **in** (εἰς can hardly have the sense of direction here but is equivalent to ἐν; these prepositions were often confused in the papyri) **the air.** The Lord comes down; the risen and the surviving are snatched up; **the air** therefore lies between heaven and earth. It is the area of the planets and the stars, the dwelling place of evil spirits and supernatural powers (Eph. 2.2). Inevitably questions are raised in our minds to which this logion provides no answer. Do the Lord and the saints remain 'in the air' or do they together ascend with him to heaven or descend with him to earth? If the Hellenistic associations of **meeting** are pushed then the saints will escort the Lord back to earth, which would accord with that strain in apocalyptic thought which envisages a reign of Christ on earth. It is unlikely that Christ and Christians remain 'in the air' because of the demonic associations of 'air', because apocalyptic imagery looks either to a new heaven or a new earth, and because 'will bring with him' (v. 14) suggests further movement. It could be that they all go up to heaven, but then why should the Lord come down half-way from heaven? The saints might as well have been snatched up the full way. Paul, as we might say, leaves the saints and the answer 'hanging in the air'.

What is certain is the continuance of the saints **with the Lord for ever**: this, probably a Pauline addition to the logion, brings out another and additional factor which is not strictly germane to the concern of the Thessalonians but accords with much that Paul emphasizes elsewhere. The saints alive on earth are not separated from the Lord but after the parousia their togetherness with him rings out with a new finality and certainty. The phrase **with him** (or **the Lord**) has appeared twice at vv. 14, 17. It was not part of the logion and Paul does not introduce it as if it was something new to his Thessalonian converts. He will previously have told them that after the coming of Christ or after their resurrection they would be with Christ. The phrase seems perfectly natural but without a belief in resurrection it could not be used in the way Paul employs it, and indeed when we examine both Greek literature and religion and the O.T. we rarely find it; and there are few parallels to it (e.g. Epictetus, *Diss.* I, 9, 16). With the rise of belief in resurrection the question would inevitably be asked, 'With whom will the risen life be spent?' Some kind of an answer first emerges in the Apocalyptic Literature (e.g. 1 En. 62.13f; 71.16) and is developed in the N.T. (e.g. Lk. 23.43; Mt. 28.20; Jn. 17.24; Rev. 3.4, 20f) implying an existence with the Messiah after resurrection or after his return. There are two Greek words for 'with', μετά and σύν, whose meaning in our period is indistinguishable; all statements in the N.T. about eschatological existence apart from those in the Pauline corpus use the first as in the texts above; Paul always uses the second, e.g. 1 Th. 4.14, 17; 5.10; Phil. 1.23; 2 Cor. 4.14; 13.4; Rom. 6.8; 8.32; Col. 3.3f, though not all of these passages are directly eschatological. Paul also uses σύν in a series of compounds which speak of dying, suffering, living, rising with Christ (Rom. 6.3–11; Gal. 2.19; Rom. 8.17; Col. 2.12–3.5). It is not accidental that Rom. 6.3–11 follows closely after Rom. 5.12–21 in which Christ was set forth as the Second Adam in whom humanity is incorporate; believers die and rise with Christ in this corporateness. Is this in any way related to the eschatological concept of being with Christ after death (or the parousia) which we have encountered in 4.14, 17? The selection by Paul of the same preposition in both cases when other Christians used the synonym is an initial argument for their relation. We have also seen that the underlying logic of v. 14 is most easily explained on such a supposition; this is probably true also of 5.10 (see notes there) and 2 Cor. 4.14; in 2 Cor. 4.10–12 Paul argues, without using compounds of σύν, the need for the daily dying of the Christian, which is the bearing of the dying of Jesus, and the manifestation of new life which is the life of Jesus, and goes on directly (v. 14) to the eschatological life with Christ which depends on the resurrection (i.e. new life) of Jesus. In Rom. 6.8; Col. 3.3f we find eschatological 'with Christ' statements in the middle of passages full of verbs compounded with σύν relating to present dying and living. It must be allowed that the clearest evidence comes from letters written after 1 Th. and that Paul may have come on the two ideas separately and eventually associated them but had not done so at the time of 1 Th. But in favour of their association as early as our letter are: (i) The evidence of 1 Th. 4.14; 5.10. (ii) The natural association of rising with Christ and of life with him after the parousia; Paul when he writes of rising with Christ here and now normally regards this as incomplete; it can only become complete at the resurrection or the parousia. (iii) Paul in 1 Th. is already using his formula 'in Christ' which goes back to the same basic conception of Christ as a representative or inclusive person as do statements about dying and rising with Christ. (iv) Paul makes no explicit reference in 1 Th. to the idea of dying and rising with Christ probably only because he has no need to do so.

With this in mind we have to ask what is the nature of eschatological life with Christ? The link between Christ and the believer began with conversion/baptism and now reaches fulfilment. It cannot, because of the idea of solidarity in Christ as corporate person, be reduced to the fellowship of two people with one another. This eschatological life with Christ is never set on the same plane by Paul as the eschatological life of Christians with one another (**with them,** v. 17, is an accidental formation and does not refer to the nature of life together). On earth it means that Christians enter into the experience of Christ's dying and living anew; we ought therefore to expect that they would continue to partake of this experience; resurrection will now be perfect. But Christ at the End is one who reigns, not just one who exists. Christians will therefore reign with him. This in fact appears in what is apparently a piece of early tradition, probably a verse from a hymn (note that it is described as a 'saying', i.e. a quotation) preserved in 2 Tim. 2.11-13. There is other evidence for this idea that Christians will reign with Christ and partake of his eternal glory (Rev. 5.10; 22.5; Rom. 5.17; 1 Cor. 4.8; cf. Mt. 13.43; Rom. 8.17f). The unique place of Christ as the creator-redeemer of the group which reigns with him still continues beyond the parousia; they reign only because he reigns. On the phrase 'with Christ' see Best, *One Body in Christ*, pp. 44-64; Dupont, *op. cit.*; R. Schnackenburg, *Baptism in the Thought of St. Paul*, Oxford, 1964, pp. 170-77.

18   With this certainty for themselves and their dead ringing in their ears the Thessalonians can go on to **encourage** (παρακαλεῖν, see on 4.1; it is no longer used in the special sense of that verse) each other. There was a charisma of exhortation or encouragement (1 Cor. 14.3; Rom. 12.8) not restricted to apostles but open to every Christian (**one another**). This 'encouraging' may have been offered in meetings of the community or as members encountered one another in other ways. It is a preaching of the word and through it the sorrow, referred to in v. 13, is replaced by true consolation.

(*e*) DATES AND TIMES? 5.1-11

Now on the subject of dates and times, brothers, you have no need to be written to; (2) for you yourselves know accurately that the Day of the Lord comes as a thief in the night. (3) At a time when men say, 'Peace and security', then sudden disaster overtakes them, just as the pain of childbirth a pregnant woman, and they will not escape. (4) But you, brothers, are not in darkness, that the Day like a thief should surprise you, (5) for you all are sons of light and sons of the day; we do not belong to the night or to the darkness. (6) Well then, let us not sleep like the rest of men,

but let us be alert and clear-headed; (7) for those who sleep do so at night, and those who get drunk do so at night. (8) But since we belong to the day let us be vigilant and put on the breastplate which is faith and love and the helmet which is the hope of salvation, (9) because God has not destined us for anger but to obtain salvation through our Lord Jesus Christ (10) who died for us in order that whether we are awake or asleep we may begin simultaneously to live with him. (11) Therefore encourage one another and let each one of you build up his fellow-Christian just as you are doing.

Although Paul had taught quite a lot about the Parousia during his visit the Thessalonians are still worried over it, not only in respect of the position of the dead, but seemingly also about the time when it would take place. On this he has no instruction to give them further than what he has already given; he repeats it in two vivid metaphors (vv. 2, 3) which bring out its unexpectedness, and consequently its unpredictability, and yet its inevitability. He therefore warns them to be alert; because they are Christians they ought not to be surprised but on guard (vv. 4–8). Their ultimate salvation however rests not on their vigilance but on what God has done for them through Jesus Christ (vv. 9f); as he encourages them so they ought to encourage one another (v. 11).

With the same phrase **on the subject of** as in 4.9, 13 Paul introduces a fresh topic (also indicated by **brothers**) which he has learnt, probably from Timothy, was perturbing the Thessalonians. They have been re-assured about the fate of their dead, a problem created by the non-arrival of the parousia; the same delay has made them worried about when the parousia would actually come. This is an obvious question once a definite End has been accepted and much of Jewish (e.g. 2 Bar. 24.4; 4 Ezra 6.59) and then Christian apocalyptic literature was taken up with its determination; an outstanding example is Daniel's re-interpretation of the seventy weeks mentioned by Jeremiah (Jer. 25.11; Dan. 9.24ff; cf. 2 Bar. 25ff; 4 Ezra 4.51ff; Mk. 13; Rev. 4ff). The problem may have been accentuated for the Thessalonians because they were afraid that if it was long delayed they might be dead and not participate in it (4.13–18). Paul refuses to be lured into a discussion of a precise time telling them that they have no further need of instruction

from him (cf. on 4.9) on **dates and times** (χρόνος, καιρός).
Both words have the definite article suggesting that they form a
phrase well-known to Paul and his readers, a technical term in
relation to the time of the parousia; they are found again, though
without the article, in Acts 1.7 which also deals with the parousia
(cf. Acts 3.19, 21). Their combination goes back to the Greek
O.T.: Dan. 2.21 (LXX and Th.); 7.12 (LXX and Th.); Wisd.
8.8; cf. Eccles. 3.1; Neh. 10.34, 13.31 (= 2 Ezra 20.35; 23.31);
Wisd. 7.18. The two words may thus be treated as a unit and it is
unnecessary to discuss their precise differentiation. The plural
may indicate a series of related events (cf. Mk. 13) comprising the
End but it may have no special significance. (Cf. O. Cullmann,
Christ and Time, London, 1951; G. Delling, *T.D.N.T.* III, pp.
455–62; J. Marsh, *The Fulness of Time*, London, 1952; J. Barr,
Biblical Words for Time, (S.B.T. 33) London, 1962, pp. 44ff.)
Although Paul says that they **have no need to be written to,** yet
as in 4.9 where they are said to love but could love more we
may suspect that he sees there is some deficiency and he now sets
out to meet it. What had Paul taught them about the date of the
parousia? A few years later it was certainly the official teaching in
some areas of the church that nothing could be known about this
(Mk. 13.32; Acts 1.7) and what these texts say probably goes back
earlier; there are possible grounds for tracing Mk. 13.32, in some
form (though not Acts 1.7), to Jesus himself. But a belief in the
imminence of the parousia was not irreconciliable for the early
church with ignorance as to its date; Jesus also probably believed
it would come soon, though he may have said Mk. 13.32. This is
Paul's position here. What he says in vv. 2ff does nothing to identify the date but describes 'how' the Lord will return.

2   **you yourselves know** (cf. 1.5; 2.1, 2, 5; 11; 3.3, 4; 4.2)
accurately: Paul regularly uses **know** (οἶδα) of himself and others
but never elsewhere qualifies it with an adverb, and there are only
two places where he may possibly do this with an adverbial phrase,
viz., 2 Cor. 12.2, where 'in Christ' almost certainly does not go
with the verb but with the noun 'man', and 2 Cor. 5.16, where it is
held by many scholars that 'according to the flesh' goes with 'no
one' rather than with the verb. At Rom. 14.14; Phil. 1.25 Paul
joins another verb to οἶδα but otherwise it is always used *simpliciter*. Probably he has abandoned his usual practice in 1 Th. 5.2
because he has picked up, as he so often does, a phrase from his

readers (cf. Findlay). Timothy has reported that they want to **know accurately** when the parousia will be; that Paul does not use **accurately** (ἀκριβῶς) elsewhere, unless Eph. 5.15 is Pauline, supports the view that the adverb comes from his readers. Paul answers their query by saying that the parousia's time can be known as **accurately** as the arrival of a **thief,** i.e., accuracy is impossible (cf. Mk. 13.32; Acts 1.7). Not a little irony thus attaches to his use of the adverb which has the connotation 'precision in detail'; the rendering of many of the EVV 'perfectly, thoroughly' can be misleading since the nuance of 'precision' is not always present in these English words.

The only knowledge that is possible of the date of the parousia is now set out in the first of two vivid images (the other is in v. 3): the **thief** who **comes** unexpectedly **in the night**—though as Schmiedel points out if Paul expects the parousia in his own life-time this itself puts a limit on the time. There is no known use of this image in pre-Christian Jewish apocalyptic material (though the idea of a sudden and unexpected coming appears in passages like Mal. 3.1; Mk. 13.34ff; Lk. 12.35–40); it is partly present in Job 24.14; Joel 2.9; Obad. 5, but is nowhere explicitly linked to the Day of the Lord. There are variant forms in 2 Pet. 3.10; Rev. 3.3; 16.15. In the last two passages, unlike 1 Th. 5.2 and 2 Pet. 3.10, it is the exalted One and not the Day of the Lord who comes, though the difference for first century Christians would not be important. In all the N.T. references apart from ours there is no mention of **night** (some MSS have it in 2 Pet. 3.10 but it is obviously a harmonization to 1 Th. 5.2). A passage in Q (Lk. 12.39 = Mt. 24.43) expands the image into a brief parable (apparently repro-duced in Did. 16.1; cf. Gosp. Thom. 21); the emphasis here lies on watchfulness in respect of the Son of man (to the evangelists identical with Jesus) so that as in Rev. 3.3; 16.15 it is Jesus who is compared to the thief. Either the Pauline expression could have been expanded into the Q parable by an imaginative preacher or the Q parable could have been summarized in the Pauline phrase; the essential difference lies in what comes, either **the day of the Lord** or 'the Son of man'. If we hold that the Q parable is a genuine logion of Jesus we shall choose the latter; if it is the creation of an early Christian prophet either is possible, as is also the possibility, in view of our limited knowledge, that the saying and idea derive from Jewish apocalyptic. Whatever the origin, the meaning is clear:

suddenly, and unexpectedly, the Lord will return. (See E. Lövestam, *Spiritual Wakefulness in the New Testament*, Lunds Universitets Arsskrift, N.F., Avd. 1, Bd. 55, Nr. 3, Lund, 1963, pp. 95–107.)

Day and **night** at first sight seem in sharp contrast in the saying, but neither is to be understood literally. **Night** adds vividness to the imagery of the thief but does not imply that the Lord will return during a time of actual darkness. Fairly soon Christians did begin to take **night** literally and, following the Jewish expectation that the Messiah would come on Passover night, began to look for the Parousia on Easter eve. **Day** similarly is not the period of day-light; it means 'time, event'. The phrase **Day of the Lord** (ἡμέρα κυρίου: already without the articles in the LXX, perhaps due to the influence of the Hebrew construct state; cf. Moulton–Turner, p. 179f; Moule, p. 117; Bl.–Deb. § 259.1, 5; the absence of the articles in Greek suggests a fixed phrase) goes back far into Jewish history in relation to a decisive or final divine intervention; there are constant references to it in the O.T. from Amos onwards, though he was not its creator since he uses it as a current term. Essentially a time of judgement (Amos 5.18–20; Joel 1.15; Isa. 13.6, 9, etc.) this can also imply a day of deliverance for the faithful of God's people (Joel 2.32; 3.18; Obad. 15–17; Zech. 14). What was the Day of Yahweh became the Day of Christ for the first Christians (Langevin, *op. cit.*, pp. 124ff has demonstrated that the Christians picked up the O.T. term); this phrase is found in Phil. 1.6, 10, though 'Day of the Lord' or 'Day of the Lord Jesus (Christ)' is much more frequent: 1 Th. 5.2; 2 Th. 2.2; 1 Cor. 1.8; 5.5; 2 Cor. 1.14; etc.; the simpler phrase 'the Day' appears in 1 Th. 5.4; cf. 2 Th. 1.10. This Day is obviously identical for Paul with the parousia of Christ. In the Gospels the normal phrase 'the day(s) of the Son of man' is equated with the coming of the Son of man (Mk. 8.38; 13.26; 14.62; Mt. 24.37–44; Lk. 17.22–7). The imagery of light and darkness which appears in vv. 4ff is associated from early times with the Day of the Lord (Amos 5.18, 20; Joel 2.1f; Isa. 24.21–3, etc.). For **The Day of the Lord** see H. H. Rowley, *The Faith of Israel*, London, 1956, pp. 177–201; G. von Rad, *Old Testament Theology*, II, pp. 119–25; E. Jacob, *op. cit.*, pp. 317ff; Russell, *op. cit.*, pp. 92–6; 264ff. On the relationship of the unheralded nature of the coming of the Day and the signs of 2 Th. 2.1ff see notes there and p. 54.

3 Paul begins with a general statement, **At a time when men**

say, 'Peace, security', then sudden disaster overtakes them,
which sounds like a proverb (cf. 'Pride comes before a fall'). It
cannot be a direct reference to the parousia since he introduces it
with a word (ὅταν) which indicates iteration and conditionality and
puts **say** in the present tense, 'as often as men say'; for a direct
reference to the parousia an aorist subjunctive would be more
appropriate (cf. 1 Cor. 15.28, 54; Col. 3.4). Years ago J. B.
Lightfoot speculated that Paul was dependent here on a saying of
Jesus and pointed out that the 'dissimilarity which this verse
presents to the ordinary style of St. Paul is striking'. There is:
(i) impersonal usage of λέγωσιν **(say)**; (ii) the meaning of εἰρήνη
(peace) as equivalent to security, whereas in Paul it has a funda-
mentally religious sense; cf. 1.1; 5.23; (iii) elsewhere Paul does not
use ἀσφάλεια (the adjective appears at Phil. 3.1), αἰφνίδιος,
ἐφίστημι. Against this it can be argued that our verse strongly
resembles Lk. 21.34 where we have 'day' and the last two words,
and in Lk. 21.36 we have ἐκφεύγειν as here, and all these appear in
an eschatological passage, though Luke's image of 'snare' gives a
different twist to the meaning. All this pre-supposes that Lk.
21.34 (Lukan special material) is earlier than v. 3; the influence
may however lie the other way and Paul's general statement have
been later made more precisely eschatological because of the
eschatological context Luke gave it (Lk. 21.34–6 contains a considerable number of Lukanisms and may well be his composition
making use of Isa. 24.17 as well as of the Pauline tradition). None
of the words of v. 3b is apart from Lk. 21.34 elsewhere an eschatological word: ἐφίστημι is a favourite Lukanism but only here used
eschatologically; αἰφνίδιος is not found elsewhere in the N.T.
(Mk. 13.36 uses a different word); ἀσφάλεια (and its cognates) are
not elsewhere used eschatologically. Paul thus uses a general statement, drawn perhaps from experience if not already formulated as a
proverb, to which he adds two comments linking it to its apocalyptic context. What is generally true is especially true of the parousia.
say has no stated subject and is most easily taken as an impersonal
plural. Most commentators see a contrast between v. 3 and v. 2
and take the subject of **say** to be unbelievers, but there is no
particle of contrast (many MSS insert one) to suggest this. If
Paul is quoting a general statement or proverb such a contrast is
unnecessary. If he is not quoting a fixed maxim but expressing in
his own words a statement drawn from experience the wording is

probably influenced by Jer. 6.14; cf. Ezek. 13.10, 16 (Jer. 8.11 is also a parallel but is not found in the LXX). The actual theme of sudden destruction in the midst of supposed security is found in an apocalyptic saying in Q (Lk. 17.26f = Mt. 24.37–9) which relates it to the sudden onslaught of the flood on men engaged in what they would regard as their normal activities. Disaster is also what overtakes the unwary householder whom the thief robs (v. 2); this is the inner connection between v. 2 and v. 3.

Does **disaster** (ὅλεθρος) imply annihilation as one of its meanings 'destruction' might suggest? This is not elucidated here and if Paul is quoting a proverb or general observation then it is wrong to look for an exact theological meaning in the word. (See further on 2 Th. 1.9 where it reappears.)

Paul expands the proverb or statement with an image, **just as the pain of childbirth,** drawn from the O.T., though it could equally have been taken by any observer from real life. It is used in the O.T. in different ways (Isa. 13.8; 26.17; 66.7ff; Jer. 6.24; etc.), often with an eschatological connection and mostly with emphasis on the pain of labour; later it came to be used of the birth-pangs of the Messiah (see on 3.3), the Messianic woes or disasters which would fall on the world before the arrival of the Messianic age; it is used in this way in Mk. 13.8. Paul employs the term (he has the singular **pain** though the plural is almost universal in the Biblical imagery) to stress both the anguish of the **disaster** as well as its inevitability, the latter being brought out by the following clause. Once a woman is pregnant the pain and the birth are inescapable. **and** men **will not escape** (emphatic both through the use of **and** and the strong negative οὐ μή): what men will not escape is not indicated but we can take it to be the judgement of God which comes with the parousia and which for the generality of men is **disaster.** Paul in no way seeks to decrease, let alone defuse, the eschatological pressure felt by the Thessalonians. He does not suggest that it may be further off than they expect but only reiterates teaching on its unexpectedness and inevitability—and of course in later letters he still expects the End to come soon (1 Cor. 7.25–31; 15.51f; Rom. 13.11; Phil. 4.5).

4   **But** Christians are not in the position of the generality of mankind for whom the Day of the Lord will be a disaster; Christians (**you** is emphatic) are prepared; only the unprepared are surprised by the unexpected.

The imagery of **darkness** and **light** (v. 5), suggested here by the reference to night in v. 2, is widespread in religion and, though Paul probably derived it from his Jewish background, would have been quickly appreciated by his Gentile converts. For those who are evil the Day of the Lord is darkness (see on v. 2) but the faithful enter a new age of light (Isa. 30.26; 60.19f). Darkness is associated with behaviour which does not please God (Job. 22.9-11; Ps. 74.20; 82.5) and light with that which does, indeed it is by the light which comes from God that men please him (Job 29.3; Isa. 2.5; Mic. 7.8). The contrast of darkness and light in relation to both eschatology and morality became especially strong in the writings of the Qumran sect (e.g. 1QS 3.13-4.26; 1 QM *passim*) and in the Apocalyptic literature generally (e.g. T. Naph. 2.7-10; T. Benj. 5.3). Taken up by the first Christians it is found throughout the N.T. (e.g. Mk. 13.24; Rev. 8.12; 1 Pet. 2.9) being especially important in the Johannine literature (cf. H. Conzelmann, *T.W.N.T.* VII, pp. 424-6). We find it in the Pauline literature in Rom. 1.21; 2.19; 13.11-13; 1 Cor. 4.5; 2 Cor. 4.6; 6.14; Eph. 5.8-11; 4.18; 6.12; Col. 1.13 in addition to our passage. Here the **darkness** is that of the unbelief in which the whole world lies apart from Christ and from which Christians are redeemed (2 Cor. 6.14; Col. 1.13). Because Christians are not in this **darkness** they are not in the state in which the **thief** may **surprise** them as he surprises the unwary householder (v. 2). The **Day** is of course the Day of the Lord (v. 2) rather than daylight. This latter meaning would have to be accepted if the variant κλέπτας (= thieves A B cop^bo) is read for the singular κλέπτης (א D G 33 81, etc.); the metaphor would then be that of thieves in the darkness caught by the sudden arrival of dawn; this is possibly a better introduction to v. 5 where the idea of the Day disappears and 'light' becomes important; but it is a change of metaphor from v. 2. This change or that between v. 4 and v. 5 is possible in Paul's vigorous style but the plural rests on less reliable manuscript evidence and probably arose from the assimilation of the ending of κλέπτης to that of the nearby ὑμᾶς; conversely it could be argued that the singular replaced the plural because the latter implied the Thessalonians were thieves. (**that,** ἵνα, is consecutive rather than final; cf. Moulton-Turner, p. 104; Bl.-Deb. § 391.5; Moule, p. 142.)

Paul introduces the ground (**For**) of his confidence that they 5 would not be surprised, emphasizing that **all** are included. This is

209

not to be taken (cf. Frame) in the sense that Paul singles out a special group who are fainthearted and deliberately includes them in the **all**. The combination **you all** occurs too frequently in Paul to allow such a deduction (cf. Rom. 1.8; 15.33; 1 Cor. 14.5; 16.24; etc.). Paul continues using the eschatologically oriented imagery of light and darkness but now in a Semitic idiom here rendered literally into Greek as often in the LXX: **sons of the light, sons of the day**. 'Figuratively υἱός **(son)** is used with a noun in the genitive in order to express a certain quality' (Moulton–Turner p. 207; cf. Moule, p. 174f; Bl.–Deb. §162.6); the idiom turns up regularly in the N.T. (e.g. Mk. 3.17; Lk. 10.6; 16.8; 20.36; Eph. 2.2; 1 Pet. 1.14). The actual phrase **sons of the light** is found in Lk. 16.8 but there is no reason to trace an influence of this verse on Paul for the phrase is frequent in the Qumran literature (e.g. 1QS 1.9f; 3.13ff; 1 QM 1.1, 3). **sons of the day** is not found elsewhere and may be a Pauline formulation; **the day** still retains something of the eschatological flavour of 'the day of the Lord' but is passing over into the sense 'daylight', which is a better contrast to darkness and more appropriate to the exhortation which follows. The two phrases denote a status; this is something which Christians are, just as they are 'new creatures' (2 Cor. 5.17) and 'sons of God' (Gal. 3.26); the status is here expressed in obvious eschatological terms as befits the context; they belong to the new age already (as v. 6 shows) and should display the conduct of that age. The final clause **we do not . . .** , joined asyndetically, puts the same point negatively using a chiasmus. It is possible that 'sons' should be understood before the two genitives **night, darkness** and the idiom regarded as continued, but it is more probable that we should take the words independently of it since the idiom seems to exist only as a complete unit. A rigid distinction is implicit here between those who belong to the light and those who belong to the darkness. This might be regarded as an empirical judgement on the observable difference between Christians and non-Christians, which was much more apparent in the early church than now. But the phrases suggest something more than an empirical judgement: Christians and non-Christians belong in different spheres of existence or possess different natures; the former are new creations (2 Cor. 5.17; Gal. 6.15). It is because Paul has now made this clear that he can move directly to exhortation. The Christian in his new position or nature is able to respond differently (vv. 6ff) from the non-Christian to the apocalyptic situation. Vv. 4, 5 are thus an essential transition from the direct answer to the question of the Thessalonians (vv. 1–3) to the exhortation of vv. 6–11. The Thessalonians know they will participate in the parousia; what is their behaviour to be? Whatever is expected they will be able to accomplish it. The transition to the exhortation is made easy by the tactful change to the first person plural in v. 5b which continues down to v. 10 (Paul associates himself with what he says of others), and by the movement of the metaphor from **Day** to **light.** Lövestam argues that **night** and **day** are eschatological terms representing the present age and the age to come (*op. cit.*, pp. 27ff, 51ff). The day is 'not yet' and does not come until introduced by the day of the Lord. The sons of the day and of the light are those destined for that **day.** While **day** may be a fitting term for the coming age of light after the parousia the whole tenor of the passage implies that Paul is stressing something which is already in existence, even if only partially.

The introductory phrase to this verse ἄρα οὖν (= **then**) always 6 indicates in Paul a new stage in the argument (cf. Rom. 5.18; 7.3, 25; 8.12 etc.); so he now moves directly to paraenesis. This is based on what the Christians are as 'sons of light'; while this may be a designation proper to the new age Christians are not yet wholly in that age and have not yet escaped the struggle of this age. The vast majority **of men** (for same phrase see on 4.13) live regardless of the parousia and the coming judgement, like those who **sleep** and into whose homes the thief can break and then escape with impunity. καθεύδειν (= **sleep** here and in v. 10) is a different word from that used in 4.13–18 (κοιμᾶσθαι) but no significance should be attached to this since they are synonyms. The word is again metaphorical (possibly suggested by the reference to night in v. 5) but in a completely different sense from 4.13–15; 5.10; it is no longer a euphemism for death but suggests an unawareness of what is happening, an unconsciousness of the coming of great events, an insensitivity to redemption; it is the sleep of false security of the householder who imagines his house is inviolable. Against this the Christian must **be alert and clear-headed.** γρηγορεῖν, **alert,** appears regularly in eschatological contexts (Mk. 13.34, 35, 37; Lk. 12.37 (39, *v.l.*); Mt. 24.42f; 25.13; Rev. 3.2f; 1 Pet. 5.8) as well as being used more generally. It is not found in Paul apart from here, v. 10; 1 Cor. 16.13; Col. 4.2, and is one of several indications ('sons of light', the thief in the night, the pregnant woman, 'for us', v. 10) that he is drawing on traditional eschatological material in this passage. The word implies wakefulness and full awareness of what is happening as opposed to sleep. νήφειν, **be clear-headed** (cf. O. Bauernfeind, *T.D.N.T.* IV, pp. 936–9; Lövestam, *op. cit.*, pp. 54ff), also comes in eschatological contexts (1 Pet. 4.7, and probably also 1 Pet. 5.8; 2 Tim. 4.5; the two words appear together in 1 Pet. 5.8). In its basic sense 'be sober' it is contrasted with actual drunkenness but it was also used regularly as a metaphor in Biblical and non-Biblical Greek; because of this widespread usage it is unnecessary to see here or in his reference to 'drunkenness' in v. 7 any dependence by Paul on the use of the word in the Corpus Hermeticum or Philo. Drunkenness can lead either to undue excitement of spirit and consequent muzziness of thought or to unconsciousness; the commentators tend to oppose sobriety to one or other of these, to the former because of the eschatological excitement in Thessalonica, to the latter because the context implies wakefulness; perhaps **clear-headed** covers both aspects when combined with **be alert;** as a word-pair they appear again in 1 Pet. 5.8.

7   Paul drives home his teaching with two facts which anyone can observe to take place **at night:** it is unusual to be **drunk** by day (cf. Acts 2.13); it is natural to **sleep** at night. A metaphorical overtone clings to these facts of observation in Paul because he has been using **night, sleep** and 'sobriety' (= **clear-headed**) metaphorically; in particular he has also argued that Christians 'do not belong to the night' (v. 5). Granted the metaphorical overtones we should not however spiritualize the words by making sleep equivalent to spiritual insensitivity, nor should we regard sleep and drunkenness as sins to which the Thessalonians were especially prone; sleep at any rate is a necessary activity for man's continued existence. The controlling thought is **night:** the Thessalonians must beware of the activities, metaphorically interpreted, which belong to it. Lövestam, *op. cit.*, pp. 34f, 56 views sleep and drunkenness as metaphors for absorption in the affairs of the present world. (On 'drunkenness' see H. Preisker, *T.D.N.T.* IV, pp. 545–8; two verbs from the same root are used and though originally distinct are here synonymous.)

8   However **(But we)** Christians do not live in the night but **belong to the day** and so their conduct will be very different from **the**

rest of men (v. 6). Paul now continues with the second of the two verbs he has used in v. 6b and because he attaches to it the metaphor of the soldier it probably shifts its meaning slightly from being 'clear-headed' to being **vigilant**. It is certainly not used in its literal sense of sobriety over against the drunkenness of v. 7. A number of factors contributed to Paul's evolution of the military metaphor, more correctly the metaphor of military equipment, which he now uses. He could quite easily have formed it from his observation of Roman soldiers but the language bears too close a resemblance to Isa. 59.17 **(put on, breastplate, helmet)** for such a simple conclusion; the same pieces of equipment are mentioned though Paul attributes a different meaning to them. In Isa. 59.17 the breastplate is that of righteousness and the helmet that of salvation, and, more importantly, it is God who wears the armour and not men (the warrior-God conception was fairly widespread in the ancient world). The image of the Christian as a warrior is found also in 2 Tim. 2.3-5; 2 Cor. 10.3-5; 6.7; Phil. 2.25; Philm 2; Rom. 16.7; Eph. 6.11ff; and goes back to Jewish thought; it is especially present in the Qumran material where one scroll, 1 QM, describes the community's eschatological existence in terms of a war (cf. O. Bauernfeind, *T.W.N.T.* VII, pp. 701ff; Pfitzner, *op. cit.*, pp. 157ff). Isa. 59 is one of those passages to which fairly frequent reference or allusion is made in the N.T. (vv. 7f = Rom. 3.15-17; 8 = Lk. 1.79; 18 = 1 Pet. 1.17; Rev. 20.12f; 22.12; 19 = Mt. 8.11; Lk. 13.29; 20f = Rom. 1.26f) and its words would therefore be well known and might therefore be used almost unconsciously to express an idea obtained elsewhere. The image also appears in Wisd. 5.17-20 which is probably an expansion of Isa. 59.17 since more items of equipment are mentioned; it is still applied to God and not man as warrior (one later Rabbinic source, b Baba Bathra 9b does apply it to man). The bridge between Isa. 59.17 where God is warrior and Paul's usage where it is man was probably made easy by the references in 1 QM to actual weapons as used in the expected eschatological warfare. (On the metaphor and its details see A. Oepke, *T.D.N.T.* V, pp. 292-315.) In our passage Paul employs the two items of equipment, **breastplate, helmet,** of Isa. 59.17 (Eph. 6.13-17 shows further development); elsewhere he uses the metaphor more generally without specifying particular items (Rom. 13.12; 2 Cor. 6.7; 10.4). Verbal dependence on Isa. 59.17 is likely, for Paul has three interpretations **(faith,**

love, hope) to attach to two items and it would have been easier for him to have used three items of equipment. He has married the triad **faith, love, hope** (see on 1.3) to the two items by replacing the 'righteousness' of Isa. 59.17 in relation to the **breastplate** by **faith and love** (epexegetical genitives) and the 'salvation' of Isa. 59.17 in relation to the **helmet** by **the hope** (accusative in apposition) **of salvation** (he also alters the LXX σωτήριον to the much more frequent N.T. σωτηρία, and interchanges genitive and accusative). We are not told towards whom **faith** and **love** are directed but since in Paul the former is always **faith** in Christ or in God through Christ and the latter is almost always **love** towards men (see on 1.3) we must assume the same to be true here. We ought not to make any general connection between the weapons and the virtues (as if the breastplate sheltered the heart which is the seat of love) but rather **faith, love** and **hope** are necessary so that the Christian may be **vigilant.** Paul sees this vigilance maintained not only by a relationship towards God **(faith, hope)** but also by a relationship, which must be an activity and not a feeling, towards men **(love).** By setting **faith** and **love** together and therefore isolating **hope** and by placing it last Paul succeeds in stressing it: to the apocalyptic situation of the Thessalonians it is the most relevant; this emphasis is further extended in vv. 9f which develop this phrase. **Hope** is directed towards **salvation** (objective genitive). Salvation can be related in Paul either to the believer's present existence or, as almost certainly here (cf. v. 9 and 1.10), to his eschatological future which is further explained in v. 9. The Christian will be maintained **alert and clear-headed** (v. 6) through his **hope of salvation** and will not be surprised by the sudden appearance of the Day (cf. v. 2); hope (cf. 1.3) is not an ephemeral emotion but a confident expectancy for the future resting on what God has done in the past.

The Christian is said to **put on** (ἐνδύεσθαι) the breastplate and helmet; this is a perfectly natural word in relation to armour. Paul uses it metaphorically elsewhere: in 1 Cor. 15.53f the believer at his death puts on immortality and incorruptibility; in Col. 3.12 he puts on various virtues (which is similar to our verse since the breastplate and helmet represent faith, love and hope; cf. in Col. 3.10, the new man); in Gal. 3.27; Rom. 13.14 he puts on Christ. Curiously in every case Paul uses an aorist suggesting the wearing of something which has not already been worn whereas we might have expected that Christians would be already armed with faith, love and hope, or already wearing Christ; the aorist is natural in Gal. 3.27 where Christ is put on at the moment of baptism. It is especially clear and surprising at Rom. 13.12 and Col. 3.9–12 where 'put on' is in each case opposed to 'put off'. In 1 Th. 5.8 the aorist appears to be one of 'identical action' (cf. Burton, §§139ff) with the main verb **(be vigilant)** and must also be taken inceptively, i.e. 'take up the armour and continue to wear it'. The armour is purely defensive (contrast Eph. 6.17; Wisd. 5.20); for what purpose does Paul envisage it being used? He does not make this clear. In so far as the Christian life was compared in the early church to a warfare waged with the personal forces of evil against the background of the great cosmic warfare of God and Satan this might be the idea here, as it is in Eph. 6.17; but then we would expect an offensive weapon to be suggested and a hint that foes exist. In Rom. 13.12f we find the same sequence of thought, viz. day, night, armour, and the struggle is against various vices; this may be so here. More probable is the suggestion that the 'alertness' of vv. 6, 8a implies the sentry on guard who, because he believes, loves and hopes, will not be surprised by the arrival of the Day like a thief; if so Paul is not really thinking of the warfare of the Christian (cf. 1 Pet. 1.13). E. Fuchs, 'Die Zukunft des Glaubens nach 1 Thess 5, 1–11', *Glaube und Erfahrung* (Gesammelte Aufsätze III), Tübingen, 1965, pp. 333–63, argues (p. 361) that the armour is not for protection against an exterior foe but against the 'flesh' (in the Pauline sense); this is allowable since the temptations which hinder vigilance come ultimately from the flesh; in the Garden of Gethsemane the disciples are exhorted to vigilance because the flesh is weak (Mk. 14.38). In Rom. 7.23f Paul does see a struggle going on within man and expresses it with a military image.

As at 4.1–12 Selwyn (*op. cit.*, pp. 375–81) finds in 5.4–8 dependence on a common catechetical tradition, itself probably remotely dependent on sayings of Jesus; the tradition is also clearly seen in 1 Peter and is related to baptism. He points in particular to the contrast of darkness and light, the idiom 'sons of' and the emphasis on vigilance, and he links these to baptism. Certainly all these three elements are common in the N.T. but the first two were also in Judaism (Selwyn wrote before the discoveries at Qumran showed how common they were); this both makes the isolation of an exact Christian catechetical tradition very difficult and also renders it highly probable that these were elements in the tradition of pre-Pauline Palestinian Christianity. A discussion of their remote dependence on sayings of Jesus lies outside our scope. Their relation to baptism is very doubtful. The clearest evidence Selwyn produces for this comes from later N.T. books (Heb. 6.4; Eph. 5.8); since such a connection is unknown in Judaism it is likely that it took place at a later stage of the development of the Christian tradition than the Palestinian period. Though the metaphor 'put on' is related to baptism in Gal. 3.27, and probably in Eph. 4.24, it is derived in 1 Th. 5 from Isa. 59.17, and is a natural word in relation to armour, and therefore need have no connection with baptism here. Thus 5.4-8 (and its contemporary parallels) does not reflect a baptismal code. The reference to the putting on of armour (v. 8) might also suggest a common tradition but this cannot be proved since it appears only in Paul and may be due to Paul's own fertile mind; there are obviously very close connections with Rom. 13.11-14.

9 Verses of tell us why the hope of the salvation of the Thessalonians is steadfast: it has been achieved by God through Christ. These verses thus supply a firm base for Paul's exhortation.

Salvation is not some exterior and unrelated blessing to which they may possibly attain; they have been **destined for** it by God (for the use of the middle of τίθημι here and for the construction, cf. Moulton–Turner, pp. 55f; Bl.–Deb. §316.1). Election (cf. 1.4; 2.12; 4.7; 2 Th. 2.13) is a conception allied to salvation. As in Rom. 9.22f **anger** and **salvation** are opposed, the negative preceding the positive and thereby emphasizing it; it is also emphasized because unlike the negative it is considerably expanded in v. 10. As in 1.10 **anger** is eschatological; it is not a process built into the world and working itself out in the present but an activity of God directed against those who have not accepted his salvation, who are now unaware how near salvation is and how suddenly it will come. The result of **anger** is not disclosed here; in 2 Th. 1.9 it is 'destruction' (see notes there and cf. Rom. 9.22).

to obtain salvation is literally 'for the obtaining of salvation' and is therefore more strictly parallel to **for anger** than our translation suggests. περιποίησις ('obtaining') can have either an active or passive meaning (Mal. 3.17; Hag. 2.9; Eph. 1.11; 1 Pet. 2.9). Taken actively it can mean either 'preserving' (Heb. 10.39; cf. 2

216

Chron. 14.12) or 'acquiring' (2 Th. 2.14); the latter is unusual but there is some supporting non-Biblical evidence for it (see L. & S.) and the cognate verb often has this sense (Lk. 17.33; Acts 20.28; 1 Tim. 3.13). In our present context the passive sense 'destined to be his possession' has to be rejected because of the difficulty of explaining the dependent genitive **of salvation.** Since within the context salvation is the salvation which comes at the parousia the active meaning 'preserve' is improbable for we cannot preserve what we do not have. Hence we choose the meaning 'acquire, obtain'. Watchfulness is necessary so that Christians do not miss what is offered but comes unexpectedly. The necessity of this vigilance does not imply that Paul is suggesting that man enters salvation through his own efforts. That **God has destined** men to obtain salvation shows such an idea to be erroneous, and the whole movement of thought within the passage is from the existing position of the Thessalonians as 'sons of light and sons of the day' to the exhortation to vigilance. Salvation may be lost through lack of vigilance but it will not be gained by its exercise alone, except by those who have already responded to the gospel. The negative possibility that lack of vigilance may lead to loss of salvation preserves Paul's doctrine of election inherent in **destined** from that absolute rigorism into which it has often been pushed so that those who believed themselves elect were certain that no matter what they did they would persevere to inherit salvation. Does our passage teach that some are **destined** for God's anger? Paul does not draw this apparently obvious logical deduction. There is of course no need for him to do so since he is not writing about unbelievers, but equally there is no need for him to deny it. That Paul allows for the possibility of some of the 'elect' failing to reach salvation through their lack of vigilance suggests he would not have drawn it, or if he had that he would have qualified it. As at 1.4 we must say that there is no place in Paul where he writes positively of the 'election' of men to God's anger.

Salvation is **through our Lord Jesus Christ.** This phrase does 10 not go directly with **salvation** for Paul normally attaches it to a verb or verbal form; here it goes more appropriately with **obtain** than with **destined.** Within the eschatological context we would have expected the phrase to lead forward to a reference to Christ's parousia; instead it leads us back to his death. Though salvation is future it is irrevocably bound to Jesus **who died for us** (the

217

meaning is unaffected whether we read περί or ύπέρ here since in
Hellenistic Greek these prepositions had become interchangeable,
as is demonstrated by the frequent way in which they appear as
variants for one another; cf. Moule, p. 63); the exalted Lord who
achieves salvation for us is the crucified Jesus. Attention is focused
on the crucifixion of Jesus though his resurrection may be held to
be implicit in the later phrase **begin . . . to live with him.** Verse
10 is the only occasion in our epistle where Paul places an explicit
interpretation on the death of Jesus, though it is not the only time
on which he refers to it (cf. 2.15; 4.14). The phrase he uses here
strongly recalls many others (Rom. 5.6, 8; 14.15; 2 Cor. 5.15;
1 Pet. 2.21 *v.l.*; 3.18 *v.l.*; cf. 1 Cor. 15.3) and almost certainly
belongs to an early stratum of tradition. It implies that through
Christ's death we are aided and that in respect of salvation. Its
casual introduction without any explanation of how Christ's death
does benefit men shows that it was a phrase well known to the
Thessalonians (for the meaning of the death of Christ in Paul see
Whiteley, *op. cit.*, pp. 130–51; L. Morris, *The Apostolic Preaching
of the Cross, passim*; V. Taylor, *The Atonement in New Testament
Teaching*, London, 1940, pp. 55–101; H. J. Schoeps, *Paul*, London
1961, pp. 126–65).

    whether (εἴτε with the subjunctive; cf. Burton, §253; Bl.–Deb.,
§372.3) **we are awake** (the same word as 'alert' in v. 6) **or asleep**
(a synonym of the word used in 4.13–15): this clause is unlikely to
be intended in a literal sense for if it was v. 10 would become a
statement of present existence, 'whatever our activity we enjoy
fellowship with Christ', and so would conflict both with the eschatological drive of the passage and the aorist subjective ζήσωμεν
(= **live**). If however the words are to be taken metaphorically
awake can hardly carry the sense it had in v. 6, 'whether we are
alert or not we . . . ,' for this would contradict all that Paul has
been saying about vigilance. Thus, though it is an unusual sense
for the word, we must take **awake** to mean 'alive'; **asleep** (cf.
4.13) easily takes the meaning 'dead'. (There is a resemblance to
but not a strict parallelism with Rom. 14.8.) Our interpretation is
confirmed by the reappearance of the phrase **simultaneously . . .
with** from 4.17 (see notes there). Paul is reaffirming here his
argument of 4.13–18 that Christians who are alive have no advantage over those who have died when the Lord comes and it is to this
that **simultaneously** refers. Both the living and the dead will

then **begin to live** (the aorist subjunctive of אB should be read here in preference to the much less well attested future indicative and present subjunctive variants and be given an inceptive meaning). With the parousia Christians enter into a new quality of life; as we saw at 4.17 this life is more than existence in fellowship with Christ. In our verse we move paradoxically from the death of Christ to the life of the believer; the same paradox is present in 2 Cor. 5.14f though there it relates to present and not future existence as here. The idea is often more fully expressed with an explicit reference to the resurrection of Christ (Rom. 6.3ff; 14.9; Phil. 3.10f; Col. 2.12ff; 1 Th. 4.14) which is essential to it and which must be assumed to underly our present passage; equally the new life of Christians is associated with Christ's risen life and therefore implies their resurrection; their new life is sometimes viewed as existing in the present and sometimes as one which is only completely fulfilled in the future (Rom. 6.8; 2 Cor. 4.14; 13.4; Phil. 3.11; Col. 3.4). It is difficult to see how we can move through the paradox of v. 10 without assuming these intermediate steps and without assuming some kind of unity between Christ and believers so that his actions (e.g. death, renewal of life) are reproduced in their lives. In Paul 'life' means more than 'existence with'; it implies 'resurrection life'; Paul envisages the Christian as entering into the resurrection life which depends on Christ's resurrection, and the Christian's life is transformed when this happens (1 Cor. 15; Phil. 3.21; cf. Tannhill, *op. cit.*, pp. 133f). On his original mission Paul must have connected the new life of Christians to the risen or new life of Christ, and this in effect means he must have spoken of the resurrection of Christians (contrast Marxsen, *art. cit.*; see on 4.13–18).

Paul ends this section of his letter with a sentence similar to **11** 4.18, throwing on the Thessalonians the responsibility of mutual encouragement for the growth of the community, a responsibility which he tactfully notes they have already been exercising **(just as you are doing)**. The End is near, they are prepared, but even the most alert can be overcome by sleep; they ought to **encourage one another** (see on 4.18) to watchfulness. Paul adds to this a new conception **build up** (οἰκοδομεῖσθαι) which goes beyond 4.18; it later became one of his favourite words in relation to the growth of the church. Originally used literally the word quickly took on a metaphorical meaning; this was made especially easy for Jews because of the description of the people of God as the house of Israel; Jeremiah speaks of God's building up the people as carried out through his own prophetic activity (Jer. 12.16f; 31(38).4). Verse 11 is the first time Paul uses it in the letters which we have from him and he attributes the activity of building up to all the members of the community: they build up one another. The phrase εἰς τὸν ἕνα is unusual and probably of Semitic origin; its meaning is clear; Paul uses it as an equivalent of ἀλλήλους = **one another** which he has just used and wishes to avoid using again (cf. Bl.–Deb. §247.4; Moulton–Turner, p. 187). In 1 Cor. 14.3–5, 12, 17, 26 (cf. Rom. 14.19; 15.2; Eph. 4.12, 16) 'building up' is applied to the charismata that members of the community possess and is even transferred to the virtues in which Christians are to grow (1 Cor. 8.1; 10.23). Later Paul used the word, almost certainly in imitation of Jeremiah, of his own apostolic activity (2 Cor. 10.8; 12.19; 13.10; cf. Rom. 15.20). But it is difficult to define precisely the distinction between this and the more general usage; presumably it is an instance of the general usage applied to the apostolic charisma which he believed himself to possess. The metaphor appears also in a variant form when the church itself is described as the 'building' (1 Cor. 3.9; Eph. 2.21), i.e. the result of the process of building. This coheres with the emphasis on Christians as building up their own community, not so much in the sense of adding new members to it, as of enabling each individual to grow in faith, hope and love. The phrase Paul uses in 5.11 (**let each of you build up his fellow-Christian; Christian** is not expressed in the Greek but is implied) contains the germ of all this future development: (i) the Christian does not build up himself, he builds up his fellow-Christians; the object of his activity is the church, and only as all grow together can one grow in particular; each knows the grace of God but only as he uses it for others and receives it from them, i.e. is built up by them, can real growth take place. (ii) Some of the building activities which Paul relates to the charismata of the church are already present in 5.12–22 (see especially vv. 14, 19, 20f), though not necessarily expressed in the same terms. Indeed the whole of 5.12–22 could be regarded as an expansion of our phrase. On οἰκοδομεῖσθε see O. Michel, *T.D.N.T.* V, pp. 136–48; P. Bonnard, *Jésus-Christ édifiant son Église*, Neuchâtel and Paris, 1948.

4.13–5.11 is the passage in our letter in which Paul approaches most closely the type of theological discussion we find in some of his

other letters, notably Rom., Gal., and 1 Cor. Yet there appear to
be also vast differences in the theology of this passage from that of
the other letters. The death of Jesus receives little attention, there
is no reference to the righteousness of God or justification by faith,
and the very frequent phrase 'in Christ' with its variants rarely
appears. Instead attention is directed towards the End, salvation
is related to this and not to the present, and the 'creed' which seems
to express Paul's initial preaching in 1.10 is different from that of
1 Cor. 15.3–5. The problem thus created has often been answered
with the argument from silence: if Paul does not mention any
particular doctrine in the Thessalonian epistles this does not imply
he did not teach it to them; he is answering questions arising out
of their situation and perforce must write in terms of a future and
not a present salvation. This is negative, but there is also some
evidence that what at first sight seems to be missing was actually
present in Paul's initial preaching. 1.9f may make no reference to
the death of Jesus but the casual introduction of a reference to
Jesus as 'dying for us' (5.10) in a traditional form implies that
Paul had taught the Thessalonians about the relevance and meaning
of Christ's death. It must be allowed that Paul does not mention
either the righteousness of God or justification by faith in our
letters but neither is prominent in the Corinthian letters. While it
would be incorrect to argue that they only found a place in Paul's
theology after our letters were written it would not be incorrect
to argue that they are the form which Paul's theology took when
faced with a particular problem, viz., the question of the Law and
the admission of Gentiles to the church; take away this problem
and Paul's theology necessarily takes a different form; the problem
in Thessalonica is eschatology and so the form will be different.
Moreover while salvation is oriented towards the End almost
exclusively in 1 & 2 Th. this same orientation can be found in
other epistles (e.g. Rom. 5.9; 1 Cor. 3.15; 5.5; Phil. 3.20). However
we can go much further than this and argue that Paul's thought in
1 Th. runs along the lines of at least some of the basic structural
elements of his theology. At least three such elements can be
isolated: (i) The believer has a new existence. In his letters this is
expressed in varying ways: he is a son of God (Gal. 3.26; Rom.
8.16f), newly created (2 Cor. 5.17), a man (1 Cor. 13.11), a temple
of the Holy Spirit (1 Cor. 6.19), in the Spirit (Rom. 8.9). In 1 Th.
it is expressed by saying that the Christian is 'a son of the light,

of the Day' (5.5); this is certainly a more purely eschatological term than the others, although there is a sense in which they are all eschatological, just because the context is more purely eschatological. (ii) The association of the indicative and the imperative based on it is found everywhere in Paul and is especially noticeable in Romans which both in its overall structure and in the details of its separate sections follows the pattern: the Christian is justified, let him be just. In 1 Th. 5.1–11 we find exactly this pattern: the Christian is a son of the light, let him live in the light. Somewhat similarly 5.11 resembles the conclusion of many of Paul's passages of theological argument in ending with a paraenetical statement (cf. Rom. 6.11; 12.1f; 1 Cor. 15.58; Phil. 2.12f). (iii) The close relationship of believers to Christ. We have seen that 4.14; 5.10 preserve the union of believers with Christ; the rationale of this does not need to be explored now, but whatever led Paul to use phrases like 'in Christ', 'dying with Christ', 'members of Christ' led him to write 4.14 and 5.10; and 5.11b implies the inter-relationship of Christians as much as 1 Cor. 12–14. None of this implies that Paul's theology did not develop or change, e.g. his ideas about the ultimate fate of the Jews (see on 2.16) and about his own position in relation to the coming of the parousia altered, and in being applied to different situations his thought was developed in new directions, but it suggests that the basic structural pattern remained the same.

(f) LIFE IN THE COMMUNITY 5.12-22

Now we ask you, brothers, to respect those who are working so hard among you by caring for you in the Lord and by admonishing you; (13) and esteem them very highly with your love because of what they do. Live at peace among yourselves. (14) And we request you, brothers: admonish loafers, encourage the worried, help the weak, be patient with everyone. (15) See that no one pays back evil with evil, but at all times seek eagerly the good of one another and of all men. (16) Be joyful always; (17) pray unceasingly; (18) whatever happens give thanks (to God); for this is God's will in Christ Jesus for you. (19) Do not extinguish the Spirit; (20) do not despise prophetic revelations; (21) but test all of them: hold fast what is good; (22) keep clear of whatever kind is evil.

We have here a series of largely unrelated exhortations; on the whole they deal with the internal life of the community, and the first part may be influenced by the exhortation to build up one another in v. 11. It is difficult to know how far they refer specifically to the Thessalonian community and not to every Christian community. Certainly the later part, vv. 14(15)–22, is very general and is derived probably from traditional material, and this may be so of the first portion also. There is a distinct resemblance to Rom. 12 both in the rapid succession of brief exhortations and in the overall structure where 5.12–14 deals with relationships between church members with reference to their responsibility for the whole as Rom. 12.3–8, and 5.14(15)–22 deals with Christian behaviour generally as Rom. 12.9–21.

The paraenetic section of the epistle was introduced at 4.1 with **12** two verbs ἐρωτᾶν (= **ask**) and παρακαλεῖν (= **request**); Paul has just used the latter in v. 11 (= **encourage**); he now therefore chooses the former alone to introduce this section although it is his normal custom when he only uses one to use the latter (2 Th. 2.1); the first now functions in the way the other is normally used (cf. Bjerkelund, *op. cit.*, and notes on 4.1).

The connecting particle δέ **(Now)** which introduces v. 12 can be taken either as resumptive in introducing a new section of the exhortation or as adversative in drawing some contrast to the preceding section, and especially to v. 11 (so Masson); but it is difficult to see what the contrast could be, unless it is the suggestion that while they are set a mutual task in v. 11 they are not to undervalue their leaders; but there is a return to the mutual task in v. 14f. It is also easier to regard vv. 12ff as an expansion of 'let each one of you build up his fellow-Christian' (v. 11) if indeed there is any strong connection between v. 12 and v. 11; v. 12 may in fact rather refer back to 4.1. **brothers** is also regularly used by Paul in introducing new sections (cf. 4.1, 13; 5.1). Faw, *op. cit.*, suggests that δέ here brings in a fresh subject to which the Thessalonians have alluded in their letter (see pp. 14f). He argues that Paul uses δέ as well as περὶ δέ in 1 Cor. (cf. 7.8; 11.2; 15.1) when answering points from the letter of the Corinthians. Even if this is granted Paul in any case uses δέ so regularly to introduce fresh sections that it provides no evidence here that he is answering a written question from the Thessalonians or even dealing with a matter reported orally to him by Timothy. He may just be giving some traditional catechetical instruction as he does in Rom. 12. οἶδα (normally meaning 'know') is employed here in a most unusual way and we are forced to translate it **respect** (cf. Ignatius, *Smyrn.* 9.1, and 1 Cor. 16.18 where another word for 'know' is used in the same unusual way in relation to leaders). The object of **respect** is a long phrase based on three participles. The second and third are subordinate to the first, since it alone is preceded by the definite article, and are themselves co-ordinate; this means that we are to see two of the activities of those who are **working so hard among** the Thessalonians as **caring** and **admonishing** rather than that we should envisage three groups each exercising a different function, **working, caring, admonishing.** The final two participles are not, of course, to be taken as spelling out all the activities of those who 'work so hard'. κοπιᾶν **(working so hard)** is used primarily of physical toil both in a passive ('tire') sense and an active ('to make great exertions'), and it stresses the greatness of the effort involved. Paul uses it of the manual labour by which he maintains himself (2.9; 1 Cor. 4.12; 2 Th. 3.8). But since he maintains himself only so that he may be free to do the work of the gospel we are not surprised that he uses the same word for his evangelical activity (1 Cor. 15.10; Gal. 4.11; Phil. 2.16). He also employs it as here for the similar activity of others (1 Cor. 16.16; Rom. 16.6, 12). The extent of the effort involved is also implicit. The following participles show that the 'work' cannot here be restricted to manual labour, implying that there are some who continue at their work while others idle (cf. 4.11f; 2 Th. 3.6ff). In 1 Cor. 16.16 Paul also asks the Corinthians to obey those who **work so hard** among them. In both places the word functions almost as a technical term for those with some kind of responsible position in the community but probably at this stage of ecclesiastical development it possessed no more exact sense than the modern term 'church workers'; these are normally voluntary workers lacking any carefully prescribed official position.

The second participle **caring for** (προϊσταμένους, cf. Bo Reicke, *T.D.N.T.* VI, pp. 700–3) has two possible meanings in our context: (i) 'preside, lead, direct'; (ii) 'protect, care for'. In the N.T. the root appears only in the Pauline corpus, most frequently in the Pastorals. In 1 Tim. 3.4f, 12, it is used of a father's relation to his children which is seen as similar to that of a church official to the community and it is put in parallel with ἐπιμελεῖσθαι; a father rules over his family and protects them; the context indicates that both meanings are present. In 1 Tim. 5.17, though often understood of 'ruling' presbyters the second meaning is more suitable; for it is difficult to speak of, presbyters who govern 'well' (καλῶς), the adverb is more applicable to pastoral care, and there is nothing in the context to exclude this meaning and much which suggests it. (A third sense of the word, viz., 'devote, apply oneself to', appears in Tit. 3.8, 14 used with an impersonal object, 'good works'; this sense is impossible in 1 Th. 5.12; Rom. 12.8; 1 Tim. 3.4f, 12; 5.17.) In Rom. 12.8 the προϊστάμενος appears among a list of those exercising various charismata within the church; it is second in a group of three of which the first relates to one who gives, presumably goods or money, and the third to one who shows mercy; within this sequence it is difficult to see a reference to one who 'presides' or 'rules'; it must then refer to someone who exercises some kind of care (cf. C. K. Barrett, *Romans*, London, 1957, *ad. loc.*). In 1 Th. 5.12 it forms the first explanation of the general term **working** and a word explanatory of the work is more appropriate than an immediate transition to 'authority'. **Caring for** forms a natural pair with admonishing, the first is positive, the second negative in emphasis; their order testifies again to Paul's tact. If the meaning were 'preside' this would be better as the first participle, 'respect those who preside among you by working so hard in the Lord for you and by admonishing you'. Paul does not specify in what the 'caring' consists; leadership is not necessarily excluded but it would not be the sole element; there would also be acts of charity, the organization and conduct of services, etc.

Whatever the duty this participle alone is qualified by **in the Lord** (if it went with all three it would be placed with either the first or third, though in its present position it might possibly be taken as governing the second and third). Paul attaches this phrase regularly to activities of the Christian; sometimes these are related to the Christian's own life ('rejoice', Phil. 3.1; 'be confident', Gal. 5.10; 'boast', 1 Cor. 1.31) but very often as here they tie the Christian to other Christians ('receive another Christian', Rom. 16.2; 'exhort', 1 Th. 4.1). The phrase sets the particular activity within the sphere of service which the Christian owes to his Lord though it is directed towards other Christians (Paul apparently never uses it of activities directed towards non-Christians); the phrase does not mean 'by the authority of the Lord', as if the Christian had

225

been appointed by him to a position within the Church. It is within the sphere of Christian existence that some exercise a special duty of caring for others, and perhaps also of admonishing them if the phrase also qualifies the third participle.

admonishing is the negative of **caring for**; those who are treated with kindness may also require to be warned about the consequences of their present life. In the N.T. the root νουθετεῖν is only found in the Pauline corpus and in Acts 20.31 (a Pauline speech). It differs from teaching in being addressed to the will rather than the mind (cf. J. Behm, *T.D.N.T.* IV, pp. 1019–22) with the intention of producing a change in behaviour; it is, of course, closely related to teaching (Rom. 15.14; cf. 1 Cor. 10.11) for wrong behaviour often follows from wrong understanding. Paul uses it of what he himself says to his churches (1 Cor. 4.14f, where it is related to a deep father-child relationship and cannot therefore be taken in the sense 'scold'; cf. Eph. 6.4; Col. 1.28) and of how those with responsibility within them should behave towards the community and also of how any Christian should act in relation to another since all are responsible for one another (Rom. 15.14; Col. 3.16; 1 Th. 5.14).

How far does v. 12 imply a ministry within the church? Those who give προϊσταμένους the meaning 'preside, rule' obviously see a group of 'leaders' who govern the church, and attempts have been made to identify them with some class of official known from other contexts, e.g. presbyters (so Rigaux). To choose, as we have, the meaning 'care for' does not absolve us from asking the general question, for quite clearly some Christians are isolated here from others and a responsibility given them towards the remainder; at the same time they are described with three participles indicating activities which would have enabled them to be picked out from the rest of the community. Yet the distinction cannot be made too rigid since **admonish** is used in v. 14 of the duty of every Christian, as is κόπος at 1 Cor. 15.58 and 1 Th. 1.3; the line between 'clergy' and 'people' is still fluid in Thessalonica. That they are identified by their activities rather than by a name suggests that at this time they did not have a name; a little later we find that the neighbouring community in Philippi had bishops and deacons (Phil. 1.1); elsewhere in his letters Paul appears chary of naming particular officials. Acts 14.23 is often taken to indicate that he appointed presbyters in all his churches but we cannot be sure that Luke here is not reading back into Paul's time the procedure of a later period. Moreover if Paul had had to leave Thessalonica as hurriedly as Acts relates then he may in any case not have had the opportunity to appoint presbyters. Any group soon throws up natural leaders and there is no reason to doubt that such appeared in Thessalonica during Paul's time or soon after he left, in which case he would have been told about them by Timothy. However we have no means of identifying them with any 'named' group (e.g. presbyter, bishop); they may not have had a 'name' at this period; we must not over-formalize organization. Elsewhere (1 Cor. 12-14; Rom. 12.3–8) Paul views those leaders as equipped for their tasks by charismata of the Holy Spirit. It is wholly in line with this that they are described in terms of their function and not of an office, though 'office' and 'charisma' do not indicate two different types of ministry. Why Paul should choose to refer to such leaders at this point in the letter is not clear; Timothy may have reported trouble between the leaders and some in the community. Schmithals (pp. 121f) argues that the authority of the leaders has been challenged by gnostic heretics (cf. 1 Cor. 16.15f; Phil. 2.29; Gal. 6.6) but if so we would expect Paul to emphasize their position somewhat more clearly. Frame suggests the leaders may have dealt tactlessly with those who neglected their daily occupations (4.11f; 2 Th. 3.6–13). But it may only be that Paul knows that friction will always arise between those in some responsible position and those among whom they work (cf. 1 Cor. 16.16 where a similar exhortation is addressed to leaders and is not related to any of the known divisions of the Corinthian church).

The thought of v. 12 continues: **and esteem** (as with οἶδα in 13 v. 12 this is an unusual sense of ἡγεῖσθαι, cf. M. & M. s.v.; it is to be taken as qualified only by **very highly**; if **with love** is attached closely it becomes equivalent to 'love', but this is a new thought and **with love** ought not then to be separated from it by the adverb) **very highly** (the word occurs in the N.T. only here and at 3.10; Paul is fond of compounds involving ὑπέρ). **respect** (v. 12) and **esteem** are offered from many different motives; Paul makes clear that such an attitude of Christians towards those working among them must be activated by **love** (ἐν, **with,** is either instrumental or adverbial) and not by fear or the thought of reward or recognition. Only **love** (see on 1.3; 3.12) can create a true and fruitful relationship in the whole community between those who exercise responsibility and those over whom they exercise it. In 1 Cor. 13.1–3 Paul makes it evident that responsibility is exercised in vain unless it is also exercised with love; here the idea is that it must be accepted with love. Finally Paul adds a reason for such loving esteem, **because of what they do;** this takes us back to and summarizes the participles of v. 12. Leaders are to be acknowledged not because of their official appointment (and the Thessalonian leaders had probably not been officially appointed) nor because they hold a particular office nor even because they exercise a necessary function for the ongoing life of the church, but because of the way they carry out the function which they exercise, **because of what they do.**

The final clause of the verse, **Live at peace among yourselves,** has no word connecting it to what precedes and there is therefore some difficulty in knowing its precise relevance. **yourselves** as a translation is itself in doubt but should be read ($\dot{\epsilon}\alpha\nu\tauo\hat{\iota}\varsigma$ is read by B A and the great majority of MSS; $\alpha\nu\tauo\iota\varsigma$, read by P³⁰ ℵ D and some others, can be taken with either a rough or smooth breathing: if the former it is the equivalent of the other reading; if the latter the translation would be 'live at peace with them, i.e. the leaders', but then we should expect $\mu\epsilon\tau'\alpha\dot{\upsilon}\tau\hat{\omega}\nu$ rather than $\dot{\epsilon}\nu$ $\alpha\dot{\upsilon}\tauo\hat{\iota}\varsigma$). Our clause has been understood as directed at both ordinary members and those holding responsibility as two groups which ought to be at peace with one another. There is however insufficient evidence to indicate any division between the two. In particular Frame's idea that the leaders have intolerantly rebuked the idlers reads far too much into the clause and also implies that the idlers compose the rest of the community over against the leaders; all the evidence suggests that the idlers were only a small group. The tone of the whole letter does not lead one to infer a serious rift within the community between leaders and people. The asyndetic nature of the clause suggests that it ought to be read as a simple imperative addressed to the whole church without any attempt to particularize **yourselves.** The thought which the clause expresses is found also in Rom. 12.18 (cf. 2 Cor. 13.11). A similar sentence appears in Mk. 9.50 at the end of a catena of sayings and is again difficult to relate to the whole context. It was probably part of the catechetical tradition (cf. Hermas, *Vis.* III 9, 10). After this diversion Paul

14 realizes he has something to say more directly related to the Thessalonian situation and returns to this in v. 14, beginning it again with **we request** (see on 4.1).

Whom is Paul addressing? Masson has recently revived the view found in some of the Fathers (Chrysostom, Theodore of Mopsuestia, cf. Bornemann, Findlay) that it is the leaders of the community already mentioned in v. 12; the first three imperatives of our verse then represent the duty of leaders and the fourth is also addressed to them because being unaccustomed to leadership they have tended to express and enforce their views too bluntly; had Paul addressed these words to the church as a whole he would only have weakened the position of the leaders which v. 12 was designed to strengthen; also **admonish** in v. 12 clearly refers to the duty of leaders and therefore ought to in v. 14. Against this we may argue: (i) The position of the leaders as a definite group is not as clearly defined in v. 12 as this view supposes; there will have been at this early stage of development in the Thessalonian community considerable fluidity as to who the leaders were and what their duties were. The much more clearly cut situation depicted in the Pastorals comes from a later date. (ii) Verse 16ff are certainly addressed to the church as a whole; there is nothing to suggest a change of subject between v. 16 and v. 15; v. 15, as Rom. 12.14–17, is most easily understood as spoken to the community as a whole, and probably a common tradition underlies both 1 Th. 5.12ff and Rom. 12.9ff (cf. pp. 241f); finally there does not appear to be any change of subject between v. 14 and v. 15. (iii) If v. 14 is addressed to the leaders then there is a change of subject from vv. 12f; but v. 14 is introduced by practically the same phrase as v. 12 (**ask** and **request** are synonyms for Paul; see on 4.1; we have another instance of the formula of 4.1 here), and if a change of subject were intended we should expect some greater contrast (von Dobschütz suggests that ὑμᾶς δέ ought then to begin the sentence). (iv) **brothers** as in v. 12 indicates the community at large and not a group within it. (v) In fact Paul elsewhere uses phrases like those of v. 14 to address communities as a whole rather than their leaders (e.g. **admonish** in Rom. 15.14; Col. 3.16; 2 Th. 3.15); although the same words are not used the conceptions of the second and third phrases are found in Gal. 6.1; Phil. 2.4; and in 2 Cor. 2.7; 7.13; 1 Th. 3.7 leaders are encouraged by ordinary church members. We thus conclude that in our verse Paul is laying a duty on all the members of the church. However the precise interpretation of the first three phrases is not easy; the difficulty in each lies not with the verb but with its object.

ἀτάκτους **(loafers)** can in our context mean 'disorderly, unruly' (and this is close to its etymological derivation) or 'idler, loafer'; there is ample evidence from the papyri for the latter meaning; cf. J. E. Frame, *'οἱ "Ατακτοι, 1 Thess. 5.14'*, *Essays in Modern Theology and Related Subjects* (Essays for C. A. Briggs), New York, 1911, pp. 189–206. C. Spicq, 'Les Thessaloniciens "inquiets" étaient-ils des paresseux?' *St. Th.* 10 (1956) 1–13, argues strongly for the former sense. This second meaning must apply in 2 Th. 3.6ff where we find the cognate verb and adverb. There is nothing in the immediate context of our verse to suggest which meaning Paul has in mind; that he uses the root in one sense on a later occasion does not imply that he must have so used it earlier when on *a priori* grounds there is an equally probable meaning. We have argued that 4.11 probably refers to the same conditions as 2 Th. 3.6ff., viz. an unwillingness to work induced by eschatological expectancy. Is this also in view here? We cannot be certain but there is a slight balance of probability in its favour; hence the translation **loafers.** Eschatological excitement might also produce 'disorderliness' and this would not be inappropriate to v. 12; disorderliness might also come from a refusal to keep the 'order' of the Christian ethic as set down by the 'leaders'. Whatever the meaning there can be no doubt that the **loafers** (or the 'disorderly') need to be rebuked **(admonish).**

ὀλιγοψύχους **(worried)** is not a widely used word; it ranges through the senses 'worried, discouraged, fearful' (cf. use in LXX and references in L & S, M & M); there is nothing in the immediate context to help us determine the exact shade of meaning and so we have chosen the fairly general rendering **worried.** We do not know what had caused this worry. Persecution had already affected them (2.14); they were perturbed by the delay in the parousia (4.13ff); they may have been tempted and sinned (4.3–8); a thousand and one other things might have reduced them to this condition. Paul is aware of all this and his exhortation is general enough to cover the many different causes which might have led them to worry. The **worried** are not admonished but **encouraged** (for the word see on 2.11); to rebuke them would not deal with the heart of their trouble.

ἀσθενῶν **(weak)** may refer to physical weakness (the word is often used for the sick) or moral or spiritual weakness (the latter are somewhat difficult to distinguish). In the light of the general context we must reject any reference to a physical condition, though, as 1 Cor. 11.30 shows, physical conditions may be closely related to spiritual. In other letters Paul uses the word of those who are hesitant about matters on which others, including himself, have clear minds, viz., whether Christians should eat food offered to idols (1 Cor. 8; 10), vegetarianism and the observance of holy days (Rom. 14.1–15.6); the weak, coming from paganism, feel that to have some rules about these problems would support them in their stand as Christians. Paul does not order them to abandon their position as contrary to the true nature of faith but instead counsels the remainder of the church to bear with them and not to enforce their own freedom from rules. While there is no evidence for such difficulties in Thessalonica they must have always cropped up whenever Christians began to enter into the freedom of their faith. While the present general reference would suit any Christian community some commentators have sought a more exact reference to 4.3–8, where Paul referred to sexual sin, by taking the sense of moral weakness; this is possible but since the phrase of v. 14 is so general and the sexual offenders of 4.3–8 are not described as **weak** the other explanation appears more probable. ἀντέχεσθε **(help)** elsewhere in the N.T. has in the middle voice the sense 'hold on to, devote oneself to' (cf. Mt. 6.24 = Lk. 16.13; Tit. 1.9) but it also has the sense **help**. The former could be appropriate here: the members are to hold on to the weak (so that they do not slip away). But the latter is more general, can easily be envisaged as incorporating the other, and so is the better rendering.

These first three clauses, each with a particular reference, have been taken by many commentators to refer to three groups in the community. Frame in particular has argued that they refer successively to 4.11f; 4.13–5.11; 4.3–8, and that Paul has had this exhortation in mind from the beginning. In that case we might have expected him to take the injunctions in the same order as the earlier more detailed passages, or possibly in reverse order. The precise connotation of each phrase of v. 14 is uncertain; the combined probability that each one of the three has the meaning he requires is much less than the probability that any particular one has, so that the probability of the triple reference is very low. It is moreover wholly in the style of Paul to set down a list of injunctions without having a precise group in mind each time, but rather an attitude which any Christian might have; this would be especially so if Paul is making use of catechetical material here; and true also if he is writing from his general knowledge of the kind of ways in which people behave in any new Christian community. The rest of the letter shows, as Frame has said, that there were many in the community who needed support and warning, though the phrases cannot be restricted to those Frame delimits. The triadic structure found here is frequent in Paul and we do not have to go outside 1 Th. to see this (e.g. 1.3, 5, 8; 5.12, 16–18, 23).

The final clause of the verse, which stands by itself and can be regarded as summing up the first part since no group or attitude of mind of a section of the community is isolated, employs an idea which in the O.T. is predicated primarily of God: 'patience', or more literally, 'length of temper' (μακροθυμία). The root is used in the LXX to render Hebrew phrases which mean 'to delay wrath'. 'There is a divine restraint which postpones' the operation of God's wrath 'until something takes place in man which justifies the postponement. If this new attitude does not eventuate, then wrath is fully visited' (J. Horst, *T.D.N.T.*, IV, p. 377). This relation to the wrath of God is still found in Paul (Rom. 2.4f; 9.22) but, more importantly, following hints in the O.T. (Eccles. 7.8f) man is expected as here to show the same patience in his dealings with others as God does with him. In Gal. 5.22 this patience is a fruit of the Spirit and in 1 Cor. 13.4 it is a quality of love. But to whom is it to be shown? **everyone** is indefinite; it can mean all men or all the members of the community; it does not mean the total of the three groups already referred to. Verse 15 certainly refers to all men but there it is made explicit; that in itself suggests that in v. 15 for the first time Paul is bringing in those outside the community. Verses 12–14 apart from this clause certainly apply only to conduct within the community. It is therefore simplest to see our clause also as applying to the community only and the wider reference as coming first in v. 15. It is all too easy to lose patience with the **loafers,** the **worried** and the **weak** even when admonishing or assisting them; and there are many others who will try patience. This is especially so when admonition and help are offered in love and rejected. Hence the necessity for a call for restraint from anger towards all who upset the sweet running of the community. If the reference is to 'all men' then patience will have been needed in the face of opposition of various kinds. It is difficult for a man to be patient when he feels innocent and is persecuted.

We note finally that here as elsewhere in his letters (e.g. Gal.

6.2) Paul lays the responsibility for the whole community on the community itself; each member, and not the leaders alone, must be aware of his or her responsibility for others and seek to help them. At no stage can the ordinary member lean back and say, 'This is the task of the ministry alone.' Paul knows nothing of an inert mass, the congregation, on which the ministry operates.

The theme of the last clause of v. 14 is now developed negatively 15 and positively and made to refer explicitly both to life within the community and to the relations of its members with those outside it. The *lex talionis* of the O.T. (Exod. 21.23-5; Lev. 24.19f; Deut. 19.21) was gradually ameliorated both in the O.T. itself and in Judaism (Ps. 7.4f; Prov. 17.13; 20.9c; 25.21f; Sir. 28.1-7; Gen. R. 38.3 (23a); Exod. R. 26.2 (87b); 1 QS 10.17f; Jos. and Asen. 23.9; 28.4, 14; 29.3; cf. Billerbeck, I, pp. 368ff). The Golden Rule (Mt. 7.12), enunciated in its negative form within Judaism at least as early as Hillel (c. 20 B.C.; Shab. 31a; cf. Tob. 4.15), is a complete denial of its validity, and we find the same denial in the teaching of Jesus (Mt. 5.43-8; 7.12; Lk. 6.27). Paul does not, as we might expect, quote Jesus for his rejection of the *lex talionis*; as a Jew before his conversion he had already accepted the teaching of this rejection and Jesus' authority was therefore unnecessary. In Rom. 12.17-21 Paul repeats in fuller form what he says here and such teaching must have formed a part of Christian catechetical instruction (cf. 1 Pet. 2.19-21; 3.9). **See that** (for the construction see Burton, §§206, 209; Moulton–Turner, p. 98; Bl.–Deb. §370.4) **no one pays back evil with evil:** the succession of plural verbs in vv. 12-14 is surprisingly broken with the insertion of this new exhortation in the indefinite third person singular. It may be that Paul is forced into this because he is quoting a known moral tag (it appears in the singular in this way three times out of four in Jos. and Asen.; it is in the plural in Rom. 12.17, but there the participial construction may require this) or he may be laying a duty on the community to see that all its members keep the principle laid down in the tag. In any case the community is to be concerned with the behaviour of each of its members; the realization that such a concern exists can in its turn be a strength to the individual.

So much for the negative development of v. 14d. The positive statement admits of no exceptional circumstances when good may be forgotten: **at all times,** in every condition, they are to **seek eagerly** (διώκειν, a strong word used of hunting and pursuing

233

but also frequently used metaphorically as here) **the good** (Paul uses ἀγαθός here; in Rom. 12.17 he uses καλός; the two words generally mean the same for him). In any concrete situation the good is expressed in loving activity for in Paul the basic element in behaviour is love (Rom. 13.8–10; Gal. 5.14; 1 Cor. 13); the good, the beautiful and the true may become ideals to be admired; love is always active. It is not a succession of 'good deeds' but the source out of which all goodness flows. It is not a moral ideal but takes its origin in the will of God. Thus though Paul employs a term **the good** which might sound as if it came from an ethical system his thought is not shaped within or by a developed system but proceeds more directly, in accordance with the Jewish tradition, from God himself, who loves and demands love.

This love or goodness must be lived out within the community **(of one another)** and outside it **(of all men** coming at the end of the verse is climactic; cf. 3.12; the variant reading which would insert a second καί is to be rejected as lacking sufficient support; it would also destroy this climactic effect). The Christian may easily be annoyed within the community by those who are idle or are sexually immoral (to instance two causes which appear as possibilities in the letter) but he is not to retaliate; it is easy to retaliate, not necessarily by some action, but with a harping admonition (v. 14a); such retaliation would destroy the peace of the community (v. 13b). Nor is the Christian to be prodded into retaliation by the dislike or hatred, mockery or even active persecution of those outside.

16–18   In vv. 16–18 we have three brief exhortations drawn together by a reference to God's will (v. 18b) which should be understood as applying to each. In their brevity and apparent lack of relation to what precedes and follows they resemble Rom. 12.9ff. Verses 12–15 were concerned with behaviour towards fellow-Christians and those outside the community; vv. 16–18 take up the inner life of each believer; an inner life is necessarily reflected in an outward attitude and in this sense it is vv. 16–18 which make possible the behaviour desired in vv. 12–15. It is this which forms the bridge, if Paul was consciously intending any, between v. 15 and vv. 16–18. Forgiveness and help (v. 15) must not be offered grudgingly even when provoked through wrongful suffering, but with joy; joy is a gift of the Spirit (Gal. 5.22; Rom. 14.17) which goes deep down into the life of the Christian, into his total approach towards

the world, an approach which emerges from his relationship to
God ('praying, giving thanks', vv. 17, 18) and which has been
created by what God has done **in Christ Jesus** (this goes with
God's will rather than with **you,** i.e. it is not primarily expressing
the existence of Christians in Christ but the locus of God's activity
towards them). Because the Christian has been redeemed in
Christ God has willed joy and prayers for him in Christ. The
whole activity of God towards the Christian can be said to be 'in
Christ' and to take place through and because of Christ, just as the
Christian's whole existence is 'in Christ' (see notes on 1.1 for the
phrase).

The Pauline letters frequently refer to joy (**Be joyful**): 1.6; **16**
2.19f; 3.9f; Phil. 3.1; 4.4; etc. There is a natural and normal
happiness which appears when things go well, but the joy of which
Paul writes is present also when everything goes wrong (e.g. in times
of persecution, vv. 15f, or sorrow, 2 Cor. 6.10, which the Thessalonians have known also, 4.13). This joy in adversity is a common
theme in the N.T. and may go back to words of Jesus (Mt. 5.10–12;
Lk. 6.22f; 1 Pet. 5.13; Acts 16.25; Jn. 16.2–22). Paul knew this joy
himself (2 Cor. 6.10; 7.4; Phil. 2.17). 'Joy' and 'grace' come from
the same Greek stem and though Paul may not consciously intend
to play on this (yet compare his change of 'greetings' to 'grace' in
the address of his letters) it is only out of the experience of the grace
of God that true joy flows (cf. de Boor), and joy is related to and
founded on the great acts of God (Lk 2.10; 24.52f; Jn. 14.28).

Paul instructs his converts to **pray**; this was probably part of **17**
early catechetical instruction (cf. Rom. 12.12; Eph. 6.18; Col. 4.2;
cf. Acts 2.42); it was advice he himself followed (3.10; 2 Th. 1.11;
etc.). προσεύχεσθαι (**pray**) is a general word including all kinds of
prayer; since the next injunction makes explicit mention of thanksgiving it is probable that it refers here to intercession by the
Thessalonians for themselves and for others. This prayer is not
however an activity of set times or places, liturgical hours or
private meditation in the morning and evening; it is to go on
unceasingly (cf. 1.2; 2.13 where the same word is used). Prayer is
an attitude towards God which while often expressed in set forms
does not need these but may be unuttered and only come spas-
modically to conscious expression. For Paul it is an essential part of
the deep fellowship which he possessed with God through Jesus
Christ. Its existence, as his joy, depends on his redemption by God

through Christ, and likewise God had intended it as a constant activity for Paul in that same Christ (v. 18b).

18   Just as Paul himself always gave **thanks** (cf. 1.2; 2.13) to God (unexpressed here but always understood) so he asks for the same from his readers **whatever happens**. This last phrase is literally 'in every' and requires to be completed by something like 'occasion' or 'circumstance'; here either is possible; at 2 Cor. 9.8 it cannot have the former meaning; mostly elsewhere in Paul it can (1 Cor. 1.5; 2 Cor. 4.8; 6.4; 7.5, 11, 16; 8.7; 9.11; 11.6, 9) though the other is usually the more probable. The temporal adverbs in the two preceding clauses might suggest a temporal meaning here but since this temporal meaning cannot be definitely established as Pauline and since as we saw **pray** (v. 17) is a general word some difference is produced from v.17 if we choose the non-temporal 'circumstance'. No matter what the circumstances (persecution, sickness, etc.) the Christian ought to give thanks to God, not of course for the difficult circumstances but for his salvation through Christ, and when he is able to do this then he also is strengthened to endure what is difficult. It is typical of unbelief that it lacks thanksgiving (Rom. 1.21). God desires the Christian to give thanks: it is his **will** (the same phrase as in 4.3; see notes there) **in Christ Jesus** (the clause qualifies all of vv. 16–18a). In his pre-Christian days Paul would still have felt bound by God's will but he would not have related it to Christ. Redeemed now by what God has done in Christ he sees his whole life, not only his outward words and actions (as in 4.3) but his inner attitude and spirit **(joyful, pray, give thanks)**, as being brought into conformity with what God wants. Law has difficulty in dealing with the thoughts of the heart; the redeemed man is so changed from within (a new creation, 2 Cor. 5.17) that he is able to begin to offer a wholly new obedience based radically on the pattern of Christ's obedience. It is interesting that in 4.3 where Paul also referred to God's will and sought conduct which would be basically in accord with Jewish ideals he did not relate God's will to Christ, but here where he seeks an inner attitude with a stress at least on the Christian virtue of joy he does so qualify the phrase.

The three injunctions though relating to the inner life should not be taken in a purely individualistic manner. They are fulfilled not only in private prayer and in a personal attitude but also in the public worship of the community (e.g. the Eucharist, Acts 2.42, 44;

Eph. 5.18-20), in its internal desires for its members and in its corporate attitude to those outside it.

There are five imperatives in these four verses. The first two 19–(vv. 19f) are linked together as negatives (μή with the present 22 imperative implying that the practices rejected are already in existence); the final three (vv. 21f) are obviously related to one another in theme. The first two are also internally related by the connection of the Spirit and prophecy; the final three might be taken in a perfectly general way of ethical behaviour but following on the other two are much more likely to continue their theme. Together the five imperatives form a unity; v. 23 is a clean break in subject; vv. 16–18 were a separate unity. These imperatives are addressed to the community as a whole and not to its leaders alone (see on v. 14). How directly do they apply to the Thessalonian community? We have reason to believe that our passage contains traditional material. This does not mean that there is no particular relevance to the Thessalonian situation for something must have induced Paul to choose this section of paraenetic material rather than another, but it certainly means that the injunctions are general enough to be applied to any Gentile Christian community of the period (just as vv. 16–18 are equally general). If there had been a particular problem facing the Thessalonian community Paul would have dealt with it in detail and with specific reference as he does with the problems of 4.3–5.11 (contrast Henneken, pp. 104ff). We can only conclude that the problem indicated in these verses, viz., spiritual gifts, was not really agitating the Thessalonians. Schmithals (pp. 124–6) assumes that it was and makes much more out of the relatively brief reference here than is justified. 'Pneumatics', i.e. men who believe they possess special powers, such as prophecy or speaking in tongues, given them through the Spirit, were probably present in many areas of the church: the problem created by their presence became prominent in Corinth and compelled Paul to damp down excessive interest in some spiritual gifts and demand that all of them should be used in an orderly manner (1 Cor. 12, 14). But it would be wrong to assume the situation in every area was the same as in Corinth. Here in Thessalonica Paul seeks more freedom for the exercise of these gifts, though he also desires their control (v. 21f). But since the material is traditional we cannot employ it to draw a full portrait of life in the Thessalonian community. Further, if as is probable the material had its origin in Jewish Christian circles whose orderliness might have quelled the Spirit, we can see the need of vv. 19f: the Jew would have rejected the excessive manifestations of the Spirit in Corinth. There are no grounds for associating the bearers of charismata with those who have been idle and disturbed the community (cf. Did. 12.3, 4); if Paul had had such conduct in mind he would have made his point much more pungently.

19   Every Christian possesses **the Spirit** (1.5f; 4.8) and to individual Christians the Spirit gives particular endowments, gifts and abilities (1 Cor. 12.4–11, 28–31; 14; Rom. 12.6–8; 1 Pet. 4.10f); it is not the general gift of the Spirit but these special gifts which are in view here. These special gifts are not virtues as the reference to prophecy shows but new capabilities in the spiritual sphere. Elsewhere we find that these *charismata* (spiritual gifts) include leadership, service, healing, prophecy, speaking in tongues, interpretation of what is said in tongues by others. In v. 20 attention is directed to one particular gift, prophecy, but here the concern is more general: no gift of the Spirit is to be extinguished (σβέννυτε). The metaphor is especially vivid—the putting out of a flame or light—and is appropriate since 'fire' is associated with the Spirit (Mt. 3.11 = Lk. 3.16; Acts 2.3f; 18.25; Rom. 12.11; 2 Tim. 1.6). If those who have been given gifts by the Spirit are either not allowed to exercise them within the community or what they say and do is ignored then in effect the fiery power and light of the Spirit is quenched and the church is not built up (1 Cor. 14.26; cf. W. C. van Unnik, ' "Den Geist löschet nicht aus" (1 Thessalonicher v. 19)', *N.T.* 10(1968) 255–69, for parallels from Hellenistic religion and culture). The main stream churches have always tended to fear an excess of charismatic activity (cf. Luther and the Anabaptists) and have hemmed it in with restrictions rather than allow its bearers to disturb and shake them.

20   One manifestation of charismatic activity is **prophetic revelation** (προφητεία). In 1 Cor. 14 Paul contrasts prophecy with speaking in tongues almost entirely in favour of the former, but his discussion was produced by the concrete situation in Corinth and there is therefore no need to see here a real or incipient contrast between them. There is however a serious undervaluation of prophecy (**despise**, ἐξουθενεῖτε, is a strong word); since Paul does not refer to 'prophets' but to 'prophecies' this undervaluation may be taken to apply to the content of the **prophetic revelations**

rather than to prophets as a class; in either case the manner of the 'prophecy' might be an important factor. Other evidence suggests that prophets as a class were highly regarded (1 Cor. 12.28; Eph. 2.20; 3.5; 4.11); their existence was a sign of the inauguration of the Messianic age (Acts 2.17; cf. Num. 11.29; Acts 19.6). Prophecy is not the same as preaching, even if the latter is understood as the forth-telling of God's word to the present situation (cf. Best, 'Prophets and Preachers', *S.J.T.* 12 (1959) 129–50), and it is certainly not the exposition of Scripture. We may describe its content as **revelation** (cf. 1 Cor. 14.25f) whether this is the inauguration of a new step in the mission of the church (Acts 13. 1–3), the exhortation and building up of the community (1 Cor. 14.3), the foretelling of events (Acts 11.27f; 21.10f), the communication of a word of the Lord (1 Th. 4.16f) or the disclosure of eschatological and apocalyptic information (the Revelation of John calls itself a 'prophecy'—1.3; 10.11 etc.). In so far as there is a direct reference to the Thessalonian situation it will probably be the latter aspect which is in mind (cf. 2 Th. 2.2). While many commentators hold that prophecies were despised in Thessalonica because of this apocalyptic element and relate them to those who were not willing to work (4.11; 2 Th. 3.6–11), it may rather be that they were despised because prophets were often ecstatics and ecstasy might too easily both become uncouth and appear too similar to pagan religious practices. If the objection had been to the eschatological content of the prophecies opponents would have been accused of rejecting this content rather than of despising it. Scorn of ecstasy would have appeared easily in Jewish-Christian circles and if, as we have suspected, the material goes back to Jewish Christianity this then is probably its meaning. Matthew's Gospel, the most Jewish of the four, has a particular interest in prophecy (7.22; 10.41; 13.17); it is in material connected with the Palestinian area that Acts mentions prophets (11.27; 15.32; 21.10); this confirms our suggested Jewish-Christian origin of 5.19–22 since it refers to prophecy and not other charismata. Paul does not write here about the positive value of prophecy; in 1 Cor. 14 where he contrasts it with speaking with tongues he argues its importance for the building up of the life of the Christian community; but linking v. 19 and v. 20 we can see that he believes that if prophecy is despised then the activity of the Spirit in the community is in part extinguished.

21 We should expect Paul to continue with an admonition to accept what the Lord says in the **prophetic relevations** (cf. de Boor) but instead he now balances (**but**, δέ, is read by אᶜ B D G it syrʰ etc. and omitted by א* A 33 syrᵖ⋅ ᵖᵃˡ; it is probably original and was omitted either because of the following ὁ of δοκιμάζετε or because a scribe did not see the connection with the preceding verses) what he has just said to encourage prophecy with an injunction to **test** what is said in it. Though Paul does speak in a similar way of judging moral behaviour (Phil. 1.10; Rom. 12.2) the general context as we have seen excludes this here. It is of course not prophecy alone which is to be tested but **all** charismata for phenomena resembling true charismata may arise spontaneously apart from God's Spirit. 2 Th. 2.2 may suggest that such parallel phenomena did appear. In contrast to Did. 11.3ff it is the prophecies and not the prophets who are tested. Paul lays down no criteria here on how the tests are to be made. Where in 1 Cor. 14 he argues the superiority of 'prophecies' to 'tongues' he implies the criteria of 'good order' (vv. 33, 40), intelligibility (v.19), and the capability of building up the community (vv. 3, 4, 5 etc.). In 1 Jn 4.1f a theological test, the reality of the incarnation, is laid down, whereas in Did. 11.10 it is the correspondence of the prophet's own life to his teaching. If prophetic revelations in Thessalonica were understood as eschatological disclosure then one test would be their future outcome—but this hardly provides an immediate criterion. Whatever the criteria it is probable that Paul would have considered that they themselves should be charismatically exercised; only he who is inspired by the Spirit can judge others inspired by the same Spirit (1 Cor. 2.13; 12.10; 14.29).

21b–
22 The end result of testing is now stated both positively and negatively—**hold fast what is good** (τὸ καλόν, **good**, is a different word from v. 15 but does not appear to have any different meaning in Paul, cf. Rom. 7.18); **keep clear of** (4.3) **whatever kind is evil**. εἶδος which we have rendered **kind** might also have been translated 'outward form' but not 'appearance' (so K.J.V., in the sense of what may not in fact be evil but appears so; cf. Milligan). Our rendering is a classical sense which re-appears in the papyri and is the most appropriate to the context. It is possible to contrast the many kinds of evil, by its nature fissiparous, with the unity of goodness (cf. Gal. 5.19–21, 'works', and 5.22f, 'fruit'). **evil** (πονηροῦ) can be either an adjective ('every evil kind') or a noun

('every kind of evil'); Pauline usage favours the former but if he is employing traditional material this may not be important; the meaning is not affected. The testing of the charismata will lead to the acceptence of whatever is valuable and the rejection of what is not.

Some commentators have seen a parallel between vv. 21f and an agraphon of Jesus, 'Be approved money changers' (cf. J. Jeremias, *Unknown Sayings of Jesus*, pp. 100–4, who rejects the parallel), which was widely known in the early church, at least from Clement of Alexandra and Origen onwards, and was used in the sense of rejecting the spurious and retaining the good. Obviously the ideas of the saying and our passage are similar but the conception is common and since our verse lacks the key-word 'money-changers' there is no reason to think of it as affected by the saying.

We have suggested the use of traditional material in 5.12–22. Rom. 12.9–13 is an obvious parallel; here we have the same succession of brief sentences but with the difference that they are constructed around participles and not imperatives. D. Daube, in an essay 'Participle and Imperative in 1 Peter' in Selwyn, *op. cit.*, pp. 467ff, has shown that this use of the participle for the imperative is Semitic and is found regularly in the N.T. Thus behind Rom. 12.9–13 lies material originating in a Semitic environment, presumably the Palestinian Jewish community. Rom. 12.14–21 continues the same type of material as in vv. 9–13 but does not use imperatival participles; C. H. Talbert, 'Tradition and Redaction in Rom. xii. 9–21', *N.T.S.* 16 (1969/70) 83–93, has suggested that material originally similar to vv. 9–13 has been heavily edited in a Hellenistic Christian context to produce vv. 14–21. The same has probably taken place in respect of the material in 1 Th. 5.12–22. Verses 16–21 can easily be thrown back into the form of Rom. 12.9–13 by the substitution of participles for imperatives. This is true also of vv. 13b, 14 (after its introduction) and v. 15. Verses 12, 13a are more directly due to Paul and therefore more directly applicable to the situation; with their reference to the internal relationships of the community they resemble Rom. 12.3–8 in content. In addition to this there are striking parallels in content between Rom. 12.9ff and 1 Th. 5.12ff: 1 Th. 5.13b and Rom. 12.18; 1 Th. 5.15 and Rom. 12.17a; 1 Th. 5.16 and Rom. 12.12a; 1 Th. 5.17 and Rom. 12.12c; 1 Th. 5.19 and Rom. 12.11b; 1 Th. 5.21b–22 and Rom. 12.9b. Thus we conclude that in

241

1 Th. 5.12ff Paul has used traditional material, probably of Jewish-Christian origin.

CONCLUDING PRAYER, EXHORTATION AND BENEDICTION 5.23–8

Now may God himself, the God of peace, sanctify you completely and may your whole spirit and soul and body be preserved without fault at the parousia of our Lord Jesus Christ. (24) He who calls you is faithful and he will accomplish it.

(25) Brothers, pray for us also. (26) Greet all the brothers with a holy kiss. (27) I charge you by the Lord to have this letter read aloud to all the brothers.

(28) May the grace of our Lord Jesus Christ be with you.

23 Paul wound up the first part of his letter with a prayer (3.11–13) and he now concludes his paraenesis with a prayer of similar form. There are prayers in the concluding sections of some of his other letters (Rom. 15.13; Gal. 6.16; Phil. 4.19; 2 Th. 3.16). Here as in 3.11–13 the prayer is focused on the holiness and blamelessness (**without fault** is from the same word) of the Thessalonians at the time of the parousia. Paul realizes that his preceding exhortations will be of no avail for those who try to carry them out in their own strength—not that the Thessalonian believers would be likely to try this, for they are believers and are therefore in a new relation to God, already being made new men and women—but he feels it appropriate to remind them of this aspect with this short prayer. 'May God sanctify you' (v. 23) balances 'sanctify yourselves' (4.3a).

Paul's prayer is directed to the God of peace, not so much because there has been disharmony in the community (5.12f?) and he wishes peace between man and man, but because God as the creator of peace between himself and man can alone save man from destroying himself; thus as in 1.1 **peace** is practically equivalent to salvation; and such salvation and oneness with God require the complete sanctification of the Thessalonians. Paul regularly describes believers as 'saints' (which comes from the same root as **sanctify;** see on 3.13; 4.3 for its meaning). They are 'holy', they need to strive for holiness (4.3) and God alone can produce holiness in them.

The second half of the verse reiterates the first chiastically and at the same time amplifies it, identifying the moment at which complete holiness is essential, the **parousia**; holiness, of course, will not come suddenly into existence then unless they are now already 'holy' (the saints) and seeking holiness. **at** (ἐν here is not to be given the sense 'up to, until', though if believers are preserved in the Day of judgement this will imply preservation until then) **the parousia** no part of them is to be lost. To the Greek for whom the body was the tomb or prison of the immortal soul its ultimate fate was unimportant; for Paul there is no existence without the body (cf. 1 Cor. 15). The relative value of **spirit** and **soul** for Paul has caused considerable discussion (for Paul's use of these anthropological terms generally cf. Stacey, *op. cit.*, pp. 121–45, 181–93). Because of the difficulty of distinguishing them in man's psychological make-up many commentators have taken **spirit** to mean the divine Spirit dwelling in believers. This is improbable; how could Paul pray that the divine Spirit should be preserved or set it in parallel with the human **soul** and **body**? Masson, 'Sur 1 Th. v. 23: Note d'anthropologie paulinienne', *R.T.P.* 33 (1945) 97–102, accepting that **spirit** is the human spirit, has argued that it means man as a person (cf. Gal. 6.18; Phil. 4.23; Philm. 25; all in liturgical contexts as here) and that **soul** and **body** then explicate this; thus we might render it: 'may your whole being, soul and body, be preserved'. This is grammatically difficult since it takes **your whole** with **spirit** alone though the Greek strongly implies that the three terms are parallel. P. A. van Stempvoort, 'Eine stilistische Lösung einer alten Schwierigkeit in 1 Thess. v. 23', *N.T.S.* 7 (1961) 262–5, divides v. 23 into two sentences placing a period after **spirit** (which like Masson he takes as the equivalent of a personal pronoun) and renders, 'May the God of peace sanctify you wholly and in every part. May both soul and body be preserved without fault at the coming of our Lord Jesus.' He detects verbal play between 'sanctify' and 'wholly' based on an alleged earlier Hebrew form. This is unnecessarily complicated, and it is very difficult to take the **and** after **spirit** as the beginning of a new sentence. If however **spirit** and **soul** are parallel and both refer to man how do we distinguish them? Is there here a trichotomic division of man? (For a discussion of suggested divisions and distinctions, see Rigaux *ad loc.*) If there is a trichotomy here this is the only place in Paul where it exists; moreover elsewhere in

Paul it is often impossible to differentiate clearly **spirit** from **soul**; it is also very difficult to press such a division in a liturgical text. Probably the attempt to make such divisions and distinctions is incorrect. It is possible that Paul is employing an accepted liturgical formulation (cf. Dibelius) and thus any such distinctions in it would not necessarily be his own. If Paul has created the verse then he is almost certainly using his terms loosely, perhaps in dependence on popular psychology (cf. E. Schweizer, *T.D.N.T.* VI, p. 435), and only implying with the use of all three terms the completeness of man's preservation by God and thereby reinforcing his use of **completely, whole** (the latter emphasizes the integrity of the preservation and perhaps has also a cultic sense since it is used of animals suitable for sacrifice; cf. Josephus, *Ant.* 3. 278f). No part of man lies outside the care of God (cf. Stacey, *op. cit.*, pp. 123f). 'This is not a systematic dissection of the distinct elements of personality; its true analogy is such an Old Testament sentence as Deut. vi. 5, where a somewhat similar enumeration emphasizes the totality of the personality' (H. W. Robinson, *The Christian Doctrine of Man*, Edinburgh, 1911, p. 108; cf. the variation of the formula of Deut. 6.5 in Mk. 12.30; Lk. 10.27). We ought not then to use this text as a source for Pauline psychology, nor deduce from the mention of the body in it any doctrine of its preservation or resurrection at the judgement.

24   It is not enough to pray; the God to whom prayers are addressed may pay no heed to them or may be powerless to assist. Not so Paul's God. He stands in a permanent relation to these Thessalonians (**calls** is a present tense; cf. 2.12); it is not that he called them once (cf. 1.4; 4.7) and has left them to their own devices thereafter. Just as God called Israel, made his covenant with them and was **faithful** to them and to it, so he is **faithful** to the Thessalonians (cf. 1 Cor. 1.9 for the association of God's faithfulness and his call and 1 Cor. 10.13 for the association of his faithfulness and his ability to **accomplish**, ποιεῖν). He will not abandon the task which he has begun but will carry it through so that they will stand faultless at the parousia of Christ (cf. Phil. 1.6). 'This verse has the ring of a magnificent confidence' (Plummer).

25-7   Paul remembers three final requests he has to make of which the first two are found regularly in his letters; only the third is unique.

25a   In other letters Paul asks that the recipients **pray** for him (Rom. 15.30-33; 2 Cor. 1.11; Col. 4.3; cf. Eph. 6.18f; Phil. 1.19;

Philm 22; Heb. 13.18). He is aware that he is in as much need of God's help as are those for whom he prays in his letters. Intercessory prayer has to be mutual if the church is to be built up, for where believers are concerned there is always a reciprocal relationship (cf. 3.6-10). This is especially emphasized if we read **also** (with P³⁰ B D* 33 81; it is omitted by ℵ A Dᶜ G; the evidence being not unevenly divided we probably ought to read it, since it is easier to see it being dropped than added). To what does it refer? Almost certainly to v. 23f for v. 17, part of the traditional material, is too remote; Paul has just prayed for the Thessalonians; let them also pray for him and his helpers.

In all his letters Paul greets his readers and often requests them 26 to **greet** one another; but in our verse who is to greet whom? Elsewhere Paul uses the phrase 'one another' rather than **all the brothers** and it has therefore been suggested (so Masson; see also on vv. 12-14) that he is here instructing the leaders of the community to greet all the others. But as we have seen there is little in the letter to sustain a distinction between leaders and people, **all** need not be emphatic, and if the instruction was restricted to a few then we should expect them to be clearly identified. We therefore conclude that Paul is addressing all the members of the community; since this is a regular request in his letters (Rom. 16.16; 1 Cor. 16.20; 2 Cor. 13.12) it can hardly be taken as suggesting that some division within the church needs to be healed. Yet if the Thessalonians were in any way disputing among themselves (e.g. over idleness) then this prescription ensures that none are left out of the greeting. In the ancient world greetings took many forms, both actions (embracing, kissing, bowing) and words (see on 1.1; cf. H. Windisch, *T.D.N.T.* I, pp. 496-502). Here the form is that of a **holy kiss** (see G. Stählin, *T.W.N.T.* IX, pp. 118-22, 124-6; 136-44). In those days kisses were given between near kinsfolk, were a mark of honour to a superior, and were used in sexual play. The kiss was given on the lips (normally only in sex), on the cheeks, brow and shoulders (among kinsfolk), on the hands and feet (in honouring a superior). Outside Judaism the kiss had also a cultic use (e.g. in the Mystery Religions) and was both a sign and a seal of reconciliation. It was used as a greeting on meeting and separation. It must have had some ceremonial significance in the early church (cf. Rom. 16.16; 1 Cor. 16.20; 2 Cor. 13.12; 1 Pet. 5.14). Later it was connected with the

Eucharist (Justin Martyr, *Apol.* 65.2) representing the reconciliation of the participants with one another, and this may well have been its meaning in Paul's churches; in any case it was very probably a part of worship. Paul's casual reference implies it was well-known to the Thessalonians to whom he must have taught it on his initial visit. As a **holy** kiss it is given between those who are **holy**, i.e. the saints or believers; it is the kiss which belongs to the **holy** community (**holy** does not signify 'non-sexual'). The origin of the rite within the church is difficult to determine; it may have been in use among the company of Jesus' disciples while he was with them (cf. the kiss of Judas, Mk. 14.44f) or it may have represented the early church's realization that it was a family (Mk. 3.31-5; 10.29f) for whom it was the traditional greeting; but it may have entered Christianity from pagan religion carrying with it something of the idea of reconciliation (cf. 1 Pet. 5.14)—of Christians to one another rather than to God. We can assume it was not on the lips because of the sexual association of such kisses.

27   Paul's final exhortation surprisingly is expressed in the first singular (cf. the sudden changes at 2.18; 3.15). Probably Paul has been using an amanuensis (Silvanus or Timothy?) or else has permitted Silvanus or Timothy to write the letter for him (cf pp. 23-8), and now at the end according to his usual custom (1 Cor. 16.21; Gal. 6.11; Col. 4.18; 2 Th. 3.17; see notes on 2 Th. 3.17) he takes the pen into his own hand and writes the conclusion (he may indeed have taken it at v. 25). Both the change to the singular and the use of the strong word **charge** (ἐνορκίζειν; for the construction see Bl.-Deb. §§ 155.7; 392.1.d; 409.5; Moulton–Turner, p.149) emphasize the importance of this exhortation. Did Paul suppose that the letter would be retained by a few and not read to **all the brothers**? (The variant 'holy' added to **brothers** in ℵᶜ A K 33 81 syr is unlikely; it is the kind of addition that takes place easily.) Does **all** imply that there was some division in the community? Harnack (cf. pp. 38-41) suggested a division between Jews and Gentiles; Masson one between leaders and people. We have seen no reason to suppose that any of these divisions were of more than minor significance; the whole tone of the letter implies that the community held together. If however we stress **aloud** (the classical meaning of ἀναγινώσκειν is 'read aloud' and it was still used with this sense in Hellenistic Greek) and recollect that many of the Christians would have been illiterate

246

we may suppose that the injunction is made lest any, even the
seemingly least important member, be ignored; this might not
happen intentionally but through carelessness. Let then those who
receive the letter (and these will be the leaders since it has to go to
somebody) see that it is read publicly. There is no evidence to
disclose whether this took place during a service of worship or not
but the hard and fast line which we draw between what is and
what is not worship would hardly have been appreciated in
the early church. The letter is certainly to be **read aloud** to the
assembled community but there is no suggestion that it forms
'canonical Scripture' or is to be put on a par with the reading
and use of the O.T. or even to be retained for regular reading
(**read aloud** is an aorist). The injunction could imply that the
letter is to be read in each of the house-churches (if there were
such) rather than, or as well as, in a general gathering (cf. von
Dobschütz).

As in all his other letters Paul closes with a benediction whose 28
exact wording varies from letter to letter: the briefest is Col. 4.18
and the most elaborate 2 Cor. 13.13. As in the initial greeting
(1.1) Paul has replaced a secular form (cf. Acts 15.29; 2 Macc.
11. 38) with a theological. For **grace** see on 1.1. See also notes on
2 Th. 3.18.

A great many MSS add 'amen' (fewer do so at 2 Th. 3.18) at the
close; this is probably a liturgical addition stemming from the
reading of the letter in public at a slightly later period in the
church.

2 THESSALONIANS
ADDRESS AND GREETING 1.1–2

**From Paul, Silvanus and Timothy to the Christian com-
munity of the Thessalonians in God our Father and the
Lord Jesus Christ:**
**(2) grace and peace be with you from God the Father and
the Lord Jesus Christ.**

The Address and Greeting of 1 Th. 1.1 (see notes there) are 1
repeated here with two additions: (i) **our** (v. 1) with **Father**; it
is found frequently in Paul where he associates God and Christ
and implies that Paul is thinking of God as the Father of believers

rather than as the Father of Jesus (the latter comes out at other
2 points, e.g. when he terms Jesus, 'Son of God'). (ii) **from God ...
Christ** (v. 2); this brings the Greeting into line with those in
most of the other letters (Rom. 1.7; 1 Cor. 1.3; 2 Cor. 1.2 etc.).
There is however one difference in that elsewhere an 'our' is
joined to **Father**. This is found here as a variant (א A 81 Orig.;
the text is read by B D 33) probably due to the influence of
the general formula and to its use in v. 1. The whole phrase is a
trifle otiose after v. 1. **God** and **Christ** are both seen as the ultimate source of grace and peace; both words depend on the
single proposition **from** and are set in parallel by **and**. While
there may be a distinction in the relationship of God (ultimate
source?) and Christ (mediator?) to grace and peace this is not in
view here.

THANKSGIVING, ENCOURAGEMENT AND PRAYER 1.3–12

**We always ought to thank God for you, brothers, as is right,
because your faith grows greatly and the love of each one of
all of you for one another abounds (4) so that even we ourselves boast about you in the communities of God, about
your endurance and faith in all the persecutions and tribulations which you are bearing; (5) this is a sure sign of the
righteous judgement of God, that you will be thought worthy
of the kingdom of God, for which you also are suffering,
(6) if it is just, as it surely is, in the sight of God to repay
tribulation to those who cause you tribulation (7) and to
you who suffer tribulation, peace together with us, at the
revelation of the Lord Jesus from heaven with the angels
of his power (8) in a flaming fire; then he will inflict vengeance on those who do not know God and do not obey the
gospel of our Lord Jesus, (9) who will pay the penalty of
eternal destruction out from the presence of the Lord and
from the glory of his might (10) when he comes to be glorified in his saints and marvelled at in all who believed—for the
testimony we brought to you was believed—, on that day.
(11) With this in mind we are also always praying for you
that our God may make you worthy of his call and may**

**powerfully accomplish every resolve for goodness and
every effort of faith (12) so that the name of our Lord Jesus
may be glorified in you and you in him, in virtue of the grace
of our God and of the Lord Jesus Christ.**

As in most of his letters Paul commences by thanking God,
in this case for the faith, love and endurance of persecution of
the Thessalonians (vv. 3f). This quickly brings him to the main
theme of his letter—eschatology. His readers know that the End
and final judgement are not too far off but they do not need to fear
for it will be a day in which God will distribute just deserts to
men: to them, entrance into the Kingdom because they have borne
their persecution; to their persecutors, exclusion from his presence
(vv. 5–10). But, though the Thessalonians have endured until
now, the End has not yet come and so Paul reminds them that he
continually prays God to make them ready for the Kingdom, for
entrance into it derives ultimately from his grace and power and
not from their own efforts (vv. 11f). Underlying this Paul is
aware that the Thessalonians are worried both about the way in
which their persecutors appear to escape punishment and they
themselves do not and about the timing of the parousia; the latter
he takes up in chap. 2.

Verses 3–10 are one long sentence in Greek; for convenience
sake it is broken up in our translation.

Paul introduces the thanksgiving in this letter differently from 3
those in his others. A sense of obligation appears in **ought** (cf. 2.13;
ὀφειλεῖν implies a special personal obligation rather than one
arising out of the nature of things; the latter idea comes in **as is
right**; cf. Westcott on 1 Jn. 2.6) and **as** (frequently causal in Paul;
cf. Bl.-Deb. §453.2) **is right**; either phrase by itself might
have been overlooked as a casual variation but together they
force the question whether something has compelled Paul to
express explicitly his sense of duty. Frame has suggested that
the Thessalonians have protested that they are unworthy of the
praise given in Paul's first letter; this is possible but we simply do
not know enough to say if it is true. Certainly the suggestion of
von Dobschütz (cf. Masson; Harnack's further extension of this
which supposes that v. 3 is phrased in the more liturgical manner
required in a synagogue cannot be sustained; see Harnack, *op. cit.*,
p. 566) that Paul's tone here is cooler than in his other letters is

unacceptable for in the following clause, **because . . .**, his words are most enthusiastic. The obligation is not one of duty alone but is forced on Paul by what he sees in the Thessalonians; they deserve this thanksgiving. Does the variation in formula imply that the letter is not by Paul? There are indeed further variations from Paul's other letters: (i) **brothers** is introduced sooner than usual; elsewhere it comes after the thanksgiving when Paul turns directly to address his readers (cf. Rom. 1.13; 1 Cor. 1.10; 2 Cor. 1.8 etc); (ii) εὐχαριστεῖν is followed here by a causal clause; (iii) **always** qualifies **ought** rather than **thank** (cf. 1 Th. 2.13; Rom. 1.8; 1 Cor. 1.5). These variations are not unrelated; the introduction of **ought** requires a stated reason (cf. 1 Clem. 38.4; Barnabas 5.3; 7.1); **always** goes easily with it. The argument is thus weaker than it looks at first sight. If we argue that 2 Th. is not by Paul because there are too many signs of imitation of 1 Th. and other Pauline letters then the argument about differences here is inappropriate for the thanksgiving formula is so fixed in Paul that anyone would pick it up. If we argue that the differences between 2 Th. and other letters suggest another mind than Paul's then the similarities which are argued for elsewhere become difficult. But conversely it is not easy to argue from the differences here that Paul wrote the letter; an author is free to vary his formulae but that is no proof he has done so, and an imitator might wish for some wholly other reason to stress obligation. We can only say that in the variations here there is nothing which strongly suggests authenticity or inauthenticity: a conclusion reached on other grounds will not have to be revised in the light of what we find here.

Paul now gives two reasons (**because**; ὅτι is here causal as in 2.13 and dependent on **ought**) why he feels obliged to thank God: (i) **your faith grows greatly** (ὑπεραυξάνειν: Paul likes compounds with ὑπέρ and uses them to intensify the normal meaning of a word; this compound is found only here in the N.T.; it is not the kind of trait or the precise word which someone imitating Paul would easily pick up). **grows** suggests an inward organic increase with which **faith** (in Paul basically the total response of the believer to God: see on 1 Th. 1.3, 8; 3.2ff) accords. It would be wrong to make too close a connection between this clause and 1 Th. 3.10 and see it as expressing the disappearance of Paul's anxiety about them. 1 Th. 3.10 had already been preceded by 1.3 in which their **faith** is praised in terms not very much less cordial than here. In 2 Th. Paul is doing no more than he does in all his letters except Galatians when he begins by thanking God for the virtues and attainments of his readers. For this same reason we should not stress **grows greatly** over against 1 Th. 1.3 and conclude that this shows our letter must follow 1 Th. (ii) **the love of each ... abounds**: if the first reason emphasized the inner aspect of Christian life this stresses the outer as action within the Christian community. Paul had prayed in 1 Th. 3.12 that their **love** should **abound**; is he then voicing now his thanksgiving for an answered prayer? Again as with (i) we cannot be certain, for this is the type of statement Paul makes regularly at the beginning of his letters and which in 1 Th. 1.3 he had already made with special reference to **love**. Thus again we cannot deduce that 2 Th. necessarily follows 1 Th. The elaborate phrase **each one of all of you for one another** includes each member of the community as an individual and shows that the **love** (ἀγάπη) which Paul has in mind can only be exercised by persons towards persons. In his prayer at 1 Th. 3.12 Paul prayed for this love not only for one another but 'for all men'; the omission of the latter phrase is not significant here; in the early church the command to love existed in the double form 'to neighbour' and 'to one another' (see notes on 1 Th. 3.12); the second appears more frequently. Possibly Paul uses it here because in his thanksgivings he tends to look at the inner life of the community he is writing to. If someone had composed v. 3 out of 1 Th. 3.12 we would not have expected 'for all men' to be omitted. This is also true with regard to 'hope'; 1 Th. 1.3 enumerates the triad 'faith, hope, love'; here we have only faith and love; a compiler would surely have introduced 'hope'. Its omission is not significant on the supposition of Pauline authorship for Paul regularly uses **faith** and **love** together without 'hope' (1 Th. 3.6; Gal. 5.6; Philm 5; Col. 1.4; Eph. 1.15; 3.17; 6.23; cf. 1 Cor. 16.13f; 2 Cor. 8.7); we do not need therefore to see **endurance** (v. 4) as a synonym for hope or to suppose that Paul deliberately omitted it because the Thessalonians were too much taken up with eschatological hope.

Knowing their growth in faith and abundance of love Paul and 4 his companions wherever they have gone have praised the Thessalonians and this is apparently now set in contrast (**even we ourselves**, αὐτοὺς ἡμᾶς: cf. Bl.–Deb. §281 and similar phrases in 1 Th. 4.9; Rom. 7.25; 9.3; 15.14; 2 Cor. 10.1; 2.13) with something else; but it is not clear with whom (or what) this contrast is. **about** (ἐν) **you** in the order of the Greek precedes **boast** and follows **we ourselves** but this may only be because Paul wishes to avoid the proximity of two ἐν clauses following the verb. If however **you** and **we** are to be contrasted the sense may be: the Thessalonians have demurred at Paul's praise in the first letter; now he re-iterates it: 'we, who really know you, boast . . .' (so Frame; this accords with Frame's suggestion on **ought**, v. 3). But **we** may be contrasted with something unstated: (*a*) 'We, with our apostolic authority, boast . . .' (cf. Wrede, *op cit.*, p. 85); this contrast however is very implicit and apostolic authority is not greatly stressed anywhere in our letters (cf. 1 Th. 2.7a and notes there; see also pp. 54f). (*b*) 'We, the founders of your community, boast . . .', it being considered very unusual for founders to boast of their own work (so Lightfoot); this again reads too much into the phrase and in any case the founders have already spoken of the Thessalonians as their crown of boasting (1 Th. 2.19; cf. 2 Cor. 8.1ff). (*c*) 'We, who ought not to boast at all, boast . . .'; boasting is sinful, we should only boast in the Lord, yet we boast about you (Rigaux); it is very difficult to see how **we** enters into the alleged antithesis at all; with whom is it being contrasted? No view is satisfactory; we lack the necessary information to resolve the issue; probably Frame's view is least unsatisfactory. Paul and his companions **boast** (ἐγκαυχᾶσθαι: elsewhere Paul uses the simple form of the verb; if 2 Th. is due to a compiler we would expect it here; this is the only occurrence of the compound in the N.T.) **about** the Thessalonians (cf. 1 Th. 2.19; see notes there), not before God (1 Th. 2.19) but **in** (possibly 'within'; cf. Moulton–Turner, p. 264) **the communities of God** (see on 1 Th. 1.1; when **God** is added it is unnecessary to preface **communities** with 'Christian'). In every other passage where Paul uses the plural **communities** he delimits it with a geographical designation; where he means the whole Christian community he uses the singular. The lack of geographical delimitation with the plural here is probably intended to create a vague phrase meaning something like 'widely among Christians'; whatever community Paul visits or writes to, he boasts to them about the Thessalonians (2 Cor. 8.1ff is an example). Just as 'every place' in 1 Th. 1.8 is not intended literally so our phrase does not refer to every church existing at that time. Rigaux notes how the Christian communities then, though geographically distant, were very much aware of what was happening in one another.

Paul now makes precise what it was in the Thessalonians about which he had boasted, viz., **about** (cf. 1 Th. 3.2) **your endurance and faith**: these qualities are picked out because they are those which enabled them to live through persecution. Paul had already referred to their **endurance** in 1 Th. 1.3, where he linked it to hope and gave it an eschatological orientation; in our present passage we move through the persecutions which have been and are afflicting the Christians to their ultimate acceptance at God's judgement (vv. 5ff); **endurance** is thus a more active quality than the 'patience' of K.J.V. suggests. With it he couples **faith**; this is one of those words which take their precise meaning from the context; if faith is essentially the total response of the Christian to God, here it is that response in a situation of persecution and so begins to pass over into the sense 'faithfulness'; part of its flavour also comes from **endurance**. Calvin wrongly suggested that **endurance** is the fruit of **faith**; it is also incorrect to understand the two words together as meaning 'your firmness in faith'; **faith** and **endurance** are rather here parallel concepts for they have a common article, and the single ὑμῶν applies to both as does the following phrase **in all the** ... (The combination of the concepts endurance and faith, but not necessarily of the words, is frequent later than Paul: 1 Pet. 1.5, 7ff, 21; Heb. 6.12; 11.1; Rev. 13.10.) Traced back to their final source the **endurance** and **faith** of the Thessalonians are not their own achievement but come from God, and so Paul returns thanks to him for both. Their **endurance** and **faith** have been displayed **in** (for the abundance of prepositional phrases cf. 1 Th. 3.7f; 2 Th. 2.9f) the midst of **persecutions** and **tribulations.** While **tribulation** has both a more eschatological and a wider connotation (see on 1.6; 3.3, 7) than **persecution** (used of religious persecution from the Psalms onwards; cf. A. Oepke, *T.D.N.T.* II, pp. 229f) the two are really synonymous here (**which**, αἵς, introducing the clause, has been attracted into their case and into the gender of the second). These sufferings are a present and a continuous reality (cf. **all** and the present tense **are bearing**); the church in Thessalonica was launched amid them (Acts 17.1–10; 1 Th. 1.6) and they still continue (cf. 1 Th. 3.3f where the Thessalonians are included in the first plural), for they are a part of the Christian's destiny. We are given no information about the identity of the persecutors. Since persecution was endemic in the early church they will certainly have been their own fellow townsfolk (cf. 1 Th. 2.14); possibly in these there may have been included some Jews, but only if Harnack's suggestion that our letter was written to Jewish Christians is correct would we expect them to have been mainly Jews.

4, 5 There are difficulties in the connection between v. 4 and v. 5 and it has been suggested that the words should be punctuated differently (early N.T. manuscripts have no punctuation; what we have in printed texts has been inserted by editors): (i) Von Dobschütz puts a comma after **tribulations** and takes **sure sign** (v. 5) as a predicate of **bearing** and in apposition to **which**, 'which you are bearing as a sure sign of . . .'; this is possible but the punctuation breaks the rhythm of the words (Rigaux) and **which** and **sure sign** are not in the same case (Dibelius); if this was the intended sense we should have expected εἰς ἔνδειγμα (cf. Rom. 3.25). (ii) Masson divides **persecutions** and **tribulations**: 'and you bear these tribulations—a sure sign of . . .' Unlike (i) this is unjustifiable since **persecutions** and **tribulations** are joined closely together as a word-pair (Mk. 4.17; Mt. 13.21; cf. Rom. 8.35; 2 Cor. 4.8f) even though **tribulations** alone is taken up in vv. 6f. If we accept the punctuation of the printed texts how do we take **sure sign** (on the meaning of ἔνδειγμα see Milligan's note)? We can either (cf. Bl.–Deb. §480.6) as in Phil. 1.28 supply 'which is' (in our translation we have assumed this solution but in order to simplify the English have begun a fresh sentence **this is**) or we can regard **sure sign** as in apposition (cf. Rom. 12.1) to what precedes; the translation will then really be much the same. The

5 clause **this is . . . judgement of God** cannot be parenthetical because vv. 6, 7a depend on it (so Lightfoot). To what then does **this** refer (or with what is **sure sign** in apposition)? We are probably wise to take it to refer at least to the whole of the preceding idea, i.e. the context of Paul's boast. This is not just that there are persecutions and tribulations (though these are 'signs' of the end, e.g. Mk. 13.19, 24; Rev. 7.14; see on 1 Th. 3.3f; it is only in 2.1ff that Paul deals with signs of the End; here he is not concerned with its proximity). Nor is **this** their endurance and faith, for Paul is not dealing with such virtues in general but only in the concrete situation of tribulation and persecution. Rather **this** must be their faith and endurance while they suffer persecution and tribulation.

It is possible to take the reference even more widely: the **sure sign** is that Paul boasts of their faith and endurance in persecutions and tribulations. As a sign this would be something more objective than their own estimation of their endurance and faith, and as we have seen in v. 3 they may have been somewhat doubtful of their own success; this interpretation would also explain Paul's boasting, which as we saw caused difficulty to commentators. The Thessalonians are not sure of their position on the day of judgement; Paul says: 'I have boasted about you; this is a sign that God will count you worthy then.'

If then this is the **sure sign,** of what is it a sign? **of the righteous judgement of God.** As the sequel shows (vv. 7b–10) this is not a reference to a judgement of God in process at that time but to the eschatological judgement at the parousia. (On judgement in Jewish thought, cf. Russell, *op. cit.,* pp. 379ff; G. F. Moore, *op. cit.,* II, pp. 279ff.) This judgement will be righteous because God is righteous, and righteous because of what takes place in it; persecutors will be punished and those they have persecuted will be vindicated. To whom is the **sure sign** given? Paul does not specify. In the similar passage in Phil. 1.28 it is given to the persecutors—that they will be lost and that those they have persecuted will be saved. Since Paul here makes no explicit mention of those to whom the sign is directed very probably he intends it for a sign to his readers, and this has been implied in our interpretation of it.

If God judges righteously then those who have suffered in persecution **will be thought worthy** (καταξιωθῆναι; the verb might mean 'made worthy' but at Lk. 20.35; Acts 5.41; 4 Macc. 18.3 it has the meaning we have given it; the passive form implies that it is God who thinks them worthy) **of the kingdom of God** (the eschatological community of the redeemed at the parousia; see on 1 Th. 2.12) and will in fact become members of it (cf. the Rabbinic phrase, 'Be worthy of the coming age'; see Billerbeck, II, pp. 254f). This clause (introduced by εἰς τό, see on 1 Th. 2.16) may give either the content of God's judgement, its result, or its purpose; it is difficult to distinguish clearly between these and all three may in fact be involved: God judges righteously with the intention that those who have suffered while righteous may be received into his kingdom, this is the actual result of his judgement, and it is stated in his decree of judgement. All this is to be expected for they **suffer** (present tense; cf. v. 4, **are bearing**) **for** (not 'in

order to obtain', cf. Phil. 1. 29) the kingdom. **also** (καί) implies some
kind of contrast or similarity: either the contrast between their
present suffering and their future glory (in the sense 'even now')
or the similarity between what is happening to them and what is
happening to others, i.e. they are not the only ones to suffer (Paul
has suffered, is probably still suffering and certainly will suffer);
this similarity comes out again in **with us** (v. 7) and for this reason
is the preferable interpretation. In any case the contrast between
present suffering and future glory appears here with the reference
to the kingdom of God and in v. 7 to **peace**; it is found regularly in
the N.T. (Lk. 6.20–6; Mt. 5.10–12; Acts 14.22; Rom. 8.17; 2 Tim.
2.11f; 1 Pet. 1.6; 3.14; 4.13f; Jas. 1.2, 12) and seems to have its
origin for Christians in Jesus' teaching, though of course it goes
back far behind him into Judaism and the O.T. It is allied in
thought to the *lex talionis* (Lev. 24.19f) and this comes out clearly in
the two-fold expansion of vv. 6, 7. Yet it is not set out here in terms
of reward as if Paul were encouraging his readers to endure so that
they should enter the kingdom; it is instead an assurance that if
they remain firm in persecution God will accept them. The persecuted will have peace, and the persecutors will be punished—
because God is righteous. In the final issue this follows from the
nature of God and not from their achievement; any other result
would entail an immoral universe. We need to remember also
that because God is righteous (the same word as **just** here) he
justifies, redeems and saves the unrighteous who respond to
him in faith. Those to whom he writes are indeed those who are
being justified through their faith called forth by God's grace in
Christ.

6   In the two-fold expansion of v. 5 (εἴπερ, **if . . . as it surely is:**
'the particle states rhetorically, in the form of hypothesis, a
recognized fact' (Findlay); cf. Rom. 3.30; 8.9, 17; 2 Cor. 5.3 *v.l.*)
Paul turns first (v. 6) to those who persecute (he expands the
original reference with the key-word **tribulation** rather than
'persecution' probably because of the former's eschatological
nuance). That God **repays** (ἀνταποδίδωμι is a strong word)
embodies a principle much wider than the present limited application to persecution. It provides an answer to the problem caused
by the prosperity of the wicked and the suffering of the innocent,
by calling in what lies beyond this world to redress what has
happened here. Though it is rejected as a principle of human con-

duct in Mt. 5.38–48 it is found in the Gospels (Lk. 16.25) and in Paul (Rom. 2.6–8; 12.19; 2 Cor. 5.10; Col. 3.25), and it seems an essential constituent of any teaching about God's judgement. While it is connected to this judgement here Paul does not use it as a threat ('Be good or you will suffer') for those to whom he writes are already Christians. He is dealing with inevitable results and not speculating about the conditions of entry into the kingdom of God. He does not specify what **tribulation** will fall on persecutors, though the repeated use of the one word would suggest a punishment appropriate to the crime; v. 9 takes the matter a little further, though not much. The other side of the picture is **peace** 7a for the persecuted. **Peace** (ἄνεσις) is not the same word as in v. 2 but one which indicates the absence of tension and trial (cf. 2 Cor. 2.12; 7.5; 8.13, where it is used of present existence and not eternal as here). This **peace** is as little explained as was **tribulation** (v. 6) but it fittingly balances the latter; from v. 5 we infer that it means being in the kingdom of God and the reference in v. 7 to the parousia combined with 1 Th. 4.17 implies that it is associated with being 'with the Lord'. Whatever it may be the Thessalonians are not the only ones who inherit it; Paul and his companions **(together with us)** will enjoy the same **peace** for they too have suffered. Paul continually remembers the common lot of Christians and is always ready to remind his readers that he and they stand together before God and his mercy. It would be erroneous to go on from this to argue that since this addition is typical of him we have evidence here for the authenticity of the letter (so von Dobschütz, followed by Frame, Rigaux, etc.). The introduction by the writer of a reference to himself when addressing his readers is a common characteristic of much N.T. writing (Heb. 12.7–11, 25; 13.7–16; 1 Pet. 2.24; 3.13–18; 5.1; 1 Jn 2.1, 24–9; 3.11; 5.13f) and is to be expected at a time when all Christians experienced strongly their togetherness.

The judgement of God (v. 5) will take place **at the** (ἐν is temporal 7b–8a but may also be instrumental if it is by means of the parousia that judgement takes place) time when Jesus re-appears: this is his **revelation** (ἀποκάλυψις; cf. A. Oepke, *T.D.N.T.* III, pp. 556–92; Rigaux, pp. 204–6). Elsewhere in these letters Paul uses the term 'parousia' and only at 1 Cor. 1.7 the present word (we find it later in 1 Pet. 1.7, 13 and the cognate verb in Lk. 17.30). Basically it carries the idea of the uncovering of a secret and so is used by Paul

257

of the disclosure of the nature of God and of his activity in accordance with the root's use in the LXX. It is not then a simple equivalent of parousia but implies the appearance of one who has been hidden since his earthly life. (The root has strong eschatological connections elsewhere, e.g. Rom. 2.5; 1 Cor. 3.13; 2 Th. 2.3, 6, 8.) There is no record of its employment in our present connection prior to Paul though the concept may go back (so Frame) to that of the hidden Son of Man who will appear (1 En. 48.6; 62.7; 4 Ezra 13.32; 2 Bar. 39.7; cf. 29.3). At the moment **the Lord** (the appropriate title in an eschatological context: cf. 1 Th. 3.13; 4.15, 16, 17; 5.2; etc.; cf. 'day of the Lord') **Jesus** is in **heaven** with God; **from** there (cf. 1 Th. 1.10; 4.16) he will come in judgement just as God himself is depicted as coming in the O.T. (Isa. 64.1; Ps. 18.9). In his descent he will be accompanied by **the angels of his power.** This is a difficult phrase: **his** by position probably qualifies **power** only but may also qualify **angels** ('his angels of power') though this is unlikely if **power** is the major concept; the phrase does not mean 'his powerful angels' (a genitive of quality) or 'the angels of his host' (implying a play on the Hebrew word חַיִל which can mean both 'power' and 'army'; cf. English 'force') or 'the angels by which he exercises power' (genitive of the object), but probably 'the angels which belong to his power' (possessive genitive). Frame argues, without much supporting evidence, that a particular class of angels is intended (cf. 1 En. 61.10; T. Jud. 3.10). The **revelation** of the Lord will thus be one of **power** (cf. 1 Th. 1.5 for **power** and Mk. 9.1 for the parousia as in power) in which he will be accompanied by **angels;** these are a constant feature of the End in apocalyptic literature (e.g. Zech. 14.5; 1 QM) and the N.T. (Mt. 13.39, 41, 49; 24.31; 25.31; Mk. 8.38; 13.27; Lk. 12.8f; see notes on 1 Th. 4.16); their presence emphasizes the majesty and might of God (or Christ).

8a Equally in the O.T. theophanies regularly take place amid **fire** (Exod. 3.2; 19.18; Deut. 5.4; Dan. 7.9f; Isa. 66.15). **a flaming fire** is literally 'a fire of flame'; we would expect 'a flame of fire', and this is indeed found in some MSS (B D Ψ G) but is to be rejected as a correction probably under the influence of Isa. 66.15; 29.6; Dan. 7.9; etc.; there is adequate support for our reading (ℵ A P K L; cf. Acts 7.30 for a similar variation). In Exod. 3.2 the LXX B-text has our phrase (cf. Sir. 8.10; on the whole textual tradition see P. Katz, "Εν πυρὶ φλογός', Z.N.W. 46 (1955) 133-8).

The **flaming fire** emphasizes the glory of the appearance of the Lord, an appearance like that of a theophany. A few commentators take the reference to **fire** with the following reference to judgement (the verse division of Greek texts is badly placed here and ought to follow **fire**) and think of fire as a purificatory agent, in which way it is certainly used elsewhere (Mt. 25.41; Mk 9.43, 48; 1 Cor. 3.13–15; 1 Pet. 1.7; 4.12), but here the structure of the sentence makes it much easier to take it with what precedes. A greater number of commentators (e.g. Lightfoot, von Dobschütz) give it both references, but **fire** has no place in the subsequent description of the judgement and 'of flame' would be unusual in this connection: we would expect something like 'of purification'; if moreover the phrase depends on Exod. 3.2 the **fire** is not there purificatory but is descriptive of a theophany. Other LXX passages have influenced Paul's words, in particular Isa. 66.15 where we find the idea of 'repayment' (cf. v. 6) and of **vengeance** (v. 8b) in association with 'a fiery flame'.

For simplicity we have commenced a new sentence here though 8b the Greek continues with a participle διδόντος (**inflict**) agreeing with **the Lord Jesus** (v. 7). In v. 5 God was judge; now it is Jesus (cf. 1 Th. 4.6; 2 Th. 2.8; 2 Cor. 5.10); Paul moves easily between the one and the other often attributing to Jesus as Lord what in the O.T. is the activity of God. Jesus' judgement exacts **vengeance**; the word (ἐκδίκησις) can take the simpler meaning 'punishment' (2 Cor. 7.11; 1 Pet. 2.14) but: (i) it has the sense **vengeance** in Rom. 12.19 (= Deut. 32.35); Lk. 18.3, 7; Acts 7.24; Heb. 10.30; (ii) in Scripture God's punishment is regularly viewed as retributory; (iii) the idea of recompense is already found in our passage (cf. 'repay', v. 6); (iv) where the phrase **inflict vengeance** appears in the LXX it has this meaning (Ezek. 25.14, 17; 2 Kgdms. 4.8; 22.48; Ps. 17(18).48). If Jesus inflicts **vengeance** Paul does not think of this as vindictive; it is 'repayment' (v. 6) to those who have sinned because of their sin; otherwise God's judgement would not be righteous (v. 5).

Before describing the nature of God's retribution Paul specifies those on whom it will fall: **those who do not know God and do not obey the gospel of our Lord Jesus.** Many commentators distinguish two groups here: the first member, drawn from Jer. 10.25, describes Gentiles, for Jews cannot be said not to **know God** and elsewhere Gentiles are described in this way

(Jer. 10.25; Ps. 79(78).6; 1 Th. 4.5; cf. Rom. 1.28); the second member then describes Jews, for disobedience is the characteristic of the chosen people (Rom. 10.16, 21; 11.30–2), or Jews and Gentiles because the latter also can be described as disobedient (Rom. 11.30–2). This latter possibility is very difficult since it destroys any sense of balanc⁎ in the total phrase and nothing in the context suggests that we interpret it in this way; the former is more natural since Paul does regularly parallel, or contrast, Jews and Gentiles. If it is to be accepted Gentiles will be seen as the actual persecutors and Jews as those who instigate them; however 1 Th. 2.14 does not suggest that the Jews had any share in the persecutions other than those of the initial period of the community's foundation. More generally there are no real grounds for dividing the phrase into two groups of people for: (i) Jews can be described as those who do **not know God**: Jer. 9.6 (LXX v. 5); Jn. 8.55; (ii) when Paul quotes Jer. 10.25 at 1 Th. 4.5 he makes the reference to Gentiles explicit by retaining the word in the quotation; here he drops it; (iii) because of this very omission it may be doubted if Paul is in fact quoting Jer. 10.25; this runs 'the Gentiles who do not know you (God) and the generations which do not call upon your name'; the second member here would have served his purpose as well as the second member he has supplied. Paul is therefore probably forming the complete phrase *ab initio*, though using O.T. words, and does not intend to categorize two classes of people (the repetition of the article does not imply two categories) but rather to emphasize the enormity of their action. It is not only that men, whether Jews or Gentiles, have persecuted Christians but in doing so they have shown what kind of people they really are: they **do not know** (though οἶδα is used, knowledge here is much more than intellectual apprehension; cf. Mk. 14.71; 2 Cor. 5.16; Tit. 1.16; Jn. 7.28; it implies faith and acceptance and so the reference is not to the 'ignorant' heathen who have never heard of the true God) **God** and they **do not obey** (obedience is the basic attitude of the Christian to God growing out of his faith; cf. Rom. 1.5; 6.16ff and can be used in places where we might expect 'faith', e.g. Rom. 15.18; 16.19) **the gospel** (obedience is offered through the gospel to God; cf. Rom. 10.16; 2 Th. 3.14; Rom. 6.17; for **gospel** see notes on 1 Th. 2.2ff) **of our Lord Jesus** (Paul normally speaks of the 'gospel of Christ'; the choice here is probably dictated by the eschatological context in which

Lord and **Jesus** have been echoing throughout the two letters). Paul is not describing how God deals with pagans as such but only with those who by their desire to persecute have shown their fundamental rejection of God; thus this passage cannot be used to argue about the ultimate fate of all non-Christians. But can persecutors really be described as those who **do not know God** and **do not obey the gospel?** Does the gospel become so apparent to them in the lives of those they persecute that they can be said to reject it? May not persecutors act in ignorance of what they are really doing? To these questions Paul would presumably have answered 'No!', but we cannot be so sure that this is the correct answer. And is not the word **vengeance** over strong? Even if we set aside any idea that God is motivated by vindictiveness does not Paul appear to suggest here that it is only when God is rejected that he takes vengeance; the persecutors are punished, not because they have persecuted (repaid by God the evil they have done), but because they have rejected God? Do such people require from God an 'eternal destruction' (v. 9)? Yet the whole N.T. stresses that ultimate issues hang on men's decision for or against God in Jesus Christ.

Paul now turns from those on whom God will take vengeance 9 to the nature of the vengeance itself: **who** (οἵτινες, generic, 'such people'; cf. Rom. 1.25; 1 Cor. 3.17; Gal. 4.24, 26; Phil. 4.3; see Bl.–Deb. §293; Moulton–Turner, pp. 47f; Moule, pp. 123f) **will pay the penalty** (a frequent idiom in classical Greek but found only here in the N.T.; as Masson remarks, it is strange to find it in the middle of so much apocalyptic and O.T. language) **of eternal destruction.** These last two words have given offence to many sensitive souls: Does Paul actually mean that the wicked will be annihilated once and for all? Does he believe that they will suffer everlasting punishment? The word **destruction** (ὄλεθρος) has already appeared in 1 Th. 5.3 (= 'disaster'); here unlike that passage it is used as a theological term. It is found also in 1 Cor. 5.5 where it refers to physical illness and death (cf. Acts 5.1ff) and implies a literal destruction of the flesh following on excommunication, and in 1 Tim. 6.9 where it is put in parallel with ἀπώλεια but where we cannot be sure that it refers to the fate of the wicked hereafter and not just their present fate. In none of these passages (including v. 9) is annihilation suggested; instead the idea is that of 'punishment' as something which takes place in an active way. This is true also of the use of the word in the LXX, e.g. Jer. 31(48).3, 8, 32; Ezek. 6.14; 14.16; the idea of annihilation may however be present in Wisd. 1.14 (cf. 2.1ff). How is this affected by the qualification **eternal** (cf. H. Sasse, *T.D.N.T.* I, pp. 197–209)? This adjective can mean 'characteristic of the age (to come)' (αἰών is used in the LXX to render עוֹלָם 'age'), or 'everlasting', and carry the nuances (*a*) 'of a different quality' (so in Jn. 'eternal life' can be life partaking of the quality of the age to come, in which case it approximates to the first meaning); (*b*) 'final, ultimate' (for the coming age is the last age); in this case the sense of infinite duration may be lost. Is Paul then referring to ultimate or everlasting annihilation? Almost certainly not, for: (i) The following phrase suggests that Paul sees the punishment of persecutors as consisting in separation from the Lord; for this to mean anything they would have to continue to exist. (ii) In many other parts of the N.T. this separation is regarded as one of suffering continuous punishment (Mt. 18.8f; 25.41; Jude 7) and nowhere is annihilation implied. (iii) Equivalent expressions to our phrase are found in 1 QS 2.15; 5.13, and in these passages the wicked are not considered to be annihilated (cf. 2.7, 8, 17; 4.12–14), and in Ps. Sol. 2.35; 15.12f (cf. 3.11), where again 2.34f; 15.10 do not suggest annihilation (cf. also 4 Macc. 10.15A). The Jew could speak of **destruction** without implying annihilation because in such a punishment 'all that makes life worth living is destroyed' (H. A. A. Kennedy, *op. cit.*, pp. 123f, cf. pp. 121ff, 314ff; cf. also Vos, *op. cit.*, pp. 294ff.) For Paul 'there would probably always remain in the background the notion of a dreary, wretched existence, removed by the whole infinitude of God from that which he designated "Life" ' (*ibid.*, p. 315), and this indeed is what is implied by separation from God. It is probably wrong to speculate too much on the meaning of **eternal**; the Jew was not interested in metaphysical infinitude; so long as existence continues in the age to come persecutors will be separated from God. (In 1 En. 10.10 eternity is defined as 500 years, and the word is even used in secular Hellenistic Greek of the duration of an emperor's reign; see M. & M., s.v.) If we allow the adjective to carry also its nuance of 'ultimate' it implies that the persecutors need not expect a change from **destruction** to salvation at some distant point in time. We cannot go on from here to the moral lesson that decision about Christ bears eternal consequences. Paul is not referring to all men but only to persecutors and he is not even addressing and warning them but describing to his readers what actually happens. The sense 'everlasting, of infinite duration' is to be rejected but the meaning 'characteristic of the age to come' may well be present; the punishment of persecutors belongs to the next and not to this age.

Persecutors will be separated **out from the presence** (cf. 1 Th. 2.17) **of the Lord** (i.e. Jesus) . . . Unlike later Christian apocalypses, contemporary Jewish apocalypses and even parts of the N.T. (Mt. 25.41, 46; Mk. 9.48f; Lk. 12.5; Rev. 14.6ff; 20.9f, 14f; 21.8; Jude 13; these passages are all very restrained compared with the detailed descriptions of later Christian writing) Paul nowhere describes the fate of the wicked as one of active torture and punishment; with him the emphasis is negative, viz. separation from the Lord. ἀπό, **out from,** has been taken in other ways: (i) As causal; cf. Mt. 13.44; Lk. 12.57; the Lord effects destruction by his presence and glory. (ii) As denoting origin (ἀπό and ἐκ are interchangeable in Hellenistic Greek; cf. Jn. 1.44–6); destruction comes from the Lord; **presence** would then seem otiose. (iii) As temporal; cf. Rom. 1.20; but when the temporal use of ἀπό is intended this is normally made clear by the immediate context and to state it now would add nothing to 'at the revelation' (v. 7). Against these alternative senses we may argue: (i) separation from the Lord as punishment balances Paul's description of the fate of Christians who are to be with the Lord (1 Th. 4.17); (ii) banishment from the Lord as punishment is also found in Mt. 7.23; (iii) our phrase is a quotation from Isa. 2.10, 19, 21 where it has our meaning; this is not affected by the omission of 'fear' from the quotation; (iv) the spatial sense is normal with the preposition (for the fuller phrase cf. Acts 5.41; Rev. 12.14; 20.11) and in the spatial the causal is included for Paul would undoubtedly hold that the Lord is the cause of the separation of persecutors from himself (the destructive effect of the presence of the Lord is seen in Ps. 34.16; Jer. 4.26). To be separated from the Lord is to be deprived of him, and therefore of all hope; the victims are abandoned completely to themselves (cf. Sartre's play *Huis Clos = In Camera*). This is a more terrible punishment than everlasting torture. Yet even allowing for the negative nature of the punishment there is a quite different atmosphere here from that of Rom. 11.25ff; we earlier noticed a similar change between 1 Th. 2.16c and Rom. 9–11; in later letters Paul modified his eschatology to a less harsh position.

By the omission of 'fear' from the Isaianic refrain (2.10, 19, 21) Paul has not only removed a possible active element in the punishment ('fear' would suggest torture etc.) but has also made the parallelism of the two phrases much stronger, as indeed it is in the Hebrew but not in the LXX. God's glory is there wherever he is present and it is the same with the **glory** of Jesus; this glory is not mere show but proceeds from his **might** (genitive of origin) and is accordingly powerful. This **glory** will only be fully revealed in its **might** at the last and it is from this glory that the persecutors will be expelled, just as it is this **glory** which the persecuted will enjoy (1 Th. 2.12; and see notes on **glory** there).

10   Paul now turns to the fate of the persecuted, not that in dealing with their fate he is any more precise than he was over the persecutors, and this again is in sharp contrast with many Jewish and Christian apocalypses. He emphasizes, not the happy condition of believers **when he** (i.e. Jesus at his parousia) **comes** (ὅταν with the aorist subjective implying a precise event whose exact timing is indefinite), but the manifestation of the glory of their Lord, in which believers will in some way participate (v. 12). This is described with two parallel phrases of which the first **to be glorified in his saints** is probably inspired by Ps. 88(89). 8(7) for the verb ἐνδοξάζεσθαι is relatively rare in the LXX and appears only here and in v. 12 in the N.T. (The regular form is the uncompounded verb.) ἐν is again repeated after the verb but its significance is not easy to determine. In Ps. 88 it clearly has the local meaning 'in' ('in the council of the holy ones') but once 'council' is omitted this local sense may disappear though it could remain with the slightly altered nuance 'among', thus incorporating 'council' into itself. If we accept this here, and it is the obvious meaning, then we have to give **in** a different sense when the verb re-appears in v. 12 (see notes there); could the meaning change so quickly with such a rare word? The preposition **in** could also be taken instrumentally (Jesus is glorified by means of his saints) or causally (Jesus is glorified because of his saints; for the idea cf. Acts 15.3; Gal. 1.24; for causal ἐν cf. Moulton–Turner, p. 253), of which the latter may be the more probable since the verb and preposition are used in this way in Isa. 45.25; Sir. 38.6. This interpretation leaves unexpressed by whom the Lord is glorified (Frame suggests the angels) but it may not be necessary for this to be either explicit or implicit since it is

not mentioned in the parallel O.T. passages. This understanding of **in** is also possible in v. 12. Yet this is not its most natural meaning nor does it fit easily the flow of the sentence which at this point is magnifying the Lord in his parousia as he judges; the causal sense draws attention away from him to his saints. Yet if we insist that the meaning is the same in v. 10 and v. 12 this sense must be accepted in view of the unique nature of the phrase. Whichever sense we adopt it is also grammatically possible in the second phrase **marvelled at in all who believed.**

What does it mean that the Lord at his parousia should be **glorified** (in the O.T. it is God who is glorified but in the N.T. the conception is also attached to Christ and in relation to his parousia, Mk. 13.26; 1 Pet. 4.13) in the sphere of his **saints**? Though in Ps. 88 the reference is to angels it is almost certainly here to believers because of the parallelism of the two phrases and because the earlier contrast of persecutors and persecuted now demands a reference to the latter; **saints** ('holy ones') has both meanings (see on 1 Th. 3.13); the parallelism also excludes any idea that Paul has Jewish and Gentile Christians in mind in the two clauses; nothing in their context or content suggests this or makes one clause more appropriate than the other to either group. It may be true that the saints participate in the glory of God (Rom. 8.18, 30; Phil. 3.21; Col. 3.4) at the consummation but this is not in view here though it does enter at v. 12, for there is no parallel possible in the second phrase (believers do not participate in being **marvelled at**). The Lord returns and meets with his saints (1 Th. 4.16f) and among them is **glorified** and **marvelled at;** it is they, of course, who glorify him and marvel at him (this solves the question of the subject of the verbs). **marvelled at** renders another word from the LXX (θαυμάζειν) but it is unlikely that Paul is inspired by any particular text, let alone that he is quoting one; Ps. 67(68). 36(35 ℵ text) is usually suggested. The Lord will be marvelled at among **all who believed** (τοῖς πιστεύσασιν; aorist participle); we would have expected a present participle, 'all believers'; the aorist focuses attention on a past act of belief; it is possible that the phrase is regarded as spoken looking back from the time of the parousia to the whole life of the believer as a single event, but this presupposes a somewhat remote parousia and no consideration of those alive at the time; it is therefore preferable to suppose that Paul has in view the actual historical position of his readers: they began to believe at a point in the past. This is confirmed in the next clause where Paul again relates what he is saying directly to them. Why does Paul say **all**? Is it a reference to the division of 1 Th. 4.13–18, the dead and those alive at the parousia, or to division within the community between some who are uncertain of their salvation or fearful at the prospect of persecution and those who are not? Paul has probably nothing of this in view. In his letters he constantly brings in **all** and similar words, stressing universality without particular significance (cf. 1 Th. 1.2).

The next clause, in which Paul takes up **believed,** is really a parenthesis, the kind of thing which takes place so easily in dictation or in the revision of the copy. The Thessalonians are reassured that though they have been persecuted it will be among ('because of', if the causal meaning of **in** is chosen) them as among nameless others that the Lord will be **glorified** and **marvelled at:** despite their present suffering they will not be separated from the final glory of Christ as their persecutors will. **brought to you** (ἐφ' ὑμᾶς) by position probably goes with **testimony;** ἐπί carries the sense of motion absent in the simple dative or in ἐν or παρά (among you). The **testimony** is of course the gospel which Paul preached to them and not merely his teaching on eschatological questions, as is shown by the references to belief, i.e. committal to Christ or God. Paul speaks of 'our gospel' (1 Th. 1.5; 2 Th. 2.14) and 'our preaching' (1 Cor. 15.14) and so here of 'our testimony' (in the translation we have absorbed the 'our' into **we brought**); he does not possess the gospel but the human agent is always necessary for its preaching; **testimony** must in every case be the testimony of someone (cf. Rom. 10.14ff).

on that day, the final words of the long sentence which began at v. 3, have often been taken to be specially stressed by their position after the parenthesis. But if Paul did intend to write them and if he unexpectedly inserted the parenthesis their position would be natural and the insertion of the parenthesis would not lay further emphasis on them. They may indeed be an echo in Paul's mind of Isa. 2; we have seen that in v. 9 he made use of the refrain from that chapter and twice it is followed by the phrase 'on that day' (Isa. 2.10f, 19f). The **day** for Paul is 'the day of the Lord' (see on 1 Th. 5.2), the day on which all that has been described in vv. 5–10 will take place.

Various suggestions have been made about the origin of vv. 6–10 in view of their rhythmic structure, especially the number of parallelisms reminiscent of Semitic poetry. Is Paul quoting a pre-Pauline Christian hymn or adapting a Jewish hymn about the coming of the Lord? If the latter then obviously certain phrases have been either altered by Paul or freshly inserted by him, e.g. in v. 7 **Jesus,** in v. 8 **the gospel of our Lord Jesus** (the original might have been 'the word of the Lord', though it is difficult to see why Paul would ever have changed such a phrase), in v. 10 **who believed** and the parenthesis. It is therefore improbable that Paul is adapting a Jewish hymn; but what of a Christian (cf. Bornemann)? Outside the sections which are clearly indebted to the O.T. almost all the vocabulary is Pauline, as a glance at R. Morgenthaler, *Statistik des Neutestamentlichen Wortschatzes,* Zurich and Frank-furt-am-Main, 1958, will demonstrate. If the hymn is pre-Pauline it is certainly Hellenistic rather than Palestinian because the quotations are not drawn from the M.T. but from the LXX; the classical expression δίχην τίνειν **(pay the penalty)** implies the same. The Pauline vocabulary is not then due to Paul's translation of an Aramaic hymn. Consequently we conclude that Paul himself is the author, though this does not mean that he was putting all of it together for the first time when he wrote this letter; he may well have used this teaching about judgement at the parousia many times and it will have gradually fallen into a rhythmic structure. There are many passages in his letters which show he had a feeling for language.

Paul has reminded the Thessalonians of Christ's coming, of the 11 judgement that will take place and of the reversal of earthly values so that persecutors will be punished and the persecuted like the readers themselves will be released to be with the Lord; now **with this in mind** (εἰς ὅ: the connection is weak, certainly not causal and probably not telic; it takes up a general reference to what precedes) he writes that he is **always praying for** them (cf. 1 Th. 5.25). Paul is not now offering his prayer, though the opening sentences in a letter can include intercession (Phil. 1.9), but informing them how regularly he prays for them; yet in actual fact his statement comes very near to being itself a prayer. What is the particular relevance of **also?** It is hardly likely that Paul is replying to a letter from the faint-hearted (so Frame) assuring them that he has them in mind (cf. pp. 249, 252) nor does **also** contrast **we** with anyone else who may be praying or **you** with anyone else who may be prayed for (i.e. 'you Thessalonians' as well as other Christians); it more probably qualifies **are praying** and indicates that as well as giving thanks for the way in which they live (1.3ff) Paul also intercedes for them. It is, however, very possible that the word has almost no significance; frequently in Paul καί after a relative pronoun may simply be omitted in translation (e.g. Rom. 5.2; 1 Cor. 1.8; 4.5; cf. Zerwick, §463). The difficulties commentators have found with it may indeed indicate that we should omit it here. Paul prays **that** (ἵνα often loses its telic sense in Hellenistic Greek and regularly has the simple meaning **that**; so here it gives the content of Paul's prayer rather than its purpose; in a prayer the two can often not be clearly distinguished; cf. 1 Th. 4.1; Moule, pp. 145f; Moulton–Turner, pp. 103f) **our God** (note the change from the second to the first person: he who prays and those for whom he prays acknowledge the same God) **may make you worthy of his call** (there is no pronoun **his** in the original but Paul could conceive of no one other than God as the 'caller'). Is God's **call** the future invitation to the eschatological kingdom (cf. Mt. 22.3, 8) or the past call which became effective when the Thessalonians responded to the gospel and which in the final analysis is a-historical or pre-historical (see on **election** in 1 Th. 1.4)? Although Paul elsewhere, with the one exception of Phil. 3.14 (where it is clearly qualified so that the future reference is brought out and where it may be passive denoting not the act of calling but its resultant state), regards God's call as past (or occassionally as continuing in the present; cf. 1 Th. 2.12) some commentators prefer the former alternative; they do so because they reject our rendering of ἀξιώσῃ as **make worthy** preferring its much more frequent meaning 'deem worthy' (where either meaning is possible it always has this latter meaning in the N.T.; Bauer, s.v. suggests Ep.Diog. 9.1 as an instance of our sense). Whatever decision we make about **call** and **make worthy** we have to force one of the words into a sense contrary to Paul's normal usage and we might hesitate to choose were it not for the following clause which speaks of the activity of God, **powerfully accomplish,** in a way that fits much more happily with **make worthy** than 'deem worthy'; the order of clauses, 'deem worthy', **accomplish,** would also be difficult; we should expect the reverse. We note that the difficulty here is somewhat similar to that with the verb δικαιοῦν, a verb of similar formation. Paul's total theology does not allow us to say that

God deems men righteous in the sense that he treats them as righteous even though they are not, which would be immoral. Nor does it allow us to say that he slowly or suddenly makes them righteous. Rather they are righteous in the same sense that they are sons of God, though just as they have to work out a son-like character so they have to work out their righteousness. This is the Pauline paradox of the indicative and the imperative. The imperative is impossible without the preceding indicative. In this sense 'deem worthy' is the necessary preliminary for being worthy and yet 'deem worthy' is not a moral fiction but something real; they are worthy. Consequently **make** is the better English rendering here since 'deem' carries a fictitious sense within it. But if God did not deem them worthy they could not become worthy and he could not make them worthy, and there would be no point in Paul exhorting them to live worthily (1 Th. 2.12).

The Thessalonians have been called (cf. 1 Th. 2.12; 4.7; 5.24) and responded at a time when they were not worthy; they are not yet worthy; they cannot make themselves worthy; only God can do this and Paul prays that he will. Does this mean that they may fail? God will not reject the prayer of Paul, but may they reject the work of God? If their freedom is to be maintained we cannot deny this possibility (see on 1 Th. 1.4); Paul leaves open the possibility of his own failure (1 Cor. 9.27; Phil. 3.11f) and that of others (Gal. 5.4; 2 Cor. 6.1; Phil. 2.12) including the Thessalonians themselves (1 Th. 3.5; 5.8–11); the very fact of prayers for the eschatological salvation of believers seems to imply this possibility (cf. 1 Th. 3.13; 5.23).

Parallel with this is the clause **and may powerfully** (lit. 'in power', but best translated as an adverb; for the idea cf. 1 Th. 1.5; the power of God is set in contrast with the weakness of men) **accomplish** (with the sense 'completely accomplish') **every . . .** The Thessalonians are moving along the way of goodness but they are by no means at the end of the journey. In 1 Th. 3.10 Paul had recognized deficiencies in their faith and wrote seeking to supplement what was lacking; there is no clash with what he writes here, for he himself, or some other missionary or pastor, will be the means through which God's purpose is fully accomplished (cf. 1 Th. 3.12). The areas in which Paul prays that God will bring to fulfilment the Christian character of the Thessalonians are identified in two parallel phrases. The second is relatively straightforward: **every** (though not repeated in the Greek **every** goes with both phrases) **effort of faith.** The phrase is the same as that of 1 Th. 1.3 ('achievement of faith'), and lacking any convincing argument to the contrary there is no reason for not taking it in much the same way, i.e. with **faith** as a genitive of the subject: the **effort** is begotten by **faith** (see on 1 Th. 1.3; it could also be taken as a genitive of apposition, 'achievement which is faith', but this does not sound Pauline). **effort** is not to be limited to endurance under suffering but should be given as wide a meaning as possible: ultimately it is love which issues from faith (Gal. 5.6). The first phrase **every resolve for goodness** is more difficult. In Biblical Greek εὐδοκία **(resolve)** on the vast majority of occasions refers to the divine will; only Rom. 10.1 and Phil. 1.15 are exceptions to this in the N.T. Some commentators therefore take this phrase to refer to God's will for (man's) **goodness** (ἀγαθωσύνη regularly denotes human goodness and the phrase cannot then be 'God's good will'). However this breaks the parallelism with the second phrase; in order to preserve it von Dobschütz forces the latter into the meaning 'God's work of faith'. In addition to the breaking of the parallelism we note that the only two places where **resolve** is used of men are both in Paul and since he only uses the word six times (four if he did not write Ephesians) it would not be surprising if he used it here in this way. If the parallel between the two phrases is strict then the first will mean 'every resolve proceeding from goodness' (genitive of the subject) but if this is not so 'every resolve whose object is goodness' would be satisfactory and make better sense. The **resolve** of the Thessalonians for **goodness** and the **effort** coming from their faith are not theirs but God's. So Paul prays that God will **accomplish** these fully in them.

12   Paul prays for God to work in the Thessalonians **so that** (ὅπως is usually confined to final clauses in the N.T.; Moulton–Turner, p. 105) **the name of . . .** Are we to take this with the majority of commentators as referring to eschatological glorification as in v. 10 or to present glorification with Rigaux, von Dobschütz, etc.? It is difficult to substantiate the latter view. Rigaux suggests that **in virtue of the grace** (see on 1.1) **of our God . . .** could not apply to the time of the parousia but must relate to the present life of believers; this is so but the phrase can be taken to govern the whole of vv. 11f, a kind of afterthought of Paul to emphasize further the point that the entrance of believers into the

future kingdom depends ultimately on God's mercy. That Paul deals elsewhere with the present glorification of the believer (e.g. 1 Cor. 6.20) is no argument that he is doing so here. If the words **that the name of** the **Lord may be glorified** are drawn from Isa. 66.5 (and this is by no means sure since Isa. 66.5 has the simple verb δοξάζειν and not the compound; see on v. 10) then we have seen already (v. 8) that Paul used words from Isa. 66.15 with eschatological reference and presumably he regarded this chapter in Isa. as eschatologically oriented. Above all the whole tenor of 2 Th. 1.3ff is eschatological and it would take strong arguments to force us to see in v. 12 a movement from this, and an alteration in meaning in a word unique to Paul in v.10 and v. 12 to make it refer to the present existence of believers. God is changing believers now (v. 11) so that glorification can take place at the End.

There is however one variation from v. 10: the introduction of **name.** This makes somewhat more precise the object of glorification. The **name** plays an important part in the religions of contemporary and earlier Hellenism and in Judaism (cf. H. Bietenhard, *T.D.N.T.* V, pp. 242–83); it is 'a power which is very closely associated with the bearer and which discloses his nature. Pronouncement or invocation of the name sets in operation the energy potentially contained in him' (*ibid.* p. 243). Thus when **the name of our Lord Jesus** is glorified it means that Jesus is glorified as Lord (cf. Phil. 2.9–11); it is the power of lordship which is operative in him. So when in John 12.28 Jesus says, 'Father, glorify your name', glorification takes place in relation to God as Father. In our text the Lordship of Jesus is openly revealed and made fully operational at the parousia, and at this time Jesus will be glorified as Lord (Phil. 2.9–11)—although naturally Christians are already glorifying him as their Lord in their earthly lives. **Lord** is the title constantly used in acclamations of Jesus (cf. Kramer, *op. cit.*, §§15ff). In the glorification of the name there is a reciprocal relationship: **in you and you in him** (grammatically **in him** could be 'in it', i.e. 'in the name' but **the name** is not an independent entity; when it is named it is its bearer who is in mind). If we assume that **in you** means 'among you' this interpretation is impossible for **in him.** If the latter is taken as 'within him' (whatever that may mean) then it is possible to understand **in you** as meaning 'within each one of you', but Paul, who normally thinks socially, would have spelt out such an individualistic conception more clearly. We could take **in** as instrumental: 'by means of you, by means of him'; glory is brought to the name of the Lord by the presence of the saved Thessalonians at the parousia and glory is brought to the Thessalonians at the same moment through their Lord; the Thessalonians could have no glory but for Christ (and this may be the significance of the following clause **in virtue of the grace ...**). The causal meaning of **in** (see on v. 10) can also be taken reciprocally: the Lord is glorified because of his saints (i.e. because of their salvation) and the saints are glorified because of him (i.e. because of his saving power). It hardly means 'by' in the sense of agent which would be differently expressed, i.e. the saints acclaim the Lord, the Lord acclaims the saints. Probably a combination of the causal and instrumental meanings is to be preferred. The participation of believers in the glory of the parousia, which is Christ's glory, is found also in Rom. 8.18; Col. 3.4; Phil. 3.21 (cf. 1 Cor. 15.43); this sharing in glory is not however confined to the parousia but already begins on earth since Christians and Christ form one body (cf. Rom. 8.30; 2 Cor. 3.4–11).

In the Greek there is only one article governing **God** and **Lord** and the final phrase could be rendered, 'our God and Lord Jesus Christ', implying that Jesus Christ is explicitly named as God. There is only one other place where Paul can be said to apply the term God to Christ, viz. Rom. 9.5. Here a great deal depends on the punctuation, but even if θεός (God) is referred to Christ it does not mean that he is identified with God but only that he is divine (cf. F. J. Leenhardt, *Romans*, London, 1961, *ad loc.*). Elsewhere Paul studiously avoids terming Christ as God and often writes in such a way as to indicate his subordination to God (1 Cor. 3.23; 11.3; 15.28; Gal. 4.4). But he also often attributes the same activities to both: like God, Christ judges men (1 Th. 3.13; 4.6; 2 Th. 1.7f); the gospel is his (1 Th. 3.2; 2 Th. 1.8) as it is God's; there is the word of Christ (1 Th. 1.8; 2 Th. 3.1) as there is the word of God; both are glorified (2 Th. 1.10, 12). By the early second century Christ was being unambiguously termed God (e.g. by Ignatius) and if our letter is non-Pauline and late this may be the meaning. But is this the meaning if the letter is Pauline? We note that 'our God' with the article is frequent in our letters and that **Lord Jesus Christ** without the article is a regular formula in Paul; he could therefore have added it to **our God;** this would be all the more likely to happen if he was dictating; anyone who has listened to extemporary prayer will know how traditional phrases pile in on top of one another and dictation of liturgical material (vv. 11f are such) is a very similar process. (There is evidence elsewhere in Paul's letters of literary carelessness probably attributable to dictation.) The words could even be a gloss added by himself when reading through the letter before sending it off. This is more probable than von Dobschütz's suggestion of a later gloss. On the question of the deity of Christ see R. Bultmann, 'Das christologische Bekenntnis des Ökumenischen Rates', *Glauben und Verstehen*, II, Tübingen, 1952, pp. 246–61; R. E. Brown, *Jesus: God and Man*, London, 1968, pp. 1–38; A. W. Wainwright, 'The Confession "Jesus is God" in the New Testament', *S.J.T.* 10 (1957) 274–99.

THE END 2.1–12

Now we beg, you, brothers, in connection with the parousia of our Lord Jesus Christ and our being gathered to him, (2) not to be readily shaken out of your sanity nor continue anxious because of a 'spirit' or oral statement or letter purporting to come from us saying that the Day of the Lord is present. (3) Let no one deceive you in any way. For unless first the apostasy takes place and there is revealed the man of rebellion, the son of doom, (4) who opposes and exalts himself against everyone called God and every sacred object so as to sit in the shrine of God proclaiming that he himself is God ... (5) Surely you remember that while I was with you I told you these things? (6) And now you know the *katechon* so as him to be revealed in his time. (7) For the mystery of rebellion is already set to work; but the *katechon* is now until he is out of the way. (8) And then the Rebel will be revealed whom the Lord [Jesus] will slay with the breath of his mouth and will destroy by the manifestation of his parousia; (9) the parousia of the Rebel is through Satan's activity in all power and signs and wonders intended to deceive (10) and in every deceit of wickedness towards the perishing, because they did not receive the love of the truth so as to be saved. (11) And for this reason God sends

273

on them a power of delusion to make them believe what is false (12) in order that all who have not believed the truth but delighted in wickedness may be condemned.

Paul has heard that the Thessalonians are in danger of being misled by some who say that the End has already taken place and he writes to reassure them (vv. 1f). He does this by reminding them of what they already know: there are certain events which must take place before the parousia of Christ (vv. 3–8); here our lack of knowledge of what he had originally taught makes it exceptionally difficult for us to pin down his allusions precisely. He envisages a final outburst of Satanic activity (vv. 6–10) which Christ will utterly defeat (v. 8); but there will be those who will be so deceived by Satan that they will not be saved but justly condemned (vv. 9–12).

1   There is no contrast with the preceding passage for Paul frequently uses **Now** (δέ) and **brothers** when introducing new aspects of his subject and even new subjects (cf. 1 Th. 2.17; 4.13; 5.1). **beg**: this is the word we have rendered **ask** at 1 Th. 4.1; 5.12. Bjerkelund (see on 1 Th. 4.1) takes our verse as another example of the formula he detects elsewhere in Paul's letters but here the phrase precedes part of the thanksgiving (2.13–17) and is differently phrased (the ὑπέρ and εἰς τό clauses are not found elsewhere). Paul is alarmed by the news of false conceptions about the parousia and so he writes **in connection with** it (ὑπέρ is equivalent to περί; cf. Moule, p. 65 and 1 Th. 3.2; there is no justification for the rendering of the K.J.V., 'by', as if it were a formula of adjuration). **our being gathered** renders a noun ἐπισυναγωγή which is closely linked to **parousia** for one article governs both; throughout the remainder of vv. 1–12 this conception is not stressed; here it explains part of the importance of the passage by giving a reason why Christians are interested in the parousia and have no need to fear it; after the parousia they will be with their Lord (cf. 1 Th. 4.13–18; 5.10); it is a point on which the Thessalonians needed encouragement. While the noun is rare in the N.T. (otherwise only at Heb. 10.25) both it and the cognate verb were used for the re-gathering of the dispersed Jews into Palestine (Isa. 52.12; 2 Macc. 1.27; 2.7, 8); in this connection it could quickly take on an eschatological significance and it is used in that way in Mt. 24.31; Mk. 13.27 (cf. Mt. 23.37; Lk. 13.34; T. Naph. 8.3; T.

Asher 7.7; Did. 9.4; 10.5). It is not clear whether emphasis lies on the act of gathering or on the community as gathered; probably on the former (cf. Heb. 10.25) since **parousia** also contains the idea of movement. This gathering together would take place at the parousia and the gathered community exist thereafter.

Verse 2 gives the object of **beg** (on εἰς τό cf. Moulton–Turner, 2 p. 143; Burton §412). Throughout the history of the church when Christians have thought too much about the parousia they have become unsettled; it was therefore only natural that in the primitive church where its nearness was especially felt believers should easily be **shaken** (σαλεύειν, used basically of what happens in a storm, was quickly given a metaphorical meaning) **out of** their **sanity**. The last phrase is literally 'shaken out of mind'; 'mind' (νοῦς) is used by Paul 'for man when the reasoning faculty is determinative, for man using his powers of judgement' (Stacey, *op. cit.*, p. 198; cf. pp. 198–205; Bultmann, *Theology*, §19.1; J. Behm, *T.D.N.T.* IV, pp. 951–60). While everyone has a mind that of the Christian has been renewed (Rom. 12.1f) and therefore he ought to be more stable and less **readily** (ταχέως, the adverb is used modally and not temporally and there is no allusion to the shortness of the period since their conversion or since 1 Th.) alarmed by thoughts of the parousia; they are in danger of being carried away by a new idea without adequately examining it. **shaken** (aorist) suggests the sudden onslaught of a storm that is quickly past but leaves its effects in insecure buildings; **continue anxious** (present tense) takes this up: greatly disturbed by some information they have had about the parousia they are now in a continuous state of nervous excitement and anxiety. **continue anxious** (θροεῖσθαι) appears only once elsewhere in the N.T. in Mk. 13.7 (= Mt. 24.6), also an eschatological context. It may well have been an accepted apocalyptic term but it goes too far to say that Paul reflects here a saying of Jesus.

The information that disturbed the Thessalonians is given in the final clause of the verse: **the day of the Lord is present** (ὡς ὅτι, **that**, is practically equivalent to the simpler ὅτι, 'to the effect that'; it does not imply any doubt about what has been reported to Paul; cf. Moulton–Turner, p. 137; Bl.–Deb. §396; 2 Cor. 11.21; 5.19). In determining what this means all we can do is to try and see what Paul thought those who used it meant by it; they may indeed have meant something different but if so we have no means of discovering what. Our understanding of what Paul thought will depend on our understanding of what he refutes in vv. 3–12. There he argues that certain events are to take place before the day of the Lord comes and he depicts that Day as a public and cosmic event. Consequently he must have believed that those against whom he was writing were saying that it had arrived and since his description of it as a public and cosmic event is not explicitly argued we must assume that he believed they also regarded it in this way. If he had thought that they were saying that it was at hand, imminent or impending (though this may be what they thought they were saying) he would have argued differently. Indeed there is no reason to think that Paul would have argued against an imminent parousia as such; there is evidence that he believed this not only in 1 Th. (cf. 1.10; 2.16; 3.13; 4.17; 5.1ff) but also in later letters (Rom. 13.11; 1 Cor. 7.25–31; 15.51; Phil. 4.5). Such an interpretation accords also with the way Paul uses **is present** (ἐνίστημι) elsewhere; it is contrasted with what is future in Rom. 8.38; 1 Cor. 3.22; 7.26 (cf. Gal. 1.4; in 1 Cor. 7.26 it has the sense 'imminent' in an eschatological context showing that Paul would not have disagreed with its use in that sense); 'presentness' accords again with the perfect tense and with the word's normal contemporary significance (e.g. it is used in the phrase 'the current year'); the attempt of A. M. G. Stephenson, 'On the meaning of ἐνέστηκεν ἡ ἡμέρα τοῦ κυρίου in 2 Thessalonians 2.2', *Studia Evangelica*, IV, *T.u.U.* 102, Berlin, 1968, pp. 442–51, to reject this evidence is unacceptable. If it is clear what Paul understood he was refuting it is not clear what those who asserted **the day of the Lord is present** meant. They cannot have believed in a 'realized eschatological' view of the parousia otherwise Paul would not have argued that certain events have still to take place before it but would have corrected their understanding of the nature of the parousia; in any case would 'the day of the Lord' with all its existing futuristic eschatological connections be a suitable term for realized eschatology? Schmithals (pp. 146ff) has argued strongly for a gnostic background. Gnostics believed that with their gnosis they were already raised (cf. 2 Tim. 2.18; Iren. *Adv. Haer.*, I. 23.5; III. 31.2; Gosp. Thomas 51; this conception may also lie behind 1 Cor. 15; cf. Lietzmann-Kümmel, *An die Korinther*, pp. 192f; Barrett, *1 Corinthians*, pp. 347f). Similar ideas are found by many commentators in the Fourth

Gospel: with the coming of the Paraclete the Lord has come and there is no future parousia. There are passages in Paul which could be misinterpreted in this way (e.g. Rom. 6.4ff; 2 Cor. 5.17) but they refer to an event within the life of the believer and not to an external event. If Paul is refuting such views in 1 Cor. 15 he does so by discussing the resurrection of believers; such a discussion, whether explicit or implicit, is not present in 2 Th. In any case gnostic views of the End were by no means as unitary as Schmithals supposes; M. L. Peel, *op. cit.*, has shown that many gnostics did believe in a real end to the universe in which individuals as such were involved and that it is wrong to think of them as interested only in the 'existence' of the individual. There are other passages in Paul apart from those dealing with the resurrection which might have been misunderstood and produced the idea that the Day has already arrived. R. Jewett, 'Conflicting movements in the early church as reflected in Philippians', *N.T.* 12 (1970) 362–90, argues that in Phil. 3.12–15 Paul 'appears to be countering the view that in the spirit one achieves an ultimacy which makes any future resurrection or parousia irrelevant' (p. 373). This again internalizes the parousia and if Paul had been answering such a position he would have used other arguments. Perhaps a better parallel is found in 1 Cor. 4.8 where Paul apparently contests the view of some of the Corinthians that they already 'reign', i.e. have reached the final state; this view could have been derived from passages where Paul suggests a future reigning by the saints (1 Cor. 6.2; Rom. 5.17; 8.17f, 30; this idea was widespread, cf. Eph. 2.6; 2 Tim. 2.11f; Rev. 20.6; Jas 2.5); if Christians could believe that they were already reigning they may have believed that in some way the Day of the Lord had come. The Thessalonians might also have misunderstood Paul's reference in 1 Th. 5.5 to them as 'sons of the day'; if they already belong to the day the Day of the Lord is present. While both these last views appear open to the objection that they to some extent internalize the Day, which Paul does nothing to answer, they do show how the phrase of v. 2 could have originated. It is also possible that those whom Paul writes against believed that the day of the Lord began when the tribulations (the Messianic woes) began, i.e. for them the day of the Lord is not a single event but a complex of events which included the parousia; it is interesting that they say that **the day** ('day' is not necessarily twenty-four hours) **of the Lord** and not the parousia is present. If they had read 1 Th. 4.13–18 they would not have claimed that the parousia had taken place, for they were certainly not raptured. On the other hand in 1 Th. 5.1ff 'the day of the Lord' is an event (whatever the 'day' may be in 5.5), and Paul is their only source of information. Mk. 13.6 is evidence that views like that of 2 Th. 2.2 could exist. Leaving aside all hypotheses about the origin of this saying it is presumably aimed in Mark at people who have been saying that the Messiah has returned and is to be seen in such and such a figure (i.e. that the period of the End has begun) and the counter-argument in Mark follows the same pattern as in 2 Th.: 'not yet . . . until . . .' (vv. 7, 14). At our distance from 2 Th. it is probably impossible for us to determine what those who held the opinion of v. 2 actually believed; and it is equally impossible for us to identify them with any group in the Thessalonian community such as the 'loafers' (1 Th. 5.14; 2 Th. 3.6–13; on the possibility that Paul is answering opponents here cf. pp. 18f, 52).

We have however to ask 'From whom did they get their belief?' **because of a 'spirit' or oral statement or letter purporting to come from us** suggests that they may have claimed that their belief came from Paul himself, or more strictly from Paul, Silvanus or Timothy because of the plural **us** (Silvanus was a prophet according to Acts 15.32). The final words **purporting to come from us** (ὡς δι' ἡμῶν) have some element of uncertainty in them (cf. Moulton–Turner, p. 158; Bl.–Deb. §425.4): either Paul has been misunderstood or the 'spirit', statement or letter was believed to come from him though it did not. We have taken this phrase as applying to all three nouns (Wohlenberg attaches it to the verbs **shaken, anxious,** but they are too remote) but it could apply only to **letter** which it follows, or more probably to **oral statement** and **letter** because these two are found together again without **'spirit'** in 2.15 and because **oral statement** without the article is better with some kind of qualification. But if it applies to the last two nouns then the balance of the sentence is preserved much better if it is in fact applied to all three. To what **letter** does Paul refer? 3.17 has been taken to imply that they have received a letter or letters allegedly from Paul but in fact forged; if Paul had thought they had been deceived in this way he would have made his denunciation of the forgery much clearer; in any case the period between Paul's visit and this letter is very brief for the creation of forgeries

(see also notes on 3.17). If then the reference is to a genuine letter of
Paul, is it to our 1 Th. (cf. 2.15)? What are the possible passages
in 1 Th. which might have been misunderstood? 2.16, judgement
has fallen on the Jews and so the End has come? 3.3f, the Messianic
woes are in existence and so the End is here? 5.4f, Christians are
sons of light and so the End has been fulfilled (suggested by
Schmithals, *Zeit und Geschichte*, p. 306f; for further suggestions
cf. Jewett, 'Enthusiastic Radicalism')? But if Paul thought that
they had misunderstood a passage in 1 Th. he would have answered
by carefully redefining his position (e.g. as in 1 Cor. 5.9–13). This
holds equally if the reference is to any letter unknown to us which
Paul wrote. (If 2 Th. itself is not genuine then 2.2 will hardly
refer to 1 Th. but to an unknown inauthentic letter.) Much more
probable than any of these is the suggestion that Paul himself does
not know where the Thessalonians received their misleading
information, and so he lists three possibilities (cf. the indefiniteness
of v. 3, 'no one'; if 2.15 represents the only two categories in which
he places his own activity this cannot govern v. 2 for here he writes
from the point of view of those he is criticizing). The other two
possible sources which may have misled the Thessalonians are
oral, and are themselves contrasted with one another. A **'spirit'**
($\pi\nu\epsilon\tilde{\upsilon}\mu\alpha$) almost certainly refers to an ecstatic utterance or spiritual
revelation (apocalyptic prophecy rather than glossolalia) inspired
by the Spirit, or possibly from Paul's point of view inspired by a
lying spirit (this may be the reason for the anarthous use of
$\pi\nu\epsilon\tilde{\upsilon}\mu\alpha$); Paul was probably known to exercise ecstatic gifts (cf.
1 Cor. 14.18) and the Thessalonians were accustomed to prophets
(1 Th. 5.19). In contrast to a **'spirit'**, **oral statement** ($\lambda\acute{o}\gamma o\varsigma$)
represents non-ecstatic rational speech (the term is wide enough to
include everything from a single sentence to a complete sermon;
cf. 1 Cor. 12.8–11; 14.6, 26 for the implied contrast). Such rational
speech does not need to be regarded as uninspired (1 Cor. 12.8).
Any oral prophecy or statement made elsewhere by Paul or one of
his associates could have been wrongly reported in Thessalonica
and given rise to the false opinion of our verse. If however we do
not attach **as purporting to come from us** to **'spirit'** and **oral
statement** then it is quite easy to imagine that some of the Thessalonians themselves believed that they had been inspired to give
the information about **the day of the Lord** (cf. 1 Th. 5.19),
probably in the course of a gathering of the community for

worship where addresses and prophetic utterances were normal
(cf. 1 Cor. 14); letters might also be read in such gatherings (see
on 1 Th. 5.27).

3   The element disturbing the Thessalonian community may have
been something other than a 'spirit', statement or letter, and so
Paul warns: **let no one deceive** (unusual prohibition in the third
person aorist singular; cf. 1 Cor. 16.11; 2 Cor. 11.16; Burton §166)
you in any way. Deceive introduces a new note; v. 2 might only
suggest that information has been wrongly understood; now Paul
implies that there may be people whose identity he does not seem
to know but who are misleading the main body of the church. We
cannot conclude that they were deliberately falsifying information,
but the way in which they understood it would bring misunderstanding. The possibility of deceit also appears in the Markan
apocalypse (Mk. 13.5; cf. Mt. 24.4f; 1 Jn. 4.1) in respect of the
nearness of the end and may belong to the apocalyptic tradition
(the Greek words are different here and in Mark but this may only
represent different Greek renderings of an original Aramaic).

Over what are the Thessalonians in danger of being deceived?
It can only be the time of the parousia (v. 2c), for it is with this
that Paul begins to deal in vv. 3, 4. **For unless . . .:** unfortunately
the sentence is unfinished; this often happens when Paul's views
are strong and he is emotionally involved (cf. 1 Th. 2.11f, 19;
Gal. 1.20; 2.4; 2 Cor. 8.13; Rom. 4.16; 5.12ff etc.). We have a
protasis which is generally completed with some such phrase as
'the day of the Lord will not come (be present)'. Recently Giblin
(pp. 122–9) has challenged this and argued that the missing
clause should be something like, 'the judgement of God will not
have been executed against the powers of deception, removing
them once and for all', or 'the Lord will not have come in judgement to end definitely the deception that is the work of Satan'.
The time element would then become relatively unimportant and
Paul would be dealing with the *'qualitative* (Giblin's italics)
aspects of the parousia relevant to the end of a process hostile to
faith, viz., divine vindication against the embodiment of the
antithesis to faith' (p. 135). We may agree with Giblin that Paul is
normally more interested in the conditions that are required for the
parousia than the chronological sequence of events which herald
its arrival (in 1 Th. 5.1ff the image of the thief in the night implies
lack of interest as to dating) yet the context created by v. 2c is such

that any answer must include a strong temporal element. Paul's readers could not be expected to see that he is answering a question other than that which lies in v. 2c unless he made this explicit. We therefore assume that the anacoluthon of vv. 3f is to be completed with a recasting of the words of v. 2c, viz., 'the day of the Lord will not be present'.

What events or conditions require to be fulfilled before the day of the Lord comes? To answer, Paul draws on the oral teaching which he had already given in Thessalonica (v. 5; and see on 1 Th. 5.1), and presumably selects from it those elements which are most relevant; by alluding to them he is able to say enough to show that the day of the Lord has not yet come. Because he selects and because he does not explain the terms he introduces, our understanding of vv. 3f, and later of vv. 6ff, is uncertain. Is there an order in which conditions must be fulfilled or events take place? **first** might suggest that the **apostasy** is to be followed by **the man of rebellion** but it more properly applies to the whole of the protasis over against the unexpressed apodosis (cf. von Dobschütz). **first** does not always have a temporal connotation and may mean 'the first matter to be dealt with'; although there is no explicit 'then' or 'secondly' in what follows, yet the temporal context of v. 2c implies it must have a temporal significance here. (**first** does not come until the end of its clause but its position is not always a safe guide to its meaning; cf. Lk. 9.59 and 9.61 and Giblin, p. 83, n.3.)

the apostasy (ἀποστασία with the definite article) is clearly a term already known to the Thessalonians. While the root is used regularly of political defection in the LXX, the intertestamental literature and the N.T., it almost always has as well a religious reference (e.g. Josh. 22.22; 2 Chron. 33.19; Jer. 2.19; 1 Macc. 1.15; 2.15; Acts 19.9; 1 Tim. 4.1; Heb. 3.12) and this must be the case here (cf. H. Schlier, *T.D.N.T.* I, pp. 512–14; Giblin, pp. 81–8; J. Ernst, *Die eschatologischen Gegenspieler in den Schriften des Neuen Testaments*, Regensburg, 1967, pp. 27–32); this excludes any allusion here to a supposed revolt in the last days by the Jews, or the nations as a whole, against the Roman hegemony. From the time of the Maccabean revolt (1 Macc. 2.15) it was used in relation to attempts by their oppressors to make the Jews forsake their God and certainly some strands of Jewish thought believed that at the End there would be a great apostasy when many of the people of God would defect (cf. Jub. 23.14ff; 4 Ezra 5.1ff; 1 QpHab 2.1ff;

cf. 2 Tim. 3.1–9; Jude 17ff; see also Billerbeck, III, p. 637; IV, pp. 977ff). It was also commonly accepted that a period of great evil would precede the End (1 En. 91.5ff; Jub. 23.4ff; 2 Bar. 27; 4 Ezra 14.16ff) and this became the accepted teaching of the early church (Mk. 13; 2 Tim. 3.1–9; Rev. *passim*). Has the apostasy then been simply transferred by the Christians to themselves, the new people of God? But was an apostasy of the church expected as a prelude to the parousia? This is possible (cf. Mt. 24.11f, 24; 1 Tim. 4.1ff; but the evidence here comes from a much later period than 2 Th.); it is hard to believe that as early as 2 Th. Paul was so pessimistic as to envisage an apostasy of Christians; moreover the N.T. gives the impression that the elect will not fail (cf. also Mt. 16.18); certainly there is nothing in the genuine Pauline letters to suggest that he expected the church to apostatize, and, in particular, he is confident of the ability of the Thessalonians to endure (1 Th. 1.2–10; 3.6–13; 4.15, 17; 5.4f; 2 Th. 1.4, 11f; 2.13). If then the **apostasy** is not of Christians of whom does Paul expect it? Mankind as a whole (cf. Frame)? But apostasy assumes an original relationship to God, and if v. 10 refers to the same event we have a deliberate rejection of the gospel and therefore some original conception of what it is; Rom. 1.18–32 may imply an original relationship to God (cf. von Dobschütz) but the defection it describes is not a future event but already in existence; moreover it is difficult to see an **apostasy** in Rom. 1.18–32 in the light of the word's background. Is it then an apostasy of the Jews (cf. Denney, B. Weiss, *Biblical Theology of the New Testament*, Edinburgh, 1885, I, pp. 305ff)? Had they not already apostatized in the crucifixion of Jesus? The N.T. never uses the term of them with this latter reference. In Rom. 9–11, though not apparently in 1 Th. 2.16, Paul still hopes for their salvation; he would not do so if he already regarded them as apostate. Perhaps, though God's punishment has caught up with them (1 Th. 2.16), he believes (contrary to Rom. 9–11) that in some future, to us unidentifiable, action (when Paul presents the tribute of the Gentiles in Jerusalem?) they will decisively reject the Christian faith which it is still a possibility for them to accept; but the break between Judaism and Christianity is not yet complete and Jews regularly became Christians. Although in the strict sense such a rejection by Jews of the gospel would not be apostasy since they never had adhered to it, yet unlike mankind as a whole their position as God's chosen people was such that they might be accounted apostate (and although a Jew would never claim to be God, v. 4, what might happen could be equivalent to this in the eyes of Paul). Nothing is said about the extent of the apostasy but clearly it will be such as to be easily identified by Christians (Cothenet, *art. cit.* also refers the apostasy to the Jews, not in relation to the parousia but to a separate prior judgement of them). Giblin's suggestion (pp. 84–8) that the apostasy relates to a separation of the good from the wicked has nothing to commend it other than its ingenuity; such a separation at the judgement is scriptural but it is not related to **the apostasy.**

Concomitant with the **apostasy** is the appearance of a figure who is opposed to the divine plan; he is described in a five-fold way:

(i) He is **the man of rebellion** (probably a Semitic phrase though it could occur in Hellenistic Greek; cf. Moulton–Turner, p. 208; Moulton–Howard, pp. 23, 441 and see 1 Th. 5.5; in vv. 8f he is called **the Rebel**), 'the rebellious one'. The name is obviously well-known to the Thessalonians and denotes a figure in whom rebellion crystallizes, who is characterized by rebellion (ἀνομίας, B ℵ 81; the variant reading ἁμαρτίας, A D G it, while strongly supported probably represents the replacement of a narrower term whose meaning was uncertain by a less specific; from it comes the phrase of the K.J.V. 'the man of sin'). ἀνομία, strictly 'lawlessness', rapidly acquired the sense 'against the law', and since the law is the law of God this implies **rebellion** against God. The term is found in other eschatological contexts (Mt. 24.12; Did. 16.4; Freer MS ending of Mk.; 1 John 3.4; cf. R. Schnackenburg, *Die Johannesbriefe*, Freiburg, 1963 on 3.4). Who is the **Rebel** or **man of rebellion?** In v. 9 he is distinguished from Satan as his tool. The attempt of Bousset, *The Anti-Christ Legend*, London, 1896, pp. 136ff, to identify him with Belial (Beliar) has been abandoned by more recent scholars. Is he a man who acts in a rebellious way or is he a supernatural figure? The use of **man** in the term cannot by itself determine the answer in view of the widely prevalent *Ur-Mensch* or primaeval man myth in which the figure is supra-human. Giblin (pp. 66ff) argues strongly that he is a false prophet: 'Man (ἄνθρωπος as here and not ἀνήρ) of God' is used regularly to denote a prophet; apart from this ἄνθρωπος with a defining gentitive does not normally appear in the LXX; therefore our term has been created over against that of 'prophet' and means 'false prophet'; false prophets are common in eschatological contexts (Mt. 24.11, 24; Mk. 13.22; 1 Jn. 4.1; Rev. 16.13; 19.20; 20.10). But is the anti-God figure not normally supernatural? The closest evidence Giblin can produce for a human figure is Or. Sibyl. 3.63–76; but in this passage the 'humanity' of Beliar is not clear and elsewhere Beliar (Belial) is not human. Moreover 'man of God' and **man of rebellion** are not direct contrasts; the genitives 'God' and 'rebellion' do not function in the same way nor are they conceptually similar since one is personal and the other is abstract; it is therefore difficult to see 'man of rebellion' as a deliberate creation to balance 'man of God'. Other characteristics of the figure, as we shall see as the exegesis proceeds, also suggest that Paul has a more than human figure in mind. Since 'rebellion' implies rejection of the law and thus also knowledge of it, and since the law is the Jewish law, the title may suggest some figure coming out of Judaism.

The **Rebel** is **revealed** (ἀποκαλύπτειν). The word (again at vv. 6, 8) is used in contrast to 'the revelation of the Lord Jesus' (1.7). Where is the Rebel before he is **revealed?** Has he a heavenly pre-existence? Is he in the kingdom of the dead or in the realm of Satan (a Nero redivivus)? Has he an earthly hidden existence? From the evidence Paul supplies it is impossible to say where he is concealed; Paul is not interested in his present existence (and we cannot be even sure that he thought of him as having a present existence) but in his appearance, character, activity, and destruction (vv. 8–12). The term 'revelation' does suggest something more than a human figure. Perhaps, however, the rigid distinction we draw between supernatural and human figures was not so clear to Paul for in 1 Cor 2.6, 8 the 'rulers of this age' can be both.

(ii) The **Rebel** is now described as **the son of doom;** this phrase is again a Semitism (cf. Isa. 57.4; 1 QS 9.16, 22; CD 6.15; 13.14); the precise phrase is not known in Hebrew or Aramaic but it would come naturally to the primitive Palestinian church or to Paul. **of doom** does not describe the place from which the Rebel comes nor suggest that he goes to or leads others to a place of destruction (contrast Satan, Rev. 17.8) but refers to his ultimate fate, 'the doomed one' (cf. Rom. 9.22) or, less probably, to his belonging to the realm of doom (as in 1 Th. 5.5 'sons of the light' belong to the realm of light). In v. 8 the nature of this figure's **doom,** in the sense of ultimate fate, is spelt out in more detail.

doom (ἀπώλεια; cf. Kennedy, *op. cit.* pp. 119ff) and 'salvation' are direct contrasts; cf. 1 Cor. 1.18; 2 Cor. 2.15; Phil. 1.28; in v. 10 **the son of doom** is related to those who are doomed **(the perishing).** In Jn. 17.12 our phrase is used of Judas but it is very improbable that Paul has him in mind; he would have to envisage him as returning from the dead to be revealed. More probably **the son of doom** was, at least in Christian circles (for there is no evidence outside these), a term used for an opponent of Christ and the use of the term in Jn. 17.12 represents the dreadful nature of Judas's act in Christian eyes. For Paul he is still future; for John whose eschatology is partially realized he belongs to the past history of the passion. The phrase itself gives us no help in the identification of the figure it represents.

The third, fourth and fifth phrases describing the figure take up 4 the first and expand it; the expansion of the second is found in vv. 8ff.

(iii) He **opposes and exalts himself,** two participles which could possibly be rendered as substantives: 'the opponent and self-exalter'. They are linked by one article and govern the same phrase **against everyone . . .** so that they must be treated in the same way; either both are substantives or both are participles. The first might be taken as a substantive and as a known phrase to denote Satan, for he is 'the opposer' (cf. Zech. 3.1) and etymologically 'Satan' is the 'opponent'; yet our figure is distinguished from Satan in v. 9, the second verb is not a known term and the flow of thought in v. 4 lays emphasis on activity rather than on being (cf. Giblin, p. 64); so both are better rendered as participles. They indicate opposition to and self-exaltation over against **everyone called God:** nothing is said as to the success of this activity and the participles may indeed imply no more than that the figure attempts to oppose and exalt himself. Against whom is this activity directed? Is **everyone called God** to be interpreted as everything to which men legitimately give the name God or as every so-called God (cf. 1 Cor. 8.5)? The former will include the God acknowledged by the Christians, the latter will not. It is difficult to see how Paul could really envisage opposition to heathen deities alone as evil, indeed he could quite easily view the true God as opposed in this way to heathen Gods regarded as evil by nature (Gal. 4.8; 1 Cor. 10.19f), and so we must choose the other alternative. Whatever men set up as their Gods to worship, and this includes the true God, is opposed by this rebellious figure, i.e. he is utterly evil and opposed to whatever is good in any religion. And so also he is opposed to **every** (taking πάντα to govern both nouns) **sacred object,** i.e. every object used in worship (cf. Wisd. 14.20; 15.17; Josephus, *Ant.*, 18.344).

(iv) Of the objects associated with worship the principal is the **shrine** (ναός, the innermost part of the temple in comparison with the whole temple area, τὸ ἱερόν) in which the God himself is believed to dwell. To **sit** (aorist, 'he takes his seat', and not, 'he continues sitting') is to display the minimum of respect and to make the maximum claim to deity, for God sits; it is not to sit alongside other Gods in a pantheon but to take a unique place. ὥστε with the aorist infinitive does not necessarily imply that the purpose was fully accomplished but only that it was intended and set in being. (The variant reading which adds 'as God' is poorly attested and unnecessary because this is made clear in what follows.) But what and where is this **shrine?** In Jerusalem? In heaven? Is it the people of God? Or is the phrase used purely metaphorically to indicate the pretensions of the Rebel? In view of the many difficulties of interpretation the last may seem the easiest solution but without positive evidence in its favour it is difficult to believe that Paul would use such a concrete term, filled with so much meaning, as a mere metaphor. Even though the preceding clause includes a reference to pagan Gods **the shrine** is certainly not in a heathen temple for the definite article **the** implies that Paul has a particular shrine in mind. This immediately suggests the Jerusalem temple. Its defilement was an apocalyptic theme (Dan. 9.27; 11.31; 12.11; Mk. 13.14), though the defiler is regarded as standing or set up rather than as sitting and may indeed not be a person but an object, e.g. the statue of himself which Caligula attempted to introduce. If the apostasy (v. 3) is that of the Jews then do we have to envisage someone whom the Jews view with high regard as taking divine honours to himself and establishing himself in the temple? The context implies that those in apostasy are linked with the Rebel. It is however difficult to conceive of any Jew seating himself in the shrine with Jewish approval unless he put himself forward and was accepted as their Messiah (cf. Targ. Zech. 6.12f, and perhaps Mal. 3.1; see also L. Gaston, *No Stone on Another*, Supplements to N.T. XXIII, pp. 147ff). The apostasy would then be the acceptance of a wrong Messiah. If instead we think of the heavenly temple (the writer to the Hebrews envisages such a temple and the idea is found more widely, e.g. Ps. 11.4; T. Levi 5.1f; 1 En. 14.16–18, 20; 2 Baruch 4.2–6; b Hag. 12b; cf. R. J. McKelvey, *The New Temple*, Oxford, 1969, pp. 25–41) we have the difficulty that this takes the Rebel away from earth and assumes a warfare in heaven; while much mythology supports such an idea it is outside the area of direct human knowledge and in 2 Th. 2 it is assumed men can be aware of it as it happens (it is one of the signs of the parousia). However the heavenly temple is often regarded as coming down from heaven at the End and becoming the new or restored temple on earth (McKelvey, *ibid.*). The attempt of the Rebel to sit in this might well be appreciated by men, but when it is put in this way there is really not so much difference between this and the view which takes it to be the existing Jerusalem temple. It is not however clear whether the heavenly temple comes down before, during, or only after the end of the holy war. Very different from both these views is Giblin's revival (pp. 76–80) of the idea that the temple is the church. It is true that Paul calls the church **the shrine of God** (1 Cor. 3.16f; 2 Cor. 6.16; Eph. 2.21) and may have taught this to the Thessalonians but the attempt of the Rebel to sit in this temple would be equivalent to an apostasy within the church, the kind of situation which earlier Protestant scholars held to be true in relation to the Pope; as we have seen Paul does not conceive in any way of an apostasy within the church.

(v) The final clause **proclaiming** ($\dot{\alpha}\pi o\delta\epsilon\iota\varkappa\nu\dot{\nu}\nu\tau\alpha$: the meanings, 'show, display, prove', though more common are unacceptable since they indicate success unless we take the participle *de conatu* 'attempting to prove') **that he himself is God** is an expression of what sitting in the Temple implies, nothing more or less than the claim to be God. Who could make such a claim? It is very difficult to see Giblin's 'prophet' doing so, especially if he comes out of a Judaeo-Christian background in this early period. A pagan might make the claim (cf. Philo, *Leg. ad Gaium*, 162; Or. Sibyl. 5.33f) but even then hardly the claim to be **God** but only the claim to be one God among others though even this would have been unacceptable and blasphemous to Jews and Christians. An eschatological opponent of God might also make the claim (Asc. Isa. 4.6) but would one do so who was not the ultimate opponent which Satan is (v. 9) and the Rebel is not? There are then many difficulties in the identification of the Rebel and our lack of information on Paul's original oral teaching prevents us solving them. These difficulties are not in any way lessened when we realize that in these verses Paul has also been dependent on O.T. passages which, even if there are no direct quotations, have influenced both his language and his thought. Dan. 11.31, 36 (Theod.); Ezek. 28.2, 6, 9; Isa. 14.13f introduce the ideas of profanation of the temple, of sitting on a throne and of claiming to be God. In all these O.T. passages the original claim related to historical personalities; Dan. 11.36 refers to Antiochus Epiphanes who first entered the temple, plundered it and later placed an altar to Zeus in the sanctuary; this left a strong impression on the apocalyptic tradition and seems to have been revived in A.D. 41 by Caligula's attempt to set his own effigy within the temple. If such eschatological language could be applied to humans may not Paul also have a human in mind? If he is making a direct reference to some person or event in the history of that period we do not know who or what this was. Caligula was dead, Nero did not become emperor until A.D. 54 and did not reveal himself as the persecutor of Christians until long after that. Unlike Dan. 11.36 the figure of 2 Th. 2.3f shows no 'royal' characteristics and there is no reason, if he is historical, to think of him as 'royal'. More probably then he is supra-human and certainly not an impersonal principle of evil (so Lightfoot) nor a collectivity of persons succeeding one another in history; the use of 'man' and son' cannot be construed in these ways, and Paul does not expect a long period of history but an almost immediate end (cf. J. Schmid, 'Der Antichrist und die hemmende Macht', *Theologische Quartalschrift*, 129 (1949) 323–43. 'The Anti-Christ': cf. Guy, *The New Testament Doctrine of the 'Last' Things*, Oxford, 1948, pp. 146–9; Vos, *op. cit.*, pp. 114ff; Billerbeck, III, pp. 637–40; B. Rigaux, *L'Antéchrist et l'opposition au royaume messianique dans l'Ancien et le Nouveau Testament* (Paris, 1932); Bousset, *op. cit.*, Ernst, *op. cit.*). The **Rebel** is often termed the Anti-Christ but Paul does not call him this. It is an appropriate term since he is the eschatological opponent of Christ (not of the historical Jesus). The term itself appears in 1 Jn. 2.18 (cf. 4.3; 2 Jn. 7) but nowhere else in the N.T.; in the Johannine epistles there is a multiplicity of Anti-Christs but Paul's Rebel is a unique figure. In Mk. 13.21f; Mt. 24.23f we have the similar term 'false Christ' which came later to be almost interchangeable with Anti-Christ. The opponent of Christ in Rev. 13.17 is more correctly an Anti-Christ, though he is not so described there, and the term may possibly also be applicable to Mk. 13.14, if this describes a 'person'. The Anti-Christ was thus a definite figure in Christian thought towards the end of the first century. It does not appear to have been either a term or an idea current among the Jews, though Judaism did envisage eschatological opponents to God. 2 Th. 2 is thus itself one of the steps in the creation of the Anti-Christ concept. Many of the characteristics of the Rebel, e.g. his self-exaltation, his entry into the temple, are also seen in some of those who had oppressed the Jews in the immediate past, e.g. Antiochus Epiphanes, Pompey, Caligula; sometimes these features are also attached to non-historical figures (e.g. the 'abomination of desolation' in Daniel) who may represent historical persons but who, once the historical period of their reference was past, might become detached from an anchorage in history and become 'mythically' oriented. It has also been suggested that the figure of Beliar (Belial) in the O.T. and in the inter-testamental literature is a predecessor of the Rebel but Beliar appears rather to be a prototype of Satan (Paul identifies him with Satan in 2 Cor. 6.15 and this is also true of the Qumran literature). In Asc. Isa. 4 Beliar is certainly Anti-Christ, but this work, or at least this section of it, is not Jewish but Christian and, dating from the end of the first century, reflects thought later than the Thessalonian letters. On the other hand the phrase 'men (man) of Beliar' could be part of the background (for the phrase cf. Deut. 13.13; Judg. 19.22; 1 QS 2.4f; 1 QM 4.2). There is undoubtedly some relation between 2 Th. 2 and Mk. 13; the latter is a combination of traditional Jewish apocalyptic ideas and prophetic or apocalyptic sayings of Jesus which have been worked over in the early church. The Anti-Christ figure may well have begun to crystallize into something like its present form around the time of Caligula's attempt to desecrate the temple. Among the ideas common to Mk. 13 and 2 Th. 2 the so-called 'abomination of desolation' is parallel to the Rebel for both appear to be involved in sacrilege and self-exaltation (cf. also Mk. 13.5 and 2 Th. 2.3, 11 in relation to deceit; Mk. 13.22 and 2 Th. 2.9 in relation to signs). This supports the view that in our passage Paul is giving traditional primitive Christian apocalyptic teaching.

Paul abruptly breaks off the sentence of vv. 3f (see on v. 3) in 5

order to remind the Thessalonians that he is not really saying
something new (**told** is an imperfect tense implying that during his
original visit he must have given repeated apocalyptic instruction).
His words, phrased as a question, have almost a touch of impatience
as he recalls them to his teaching. Since they themselves know the
conditions of the parousia they ought to have been able to answer
those who said that the Day had come. He drops into the first
person singular but the change from the plural is not nearly so
sudden as in 1 Th. 2.18; 3.5, in both of which it is emphasized
by the use of ἐγώ; there are no plurals in the immediate vicinity of
v. 5 and the singular may well represent a moment of forgetfulness
on Paul's part as he animatedly drives home his point (cf. the
anacoluthon of vv. 3f); he was very conscious of what he himself
had taught.

6   In Greek as in English **now**, νῦν, can often be a logical particle
introducing a new point, but it is almost certainly temporal in the
present context which deals largely with the relation of events and
'persons' to one another. What is the temporal contrast? (i) It
may refer back to v. 5, 'you now know . . .' as opposed to earlier
instruction given 'while' Paul had been with them. If this means
that they are now being given information which they had not
previously known so that they may have an answer to v. 2c, then
we would expect νῦν δέ ('but now'); further, the information about
the **katechon** which follows does not read as if it was new to them
for: (a) **katechon** is clearly a term with which they are familiar;
(b) details in vv. 6f are so slender as to be incomprehensible without
earlier teaching. Finally, if **now** is as closely associated with **know**
as this interpretation requires then the two would probably be
together in the Greek. (ii) **now** may contrast with **time,** but **time**
is balanced much better against **already** in v. 7 and **now** would
then have to be closely associated with the **katechon** ('the present
katechon') which is difficult because of its position (cf. Bl.–Deb.
§474.5c). (iii) **now** should be given a perfectly general reference,
'and at this present time', contrasting with the discussion of future
events in the remainder of the passage (cf. Frame). Such a solution
is grammatically the simplest and is assisted if we accept the
understanding of **know** (οἴδατε) for which Giblin (pp. 159–66;
cf. Plummer) has argued: **know** does not relate to information
which Paul gave on his visit or is giving now but to 'experience' or
'awareness'. They are **now** aware of, experience, understand, the

katechon. Earlier Paul had taught them about the **katechon** (it is included in 'these things', v. 5); since then they have come to understand or experience his activity, and so they ought to be able to appreciate why the day of the Lord has not yet come. **katechon** (for the meaning of this term which we transliterate because of its difficulty see note after v. 7) reappears in a slightly altered guise in v. 7; both here and there it is a present participle; here a neuter and there a masculine.

The relationship of the following clause, **so as . . .,** is difficult. Does it depend on **katechon** or on **know?** Who is **him?** The clause is introduced by εἰς τό with the verb in the infinitive; Paul normally uses this (cf. Burton, §§407–11) to indicate purpose but sometimes to indicate result or tendency and even sometimes for the direct object (cf. 1 Cor. 11.22). Giblin (pp. 206f) has shown that when Paul uses it elsewhere it depends on the nearest verb, which here is **know; katechon** moreover would not have a clause depending on it because though a participle it does not in fact behave as a verb; it is really a title (note the use of the article with it and the assumption that it is familiar to the Thessalonians). But to attach the clause to **know** is awkward since **know** already has a direct object; nowhere else does Paul use εἰς τό after **know,** and only at Phil. 4.12 (*bis*) and 1 Th. 4.4 does he use an infinitive in any construction after it. If we examine the occasions where Paul uses a noun as direct object of **know** and then follows it with another dependent clause (e.g. Rom. 13.11; 1 Cor. 2.2; 16.15; 2 Cor. 9.2; 12.3; 1 Th. 1.4f; 2.1; cf. 4.2ff) we see that the dependent clause relates to, amplifying or explaining, the idea contained in the noun. We must allow that in each case (except 1 Cor. 2.2. where the textual evidence is uncertain) the noun follows **know** but there are too few instances to create a rule and if Paul wished to stress the noun, as he seems to here, there is no reason why he should not allow it to precede the verb.

Who is to **be revealed?** Within the context it could be Christ (in his parousia, v. 2), the man of rebellion (vv. 3f) or the **katechon** (v. 6). The first is improbable because of its remoteness. The third is unlikely because **him** would not then be normally expressed in Greek as it is here and because it is masculine whereas **katechon** is neuter; it is possible that since in v. 7 the **katechon** does become masculine the masculine **him** might be intended to prepare for this and deliberately expressed because of the change of gender.

However since vv. 3, 8 also refer to the revelation of 'the man of rebellion' the reference is most probably to him here also. The revelation of the Rebel is thus in some way related to the **katechon**. At whose **time** does this revelation take place? There is a difference of reading in respect of **his**: either ἑαυτοῦ (reflexive, 'his own': B אᶜ D G 1739, *et al.*) or αὐτοῦ ('his', א* A K P); if we read the former the reference must be to **him**, i.e. the Rebel; if we read the latter it could be either to **him** or to the **katechon** (either is grammatically possible since the masculine and neuter are indistinguishable in the genitive). **time** (καιρός, see on 1 Th. 5.1) in addition to its general meaning relating to dates and the passage of time has the special meaning 'appropriate, appointed, decisive, due time (moment, hour)' and this is the sense here; almost invariably elsewhere in Scripture it is God who determines the time of events and people, especially of those with an eschatological reference. The **his** of **his time** cannot refer to God but **his time** may mean that God has appointed a time for whoever is referred to in **his**: since some relationship exists between the **him** and the **katechon** it may not be important to decide to which of them **his** refers for the **time** of both will be controlled by God; all Jewish and Christian apocalyptic testifies to God's ultimate control over even Satan the final enemy. But it is possible that in the present instance the controller of the **time** is not God; a number of terms (revelation, parousia, mystery, signs and wonders) which are normally applied only to God are here applied to anti-God forces and **time** may be also if the **katechon,** as Giblin holds, is opposed to God. If the **katechon** is friendly towards God the **time** will naturally be that set by God, and of course God may also fix the time of hostile powers and forces.

7   An explanation **(For)** is now given of the preceding: evil is at work and a limit is set to the time of its activity.

the mystery of rebellion is a strange phrase to which there is no exact parallel in the N.T. though there are many references to the **mystery** of God (1 Cor. 4.1; Col. 2.2; Rev. 10.7), of Christ (Eph. 3.4; Col. 4.3), of the kingdom (Mk. 4.11), of the gospel (Eph. 6.19), etc. All these suggest something which has been previously secret but is now known to believers. On **mystery** see G. Bornkamm, *T.D.N.T.* IV, pp. 802–28; R. E. Brown, 'The Pre-Christian Semitic concept of "mystery"', *C.B.Q.* 20 (1958) 417–43; 'The Semitic Background of the N.T. *mystêrion*', *Bib.* 39

(1958) 426–48; 40 (1959) 70–87; J. Coppens, '"Mystery" in the theology of Saint Paul and its parallels at Qumran' in *Paul and Qumran* (ed. J. Murphy O'Connor), London 1968, pp. 132–58. The closest parallels to our phrase appear in 1 QH 5.36; 1 Q 27.1, 2, 7; 1 QM 14.9, but in each case we have the plural 'mysteries of sin (etc.)'. If there is any parallel in the usage of v. 7 to that of the N.T. generally it will imply that believers know about the **rebellion** though it is a mystery to outsiders. It does not mean 'the mysterious rebellion'; possibly it means 'the mystery which consists in rebellion' (i.e. **rebellion** is a genitive of apposition); more probably it means 'the secret rebellion' (cf. Frame, Rigaux, p. 272; this view may be supported by the frequent reference to 'revelation' with which it contrasts). Just as salvation is now an open secret to Christians so also is the force which works against God. This mystery of rebellion is **already** active. Paul is not making here a general statement about the universe, viz., evil is working in it, or he would not have added **already**; he is writing instead about the eschatological period which has begun and in which he and his readers live. The apostasy has not taken place, nor has the Rebel appeared (vv. 3f) but **rebellion** even now opposes God; this rebellion will culminate in the revelation of the man of rebellion who will be utterly vanquished by Christ in his parousia (vv. 8ff). Is the **mystery of rebellion** at **work** (ἐνεργεῖται) on its own or has it been set to work by God? This depends on whether the verb is treated as middle or passive (see on 1 Th. 2.13; in the N.T. the root is reserved for the activity of supernatural powers, satanic and divine). If the verb is passive then we should probably regard God as the one who sets the mystery of rebellion to work (to the apocalyptic writer even evil is under God's control) or less possibly it is the **katechon** or the Rebel who does so. If the verb is middle then the clause is descriptive, and does not specify the origin of the activity. In favour of the passive is the subject **mystery;** in the other passages where this appears as a subject it always governs passive verbs; if **the mystery of rebellion** is a fixed phrase it may be middle and take the sense 'rebellion is at work in secret'. Will the Thessalonians see the mystery of rebellion active in the work of heretics who mislead them with false teaching or in their harassment by the Jews or their fellow-countrymen (1 Th. 2.14) or in a 'holy war' waged in the supernatural sphere? (The suggestion of von Dobschütz that Paul refers to the general moral decay of the time is most improbable; see on **apostasy,** v. 3.) We lack the information to give an answer; history has shown that almost any evil can be seen as eschatologically oriented by someone who thinks the End is near.

The remainder of this verse runs literally 'only the **katechon** now until he (it? cf. A. Strobel, *op. cit.*, pp. 107f; the translation will only be 'it' if, as is most unlikely, the subject of 'out of the way' is the 'mystery of rebellion') is out of the way'. The first part of this requires a verb but what is to be supplied? It must either come from the context or be a part of the verb 'to be'. If **katechon** is treated as primarily verbal (it is a present participle) and not as a name it could provide the verb, 'the **katechon** exercises his function . . .' (cf. Giblin, pp. 210–16; he actually prefers an imperative using Rev. 22.11 to suggest a 'law' operative under apocalyptic conditions and he gives 'only' concessive force). The Vulgate runs along this line '. . . qui tenet nunc, teneat donec . . .' If however **katechon** is primarily a substantive it is easier to take either 'is' (γένηται) from the following clause (or to supply 'is' = ἐστίν which gives the same meaning) or 'is at work' from the preceding clause: 'only the **katechon** is now until he is out of the way' or 'only the **katechon** is at work now until he is out of the way'. The latter by using the same verb may identify too closely the **katechon** and **the mystery of rebellion** which would be impossible for some theories of the identity of the **katechon;** the former is both easier and implies no such identity and by giving **out of the way** a future reference indicates that the **katechon** (which if a substantive is also a functional substantive) is present and active. But there is yet another possibility; there may be no ellipsis of the verb; Gal. 2.10 suggests that the **katechon** may be placed out of position for emphasis and we could render 'only until the "now" **katechon** is out of the way' (cf. Plummer, Lightfoot). This gives practically the same meaning as when we supply 'is' and leads to something like our rendering though this is based on the supposition of an ellipsis of 'is': but ('only', introducing a unique condition) **the katechon** (a masculine form; though the form is different we assume that it has the same ultimate meaning as the neuter in v. 6) **is now until he** (the subject of this clause is unexpressed and must therefore be the same as in the first) **is out of the way** (ἐκ μέσου is not found elsewhere in Biblical Greek in this way but similar phrases suggest this is its meaning; cf. Rigaux). **is out of**

the way is a statement of fact with no indication how it will be carried out; there is no reason to take it pejoratively. It implies that whatever the activity of the **katechon** it will eventually cease.

The Katechon

From our exegesis of vv. 6f we can set down certain factors which must be taken into account in discussion of this term.

1. **katechon** appears only as a present participle, once in the neuter (v. 6) and once in the masculine (v. 7). Lacking any evidence to the contrary we assume that both refer to the same reality under different aspects and for simplicity we have referred to this reality as 'it'.

2. The term is already known to Paul's Thessalonian readers.

3. The term has not been found elsewhere in Jewish or Christian Greek eschatological writings except those dependent on 2 Thess.

4. The meaning of **katechon** will be a normal and not an unusual meaning of the verb, unless there is strong evidence to the contrary.

5. The term, though a participle, is not given a complement.

6. It is now active (cf. **is now,** v. 7) and exercises its function in such a way that believers know (cf. **know,** v. 6; **mystery,** v. 7).

7. There is a temporal limitation on its activity (cf. **until he is out of the way,** v. 7; **and then,** v. 8).

8. It stands in some relationship to the **Rebel** (vv. 6b, 7b–8a).

9. The **mystery of rebellion** is active in at least a part of the same period as the **katechon.**

10. After Thessalonians it apparently disappears from Christian teaching (any satisfactory theory ought to account for this).

11. An individual is involved (the masculine participle). Attempts to define the **katechon** as a collective body of people have usually been dogmatically motivated in order to account for the period between Paul and the present, and reveal an unwillingness to admit that Paul expected the parousia soon. They have been severely criticized by J. Schmid, *art. cit.* If it was a succession of individuals the **katechon** could not be a true sign of the nearness of the parousia.

Since **katechon** is a verbal form its meaning must derive from the verb and will not have changed through frequency of use, for it was current during only a short period. The verb has a wide range of meanings in the area 'hold fast, gain possession of, be master of, occupy, prevail' (cf. L & S; Giblin, pp. 181ff). The interpretation of **katechon** is necessarily related to its meaning.

The traditional interpretation which goes back at least to Tertullian and was widely accepted among the Fathers thereafter takes the verb in the sense 'restrain' and regards the Roman empire as the restraining power (neuter) and the emperor as the restrainer (masculine). This gives a simple explanation for the appearance of both neuter and masculine forms and clearly fulfils (6) above. It is supported by the undoubted protection Paul received from the Roman power against Jewish persecution (e.g. Acts 18.12ff; 25.1–12; cf. 1 Macc. 8; 12.1–4; Josephus, *Ant.* 12. 414–19) and the favourable view which he had of it (Rom. 13.1–7). The very vagueness of the reference accords with similar vague references in apocalypticism, for the civil authorities must not know they are intended. Daniel and Revelation show that historical personages and powers could quite easily play apocalyptic roles. It has indeed been supported with the suggestion that **katechon** is a word-play on Claudius = *claudens*, the restrainer. Despite its early acceptance this interpretation faces grave difficulties: (i) The whole tone of the passage is against the identification of anything or anyone in it with historical events, powers or persons. (ii) There is no idea of Rome as a restraining force in other parts of the apocalyptic writings, though the fall of Rome is an apocalyptic sign; where Rome does appear in this literature it is almost always as an enemy of the people of God (e.g. Rev. 17). (iii) It is hard to see what is meant by saying that the Roman emperor will be 'out of the way' (v. 7). (iv) There does not appear to be any real connection between the empire or emperor and the date of the parousia of the Rebel or that of Christ.

Since the late nineteenth century the historical interpretation has gradually been rejected in favour of a mythological. In the form suggested by Dibelius (see his excursus on 2.10) and widely accepted the background to this view is the myth of the binding of Satan who, released at the End to persecute the saints, is defeated by Christ in his parousia. Clearly in 2 Th. 2 mythological overtones surround the figure of the Rebel. The binding and release of Satan is a well-known eschatological theme (Tob. 8.3; 1 En. 10.4f, 11f; 18.12–19.2; 21.1–6; 54.4f; T. Levi 19.12; Jub. 48.15; Rev. 20.2); in one Christian apocalypse, Acts of Pilate 22(Descensus 6).2, the very root **katechein** is used of Satan's detention. On this mythological view we must assume that it is the Rebel and not Satan who is held fast by the power of the **katechon**; this is a minor variation since there are forms of the myth in which evil spirits are bound. There are more serious difficulties (though it must be allowed that whatever the solution mythological ideas had already certainly coloured the eschatological climate): (i) This interpretation does not satisfactorily identify the **katechon**; in Rev. 20.2 it is an angel who binds Satan; is the katechon then an angel? Angelic powers might be referred to by this term. Otherwise the **katechon** must be God, Christ or the Spirit and the term is surely a very odd way to refer to any one of them; there would appear to be no reason for not introducing them directly by name. (ii) 'out of the way' is a very strange way of referring to the release of the Rebel by a heavenly power. (iii) No explanation is offered for the use of both masculine and neuter forms of **katechon**. (iv) In so far as the man of rebellion is held fast this would suggest that 'rebellion' would be absent, yet 'the mystery of rebellion is' at 'work' (v. 7). (v) How can the Thessalonians be said to experience or understand (**know**, v. 6) this **katechon?** (vi) 'Detain' in prison is not a normal meaning of **katechon**. (vii) In the myth the 'restraining' or 'detaining' is linked to punishment of the evil power; there is no trace of this here.

Dissatisfaction with both these interpretations has led recently to the development of a number of new theories; many of these had been suggested or hinted at in earlier writers; it will not be possible to trace back their history or even to outline all of them.

O. Cullmann, 'Le caractère eschatologique du devoir missionaire et de la conscience apostolique de S. Paul', *Revue d'Histoire et de Philosophie religieuse*, 16 (1936) 210–45 (cf. *Christ and Time*, pp. 164–6), has argued that since early Christianity believed that the end was delayed until the gospel had been preached to the Gentiles (e.g. Mk. 13.10; Mt. 24.14) the **katechon** (neuter) was this preaching. This itself was a transformation of the Jewish idea that the End was delayed until Israel would repent. Paul was intensely conscious of his own apostolic position as the preacher *par excellence* to the Gentiles (Gal. 1.16; 2.7) and therefore he saw himself as the **katechon** (masculine). Obviously this interpretation is impossible if Paul did not write 2 Thessalonians. Cullmann fails to integrate Paul as **katechon** into Pauline theology and he does not show clearly how Paul's being 'out of the way', presumably his death, permits the Rebel to be released. J. Munck, *Paul* *and the Salvation of Mankind*, London, 1959, pp. 36–42, accepted Cullmann's view of **katechon** and sought to support it by a wholly new interpretation of Paul in which he is seen as the one who offers up the Gentiles to God and by his death brings in the End. This interpretation has come under severe criticism. Special difficulties for our problem arise because the basic idea of the delay of the parousia until the repentance of Israel, by which all Israel was meant, is replaced by the conversion of a few 'representatives' of the Gentiles. Moreover as we have seen it is in the Thessalonian epistles that Paul is least conscious of his apostolicity (cf. use of **apostle** in 1 Th. 2.6f and its omission in the address of both letters). In 1 Th. 4.13–18 Paul expects to be alive at the parousia and therefore can hardly be 'out of the way' (v. 7), i.e. die, in order to allow the End to take place. The meaning 'delay' for **katechon** while possible is not one of its more common meanings and if Paul had been translating the alleged Hebrew equivalent עבל he would hardly have chosen **katechon.** If this is the explanation why should Paul have been so secretive about it? Though many references in the apocalyptic writings are deliberately vague because of fear of the civil authorities openness here would have caused no trouble. Would the Thessalonians so soon after Paul's departure have been able to believe that he had already preached the gospel at least representatively to the Gentiles ('the day of the Lord is present'), and if this was the meaning would Paul not have denied it more clearly?

Giblin has made a clean break with most current interpretations by proposing to take the **katechon** as a force and/or person hostile to God (see especially pp. 167ff). Such a hostile sense had been suggested earlier but never developed with so much detail; cf. L. Sirard, 'La Parousie de l'Antéchrist, 2 Thess. 2.3–9', *Analecta Biblica* XVII–XVIII, Rome 1963, pp. 89-100; D. W. Robinson, 'II Thess. 2.6: "That which restrains" or "That which holds sway"?' *Studia Evangelica*, II, *T.u.U.* LXXXVII, 1964, pp. 635-8. Giblin points out that the whole passage is taken up with hostility and translates the term as 'seize', arguing that it has normally a pejorative force in Paul; he then links this to a use of the word in relation to the ecstasy or frenzy of a prophet. He supposes that falsely inspired prophets had misled the Thessalonians about the day of the Lord (v. 2). This 'seizing force' was most apparent to them in one particular 'prophet', the **katechon** (masculine). His ousting is a condition of the manifestation of the man of rebellion who is destroyed by the Lord Jesus, and this is the day of the Lord. This explanation must be commended for the attempt to derive it out of the Thessalonian situation which would explain why we do not hear of it elsewhere in Paul. But there are grave difficulties: (i) If the **katechon** is a hostile figure why is a stronger expression than 'out of the way' not used in v. 7? Giblin accepts that this phrase is neutral and should be rendered in a neutral way but immediately employs the translation 'ousted' which has a pejorative sense. (ii) As Giblin admits (p. 240) while the passive of **katechein** can mean 'be possessed' it is unusual for the active, as here, to have this meaning. (iii) In 1 Th. 5.21 Paul uses **katechein** in relation to the ecstatic activity of prophets but in a good sense; could he have expected the Thessalonians to see an evil sense in the word when he uses it next? (iv) While it is easy to think of a 'possessing' force as misleading the Thessalonian church Giblin is very vague about whom the **katechon** (masculine) is. Paul's use of the term implies a definite figure, but if we interpret this 'locally', i.e. out of the Thessalonian situation, how does this figure have a 'universal' significance and how can it be worked into an eschatological pattern which is definitely Jewish in its other details and which suggests a world-event? (v) Why should the 'Seizer' be ousted so that another evil figure, the Rebel, may appear? Giblin has not successfully distinguished the evil figures of the passage from one another. (vi) As we have pointed out in the notes on the text there are quite a number of details of the exegesis which Giblin offers which are open to criticism; it is almost impossible to accept his elimination of the temporal element from the passage; he has to do this so that the **katechon** personality in Thessalonica may be only an eschatological 'condition' and have no temporal significance in relation to the End—otherwise Thessalonica itself becomes the central eschatological scene (cf. iv *supra*).

If the **katechon** is to be regarded as an evil person or power (cf. also Frame, pp. 261f who adapts an earlier theory of Schaefer) this makes it fall into line with the other forces and figures in vv. 3–8, all of which, except the Lord, are evil, and would give the word one of its regular meanings 'rule, hold sway, possess'. That the forces of evil possess or hold sway in the universe is a commonplace of apocalyptic thought. The exegesis of the passage forbids us seeing the **katechon** as Satan (as Schaefer does according to Frame) but it is possible to imagine another evil power or person (cf. the beasts of Revelation) to whom Satan has given present authority and who will step out of the way when the Rebel appears (vv. 7f). This **katechon** will be in some way related to the mystery of rebellion, i.e. he will be the force of rebellion at present in the world, and this allows us to account for the presence of 'rebellion' in the world though the man of rebellion has yet to appear. The difficulties lie in the identification of this **katechon** (masculine) with any known historical or super-historical figure and with the understanding of the **katechon** (neuter); it is not clear why the two forms are used.

Three recent interpretations have reverted to a view already found somewhat hesitantly in the Church Fathers: the **katechon** (masculine) is God: so Strobel, *op. cit.*, pp. 98–116; Ernst, *op. cit.*, pp. 55ff; D. J. Stephens, *Eschatological Themes in 2 Thessalonians, 2.1–12,* (an unpublished thesis in the Library of the University of St. Andrews). The former two take **katechon** in the sense 'delay' and use Hab. 2.3 and the speculation deriving from it which speaks of the delay of the End; the third takes the word in the sense 'restrain' and argues that when God withdraws ('is out of the way') the Rebel comes on the scene. Up until then God has restrained the mystery of rebellion (v. 7). The Rebel however will be revealed in God's time (v. 6), at the moment he withdraws his restraint. Stephens quotes instances of God withdrawing and giving way to evil (Judges 16.20 LXX (A text); 1 Sam. 16.14; Acts 7.42; Rev. 11.2; 13.5) and of God restraining or confining evil (e.g. the seventy years of Jeremiah). As with all other theories there are difficulties: (i) What is the **katechon** (neuter)? To get a meaning we have to objectify some 'will' or 'plan' of God and make it into a force. Would Paul have done this and if he had would he not have used the word (will, plan) itself? Why, in fact, are there masculine and neuter forms? (ii) Why should Paul refer to God in this odd way? There is no reason for secrecy; to have said 'God' would have betrayed no one nor allowed the Roman authorities to take action for treason. In other words this theory does not really account for the use of **katechon.** (iii) The evidence that 'is out of the way' can mean 'withdraw' is scanty and seems to be implied by the context in each case where it is found; could Paul not have said much more easily, 'until the **katechon** ceases to control'? The views of Strobel and Ernst encounter the first and second of the above difficulties and also: (iii) 'Delay' is not a normal meaning of **katechein**; the LXX of Hab. 2.3 uses $\chi\rho o\nu i\zeta\epsilon\iota\nu$. (iv) The 'delay' is in the coming of the final salvation of God; in our context it would be a delay in the coming of the Rebel.

Many other attempts have been made to solve the riddles of our passage but it is impossible either to enumerate them in full or to examine them critically. Giblin has done this fairly fully (he missed Strobel); in particular see his criticisms of Coppens, *op. cit.*, on pp. 176–81 and of O. Betz, 'Der Katechon', *N.T.S.* 9 (1962/3) 276–90, on pp. 168–76. No theory can be held to be satisfactory and as Augustine realized long ago (*De Civ. Dei* 20.19) we must acknowledge our ignorance. Any stray letter on which we may chance between correspondents whom we do not know well will contain allusions, words and phrases which we shall not be able to decipher; moreover much apocalyptic writing was deliberately mysterious lest it should fall into wrong hands. It is not as if **katechon** was the only term we find it difficult to understand in our passage; there are others and **katechon** cannot be solved apart from these. Somewhat hesitantly we suggest that there is much to be said for taking **katechon** in a hostile sense; it then falls into line with the other forces referred to in the passage and its meaning does not have to be forced. We suggest the meaning 'occupier' or 'possessor'. The **katechon** is the one in possession. That the force of evil 'possesses' or 'occupies' the present world fits suitably into apocalyptic thought. This **katechon** is in some ways related to 'the mystery of rebellion' as perhaps the force of rebellion at work in the world; this allows us to account for the presence of 'rebellion' in the world though the 'man of rebellion' is yet to appear. Paul also envisages the **katechon** as embodied in some person, human or supernatural; we cannot identify him but apocalyptic thought allowed for a multiplicity of such figures. This present force of rebellion is later to come to a climax in the figure of the man of rebellion and at that stage the lesser figure of the **katechon** disappears. The **katechon** thus 'ministers' to the man of rebellion. An interpretative translation might run as follows:

And now you are aware of the hostile occupying power so that the man of rebellion will be revealed at his proper time.

For the mystery which is rebellion is already at work; only until the hostile power at present in occupation is out of the way. And then the Rebel will be revealed.

8   That the activity of the **katechon** is viewed as coming to an end is emphasized by **And then** (Giblin's attempt, p. 232, to rob this phrase of temporal significance fails completely). This brings us to the next stage in the eschatological drama, viz. the revelation of **the Rebel** (to be identified with **the man of rebellion**, v. 3; the Semitic idiom is now dropped); this revelation appears to follow without interval directly on v. 7. This brings us back to vv. 3,4 after the parenthesis of vv. 6f and to the man of rebellion and the depiction of the future.

But if Paul has returned to the **Rebel** it is not to concentrate attention on his activities and so he at once refers to Christ. There is a minimum which the Thessalonians must know about the Rebel but their gaze is not to be on him but on the Lord. So in parallel clauses **whom the Lord . . . his parousia** he describes his liquidation. The imagery of warfare goes back to the Jewish concept of the Holy War (cf. R. de Vaux, *Ancient Israel: Its Life and Institutions*, London, 1961, pp. 258–67); in later Judaism this became almost entirely eschatological (cf. 1 QM): a conflict between the forces of good and evil, of God (or the Messiah) and his angels against the devil and his angels. In 2 Th. 2 only the principal contestants, the Messiah and the Rebel, appear. While the N.T. often describes the cross and resurrection of Christ as a victory over the powers of evil (e.g. Phil. 2.9–11; Col. 2.15) it also conceives of a final battle associated with the parousia (cf. 1 Cor. 15.24–8; Rev. 12ff). Paul draws part of his imagery here from Isa. 11.4, 'he will smite the earth with the word **of his mouth** and with **the breath** of his lips he **will slay** the wicked' (LXX); he has combined the two clauses into one and has then added to it another in parallel; this parallelism may indeed suggest that he is using an early Christian Palestinian source. If **slay** (ℵ A B P 81) is the wrong reading and we ought to read a part of ἀναλίσκειν 'consume' (Dᶜ K Ψ syrᵖ⋅ ʰ) then there is probably no allusion to Isa. 11.4. It is easier to see **slay** being changed to 'consume' once the allusion to Isa. 11.4 is not recognized since 'consume' goes more naturally with **breath of the mouth** than to see 'consume' changed to **slay** in order to bring a very vague allusion into line with the text of Isa. 11.4; and the textual development is more easily explained if **slay** is the original reading (see Frame's note). In Isa. 11.4 'wicked' is a collective singular; Paul has ignored this and taken it as a real singular and referred it to **the Rebel.** Isa. 11.1ff was understood by the early church as a Messianic prophecy and so Paul connects it to **the Lord Jesus** (though **Jesus** is widely and anciently attested it is not clear if it is the true reading: the whole phrase, **the Lord Jesus,** appears so often in this letter that scribes could easily have added **Jesus** to **the Lord;** in any case **the Lord** is certainly Jesus). Why has Paul amalgamated the two clauses of Isa. 11.4? Obviously the first clause with its reference to 'smiting the earth' is inappropriate, but why has he changed 'lips' in the second to **mouth** drawn from the first? In 1 En. 62.2 the clauses are combined differently 'the word of his mouth slays all the sinners' (cf. Ps. Sol. 17.24). Probably Paul is quoting from memory under the influence of Ps. 32(33).6 and no importance should be attached to the alteration. The **breath of his mouth** is not something weak and ineffective for God's breath is powerful (cf. Ps. 32(33).6; contrast Ps. 134(135).17, idols have no power; see also Exod. 15.8; 2 Sam. 22.16; Job 4.9); the image is thus not one of the Rebel being easily blown over, as by a mere breath, nor is it of a word coming out of Christ's mouth; it is an image of war (cf. Rev. 19.15) where the breath is a fierce weapon (cf. Isa. 30.27f; Rev. 2.16; 1 QSb 5.24). 'Spirit' and **breath** are translations of the same Greek word ($\pi\nu\varepsilon\tilde{\upsilon}\mu\alpha$) but it is unlikely that Paul is referring here to the Spirit of God (Christ) as Giblin holds (pp. 92ff) for the Spirit in Paul is not a destructive power (Rom. 8.13 is not an adequate parallel to v. 8) and **breath** combines easily with **mouth** into a natural metaphor.

If this clause has stated metaphorically how the Rebel will be defeated the next repeats this and also states when this will happen —**by the manifestation of his parousia** (see Appendix, pp. 349–54). The two terms **manifestation** ($\dot{\varepsilon}\pi\iota\varphi\dot{\alpha}\nu\varepsilon\iota\alpha$) and **parousia** are practically synonymous. Like the second the first (cf. Rigaux, pp. 201–4; Dupont, *op. cit.*, pp. 73–7) has a Hellenistic background in the visitations of deities to save and help men, and is applied in a similar way to the visitations of kings and emperors to cities. Their equivalence is seen in the use of epiphany (= **manifestation**) in the Pastorals in places where Paul would have used **parousia** (1 Tim. 6.14; 2 Tim. 1.10; 4.1, 8; Tit. 2.13). What is the significance of the combination of the terms? In Jewish Greek **manifestation** has a more hostile sense than **parousia** (cf. 2 Macc. 2.21; 3.24; 12.22; 14.15; 3 Macc. 5.8; cf. Joel 2.11; Mal. 3.22 LXX) and this would be appropriate in the present context; it is too weak to say that it describes the onset of the parousia (Rigaux) or is simply pleonastic (Dibelius). If then the technical Hellenistic usage is played down and the words are not taken as synonyms it means that the Rebel is destroyed by the 'glory' of Christ's appearance (cf. N.E.B.). Whatever its precise significance, it is at the time of **manifestation** that the Rebel is **destroyed** (καταργεῖν, rare in LXX and N.T. apart from Paul with whom it is a favourite; for its meaning here see 1 Cor. 15.24, 26; 2 Tim. 1.10; Ep. Barn. 15.5; in Paul it very often means 'render powerless, inactive', but **destroy** suits the parallelism and the order better for **slay** would succeed rather than precede inactivation). There is no long battle, victory comes at once.

9   The grammatical structure of vv. 9f is not clear. There are three possible complements to **the parousia of the Rebel is;** the first two are the adverbial phrases **through Satan's activity** and **in all . . . and in . . . wickedness** and the third the present participle **towards the perishing.** (1) If the third is chosen the two adverbial phrases will be in apposition to parousia and it will be firmly implied that the Rebel's parousia is for the disadvantage (*dativus incommodi*) of the perishing; this construction separates **is** very far from its complement. (2) If we take **in all . . .** as the complement then **through Satan's activity** will be explicatory of this and **the perishing** will also depend on it. (3) If we take **through Satan's activity** as the complement the other adverbial phrase will depend on this and **the perishing** again on the latter. It is difficult to choose between these three; whichever we select the overall meaning is not greatly affected; probably this last is the easiest.

    Satan's (see on 1 Th. 2.18) **activity** (this noun comes from the verb of v. 7, **is at work**; in the N.T., like the verb, it denotes supernatural activity; see on 1 Th. 2.13) will produce (**is:** a present tense because at the time of the parousia Satan's is a present activity; cf. 1 Th. 5.2, 'comes'; the aorist in v. 10, **did not receive,** is a past tense from the point of view of the parousia; neither are viewed from Paul's present) **the parousia of the Rebel.** Behind the Rebel there is thus a greater source of evil;

curiously Paul does not describe the ultimate defeat of this source (cf. Rev. 20.7–10), though it is implicit in passages like 1 Cor. 15.24–8. Since it will come after the defeat of the Rebel which takes place with the parousia of the Lord and since Paul as a pastor is only concerned to deal with the confusion in the Thessalonian church caused by the false belief that the Lord has come, he has no need at this point to go beyond the conditions presaging the Lord's parousia into the defeat of the ultimate eschatological opponent of God. Satan will not only be active in producing the parousia of the Rebel but he is active in the present, for he has hindered Paul's attempts to revisit Thessalonica (1 Th. 2.18); he may be assumed also to lie behind 'the mystery of rebellion' which is already at work (v. 7). The **Rebel** is in some respects the mirror image in evil of the Lord; so he also has a **parousia;** the word seems deliberately chosen for after the previous references to his 'revelation' (vv. 3, 6, 8) the latter would have been the natural word to use here. Although **parousia** was later used in relation to the incarnation this is not the idea here and there is nothing to suggest an 'incarnation' of the Rebel.

The **parousia** of the Rebel is accompanied by and made visible in miracles (**signs and wonders** are a word-pair normally denoting supernatural happenings; Rom. 15.19; 2 Cor. 12.12; Jn. 4.48; Acts 2.22, 43; 4.30; 5.12; 6.8; 7.36; 14.3; 15.12; Heb. 2.4). What is the relationship of **power** ($\delta\acute{\upsilon}\nu\alpha\mu\iota\varsigma$) to these miracles? Used in the plural **power** itself means 'miracles' (Mt. 7.22; 11.20; Acts 2.22; 2 Cor. 12.12; Heb. 2.4; etc.) but this is rarely its meaning in the singular which we have here; the singular means 'power'; in Rom. 15.19 it is the power by which Paul performs signs and wonders and although in our text it is set in parallel with **signs and wonders** it probably again has this meaning (see on 1 Th. 1.5). It is really irrelevant whether the **all** (singular) goes only with **power** or also with **signs and wonders** (in which case it means 'all sorts of'); if **all power** is seen in **signs and wonders** then we ought to think of all sorts of signs and wonders. These **signs and wonders** are clearly associated with the parousia of the Rebel which suggests that they take place at the time of his parousia rather than that they precede it and lead up to it; in the latter case they would be the activity of 'the mystery of rebellion' (v. 7). But if they accompany the parousia of the Rebel then this indicates that there is a period between his parousia and his destruction (and therefore between his parousia and that of the Lord) during which they take place and during which **the perishing** (v. 10) are deceived and led to their destruction. Satan is of course the ultimate source of the **signs and wonders.**

These miracles are **intended to deceive**: ψεύδους, a genitive, might describe (a) the nature of the miracles, i.e. they are fakes and unreal, or (b) their origin, i.e. they proceed from a false source, the Rebel (or Satan behind him), or (c) their intention. (a) is unlikely for Paul seems to regard them as real happenings. Perhaps both (b) and (c) are present in the vague use of the genitive; the context demands (c) at least, and if they are intended to deceive they must also proceed from a false source. Even if we accept (b) alone we should not see it in such definite terms as the N.E.B. 'of the Lie'; the noun has no article and such a translation unnecessarily introduces a new character to the scene. Because the miracles are intended to deceive, the **perishing** do not receive the truth (v. 10); truth and deception are opposites (Rom. 1.25; Eph. 4.25). What are these **signs and wonders?** In Mk. 13.22; Mt. 24.24 false Christs and prophets perform them in the period of the end (cf. Did. 16.4) and in Rev. 13.13 the second beast does so. The use of the words which describe the healing activities of the apostles and the early church (the word-pair is only used in Jn. 4.48 and Acts 2.22 of Jesus) suggests that healing activities are understood. Healing activities were well-known in the ancient world taking place through the hands of 'inspired' men and magicians and within the temples of Aesculapius; in Judaism Rabbis were known to heal. Granted that **signs and wonders** are healing activities we cannot be any more precise as to what Paul has in mind. These miracles would accredit those who performed them just as the apostles were accredited by their miracles (2 Cor. 12.12; Rom. 15.18f; Acts 15.12). It would however be wrong to over-stretch the parallel between the Rebel and Christ: Christ's miracles are associated with his incarnation and not his parousia; the miracles of the time of the Rebel are parallel rather to those of the primitive church than to those of Christ. Perhaps the Rebel has his servants who at his coming perform miracles. If we were entirely to dissociate the clause **in all . . .** from **parousia** and link it only to **Satan's activity** it might be argued that these miracles are Satan's activity prior to the parousia of the Rebel; they might thus be going on even while Paul was writing.

But such an interpretation makes **Satan's activity** function in a twofold way: as complement of **is** where it refers to one period and in relation to these miracles where it refers to another. (On the miracles, cf. K. Gatzweiler, 'La conception paulinienne du miracle', *Eph. T. L.* 37 (1961) 813–46.)

In a phrase **and in . . . perishing,** parallel to v. 9b but laying 10 the emphasis not on the outward activity of evil power but on its inward, Paul continues his description of Satanic activity. **wickedness** could be a genitive of quality, 'every wicked deceit' (this is a common Semitism, cf. Moulton–Turner, pp. 212–14; Bl.–Deb. §165), but it would be to some extent pointless since every **deceit** is wicked. We therefore take it as a genitive of origin: the **deceit** which originates in **wickedness.** This might also seem pointless, but **wickedness** (ἀδικία) is a term with a strong eschatological orientation. Its development is similar to 'rebellion' (vv. 3, 6) to which it is practically equivalent (cf. Rigaux). Satan is wickedness pure and undefiled. Deceit which originates in Satan is wickedness, and vice versa. The last days are days of deceit (v. 3; cf. Mk. 13.5). The way in which this **deceit** takes place is not made clear (Satan can turn himself into an angel of light!) but it results in men's rejection of the gospel (v. 10b; cf. 1QS 4.23, where the spirit of evil contends for men). Not all men are deceived, only those who are **perishing** (τοῖς ἀπολλυμένοις); believers are forewarned and remain faithful to the truth. The **perishing** (present participle; cf. 1 Cor. 1.18; 2.15; 4.3) can be taken either as a description of a process going on during the evil activity at the time of the parousia of the Rebel (those who are in process of perishing) or as a class of men, 'those who perish' (or 'those who are doomed'; the root is the same as in 'the son of doom', v. 3; the Rebel brings on those who are his followers the fate for which he himself is destined). If it is taken in this latter way it does not imply that there are two groups of men, 'the saved' and 'the doomed', and each man from all eternity belongs to one or other group, for in the next clause Paul goes on to describe why the doomed, are doomed—through their own deliberate rejection of the truth: **because** (ἀνθ' ὧν; cf. Bl.-Deb. §208.1) **they did not receive** (aorist tense from the point of view of the later parousia) the word of God as the Thessalonian readers had done (1 Th. 1.6; 2.13). As complement of the verb Paul does not use the customary 'the word' (cf. 1 Th. 1.6; Acts 8.14; 11.1; 17.11) but forms a new phrase with **the love of the truth;** he possibly intends it to balance **deceit of wickedness** (all four nouns begin with the Greek letter *a*). **Love** of the truth implies much more than its admiration, whether intellectual, emotional or aesthetic; it is committal to the truth. To accept **the love of the truth** is therefore equivalent to obeying the truth. Though Paul and other leaders of the church perform 'signs and wonders' he does not draw the contrast between these and those of the Rebel (v. 9). Truth is accepted not through the compulsion of miracle but through **love** of it. Those who love the truth are **saved.** The result (**so as,** εἰς τό, probably consecutive) of its rejection is doom and those who reject it are the **perishing.** These (and those of vv. 11f are the same) are presumably those who apostatize (v. 3); they are not those who say that the day of the Lord is present (v. 2), for at no point (see notes on **apostasy,** v. 3) does there appear to be a group of 'heretics' against whom Paul directs an attack in the letter. They cannot be mankind in general for not all men have had the opportunity of receiving the gospel. They could conceivably be those in the various towns where Paul and others have preached who rejected their message. But it is much more likely that Paul means the Jewish people who in his eyes (cf. 1 Th. 2.16) have definitely rejected the truth and who probably form the apostasy (v. 3).

11   **And for this reason** (the same phrase introduces 1 Th. 2.13; in Paul it normally refers backwards as here), viz., that they had not accepted the gospel (v. 10b), **God** (the word is emphatic by position) **sends:** it may have looked as if evil was the result of Satanic activity alone (vv. 9f); now behind Satan, though opposed to him, appears the figure of God. While the N.T. recognizes the opposition of God and Satan the resultant dualism is never viewed as absolute. In the last resort Satan is subject to God and his rebellion cannot be final (cf. the similar dualism in the Qumran writings); consequently Satan cannot be held ultimately responsible for the doom of those who reject salvation. Apart from Satan's **activity** (v. 9) there is the **power** (the same word as in v. 9) which God **sends** (or 'will send'; cf. **is** in v. 9) to delude (**delusion** is the same word as 'error' in 1 Th. 2.3). **God sends** is positive; God does not just permit evil to exist and men to go to their doom with the 'son of doom' (v. 3) nor is it that he has made the world in such a way that every sin inevitably receives its punishment as failure to eat leads to starvation and death.

God intervenes with definite action; in Rom. 1.24, 26, 28 the rejection of God is punished with sin, i.e. each stage in sin leads on to
a further stage and this takes place by God's action (cf. Ps. 81.11f;
Ezek. 14.9; 1 Kings 22.23; in this last passage the 'lying spirit'
enters those who are already false prophets). The **power of
delusion** which God sends on the wicked is almost parallel to
the Spirit of truth which he sends on believers; 'Spirit' (despite
1 Kings 22.23) would not be a possible term for Paul here but
'Spirit' is 'power, activity'. The precise choice of ἐνέργεια,
power, is suggested by the use of the word in v. 9 in relation to
Satan.

The purpose (εἰς τό is final) of God's delusive **power** is to
make those who are perishing **believe what is false** (lit. 'the
lie'). The source of falsehood is Satan (cf. Jn. 5.43) and **what is
false** is therefore not just error in general but in contrast to 'the
truth' (v. 10; cf. Rom. 1.25) which is the gospel it is that which
lacks all truth, is false through and through and proceeds directly
from Satan himself. Those who **believe** this submit themselves
(**believe** is followed here and in v. 12 by the dative, which is
unusual in Paul; cf. Moulton–Turner, p. 237f) to it as completely
as those who accept the gospel do to it.

The ultimate purpose of this part of God's activity is now 12
stated: **in order that** they **may be condemned** (κρίνειν is
strictly a neutral concept, 'judge', but very readily takes into itself
the verdict, which when men stand before God must be condemnation; Jn. 3.17f; Rom. 2.12; 1 Cor. 11.31f). The subject of **condemned** is quite clear from the context but Paul repeats it to
bring home the gravity of the action and of God's judgement.
This subject is stated both negatively, they **have not believed
the truth** (aorist tense from the point of view of the parousia of
Christ), and positively, **but delighted** (= 'gladly determined',
1 Th. 2.8, and implies their willing choice of wickedness instead
of truth) **in wickedness;** they have acted evilly not through
pressure of circumstance but because they have gladly chosen
evil. The antithesis of **truth** and **wickedness** is found elsewhere
in Paul (Rom. 2.8; 1 Cor. 13.6) and in the context implies that
neither does truth mean truth in general (intellectual or philosophical truth), but the truth of the gospel, nor is wickedness
misbehaviour in general but the choice of Satan instead of God
(cf. Rom. 1.18ff).

Does God's power operate simultaneously with 'Satan's activity' (v. 9)? Though on the surface it looks as if Satan deceives and after men are deceived God steps in to deceive them further, more probably Paul is looking at the same process from two sides. On the one hand men at the parousia of the Rebel appear to be led astray by the work of Satan; on the other hand God's ultimate control cannot be set aside, so when they go astray it is God's **power** of delusion that is responsible. But there is another factor of which Paul must take account and it is this which really produces the present complication: this factor is human responsibility. Of their own freedom men reject the gospel, are beguiled by Satan and even delight in wickedness (v. 12); Paul does not wish to rob men of their freedom and so it seems God's action follows on their decision (**for this reason,** v. 11a) and leads to their judgement. Paul is not saying that men having chosen Satan are made by God to sin so that his condemnation may be justified, but he is trying to hold together the antecedent nature of all God's action and yet leave his judging activity subsequent on man's responsible action. Hence the difficulties of the passage (see also notes on 1 Th. 1.4 re 'election').

ASSURANCE OF SALVATION 2.13-17

Now we ought to give thanks to God always for you, brothers loved by the Lord, because God chose you from the beginning for salvation through sanctification by the Spirit and your faith in the truth, (14) to which he called you by means of our gospel, to obtain the glory of our Lord Jesus Christ. (15) So then, brothers, stand firm and hold fast the traditions which you were taught both in our oral statements and our letter. (16) Now may our Lord Jesus Christ himself and God our Father who has loved us and given us in his grace eternal encouragement and good hope (17) encourage and strengthen your hearts in every good deed and word.

The theme appears to change abruptly. Paul has answered the explicit and implicit questions of the Thessalonians about the parousia but his real interest does not lie in this but in their salvation. Evil works in the world but God's work of love is also there and indeed was there before evil was. So though Paul has spoken of those who are doomed when Jesus returns he can thank God that his Thessalonian converts are not among them for God himself has set them on the way to salvation (vv. 13f); they for their part need to persevere on this way (v. 15), and since they cannot do this alone and unaided he prays once more for them (vv. 16f).

There is no contrast (**Now,** δέ, see on 2.1) with the preceding 13 passage for there is nothing with which to contrast **we** (Paul, Silvanus and Timothy) in the immediately preceding context. The main theme of vv. 13–17 is the salvation of the Thessalonians and there may be some contrast with the punishment of the doomed of vv. 9-12, but had Paul wished to bring out this contrast he would have begun with 'you' and not **we. Now we ought to . . . you** is identical with the initial clause of 1.3 except for the addition of **now,** an emphatic **we,** and some variation in word order. Paul is apparently returning deliberately to the theme of thanksgiving and making a new beginning (Schmithals takes this as an indication that two letters have been joined here; cf. pp. 31ff, 45ff). In 1.3ff Paul centred his thanks on the way the Thessalonians had lived, here on what God has done for them; these two aspects are complementary. It has been argued that since Paul does not use elsewhere the expression of 1.3 and 2.13 we may infer that the letter is pseudonymous; but would an imitator have imitated himself and not a known expression of Paul? The argument for pseudonymity can however be put more cogently by saying that as 1 Th. 2.13 picks up 1 Th. 1.2 so 2 Th. 2.13 is made to pick up 2 Th. 1.3, that is that the author has deliberately introduced at 2 Th. 2.13 a return to 1.3 in a way similar to what he found in the first letter.

A second expression is now introduced, **brothers loved by the Lord,** which recalls the phrase of 1 Th. 1.4. There is one important change: **God** (1 Th. 1.4) has been changed here to **the Lord** (in v. 16 both are linked in their love of man). As usual in Paul **Lord** refers to Jesus and not to God; this is confirmed by the previous explicit mention of God and by the similar mention in the next clause **(God chose)** where a simple 'he' would have sufficed if **the Lord** meant God. As in 1 Th. 1.4 (see notes there) it is closely related to election; it is because God (or Christ) loves men that he chooses them; there is incidentally no equivalent phrase that God hates men and therefore dooms them. It is not clear why **Lord** replaces **God** (von Dobschütz remarks that it makes the passage sound more like the O.T.; cf. Deut. 33.12); if someone was writing in Paul's name and recalling his phrases it is not the kind of alteration he would make. Similar changes may be noted between 1 Th. 5.23 and 2 Th. 3.16; the order of names is interchanged in 1 Th. 3.11 and 2 Th. 2.16; and in 2 Th. 3.3 'the Lord is faithful' is elsewhere in Paul 'God is faithful' (cf. 1 Cor. 1.19; 10.13; 2 Cor. 1.18). On the equivalence of Jesus and God for Paul see on 1.12. That **Lord** is used more frequently in 1 & 2 Th. than in the other epistles may have no deeper significance than that it is the title appropriate to eschatology and these letters deal with this topic more than any of the others (see notes on **Lord** at 1 Th. 1.1; 5.23 etc.). Moreover Paul regularly alternates God and Christ in relation to what they do (see also on v. 16), e.g. both act as Judge of men; we ought not then to make too much of this variation between our passage and the passages in 1 Th.

The Thessalonians' assurance of salvation does not rest on their own decision or conversion but on the fact that **God chose** them. The thought is the same as in 1 Th. 1.4; there Paul followed it up by pointing to the way they were living as Christians, here by emphasizing God's further work in their redemption. Paul, indebted to Jewish thought, regularly refers to God's choice of believers though he never uses exactly the same expression twice; cf. Rom. 8.29f; 1 Cor. 1.27f; 1 Th. 1.4; cf. 5.9; 1 Cor. 2.7; Eph. 1.4, 5, 11. In each case it is God, and not Jesus, who elects. The belief of Christians in their election has often been an important element enabling them to endure trial and persecution steadfastly, as Paul obviously intends it to be here (see notes on 1 Th. 1.4).

In many of the references to election though not all (cf. 1 Th. 1.4; 5.9; 1 Cor. 1.27f) the antecedent nature of God's action is brought out either by the use of the proposition $\pi\varrho\delta$ (Rom. 8.29f; Eph. 1.5, 11) or by an adverbial phrase (Eph. 1.4; cf. 1 Cor. 2.7). As our translation reads we have such an adverbial phrase here in **from the beginning,** but the underlying Greek is uncertain. We have read $\dot{\alpha}\pi'\dot{\alpha}\varrho\chi\tilde{\eta}\varsigma$ as in א D K Ψ syrᵖ copˢᵃ but $\dot{\alpha}\pi\alpha\varrho\chi\dot{\eta}\nu$ is read by B Gᵍʳ 33 81 syrʰ copᵇᵒ (the Old Latin and the Fathers are divided); this would be translated 'as first-fruits'. Since the manuscript evidence is inconclusive we must consider what Paul would have been most likely to write and what would have been most likely to be changed. In defence of 'as first-fruits' Dibelius argues that the Fathers tended to think of election as pre-temporal and seeing a reference to election would then change the text to bring this out. If then we read 'as first-fruits', a good Biblical image, what does it mean? We would expect 'first-fruits' of something, e.g. firstfruits of Thessalonica, i.e. the first converts in the community; this is excluded since the letter is addressed to the whole church (Harnack, *op. cit.*, pp. 575–7, referred it to the original nucleus of Jewish converts to which 2 Th. was addressed and on this hypothesis the reading has real significance; the hypothesis itself is unacceptable, cf. pp. 38ff). The first-fruits cannot be those of Macedonia because these were the Philippians whom Paul evangelized earlier. If the first-fruits were the Gentiles who are saved (contrasted with the **perishing** of vv. 10–12) then we would expect some qualification to bring this out. When Paul uses first-fruits in any of these senses he qualifies the word with a genitive to make his meaning clear (cf. 'of Asia' etc. in 1 Cor. 16.15; Rom. 16.5). Those who defend this reading therefore argue that 'first-fruits' must be taken as a value judgement without any idea of temporal priority, and point out that Philo, *De Spec. Leg.* IV, 180, uses it in this way. But it is doubtful if in Paul the sense of 'firstness' ever entirely disappears from the word; the first-fruits imply there is a full harvest to follow; cf. Rom. 8.23; 11.16; 16.5; 1 Cor. 15.20, 23; 16.15. In Jas 1.18; Rev. 14.4 Christians as a whole are 'first-fruits' in respect of all mankind but this does not suit the present context. (On the term see G. Delling, *T.D.N.T.* I, pp. 484–6.) It would have been easily possible for a second century Christian looking back to think of the original converts in Thessalonica as possessing some kind of firstness but to someone writing at the time this would have been impossible. The change in reading to 'as first-fruits' could easily have been influenced by Jas. 1.18; Rev. 14.4, and since it superficially looks full of meaning this may have been what happened. M. J. Suggs, *art. cit.*, argues on the basis of John Knox's chronology for Paul (cf. pp. 11ff *supra*) that Paul's Macedonian ministry may have been the actual beginning of his ministry and therefore 'first-fruits' here is to be taken literally of Paul's first converts. But this is again open to the objection that the Philippians and not the Thessalonians were the first-fruits. Unless we were to hold that 2 Th. came from a period considerably after the Macedonian mission (and Knox does not hold this if 2 Th. is authentic) Paul would hardly have lumped together all his Macedonian converts as 'first-fruits'; he would have been too near the time to isolate them in this way. If Knox's chronology is rejected the words can hardly be taken as Suggs suggests. If then we accept the reading **from the beginning** what does this mean? It could conceivably refer to the beginning of Paul's preaching in Thessalonica but it much more probably carries the nuance 'beginning of time' as in Isa. 63.16; Sir. 24.9 *v.l.*; Mt. 19.4; 1 Jn. 2.13. It is sometimes alleged that Paul uses other phrases elsewhere to denote this conception (1 Cor. 2.7; Col. 1.26; Eph. 1.4; 2 Tim. 1.9) and therefore **from the beginning** is the more difficult and thus the correct reading; leaving aside the question of the authorship of Col., Eph. and the Pastorals Paul has no consistency of usage and the number of instances is too small to suggest that **from the beginning** is a hard reading according to his general usage. But this does not affect the conclusion that it is indeed the better reading. Suggs, *art. cit.*, argues that even if it is the correct reading (he prefers the other) it can still be used to support his position. For ἀρχή in Paul, when used temporally and not in reference to supernatural powers, relates to a definite point in history and therefore here to the beginning of Paul's ministry. However Paul, according to Suggs, only used the word once with temporal significance (Phil. 4.15); one instance is not enough from which to fashion a rule, especially since we know that the word frequently has the nuance 'beginning of time' and that the particular phrase used here has it; in Phil. 4.15 Paul clearly identifies the period in history to which he ties the word but he does not do so in the present context.

This election by God is for their **salvation** (see on 1 Th. 1.10; 2.16; 5.8; 2 Th. 2.10; the word must be given here its widest possible meaning embracing both the present life and the life of the End) which is achieved by God's **Spirit** and their **faith.** The end result is their eventual and complete participation in Christ's glory (v. 14b). Although we have translated **sanctification** (see notes on 4.3, 7) **by the Spirit** (lit. 'sanctification of spirit', a genitive of the subject) as a reference to the Holy Spirit some commentators prefer to refer 'spirit' to the human spirit (as in 1 Th. 5.23), and translate, 'sanctification of spirit' (genitive of the object), because 'spirit' lacks the article. This absence is not a barrier to its application to God's Spirit, cf. Rom. 8.4, 13; if 1 Pet. 1.2

depends on our phrase this view is confirmed. While Paul could easily have thought of man as sanctifying himself he regarded sanctification in the final issue as the result of God's work in man (on the relation of these two aspects see Phil. 2.12f) and since the present context lays so much stress on God's work it seems appropriate to take the phrase with this meaning (on the role of the Spirit in sanctification see 1 Th. 4.7f; Rom. 15.16; 1 Cor. 6.11f; cf. 1QS 3.7; 4.20f; that the Spirit should have such a role is obvious from the fuller title 'the Holy Spirit'; although God, Christ and Spirit are all mentioned in vv. 13f we should not think of Paul as adopting a conscious Trinitarian position). The parallel phrase (**your faith in the truth,** lit. 'faith of the truth') can also be interpreted in a number of ways. **Faith** can range in meaning through 'the Faith' (i.e. the objective content of what is believed), 'faithfulness' and 'trust' (i.e. the total response of the believer to God) and truth can be either that which creates **faith** (genitive of the subject) or that in which **faith** is placed (genitive of the object), or possibly that which gives its quality to **faith,** i.e. 'truthful faith' (genitive of quality). If the parallelism with the first phrase is to be maintained then we ought to take **truth** as that which creates faith and the latter in the sense 'trust'; **truth** then stands for the gospel (cf. v. 12) which awakens faith. But there are difficulties in maintaining the parallelism; **sanctification** is a continuing and growing process, **faith** in the sense of 'trust' is for Paul a total response and not a process. It may then be better to take **truth** as a genitive of the object; the salvation of the believer takes place through his **faith in the truth** (the latter again in the sense 'gospel'); this interpretation produces a balance between the two phrases, the first stressing the work of God in the believer, the second his own response to what God has done for him, and the second is then in essence similar to **believed the truth** in v. 12.

In **to which** (the phrase is the same as that of 1.11, **with this** 14 **in mind,** but the meaning is not quite the same; more of its relative sense adheres here to δ) the reference back is not to any single word, **salvation, sanctification** or **faith,** but to the whole preceding idea; God has chosen the readers, he desires their salvation, he sanctifies them, they believe—all this came into being when Paul and his companions preached to them. At that time God **called** (see on 1 Th. 2.13; 4.7; 5.24; 2 Th. 1.11) them **by means**

of our gospel (see on 1 Th. 1.5 for **our gospel**). The pre-historical or meta-historical choice by God became actual in the historical event of Paul's visit to Thessalonica and his preaching of the gospel (Dibelius who took **chose**, v. 13, in the sense of this temporal act now takes **called** as its synonym and sees the discussion advanced through the addition **by means of . . .**). But the conversion of the Thessalonians does not complete God's choice; this is only realized when believers **obtain** (lit. 'for possession of'; see notes on 1 Th. 5.9 where the concept is also related to God's plan) **the glory of our Lord Jesus Christ.** This clause is in apposition to **for salvation** (v. 12; a simple εἰς introduces both, whereas **to which** is εἰς ὅ) and amplifies it by bringing out the final purpose of God's choice. Christ has already been glorified and it is in his glory that believers now participate and will fully participate at the End (Rom. 8.17f, 29f; 1 Cor. 15.43; 2 Cor. 3.18; Phil. 3.21; see notes on 1.9, 10, 12; 1 Th. 2.12); when this takes place their salvation is fulfilled.

Paul has allowed his thought to range from the pre-historical choice of God to its post-historical fulfilment, from everlasting to everlasting. Denney comments that vv.13f 'are a system of theology in miniature'; yet much is missing; there is no reference to the death and resurrection of Jesus; even if these are held to lie implicitly in the term **gospel** their explicit omission shows that Paul, for whom they are the centre of theology, is stressing something else, viz., the engineering of man's salvation lies in God's hands. While this will sustain the Thessalonian Christians through a period of trial it would never have won them to Christianity; the gospel for unbelievers begins and ends with what God has done in Jesus Christ, and not with what he has done, or may do, to men.

15 We might perhaps expect that Paul would move directly from what he has said of God's love for and activity on behalf of the Thessalonians to his prayer that he would preserve them but this would be to omit a vital factor, for balancing God's activity must be the responsive activity of the Thessalonians; vv. 13f are not intended merely to make the Thessalonians rejoice but to lead them to action. And this action is expressed in terms appropriate to the context: Paul has been worried that they might be shaken (v. 2) from the faith and so he calls on them to **stand firm** (for the word cf. 1 Th. 3.8) **and hold fast** (both are present imperatives implying a continuous effort) **the traditions.** The movement of

thought reproduces in miniature that at Rom. 12.1f—from God's mercy which has been explained in detail in Rom. 1–11 to the duty of the Christian in Rom. 12.3ff. If he does not know God's love the Christian cannot love his neighbour and if he is not established by the choice of God (vv. 13f) he cannot **stand firm and hold fast.** The logical nature of the transition is made clear by **So then,** ἄρα οὖν, a favourite Pauline expression, while the change of thought is brought out by the renewed **brothers.** To **stand firm** is not of itself a virtue for it is possible to stand firm in evil; so Paul clarifies this phrase with the addition **hold fast . . .** We might almost render 'stand firm by holding fast . . .' To what are they to hold fast? Paul does not simply say 'what we taught you', but **the traditions** (cf. 1 Cor. 11.2; 15.1f) which he, Silvanus and Timothy had **taught** them (for the accusative with the passive cf. Moulton–Turner, p. 247; Bl.–Deb. §159). **Tradition** is another word from the Rabbinic vocabulary for the transmission of religious and legal material (see on 1 Th. 2.13) and indicates that Paul refers here to what was generally passed on in the primitive church by missionaries to their converts and not just to special teaching of his own or to occasional teaching which might arise out of a particular situation. (Paul can express the same idea without using this Rabbinic vocabulary, e.g. Rom. 6.17; 16.17; 1 Cor. 4.17; Phil. 4.9; Col. 1.7; 1 Th. 4.11; the idea, if not the particular Rabbinic terminology, was part of the life of the early church.) These **traditions** consisted of brief confessions of belief (e.g. 1 Cor. 15.3–5), liturgical material (e.g. about the Eucharist, 1 Cor. 11.23–25; cf. 1 Cor. 11.2) and ethical instruction (1 Th. 4.1f; 2 Th. 3.6, 10; 1 Th. 5.12ff and Rom. 12.9ff; the *Haustafeln* of 1 Pet. 2.13–3.7; Col. 3.18–4.1; Eph. 5.21–6.9; and the Two Ways of which the clearest example is the first part of the Didache). The material passed on need not necessarily be in rigid form (cf. the variations in the *Haustafeln* and between 1 Th. 5.12ff and Rom. 12.9ff) but would follow accepted general lines. In our passage **traditions** relates to doctrine rather than to worship or behaviour. These traditions cannot however be limited to teaching about eschatology alone; **our gospel** (v. 14) shows that Paul is thinking of the central teaching of the meaning of Jesus Christ (cf. 1 Th. 2.13; Col. 2.6; Gal. 1.9).

There is always a danger that traditions will turn into dead forms controlling and then killing the life of the church. Jesus spoke against 'the traditions of men' (Mk. 7.1–13; cf. Gal. 1.14). Paul could have defended himself against such a charge by arguing that the traditions which he handed on, though he may have received them from men and though he, a man, transmitted them, yet had their origin in God and his actions (cf. 1 Cor. 11.23; here Paul speaks of receiving the Eucharistic tradition from God; he can hardly have meant that he had a special revelation but rather that God was the real source though men passed it on to him). This is true but it also needs to be remembered that traditions arise within certain historical settings and if the settings change then the traditions may become dead and in turn destroy the life of the church. Every church gathers traditions from its history; these become a peril to its thought, if it attempts to defend itself in their terms when the basic cultural patterns in which the traditions arose have changed (e.g. the creeds of the fifth century), and to its worship, if it falls into the illusion that the drama and language of one age are appropriate to all ages. Nevertheless not all traditions can be discarded. In whatever ways Christianity is expressed and lived it cannot be dissociated from Jesus; the traditions about him are embedded in a first century Palestinian setting which is very different from ours; yet they cannot be rejected, which would be to throw out the baby with the bath water, but must be re-interpreted. Other traditions, coming from later periods, and some from that very period and from within the N.T., may have to be rejected *in toto*, but never those about Jesus, though few of them can be accepted *simpliciter*. We note that while the Thessalonians are urged to receive the **traditions** they are not urged to pass them on; this emphasis (cf. 1 Tim. 6.14, 20; 2 Tim. 2.2; Tit. 2.1ff) belongs to a later age when the pressure of the parousia is lessening; this absence of an instruction to transmit the traditions confirms the early date and therefore the authenticity of our letter.

The **traditions** to which they are to hold fast have come to them both as **oral statements** and in written form **(our letter)**, referring respectively to Paul's teaching during his visit and to the first letter (the absence of the definite article shows it cannot be the present letter; contrast 3.14; Rom. 16.22; Col. 4.16; 1 Th. 5.27; if, as Schmithals holds, there were a number of letters it could cover them all and be rendered 'oral and written statements'). There is no attempt here to authenticate the first letter, let alone canonize it as Scripture. It is significant that when Paul refers to the traditions he has handed on there is no reference to a 'spirit' (cf. v.2). Do the traditions not include ecstatically inspired statements? What of 1 Th. 4.15–17? It may be that Paul does not think of himself as receiving the traditions in this way or 1 Th. 4.15–17 was not his own inspired utterance.

The Thessalonians have been chosen for salvation and for that 16 reason bidden to stand firm in their Christian faith; knowledge of their choice will not itself enable them to do so; they can be too easily shaken (v. 2) or deceived by wickedness (v. 10); God's help is required. So Paul prays that the God who selected them will give them the power to endure (Paul moves easily from thanksgiving to intercession: 1 Th. 3.9–13; Rom. 1.8–10; Phil. 1.3–9; Col. 1.3–14). In a sense the passage ends where it began: with God's action. The prayer itself is structurally similar to that of 1 Th. 3.11–13 (see notes there) and as in that letter comes at the end of the thanksgiving. There are some changes; the most striking is the inversion of the order of the names **our Lord Jesus** (to it is added **Christ**) and **God our Father.** No significance should be attached to the addition **Christ,** since Paul so regularly uses the full formula **our Lord Jesus Christ.** Nor may the inversion in order be significant; Paul generally puts the name of the Father before that of Christ but in Gal. 1.1 and in 2 Cor. 13.13 Christ's comes first. He may have been led to put it first here under the influence of v. 14 which ended with it. Rigaux points out that 2.13–3.5 is oriented christologically rather than theologically (Christ's name is mentioned eight times, God's four) and that in 2.1–12 Christ has been the leading figure as the victor over evil. As in 1 Th. 3.11–13 we have the singular **himself** and the verbs in the singular form. The precise formula **God our Father** (ὁ θεὸς ὁ πατὴρ ἡμῶν) is unique and this has led to a number of textual variants none of which really affects the meaning. The fact of, and the apparent meaninglessness of these alterations from 1 Th. 3.11–13 reinforce the argument for the authenticity of the letter; it would have taken a very subtle imitator to produce them. Another important change from 1 Th. 3.11–13 is the addition of a participial clause before the petition proper; although this is not found at 3.5 or 3.16 it is a regular characteristic of the 'collect' type of prayer and is a feature of many Jewish prayers of the form 'Blessed be God who . . .' (e.g. 2 Chron. 2.12; Ps. 72.18; cf. the

Shemoneh 'Esreh or 'Eighteen Benedictions'; cf. W. O. E. Oesterley and G. H. Box, *The Religion and Worship of the Synagogue*, London, 1911, pp. 356–72; J. Singer, *Authorised Daily Prayer Book*, London, various dates). We find the form in Paul in 2 Cor. 2.3ff (cf. Eph. 1.3ff; 1 Pet. 1.3ff).

Paul can intercede with God and Christ because they have **loved and given** (aorist participles referring to an action in the past) **us . . .** (Note the change from the second person and the return to it in v. 17; Paul cannot limit Christ's love to the Thessalonians; his real knowledge of it comes from his own experience, Gal. 2.20.) The verbs, **loved, given,** are singular but as in 1 Th. 3.11–13 they are to be applied both to the Lord Jesus and to God our Father. It would be difficult to apply them to either alone though we need to recognize that for Paul all divine activity is initiated by God (for that reason we have preserved the singular in the translation), and certainly wrong to apply **loved** to Christ and **given** to God. Paul writes both of Christ loving men (Rom. 8.35, 37; Gal. 2.20; 2 Cor. 5.14; 2 Th. 2.13) and of God doing so (Rom. 5.5, 8; 8.39; 2 Cor. 13.13; 1 Th. 1.4; 3.5); Rom. 8.34–9 shows how difficult it was for Paul to keep the two distinct. The 'love' may be that of God's pre-existent choice but is more probably that of the death and resurrection of Christ; because of the past tense it cannot be God's present care. **given** really explains **loved:** 'who has loved and *so* given us' (cf. Frame, von Dobschütz). God's love and gifts are always 'of **grace**' (**in his grace** is an adverbial qualification of both verbs with **in** giving the ground or cause); men cannot earn God's love or gifts; they receive them only because God is gracious (see on 1 Th. 1.1 for **grace**).

God (or Christ, for both are said to give encouragement, Rom. 15.5; 2 Cor. 1.3; Phil. 2.1) has given them: (i) **eternal encouragement.** This could mean 'God has encouraged unfailingly' (cf. N.E.B.) or 'God has encouraged in respect of eternity'. The first is made difficult both by the aorist form of **given** and by the normal eschatological reference of **eternal** (αἰώνιος, see on 1.9). The **encouragement** (see note on 1 Th. 4.1; this meaning suits the context better than 'comfort' or 'exhortation' because the Thessalonians require to be built up for what faces them; cf. 1 Th. 3.2, where it is linked to **strengthen** as here; 4.18; 5.11) then is eschatologically oriented. The age to come may bode ill for

persecutors (1.9) but its existence is an encouragement to believers. (ii) **good hope** (for **hope** see on 1 Th. 1.3); again this is a
phrase with a strong eschatological orientation (cf. 1 Th. 2.19;
4.13; 5.8) and is almost synonymous with **eternal encouragement.** **good** has caused commentators and translators some
difficulty ('bright', N.E.B.; 'sure', Jerusalem Bible; 'unfailingly',
Phillips). However the whole phrase **good hope** was current in
the ancient world for life after death being probably derived from
the mystery religions (cf. F. J. Cumont, *Lux Perpetua*, Paris,
1949, pp. 240–2; 401–5; P. Otzen, *Z.N.W.*, 49 (1958) 283–5).
Paul thus uses a phrase of his own, **eternal encouragement,**
and as an explanation adds to it another which his readers will
know: 'God has given us an encouragement in respect of eternity,
or, as you are accustomed to say, a good hope'. We should not
then try to see some special meaning in **good.** For the Christian
it is of course good because he will be with his Lord (1 Th. 4.17;
2 Th. 1.5). When these Thessalonians believed they became aware
of God's love for them not only in their election and in the cross
but also in his care for their ultimate end in the parousia. The
whole phrase, **who has loved . . .,** is in the solemn elevated style
of prayer appropriate to the qualifying clause of this form of
prayer (cf. 2 Cor. 1.3 and the references cited above).

The prayer concludes with its petition: **encourage and 17
strengthen . . .** The verbs (in the optative as in 1 Th. 3.11–13)
were also linked in the reverse order in 1 Th. 3.2 and **strengthen**
is found in the prayer of 1 Th. 3.11–13 (see notes on 3.13 and
2 Th. 3.3). Paul uses it much more in Thessalonians (four times)
than elsewhere (Rom. 1.11; 16.25; the latter may not be Pauline;
it is however a word appropriate generally to the apocalyptic
atmosphere of the Thessalonians letters and more particularly in
the context to the exhortation of v. 15, to 'stand firm and hold
fast'. The same idea though expressed with different words is
found both in Paul and in other parts of the N.T.: 1 Cor. 1.8;
2 Cor. 1.21; Eph. 3.17; Col. 1.23; 1 Pet. 5.10. Apart from the
apocalyptic atmosphere Christians needed staying in the prevalent
immorality of pagan culture and continual threat of persecution.
(On the association of **hearts** with the verbs see on 1 Th. 3.13.)
The Thessalonians are to be strengthened and encouraged **in
every good deed and word** (**every** and **good** go with both
nouns and it is not 'in every deed and good word') of their daily

lives; the phrase is comprehensive. They have been given a **good hope** (v. 16) but they are not to let their minds linger on this and neglect their ordinary and everyday duties; a good hope ought to work itself out in a good life. We always find in Paul this inter-relation between what God has done for men or given to them and the conduct which ought to correspond to and proceed from his action.

The prayer of 1 Th. 3.11–13 ended in the eschatological petition that the Thessalonians might be blameless at the parousia; it is incorrect to speak (cf. Masson) of the present prayer as less eschatological; **eternal encouragement and good hope** pre-serves this note here. It is even more erroneous to deduce from this that our letter belongs to a different apocalyptic context from the other because this prayer is directed to life in the present and the End is therefore not felt as near; the first letter is equally con-cerned about present living, e.g. 4.1–12 (especially v. 11 if its background is work abandoned because of the assumed nearness of the parousia); 5.8, 11 (set in an eschatological passage); 5.12–24. The difference in the petition does nothing to support the assump-tion of the letter's inauthenticity.

MUTUAL PRAYER 3.1–5

Finally, brothers, pray for us, that the word of the Lord may spread swiftly and gloriously just as among you, (2) and that we may be delivered from perverse and wicked men; for not everyone has faith. (3) But the Lord is faithful, who will strengthen you and guard you from the wicked One. (4) We have confidence in the Lord about you that you are doing, and will go on doing, what we instruct. (5) May the Lord direct your hearts to God's love and to Christ's steadfastness.

This section is somewhat loosely attached both to the preceding material and to the following. The prayer for the Thessalonians (2.16f) may have put into Paul's mind the need for prayer by the Thessalonians for himself and his companions in their missionary work (3.1f); but he swiftly moves back again to pray for them basing his intercession on the faithfulness of God (3.3–5), and in

large part he repeats 2.16f. The transition from v. 2 to v. 3 seems
to be brought about simply through play on 'faith' and vv. 3–5
are loosely connected internally by a δέ at the beginning of v. 4
and v. 5. The prayer for the Thessalonians, while it leads on to
the following warning about idleness (vv. 6ff), cannot be said to
be specially directed towards it. Paul may have made a break in
dictation at 2.17 and be finding his way back into the letter again
(this might explain the initial **finally**) or some of the original
material may be missing (Harnack) or he may be answering the
points in a letter from the Thessalonians (Frame); none of these
suggestions is capable of anything like a viable proof.

It is not clear why Paul begins this verse **Finally** (almost the 1
same word as 'as our last matter' in 1 Th. 4.1; see notes there).
Probably he considers he is moving into the last section of his
letter; this does not imply that 3.1–5 and 3.6–16 are necessarily
related in content (the contents of 1 Th. 4.1–5.28 are not closely
related) but that the end of the letter is in view. He has only a
couple of further matters to raise and they are no longer directly
related to the preceding eschatological teaching. **Finally** suggests a
clean break between 2.17 and 3.1 which is reinforced by the use of
brothers and, if 2.16f corresponds to 1 Th. 3.11–13, then it falls
at the same point as in the first letter. This might support the
conclusion that someone other than Paul has been shaping the
second letter to resemble the first were it not that the two phrases
finally and **as our last matter** (1 Th. 4.1) are not precisely the
same, that of 1 Th. 4.1 lacking the article, and that the structure
of the letter after 2 Th. 3.1 is different from what follows 1 Th. 4.1
since at 3.5 we have a return to prayer. Schmithals uses the very
same evidence to support his partition theory.

Paul is not only aware that the Thessalonians need God's help
(cf. 1.11f; 2.16f) but also that he himself does. If he prays for
them, let them **pray for** him in mutual intercession. He had made
the same request in 1 Th. 5.25 (see notes there); he renews it
now with minor variations and defines the areas of intercession,
which he had not done there. The variations are of no real significance; the verbal order is altered and the 'also' of 1 Th. 5.25 is
omitted here (we saw that there were difficulties in explaining it
there). As in 1 Th. 5.25 the present imperative is used but it
goes too far to say that it should be taken as 'Keep on praying . . .'
on the grounds that in some letter to him the Thessalonians have

said they were already praying about him or that Paul is assuming that 1 Th. 5.25 has been carried out and now he wants it continued. Neither of these reasons would apply to the earlier present imperative of 1 Th. 5.25 and it is easier to explain both in the same way: as signifying a continuous activity of prayer (cf. 1.11f; Phil. 1.9) rather than one prayer for a particular situation which may quickly pass. The situation of Paul's need is his ever-present situation as a missionary.

The Thessalonians are to pray for two objects (ἵνα here and in v. 2 is used of the content of the prayer, as in 1.11): (i) that the gospel may spread quickly and successfully (v. 1b); (ii) that Paul and his companions may not be hindered as they spread it (v. 2). (i) While Paul says **pray for us** his primary desire is not for the safety of himself and his companions but **that the word of the Lord** (a phrase used regularly as equivalent to the gospel; see on 1 Th. 1.8) **may spread swiftly and gloriously** (lit. 'may run and be glorified': the two verbs are closely linked but are not strictly a hendiadys). The image of 'running' (not a slow or gentle spread and not suggestive only of freedom from hindrance) appears regularly in Paul (Rom. 9.16; 1 Cor. 9.24; Gal. 2.2; 5.7; Phil. 2.16) and occasionally in the O.T. (Ps. 147.15 (LXX v. 4); 19.5; cf. Isa. 55.11). Paul is probably influenced verbally by Ps. 147 since it is **the word** that 'runs' (cf. Wisd. 7.24; Pfitzner, *op. cit.*, p. 108); elsewhere he is more indebted in his use of the metaphor to the athletic stadium from which it was derived as an obvious and current metaphor (cf. Pfitzner, *passim*). Such a spread of the Gospel is its 'glorification', its triumph (Paul is not making a direct reference here to the prize of victory; it is not the word which receives 'crowns' but men); 'glorify' is thus used more loosely here than as a specific reference to the glory of God (or Christ); it is of course true that the triumphant onrush of the Gospel brings glory to God, and in its success his glory is seen because it is God who spreads the gospel (Rom. 9.16; in Ps. 147.18 (LXX v. 7) God sends his word) and brings it to success or glory (Isa. 55.11; 'be glorified', a passive voice, suggesting that it is God who gives the glory; it certainly does not refer to men as praising the success of the mission); God of course uses men to accomplish this; because God is the ultimate cause Paul prays primarily for the spread of the gospel rather than that he himself may spread it (on the whole phrase cf. L.-M. Dewailly, 'Course et gloire de la parole (II Thess, iii. 1)', *R.B.* 71 (1964) 25–41). The 'mystery of rebellion' (2.7) is active; the gospel therefore needs to spread quickly (cf. de Boor). Behind this there may be something of the same thinking which produced Mk. 13.10—the coming of the End is related to the spread of the gospel. If the Thessalonians knew this (and as we have seen they were aware of some of the apocalyptic thought of the Gospels) they would have seen here a deeper significance than a mere desire for the growth of the church. They themselves have seen the word spread and triumph in their own city **(just as among you)** and the gospel 'sounded out' from them into a wider area (1 Th. 1.8); **just as among you** lacks a verb and Paul may be including both the present spread of the gospel in Thessalonica as well as that which took place on his initial visit; the story of Acts 17.1–10 may not suggest that the original mission was very successful but we have seen (pp. 2–7) that that account cannot be fully trusted. Out of their experience let them pray for an even greater success for God's word; joy and thankfulness should urge them to it.

(ii) The swift spread of the gospel depends on the freedom of its 2 messengers to fulfil their task and so Paul now prays that he and his companions **may be delivered** (cf. Rom. 15.31; 2 Cor. 1.10) **from perverse and wicked men.** The petition of v. 1 shows that here Paul is not seeking an easy time for himself and his companions but the speedy progress of the gospel through them; the mission and the missioner can never be separated. Paul himself never had an easy time in the proclamation of the gospel (cf. 2 Cor. 1.8–11; 11.23–9). Who are these **perverse** (Paul employs an unusual word, ἄτοπος; the K.J.V. and R.V. renderings are incorrect because they do not take account of the meaning of the word in contemporary Greek where it was used almost synonymously with **wicked;** ordinarily this last word forms a word-pair in the LXX with 'rebellious', ἄνομος (2.8); Paul probably avoids the latter because of its technical use in 2.3–8) **and wicked men?** Deliverance from evil men is a frequent O.T. theme (cf. Isa. 25.4 LXX; Ps. 139(140).1 which use very similar words); Paul himself prays for or seeks the prayers of others for this in Rom. 15.31; 2 Cor. 1.10. The reference then may be quite general since Paul was constantly hindered in his preaching (1 Th. 2.15f). However because (*a*) the definite article is used with **perverse and wicked** suggesting particular men, (*b*) **delivered** is an aorist (the verbs of v. 1 were in the present) suggesting a definite event, and (c) Paul refers in 1 Th. 2.15f to hindrance from the Jews, the vast majority of commentators have been led to assume that Paul has the Jews in mind here. The case for this is stronger if our letter was written from Corinth at a time when Paul was experiencing trouble from the Jews there (cf. Acts 18.5ff). Yet we should not make this identification too hastily (cf. Masson); although the use of the definite article and the aorist almost certainly imply that Paul's situation is a concrete one known to the Thessalonians and that he is not alluding to a general hindrance, yet Paul ran into so much trouble from both Jews and Gentiles that it is perhaps better to be agnostic as to those who were troubling him. The following phrase excludes any idea that they may be Christian deviationists, whether Judaisers or gnostics. All we can say with any certainty is that as Paul writes there are difficult circumstances caused by unbelievers. Nothing else could be expected **for not everyone has faith** (lit. 'faith is not of all'; we take **faith** as the response of man to the gospel and not as the objective system, 'the Faith'; the former leads more naturally to 'faithful' in v. 3 though the other sense would not alter the general meaning of v. 2). It is a simple fact of observation that many men reject the gospel; those who persecute have come into contact with it and therefore can be said to reject it and not have faith. We would be extending this too far if we were to conclude that here Paul divides humanity into two classes, believers and unbelievers, implying that the latter are all **perverse and wicked,** or that he abandoned here the idea that all men can be saved; he is passing a judgement on one definite situation. If the Jews are intended (and the reference to 'faith' may reinforce the belief that they are since Paul would not expect faith from Gentiles in the same way as from Jews) then later we find Rom. 2–3 is a development of the idea that they are **perverse and wicked** as Rom. 9–11 is of the idea that they are not of the faith. (Harnack, *op. cit.* p. 570, arguing that this only makes sense if Jews are intended, uses this to support his theory that 2 Th. was written to Jewish Christians.)

3   Paul suddenly switches back from himself and his companions to the Thessalonians; he might have been expected to go on to write of his confidence that the Lord would strengthen and guard him but instead says this of the Thessalonians; he does not write to build himself up but them; they need strengthening because of

persecution, uncertainty about the parousia, and the difficulties
caused by those who do not work. As he did not pray for his own
freedom from trial (cf. 1 Th. 3.4) so he does not pray for that of
the Thessalonians, but that they may be strengthened to endure it
(cf. 1 Th. 3.13). Paul knows that God will supply the necessary
endurance (1 Cor. 10.13). **But** (the same word δέ opens vv. 4 and 5
and in each case has hardly any more value than 'here is the next
item'; however the context in v. 3 demands that it be given
adversative value; in the concluding sections of his letters Paul
tends to jump abruptly from one subject to another, cf. 1 Th.
5.12ff; Phil. 4.2ff; Rom. 12–15; there is no need then to suppose,
as Frame does, that he is answering points in a letter from the
Thessalonians) **the Lord is faithful:** the formal connection
with v. 2 is made by a play on words, **faith, faithful** (cf. Rom. 3.3).
But it is more than formal (cf. von Dobschütz); it lies in the nature
of the content; men who persecute are without faith; God is
faithful and therefore those 'of faith' who are persecuted, or
troubled in any way, may take courage. Paul uses this phrase in
1 Cor. 1.9; 10.13; 2 Cor. 1.18 (cf. 1 Th. 5.24 and see notes on
2.13) but in the variant form 'God is faithful'; there seems no
apparent reason for our form other than the emphasis we have
seen Paul has been laying on **Lord** throughout 2.13–3.5. It is
incorrect to say, as many commentators do, that **Lord** forms a
better antithesis to **the wicked One** than God, for God regularly
appears as the eschatological opponent of Satan. Anyone writing
this letter in the light of Paul's other letters would have used the
regular form.

The anxious Thessalonians may waver but the Lord does not
and in his faithfulness he **will strengthen** (cf. 1 Th. 3.2, 13;
2 Th. 2.17) them **and guard** (elsewhere in Rom. 2.26; Gal. 6.13
Paul uses this word of men observing the law and in the Pastorals
it is employed of the preservation of the faith, 1 Tim. 5.21; 6.20
etc; in the LXX it is used of God's guardianship of man, Ps.
11(12).8; 120(121).7; 139(140).5; 140(141).9; cf. Jn. 17.12) them
from the wicked One. It is impossible to determine the gender
of **wicked;** though we have translated it as masculine it could be
neuter, 'wickedness'; the same grammatical uncertainty exists in
Mt. 5.37; 6.13. Dibelius and others have argued strongly for the
neuter: (i) **the wicked One** (ὁ πονηρός) is not found as a customary designation of the devil in Judaism; (ii) in Did. 10.5 it

must be taken as neuter (but there it is qualified by 'every'); (iii) Mt. 6.13b is probably an addition to the original form of the Lord's Prayer; both it and our text go back to a Jewish prayer for freedom from the 'evil impulse' (cf. G. F. Moore, *op. cit.*, I, pp. 474ff; W. D. Davies, *op. cit.*, pp. 20ff; Billerbeck, IV, pp. 466ff); (iv) **strengthen** throws us back to 2.17 where its object is not personal and v. 3 picks this up (but **wicked** is not the object of **strengthen** in v. 3 as 'hearts' is in 2.17). Our translation may be defended: (i) the title came to be used very early by Christians for the devil as Eph. 6.16 shows (cf. Mt. 13.19, 38; 1 Jn. 2.13f; 5.18f) even if it is not Pauline; (ii) the devil is depicted in our letters as active, 1 Th. 2.18; 3.5; 2 Th. 2.9; (iii) Ps. 139(140).5 probably had some influence on our verse and deliverance there is from men and not impersonal evil; (iv) Judaism, and Christianity after it, was in this period tending more and more to see a personal force as the centre of opposition to God; (v) the context of the passage is 'personal', cf. **perverse and wicked men** (v. 2); (vi) **the wicked One** is a suitable antithesis to **Lord** in expressing the eschatological warfare of which we have evidence in chs. 1, 2. The reference may be wholly eschatological if Paul is thinking of the period of severe stress for the faithful before the parousia in which Satan will be especially active; it is then above all that Christians need protection (cf. A. L. Moore). While we reject the translation of Dibelius we must allow him that there is no necessary dependence here on the Lord's Prayer.

4   Again, the thought changes in a way similar to the transition from 2.13f to 2.15: from Paul's certainty that God will preserve them to his **confidence** (perfect tense; Paul's confidence began at their conversion and still continues) in their obedience to his instructions. But Paul's **confidence** is not an unqualified confidence; it is not a confidence in them as human beings or in his own judgement of human character; it is a **confidence in the Lord.** Paul is fond of this formula (Rom. 14.14; Gal. 5.10; Phil. 2.24; and possibly Phil. 1.14), but it is difficult to know whether **in the Lord** goes with **confidence** or with **about you** or with both. Word order here suggests the first possibility but in the closest parallel (Gal. 5.10) it suggests the second. Perhaps it is easiest to take it as governing the whole clause. Paul and the Thessalonians are within the Body of Christ, the Christian community, and in consequence relationships exist among them that

328

could not exist outside; but such relationships do not exist at the
human level alone; they have being only because Christ is their
exalted Lord in whom and because of whom every activity takes
place, including mutual trust (in v. 3 Paul has already said that the
Lord strengthens). Paul's confidence is particularized as a confidence that they will continue to do what they have been doing,
and keep the instructions he gives them. The root **instruct** (see
notes on 1 Th. 4.2, 11) recurs repeatedly in the next section
(vv. 6, 10, 12). The 'instructions' to which Paul refers are those
which the Thessalonians are already keeping (**are doing,** present
tense; on the variant readings see Dibelius's note) and will continue to keep (**will go on doing,** future tense; for the combination
of the two ideas cf. 1 Th. 4.1, 10; 2 Cor. 1.10, 13f). This might
suggest that they are Paul's teachings during his first visit and in
his first letter but then **instruct** would be a past tense as **taught**
was in 2.15; but it is a present tense and so must include what
Paul is teaching in the present letter; yet the present tense **are
doing** cannot be restricted to a present sense alone; **instruct**
therefore includes both past instructions (as in 2.15) and the
present instructions. In view of the frequent repetition of the
word in vv. 6ff and its use in 1 Th. 4.2, 11 it seems wise to limit
its extent to paraenetic teaching and not to include doctrinal (Paul
uses it elsewhere only in 1 Cor. 7.10, where its use is again paraenetic, and in 1 Cor. 11.17, where it refers to liturgical instruction).
Verse 4 then looks forward to vv. 6-15 where Paul warns against
idleness. (The interruption of the prayer of v. 5 does not prohibit
such a reference.) His present commendation of the Thessalonians
prepares them for his admonitions in vv. 6ff.

But before he dares to admonish those among them who are 5
failing he turns their thoughts in a prayer to the source of their
ability to carry out his instructions, whether those they have
already been carrying out or those he is now about to give them.
The prayer follows the same general pattern as those of 1 Th.
3.11-13; 5.23; 2 Th. 2.16f; 3.16. Unlike 1 Th. 3.11-13; 2 Th.2.16f
it is addressed to **the Lord** alone. **direct** (optative, see on 1 Th.
3.11) is also picked up from 1 Th. 3.11; this might suggest literary
dependence for Paul does not use the word elsewhere yet its sense
is different here; in actual fact it is difficult to argue from it for or
against authenticity because **direct your hearts** (= 'you', see on
1 Th. 2.4) is frequent in the LXX (1 Chron. 29.18; 2 Chron. 12.14;

19.3; 20.33 etc.) and can have been picked up from there by either Paul or an imitator. The Lord is prayed to direct the Thessalonians to **God's love and to Christ's steadfastness**—two phrases each with an internal genitive and each subject to more than one interpretation. The first is literally 'the love of God'; within the context it may appear more natural to understand this as love towards God (objective genitive) but Paul rarely writes of men loving God (see on 1 Th. 1.3); when he uses our phrase in other passages it means that God loves men (subjective genitive; Rom. 5.5; 8.39; 2 Cor. 13.13); when he does speak of men loving God he uses a verbal form (Rom. 8.28; 1 Cor. 2.9; 8.3); and if he had intended to say that men should love God an infinitive after **direct** would have been much more natural (cf. 2 Chron. 12.14; 19.3; Ps. 118(119).5). Moreover the rendering **God's love** is not without meaning in the context: if the Thessalonians continually remember how God loves them their hearts will be steeled to keep the instructions he has given and is about to give them through Paul. The difficulty of the second phrase is increased because **steadfastness** can also mean 'patient expectation' and the whole translated in a way which fits such an eschatological letter as 'the patient expectation of Christ' (i.e. the expectation of his parousia, cf. Ign. *Rom.* 10.3; so von Dobschütz). Against this we may argue: (i) the word (*ὑπομονή*) though appearing twelve other times in Paul never has this meaning (cf. 1 Th. 1.3; 2 Th. 1.4 where it means 'endurance'); (ii) it is again associated with **love** in 1 Th. 1.3, and this would tend to hold it to the same meaning here as there; (iii) the interpretation of von Dobschütz would have been more easily expressed with an infinitive; (iv) it involves taking 'of Christ' as an objective genitive and thus breaking the parallelism with the first phrase. The last two objections are still valid if we render it 'steadfastness to Christ' (Moulton–Turner, p. 212). If then we accept the translation **Christ's steadfastness** this could mean either (a) taking his steadfastness as an example (cf. Polycarp, *Phil.* 8.2; Jas. 5.11) or (b) receiving the steadfastness which he imparts. The actual difference in meaning is slight; if the readers take **Christ's steadfastness** as an example that steadfastness will be theirs because they are 'in Christ'. Yet the parallel of (b) to the first phrase, **God's love,** is preferable and is supported by Rom. 15.4f. Given **Christ's steadfastness** they will endure their persecutions, the internal troubles of their church and be enabled to keep Paul's instructions. It is possible that we should not make too great a distinction between objective and subjective genitives and that the ideas of both are present in each case: both steadfastness to Christ and steadfastness deriving from him, both love to God and love deriving from him.

IDLE BROTHERS 3.6-15

Now, brothers, we instruct you in the name of the Lord Jesus Christ to hold aloof from every brother who behaves as a loafer and not according to the tradition which he received from us. (7) For you yourselves know how you ought to imitate us for we did not live as loafers among you (8) nor accept our keep from anyone without payment but worked with hard labour and toil day and night so as not to be a charge on any of you; (9) (it is) not that we do not have the right (to our keep) but we (did it to) offer ourselves as an example for you to imitate. (10) For also when we were with you we used to instruct you: 'If anyone is not willing to work, he shall not eat.' (11) For we have heard that there are some among you who are behaving as loafers, doing no work but being busybodies. (12) Such people we instruct and request in the Lord Jesus Christ to work quietly and earn their own keep. (13) But you, brothers, do not be slack in helping them. (14) Now if anyone does not obey our command in this letter take note of him not to associate with him so that he may be ashamed; (15) do not treat him, however, as an enemy but admonish him as a brother.

Paul had already given the Thessalonians some instruction on his first visit (1 Th. 4.11f) and in his first letter (5.14) on the second major subject of the present letter, viz., the failure of a minority to continue at their daily work, apparently caused by a belief in the nearness of the End (see on 1 Th. 4.11). Since the writing of 1 Th. he has received fresh reports (cf. v. 11) which lead him to amplify his earlier teaching and demand its enforcement. He now recalls them to that teaching (vv. 6, 10) and also reminds them of his own example (vv. 7-9). It is not enough to instruct the culprits themselves (v. 12); it is necessary also to tell the majority how to treat this erring minority (vv. 13–15). The whole tone is sharper here than in 1 Th. 4.11 for nothing has been done in the interval to deal with the situation; by this failure alone it has grown worse whether the numbers involved have increased or not. These verses raise many problems: what was the precise failure of the minority? how are those who behave in a clearly wrong way to be disciplined? what is the importance of work?

Schmithals joins vv. 6–16 to 1.1–12 to form his letter A (cf. pp. 31ff, 45ff).

6   **Now, brothers,** as often in these epistles (cf. 2.1; 1 Th. 2.17; 4.10; 5.1, 12), denotes the beginning of a new section, though not of one wholly unrelated to what precedes; the use of **instruct** here and in v. 4 (see notes on 1 Th. 4.11) confirms this (see also on **will go on doing** in notes on v. 4). Though we could easily move directly from v. 5 to v. 16 it is incorrect to argue as de Boor does that 3.6–15 is an after-thought caused by new information which has reached Paul. Information has certainly reached him but there is no need to distinguish the time at which this reached him from the time at which that on the difficulties of the Thessalonians about the parousia did so. Since Paul regularly uses **brothers** to introduce new sections of material and since this is a new section we cannot agree with the majority of commentators that he uses it here to soften the severity of what he is about to say. It serves rather as a renewal of address, though it is true that it is because they are **brothers** in Christ that Paul claims the right to instruct (cf. the image of the body of Christ and the conception of authority within it, 1 Cor. 12.12ff; Rom. 12.4ff). He does not however **instruct** on his own authority but on the authority (**name;** see notes on 1.12, Bietenhard, *op. cit.*, pp. 278f and 1 Cor. 1.13; 5.4; Acts 16.18; Lk. 10.17; cf. 1 Cor. 6.11; Eph. 5.20; Col. 3.17; Ign., *Polyc.* 5.1; see also on 1 Th. 4.2) of **the** (many MSS, ℵ A G etc., add 'our'; it is easier to assume its later insertion to create Paul's normal phrase than its accidental omission) **Lord Jesus Christ** (for Paul's belief that this preaching and teaching is given with God's authority see on 1 Th. 1.5; 2.4, 13). Paul is God's servant authorized through Jesus Christ (Rom. 1.5; 1 Cor. 1.1; 2 Cor. 1.1; Gal. 1.1); thus God is the ultimate source of Paul's instructions to the Thessalonians. He does not distinguish here between himself on the one part and Timothy and Silvanus on

the other as if he had been authorized by God in a way in which
they had not (cf. 1 Th. 2.7; all three are apostles). The whole
community has not been at fault, probably only a small part of it
(cf. v. 11, 'some'); slaves naturally could not have abandoned
their work nor could they have supplied the needs of those who
had done so and were hungry. (Does the existence of the problem
suggest that the number of Christian slaves was a smaller proportion of the congregation in Thessalonica than elsewhere in
the church?)

Paul not only reminds the minority of his teaching on work and
food but he also sees the need to **instruct** the majority how they
are to treat those who reject that teaching. It will help the community to mature if it itself deals with the fault rather than that
Paul should directly intervene against the offenders. Some faults
are much more destructive of community life than others, and the
abandonment of work and dependence on others for food is one;
indeed its continued success for those who adopt it depends on
others not adopting it! How then is the rest of the community to
treat those who fail to work? It would be possible to copy them,
but that would only lead to the total collapse of the community in
a relatively brief period, even before the Lord had come. The
majority might grow so envious and embittered at the laziness of
their brothers that they would eject them from the community in
order to purify it and relieve themselves of an intolerable burden
(cf. v. 13). The majority might be in such doubt on the issue that
they would take no action at all, perhaps secretly admiring the
great faith which allowed others to cast themselves on God's
supply for all their needs. The majority might simply disregard
the whole matter and complacently hope it would solve itself. By
the very fact that Paul suggests action he eliminates this last possibility outright as one not even worthy of consideration. As for the
others he instructs the majority neither to eject or excommunicate
the minority (contrast 1 Cor. 5.3–5, 13) nor to admire them
secretly and adopt the same practices. Instead they are to **hold
aloof** ($\sigma\tau\acute{\epsilon}\lambda\lambda\epsilon\sigma\theta\alpha\iota$: for the meaning see Bauer, s.v., and notes by
Milligan and Rigaux) from them. They are to continue to treat
them as brothers (**every brother;** cf. v. 15), which implies they
are to regard them as within the church, and they are to warn
them of the consequences of their conduct (v. 15). **holding aloof**
(cf. v. 14) must therefore at least mean that they are not to supply

food to these non-working brothers, i.e. the command of v. 10 is
to be rigorously enforced. This may bring them to their senses (if
so it implies they are not the 'idle rich'). Is such a refusal to share
food the way to treat a **brother?** In circumstances like these it
may be the only way, but it must not be exalted into a political or
sociological principle nor are political and economic lessons to
be drawn from it; conclusions in these areas cannot be so easily
deduced from Scripture. The situation of the first Christians was
not only politically and socially different but Paul was writing in
a period of economic scarcity to a community of believers in
Christ and not to a political or national group; and this community
is dominated by a belief that for it, and everyone else, physical
existence is soon to end.

Our emphasis so far has lain on the failure of some to work
(**behave as a loafer,** lit. 'walk idly') but some commentators
(e.g. Rigaux, cf. Spicq, *op. cit.*, see on 1 Th. 5.14) dispute that
this is the central thrust of the passage. The adverb 'idly' comes
from the same root as 'loafer' which appeared in 1 Th. 5.14; it
can also mean 'unruly', 'disorderly'. There is however only one
word in the passage, 'busybodies' (v. 11, cf. also 'quietly', v. 12)
which clearly suggests that the fault of these people may be
anything other than a failure to work; they themselves may have
given positive value to their inactivity in view of the nearness of
the End, but in the eyes of Paul and others who laboured hard it
looked like shirking a necessary duty; so they could be described
as loafers (English has no suitable adverb). Rigaux argues that
behaves (*lit.* 'walk', see on 1 Th. 2.12; 4.1, 12) is so positive a
term that a negative or passive word like 'loafer' cannot be associated with it; but 'loafer' is neither negative nor passive looked at
from the point of view of those who work; it is a positive and active
failure; wickedness is never merely negative or passive.

We are not told why the minority does not work, and as at
1 Th. 4.11 we can only surmise from the completely eschatological
atmosphere that they reasoned within themselves, 'The End is
near, work is a waste of time.' Perhaps they also had the Hellenistic scorn for manual work (see on 1 Th. 2.9); as Christians they
are the free children of God and cannot be expected to work like
slaves. The letter does not associate these 'loafers' with those who
believed that the parousia had taken place (2.2) yet it is possible
that such a connection may have existed, for in 1 Cor. 4.8 Paul

rebukes some Corinthians who believed they had reached some kind of eschatological fulfilment and in opposition to them he emphasizes how he worked to support himself (4.12). On the other hand 'loafing' was a problem at the time of 1 Th. (cf. 5.14), if not during Paul's original visit (2 Th. 3.10), before there was any mention of the strange idea of 2.2. The way in which the loafers are treated by Paul eliminates any idea that they were attempting to reproduce the so-called communistic experiment of the primitive Jerusalem community. Schmithals (pp. 142f; cf. Jewell, 'Enthusiastic Radicalism') sees the 'loafers' as religious enthusiasts, *pneumatikoi*, arguing that if they had been excited by the proximity of the End Paul would have said something about this in vv. 6–15 and told them that despite its nearness men must still work; equally on Schmithals view Paul ought to have referred to the Spirit in vv. 6–15.

The failure of the 'idle' Thessalonians did not come from ignorance; already while Paul had been with them he had taught them (v. 10) and supplied them with his example (vv. 7–9); together these form **the tradition** (less probably **tradition** refers only to Paul's teaching and not his example; if so v. 10 ought to have preceded vv. 7–9; **traditions** may be passed on by example as much as by instruction; our verse has the singular **tradition** referring to one particular field of behaviour; see also on 2.15) **which he** (lit. 'they') **received** (a technical work for the transmission of tradition; see on 1 Th. 2.13; 4.1). There is here a complex textual question which in the end boils down to the choice between the second (B G) and third (א A 33) persons ('they received' or 'you received'). In favour of our reading are: (i) the unusual form of the third person plural (-οσαν, cf. Moulton–Howard, pp. 194f, 209; Bl.–Deb. §84.2; the reading -ον is almost certainly a smoothing) which it is difficult to view as a correction; (ii) the hardness of the reading itself, for v. 7 suggests we should have a second plural here; (iii) the difficulty of seeing how the third plural could ever have appeared by accidental error; (iv) the plural 'they' comes uneasily after the singular **brother;** anyone altering the second plural would probably have changed it to the third singular (this does appear in a few MSS), though the plural after the virtual plural **every brother** would not be too unusual in Greek. The main argument for 'you' is its suitability in the context.

7   In vv. 7–10 Paul gives the grounds **(For)** why the majority
should discipline the 'loafers': his own example (vv. 7–9) and his
original teaching (v. 10). Since they **know** (cf. 1 Th. 2.1; 3.3;
4.2; 5.2) their duty to imitate him they can offer no excuse. Though
Paul does not directly address the loafers themselves they will
learn what he writes here and so these words form an indirect
appeal to them; he probably hopes this will bring them to their
senses. Paul argues that all of them **ought to imitate** himself and
his associates in working for their livelihood just as earlier he had
congratulated them on the way they had received the word like
himself (1 Th. 1.6; see notes there), continued to imitate other
Christians despite persecution (1 Th. 2.14) and become an example to others (1 Th. 1.7). The 'tradition' is embodied in Paul;
his example is their access to it as 'life' rather than as dead teaching. Thus Paul can speak of an obligation **(ought)** to imitate himself. In this instance the obligation relates to the manual work he
did in Thessalonica **for we did not live as loafers (live as
loafers** is the verb from the same root as **loafer** in v. 6) **among
you.** This, phrased negatively, is a 'classic understatement'
8 (Morris) of Paul's normal activity when engaged in mission. Paul
has to go further than saying that he and his associates did not
'loaf' their time away; they might have been so feverishly engaged
in spiritual work (as perhaps the 'loafers' would have claimed to
be) that they lived on other people, accepting their **keep without
payment** (lit. 'as a gift'; cf. Exod. 21.11; Rom. 3.24). To **accept**
one's **keep** reflects a Semitic idiom, 'to eat one's bread', which
passes into the wider sense 'to eat' without specific reference to
what is eaten (e.g. 2 Sam. 9.7; 2 Kings 4.8). Paul may have in
mind Gen. 3.19 where the phrase occurs and be implying that
he has not sought to escape the fate that fell on man through
Adam's sin. Acts 17.7 suggests that Paul and his companions
stayed with Jason; whether it was with Jason or not, they paid
for their lodging fulfilling the precept of 4.12b. This they were
able to do because they **worked** (see on 1 Th. 2.9 for Jewish
attitudes to work). In almost precisely the same terms Paul had
referred in 1 Th. 2.9 to their manual work in Thessalonica; it
had been burdensome **(hard labour and toil)** and continuous
(day and night: A P D K L read the accusative here instead of
the genitive as in 2.9; Paul normally uses the genitive, e.g. 1 Th.
2.9; 5.7, but the accusative is found at Lk. 2.37; Acts 26.7;

Mk. 4.27; either might have been accommodated to the other; there is no essential difference in meaning; but since the weight of MSS evidence, B ℵ G 33 etc., favours the genitive it is to be preferred) and carried out with a purpose (**so as not to be a charge on any of you**). It has been argued that the verbal reminiscences of 1 Th. 2.9 imply that these terms have been drawn from it by a compiler; but Paul uses one of these phrases again in 2 Cor. 11.27 and he uses both of them here with a slightly different reference from 1 Th. 2.9 (in 1 Th. 2.9 they are related to the purpose of his mission; here to his example and the need for every Christian to work; cf. von Dobschütz); a compiler would tend to use them in the same way. (If the accusative is read in **day and night** then there is much less imitation and we have the type of alteration a compiler would not make.) Work not only then gives the worker independence and preserves his freedom in mission (1 Cor. 9.12, 18; 2 Cor. 11.7ff; 12.13ff) but more positively it is a service to the community (Eph. 4.28). Paul feels the **9** need of further explanation and adds parenthetically **it is not that we . . .** The verse is very compressed and we have had to supplement it to bring out its meaning (ellipses are not uncommon in Paul; see on 2.3; cf. Bl.–Deb. §480.5; Moulton–Turner, p. 303). In 1 Th. 2.7 Paul had already hinted at a right which he had to maintenance and in 1 Cor. 9.4ff (cf. 2 Cor. 12.13–18) he explains this in more detail arguing that he has the same right as the apostles and brothers of Jesus; he bases his argument on analogies drawn from daily life (9.7, 11), on the O.T. (9.8–10, 13) and on a saying of the Lord (9.14); later, within N.T. times, this was a clearly recognized right of church leaders (1 Pet. 5.2). In 1 Cor. 9.4ff Paul says that he renounced his **right** (for this meaning of ἐξουσία, see Bauer, s.v.) to further his mission work; in 1 Th. 2.7 his renunciation is linked to the purity of his motives and in v. 9 it is set out as an **example** (see on 1 Th. 1.7; cf. 1 Pet. 5.3 for the minister as example) to others. Perhaps if he did not insist on his right to maintenance (1 Cor. 9.4ff) he might cast doubt on his own apostolic position and make it more difficult for others to exercise this right; but in Thessalonica his point is simply that if he who as a missionary had the right to maintenance had worked for his living why should not the Thessalonians who have no similar right? The **example,** of course, is not his renunciation but his manual work and refusal to be a burden on others (cf.

Gal. 6.5). In referring to his example he uses a strong word **offer**
(δίδωμι; contrast Phil. 3.17); the Thessalonians do not just 'have'
this example; it has been deliberately set before them.

10   Paul now goes back to the **tradition** with which he began in
v. 6; having shown that it was fulfilled in his own example he
now states it in basic and bare form as the second ground **(For
also)** for the disciplining of the 'loafers'. It is not the first time
he has taught them this: not only did he refer to it in his first
letter (4.11) but even at the time of his initial mission he had
instructed them, and it is to this rather than to the letter that he
now refers **(when we were with you**; cf. 1 Th. 3.4; 2 Th. 2.5).
The fact that he instructed them then and that he refers to this
as **tradition** (v. 6) implies that this was a part of the ordinary
catechetical instruction of the church (cf. Did. 12.3f; there is no
evidence that Did. used 2 Th.), probably not originating with
Paul but with earlier missionaries and certainly not created
especially for the Thessalonians; its absence from other N.T.
letters is no reason to reject it as being part of early tradition;
it may have been replaced later by the section on 'servants' in the
Haustafeln (Eph. 6.5–9; Col. 3.22–4.1; 1 Tim. 6.1f; Tit. 2.9f;
1 Pet. 2.18–25). Such teaching would have been necessary in view
of the Hellenistic dislike of anything other than intellectual labour
for free men; Christians, taught that they were free, would have
run the danger of thinking they ought to cease manual work; this
is more probable than that they would think themselves too pious
to work (Schlatter) or too 'spiritual' (cf. Schmithals, Jewett). The
danger was probably inflamed by the apocalyptic atmosphere of
the Thessalonian community and so became an acute problem
for it; lacking this atmosphere Paul did not need to take up the
point in other letters; the initial teaching was sufficient to control
the situation. The present urgency to recollect the original instruction is brought out by the imperfect tense **(used to instruct**;
contrast 1 Th. 4.11) implying repeated instruction. The instruction itself, **'If anyone is not** (for οὐ in conditional clauses see
Moulton–Turner, pp. 283f) **willing to work, he shall not eat'**,
appears a straightforward piece of common sense, yet it is not
found in that form in extant literature. It may have been a popular
proverb (Jewish or Hellenistic) taken over by the primitive church
or adapted from one, or it may have been created by Christians.
The closest parallels are of the form, 'If anyone does not work

he will have nothing to eat' (cf. Prov. 10.4; Gen. R. 2 (on Gen. 1.2), a saying of R. Abbahu; Phaedrus, IV, 23; for Jewish sayings on work cf. Aboth R. N. XI). The present form differs in its stress on 'willingness' and in its ethical (**he shall not eat** is an imperative) rather than prudential nature. Those who do not work are a burden on the community and threaten its life and mission, if not its very existence; they fail to love their neighbours as themselves. On v. 6 we pointed out that it is impossible to move from the teaching of this passage to political or social conclusions for today; it is equally impossible to draw conclusions about the dignity of labour, of its value for the worker himself, or of its economic and social importance. What Paul says relates to a community held together by bonds of religion in a period of economic scarcity; nations in the West are not held together in this way nor is there the same economic scarcity. For the place of work and leisure in the Western world cf. A. Richardson, *The Biblical Doctrine of Work* (Ecumenical Biblical Studies, No. 1), London, 1952; J. H. Oldham, *Work in Modern Society*, London, 1950; and for the wider issues, *Economic Growth in World Perspective*, edited Denys Munby, London, 1966.

Paul has completed the 'tradition' (v. 6); now its application, 11 **for** there are offenders in the community. He and his companions **have heard** (a present tense equivalent to an aorist; cf. 1 Cor. 11.18; Burton §16; Moulton–Turner, p. 62; for the use of the participle after it cf. Bl.–Deb. §416.1; Moulton–Turner, p. 161) of those who are not earning their keep in accordance with the example and teaching given them. We do not know how Paul heard for **heard** can be used either of oral or written information; nor do we know the source of his information or how reliable it was. We can infer that the offenders are a minority since very little direct appeal is made to them and the rest of the church is expected to take action, and since they are termed **some among you** (cf. v. 6). Whether **among you** (ἐν ὑμῖν) goes with **some** or with **behaving as loafers** (same phrase as v. 6) is not clear. Paul does not use this verb elsewhere with ἐν but it is a natural usage; that **among you** does not directly follow **some** is no argument against their association (cf. 1 Cor. 10.27; 3.18). Although Paul mentions no names there is nothing to suggest he does not know who the offenders are; even in 1 Cor. 5.1ff where he must have known the culprit and where he demands much more severe action on the part of the church against him he does not name him. It is almost impossible to reproduce properly in English the final phrase, ἐργαζομένους . . . περιεργαζομένους (a paronomasia; cf. Bl.–Deb. §488.1b), and we have made no attempt to do so. Moffatt's 'busybodies instead of busy' is probably the nearest we can come to it. Word play like this was a common rhetorical trick in the ancient world (in Paul cf. Rom. 12.3; 1 Cor. 7.31; 11.29ff; 2 Cor. 1.13; etc.). These people are **doing no work** and this might seem to be the sum total of their offence; but by **doing no work** they inconvenience the rest of the community who have to maintain them (1 Th. 4.12). The word employed here (**busybodies**; cf. L. & S., Bauer, s.v.) goes beyond this in suggesting that they actively interfere in the life of the community. We can only guess at the nature of their meddling: did they attempt to persuade others to cease working either because of the presence of the parousia (2.2) or, much more likely since there is no real suggestion that they hold that opinion, because of its nearness (cf. 1 Cor. 7.20–4, where again the underlying cause seems to be eschatological excitement)? Or do they attempt to dissuade them from work because work is ignoble for free men, the children of God, as they now believe themselves to be? Or is it because when they are not working they have time on their hands to talk to others (presumably about religion) and keep them back from their work? Inactive where they ought to be active, they are over-active where they ought to be passive.

12 So far Paul has addressed the responsible majority; now he turns (δέ marks the change) briefly to the offenders themselves (**Such people**: there is no trace of contempt; they are only being identified) who if they were present, as they almost certainly were, when Paul's letter was read out must also be addressed. A last appeal and command may lead them to change their ways and the discipline suggested in vv. 6, 14f become unnecessary. So Paul, Silvanus and Timothy **instruct** (see on 1 Th. 4.2; the word appears regularly in this section of the letter: 3.4, 6, 10, 12) and **request**. The difference between these words is much less than many commentators suggest (Paul first 'orders' and then tactfully softens this to 'ask, beseech') if we accept the view of Bjerkelund (see on 1 Th. 4.1; Bjerkelund does not give our verse as an example of his formula but there are good grounds for taking it in this way: the 'address' is implied in **such people** and the adverbial

phrase is **in the Lord Jesus Christ**) that **request** is the term used by a superior to those inferior to him but who are linked to him by some tie (**in the Lord Jesus Christ**: see on 2 Th. 1.1; 2.14; cf. 4.1; it is different from the phrase of v. 6; Paul can address them in this way because both he and these erring Christians are 'in Christ'; indeed the fact that he can and does so address them is part of his appeal to them). Indeed with **instruct** Paul uses a word no stronger than he has used to the responsible majority and **in the Lord . . .** is weaker than 'in the name (authority) of . . .' (v. 6). Concentration on their **work** will steady the non-workers, keep them occupied so that they do not interfere with others and enable them to **earn their own keep** (lit. 'eat their own bread', the same phrase as in v. 8), and so ease the burden they have placed on the remainder of the community. The emphasis ˊon working **quietly** (lit. 'with quietness, calmness') implies that there had been an absence of this quality when they were not working. It does not refer to an inner attitude of spirit on the part of individuals but to the life of the community and so links with 'busybodies' (v. 11). The reference to 'quietness' strengthens the suggestion that its opposite was 'excitement', caused by the belief in the nearness of the parousia.

After briefly addressing the loafers Paul swings back (**But you, 13 brothers**) to the remainder of the community. In vv. 14f he makes more precise the positive action they are to take. Does he begin this in v. 13, '**do not be slack** (the origin of the word, ἐγκακεῖν, suggests that it should mean 'behave badly' but it came to have the sense 'be discouraged, be slack, fail, grow weary'; cf. Gal. 6.9; 2 Cor. 4.1, 16; Eph. 3.13) in doing good to them' (cf. von Dobschütz), or is he giving a general warning, 'do not be slack in your pursuit of good' (cf. Rigaux), or is it in contrast to v. 12, 'do not be slack in doing that good thing which is earning your living' (cf. Dibelius)? The last though attractive would have been more easily understood if Paul had finished with a direct reference to the community as working or earning its keep. The first and second possibilities depend on the meaning we give to καλοποιεῖν: 'act correctly' or 'treat well'. The word itself occurs very rarely but its separated parts appear more regularly as adjacent words and then in the N.T. they have both meanings: 'act correctly' in 1 Cor. 7.37f; Jas 2.8, 19; Rom. 7.21; 2 Cor. 13.7 etc.; 'treat well' in Mt. 12.12; Lk. 6.27; Acts 10.33; Gal. 6.9 (cf.

v. 10); Phil. 4.14. We prefer the second meaning in the present
context, for: (a) Gal. 6.9 is very similar as a whole to our passage;
(b) even if we assume the former rendering it is very difficult to
see how Paul could intend it in any other way than as an instruction to 'act correctly' towards the loafers, which by the very
nature of the Christian ethic must mean to treat them well; Paul
is not enunciating a general ethical principle but speaking to a
particular situation; (c) that it is not a general principle but a
particular application is suggested by the aorist subjunctive: 'do
not begin now to be slack' (on the aorist subjunctive in prohibi-
tions, cf. Burton, §§162-5; Moulton, pp. 222-4; Moulton–Turner,
pp. 76-8). The loafers are a burden on the community (v. 12) but
though it disciplines them (v. 14f) it is not to ill-treat them; every
action it takes is to be for their good. It is impossible to be precise
about what the 'good' of the loafers is; Chrysostom's suggestion
that it means their food is not to be cut off is too narrow. It relates
rather to the general attitude of the majority which may include
action on food but also certainly includes a more general discipline.

14   Paul is conscious that though he has re-stated the tradition by
example and word, has made his appeal and exerted his authority
there may well still be a few **(Now if anyone)** who will not
respond; his words suggest that he does not see them as a
definite group but rather as individuals. What is to happen to
them? He had earlier answered this summarily by saying 'hold
aloof' (v. 6); now he explains with a little more detail (v. 14) and
indicates the spirit in which it is to be carried out (v. 15). Failure
is stated simply as disobedience to a **command** (lit. 'our word');
'word', λόγος, was used occasionally in classical Greek of a command or order (see L & S, s.v.) but Paul is more probably indebted to the Hebrew *dābhār*; the ten commandments are termed
the 'ten words' in Exod. 34.28; cf. Deut. 1.1. ('word' is of course
used in v. 14 quite differently from 1 Th. 1.5, 8; 2.13). Although
Paul says **our** command he would not have thought of it as
especially his own; it was God's command of which he was now
the spokesman in the church and as such it ought to be obeyed
(cf. Rom. 6.17)—just as obedience was demanded to the gospel
as God's gospel though Paul proclaimed it (cf. 1.8; Rom. 15.18).
The **command** had already been given (see on 3.6, 11) during
Paul's original visit and renewed in 1 Th.; and it has been re-
stated firmly and clearly **in this letter** (the absence of τῷ before

this letter led some commentators to link it to 'take note of'; the omission is not exceptional; cf. Bl.-Deb. §269.2; Moulton–Turner, p. 187; the connection with the verb would be very difficult in view of the article with **letter**). The time for warnings has ceased. Those who disobey are to be picked out **(take note of)** presumably by the community as a group (Mt. 18.17f; 1 Tim. 5.20; 1 Cor. 5.4, 12; 2 Cor. 2.5–11 all suggest the part played by the community in discipline; 1 Cor. 5.3; 1 Tim. 1.20; Acts 5.3ff; Tit. 3.10 the part played by individuals acting as 'ministers', and not merely as individuals) rather than by individuals acting independently. Paul does not say how or when this is to take place; the community had opportunities for joint action when it met for its agape, worship and instruction. We do not know whether the community officially named those who were in error or officially instructed the remainder on their attitude towards them. The whole matter will have been carried out much more spontaneously than 'officially' suggests.

Paul goes on to detail the action the community ought to take— **not to associate with them** (it is almost certainly correct to read the infinitive here with B ℵ A 33 D, etc.; it has much the better support and the imperative would easily arise through auditory confusion over the ending and the influence of the preceding imperative). The word, συναναμίγνυσθαι, is rare and only occurs elsewhere in the Bible in the LXX A-text at Hos. 7.8; Ezek. 20.18; 1 Cor. 5.9–11; in the last passage Paul is obviously clarifying an earlier instruction. In 1 Cor. 5.11 non-association includes the rejection of common meals (cf. 1 QS 6.24–7.25). Does it mean this here? It would not be inappropriate. The loafers did not earn their keep and depended on others for their food; if there was a common meal in the community (cf. 1 Cor. 11.17ff) then they would have received their share and would not have starved. If **our command** is 'If anyone is not willing to work, he shall not eat' (v. 10) then exclusion from the common meal would be an effective way of achieving it. Would this imply exclusion from common worship? If the meal was integrated into worship it would be difficult to avoid this; if the meal preceded the worship it would not be impossible. Verse 15 implies that the common worship con- 15 tinues for the community is to **admonish** (see on 1 Th. 5.12, 14 for the word) the erring **brother;** this can hardly mean that as individuals meet him on the street they are to speak to him but refers rather to action when the community is gathered (there is nothing in the use of **admonish** elsewhere in the N.T. to suggest that admonition was carried out on an individualistic basis; cf. Acts 20.31; Rom. 15.14; 1 Cor. 4.14; Col. 1.28; 3.16; 1 Th. 5.12, 14). The purpose of non-association with the loafer is not the preservation of the purity of the community but the winning back of the offender by making him **ashamed** of his conduct; the sudden cessation of some of his normal communal activities may bring him to his senses. However the spirit in which this is carried out is important; it would be possible to treat the offender with scorn, to censure him angrily, to despise him, or to **treat** him as though he were **an enemy** (cf. Bl.–Deb. §416.3; Moulton–Turner, p. 161, for the construction). The church is always responsible for its sinners and cannot act in such ways (cf. Gal. 6.1). The offender may be excluded from the common meal but he is not outside the community; he is still a **brother** and has to be treated as a brother.

Paul's final word to these 'loafers' is **brother**; they are excommunicated neither temporarily nor permanently; they are still Christians and cannot be ignored. Because of this it is wrong to parallel our passage with Mt. 18.15–17 where the recalcitrant church member is to be treated as a pagan or a tax-collector. There is also an essential difference from 1 Cor. 5.9–13 where, though the same verb **(associate with)** is used, the final emphasis is quite other—'expel the evil man from among you'. But the offences and therefore the action to be taken are different in each case; non-association is fitting in Thessalonica because association (giving food to the offender) will make him think the community wants to encourage him in his offence; non-association is fitting in Corinth in order to preserve the purity of the community—the impure is expelled for the community's good and not just his own. The more severe judgement by expulsion in 1 Cor. 5.9–13 is also found in 1 Cor. 5.3–5; 1 Tim. 1.20; Mt. 18.17. Parallels from Judaism are not at all clear; cf. D. R. A. Hare, *op. cit.*, pp. 48–56; the best contemporary evidence comes from Qumran (1 QS 6.24–7.25; 9.1; CD 9.23; 20.3) where exclusion could be either temporary or permanent. When temporary it was always inflicted in the hope that repentance would follow, and even in such severe sentencing as we find in 1 Cor. 5.3–5 the hope of ultimate salvation is at least part of the reason for action. 2 Cor. 2.5–11 envisages the re-acceptance of an offender (it is not clear if it is the same person as in 1 Cor. 5.3–5). In 2 Th. as in 1 & 2 Cor. it is the community itself which appears to be responsible for discipline; we saw in 1 Th. 5.12 that there were leaders in it but no special appeal is made to them to take action. In 1 Tim. 1.20 it is the ministry which acts. This suggests that 2 Th. is early. It also fits in with Paul's teaching on the community as the body of Christ: the loafers have injured the life of the body and so the body must act. The precise action which Paul desires does not appear to be clearly thought out. How is it possible to **hold aloof** (v. 6) from someone and **not associate** (v. 14) with him and yet continue to treat him as a **brother?** This suggests a very early stage in the development of discipline.

CONCLUDING PRAYER AND BENEDICTION
3.16–18

Now may the Lord of peace himself give you peace all the time and in every circumstance. The Lord be with you all. (17) The greeting in my own, i.e. Paul's, handwriting, which is a sign in every letter; this is the way I write. (18) May the grace of our Lord Jesus Christ be with you all.

The final prayer, greeting and blessing close the letter; each of these is found in many different forms in the conclusions of contemporary letters.

The form of the prayer with the use of the optative is the same **16** as in 2.16f; 3.5; 1 Th. 3.11–13; 5.23. It is nearest to 1 Th. 5.23 in its reference to **peace** but unlike it in being addressed to Jesus (**the Lord;** cf. 2.16f; 3.5; on the variation between 'Lord' and 'God' in these letters see on 2.13). Since our letter refers so much to the parousia we might have expected Paul would mention it here as in 1 Th. 5.23f (cf. Rom. 15.33; 16.20); its absence is another of those slight indications favouring authenticity. At first sight the description of Jesus as the **Lord of peace** seems appropriate to a situation in which there is some disorderliness (vv. 11f) but this cannot be stressed for Paul regularly refers to God in this way without any apparent allusion to particular circumstances in the church to which he is writing (cf. 1 Th. 5.23f; Rom. 15.33; 16.20; 2 Cor. 13.11; Phil. 4.7, 9; Col. 3.15; cf. Gal. 6.16); in any case the primary failure here is not disorderliness but idleness. Paul's confidence about them in 1.3f; 3.4 does not suggest any deep dissension, although it is possible he may suspect there will be some after the 'loafers' have been disciplined. **Peace** is the normal Jewish greeting and for this reason also it would be wrong to read too much into it here. **Peace** is much wider than the absence of conflict (cf. Morris); it is almost equivalent to salvation (see notes on 1 Th. 1.1) because its primary reference is not to a condition between men or within man but a condition between God and man; yet because the Lord is the Lord of peace and creates peace with man it becomes possible for peace to exist between man and man. Such peace is not for special occasions of unrest only but for every **time** and **every circumstance** (the *v.l.* τόπῳ for τρόπῳ probably originated under the influence of 1 Th. 1.8; 1 Cor. 1.2; 2 Cor. 2.14; 1 Tim. 2.8, or may be accidental); this very wide reference reinforces the view that Paul is not thinking of vv. 11f only. Neither time, place nor event control or exclude God's help.

The second prayer, **The Lord be with you all,** is again general: the Lord creates peace between himself and the community; this still seems to leave him outside the community; the present prayer brings him into it; for this reason it is also different from v. 18; the latter is the more usual form: some quality of God (peace, mercy, grace) is said to be with men. Rom. 15.33; Phil. 4.9 approximate to the form of v. 16 but refer to God rather than to **the Lord** (Christ). Closer still are the explanation of 'Emmanuel' as 'God with us' in Mt. 1.22 and the saying of Jesus, 'I shall be with you' in Mt. 28.20 (cf. Acts 18.10). There is no reason to suspect a direct link with Matthew since both Matthean verses are late reflections on the meaning of Jesus, but the idea is similar. The prayer is not a statement of the Pauline conception of dying and living with Christ, for in the latter Paul uses a different preposition, σύν, for **with.** For the third time in the verse we have **all** (**every** is a translation of the same Greek word); as we saw on 1 Th. 1.2 Paul likes to repeat this word: God's activity is all-inclusive.

17   Apart from Galatians, which Paul wrote when he was angry, and Ephesians, supposing it to be by Paul, a circular letter, none of his letters lack a **greeting.** Elsewhere the greetings are always expressed using the cognate verb; only here is the noun used by itself (an identical phrase is found in 1 Cor. 16.21; Col. 4.18 but

3.17   CONCLUDING PRAYER AND BENEDICTION

in each case there are also verbal forms). To those from the Middle East, and especially the Jews, the content of a greeting was 'peace' (see H. Windisch, *T.D.N.T.*, I, pp. 496–502). The greeting itself is therefore v. 16 with its reference to peace. It was in Paul's handwriting, as are presumably vv. 17f. The noun **greeting** thus describes v. 16 and is not itself the greeting. It is thus difficult to split v. 16 from v. 17 as Schmithals's theory (pp. 145f) requires. At v. 16 Paul took the pen from his secretary's hand and finished the letter himself. Ancient letters often show the writer, after he has used a scribe for the main body of the letter, writing the final words in his own hand. Obviously the difference in hand-writing does not appear in a copy but a photograph of an original in which this has happened can be seen in A. Deissmann, *Light from the Ancient East*, London, 1927, facing p. 170. Evidence that Paul used a scribe is found in Rom. 16.22 and that he wrote the con-cluding words of his letters in 1 Cor. 16.21; Gal. 6.11; Col. 4.18 (Philm. 19 may indicate that in some cases he wrote the whole letter). Our phrase reappears in 1 Cor. 16.21; Col. 4.18. It is stressed here by the addition of **which is a sure sign in every letter. which** refers back neither to **greeting** nor to **handwriting** (lit. 'hand') but to the whole of the preceding clause: the greeting in Paul's hand is the **sign** (not the fact that it is in **handwriting** for this was true of many letters, but that it is **his** handwriting). Is Paul attempting to distinguish his letters from forgeries? At 2.2 it was pointed out that Paul believed the Thessalonians may have received misleading information as to his views but that he did not know from what source or even whether oral or written. Now concluding the letter he draws attention to **the way** in which he writes; since he closes all his letters in his own hand they can check his **handwriting.** This does not however imply that forgeries were actually in existence, but on the vague chance that there may have been some this provides reassurance (a reassurance about a 'spirit' or oral statement is irrelevant at this point). 2 Th. may be the second or third earliest extant letter (depending on the date of Galatians) but Paul must have written many others which are lost to us (he had been an active missionary for many years before this): hence the words **every letter.** If he had written a number of letters it would have been very easy for one of them to have been misinterpreted or a forgery to have been passed off. That he does not refer to this possibility in other letters may only be because he had no reason to deal with a matter of false interpretation (as in 2.2) of whose source he was ignorant. Harnack uses this reference to support his theory that 2 Th. was written to Jewish Christians; if it was written along with or just after 1 Th. to a different group in the church some certification of its Pauline authorship would be needed to explain its existence.

18 This benediction is identical with that of 1 Th. 5.28 (see notes there) but for the addition of **all**, an addition found also in 1 Cor. 16.24; 2 Cor. 13.13. The basic form of the Pauline closing benediction is subject to considerable variation in respect of the titles used of Jesus and the object of the grace (cf. Rom. 16.20; 1 Cor. 16.23; 2 Cor. 13.13; Gal. 6.18; Eph. 6.24; Phil. 4.23; Col. 4.18); little emphasis should therefore be laid on the addition; it implies that none of those to whom Paul writes, and this includes the loafers, is outside its purview.

APPENDIX: THE PAROUSIA

For Paul the parousia is an event associated with the End. Christ will re-appear coming down from heaven; Satan and his forces will be destroyed; believers will be re-united with their dead in the presence of Christ; judgement will be completed. A number of terms are used to describe this event: the day of the Lord (= Jesus), the coming of the Lord, the revelation, the parousia. Before we look at this last term we need to enquire after the origin of the conception itself. It is not an invention of Paul; it is already present in the primitive creed which he uses in 1 Th. 1.9f. This creed belonged to the Jewish Christian stage of the church and so the idea goes back at least as far as this. The survival of the Aramaic phrase of 1 Cor. 16.22, *Marana tha* (or *Maran atha*), indicates that it goes back to the Palestinian Jewish Christian community. But does it go back to Jesus himself?

Some scholars who have adopted a position of thorough-going realized eschatology have held that the idea is not in the teaching of Jesus. A good statement of this view is found in T. F. Glasson, *The Second Advent*, 2nd edn., London, 1947. 'All the evidence brought forward . . . encourages the view that He (Jesus) looked forward to a long period in which the Kingdom of God would spread through the world until at last the old prophecies would come to pass and the knowledge of the Lord would cover the earth . . . and the will of God would be done in earth as in heaven' (pp. 148f). In support of this he contends that pre-Christian Judaism did not teach a parousia in glory for the Messiah nor did the primitive Christian kerygma contain the idea. In the primitive church a number cf factors worked together to produce it: (i) O.T. passages which speak of the coming of the Lord were transferred from Yahweh to Jesus and placed in the future; indeed many of the expressions used of the parousia can be paralleled in expressions about Yahweh in the O.T. (ii) The adoption of the antiChrist legend would lead to the idea of the coming of the Messiah. (iii) A partial misunderstanding by the disciples of the teaching of Jesus. (iv) The widespread expectation in Judaism that the End was not far off.

Glasson's arguments on the teaching of Jesus are only obtained

349

by forcing the material into a non-apocalyptic strait-jacket through the omission as non-genuine of those pieces that do not fit. This is ground which has been gone over many times and we shall not retread it; those who hold the other views we list have refuted it in detail. The period which Glasson leaves for the development of the idea is very brief; he finds it appearing first in 1 & 2 Th. but we have seen it dates back to the Palestinian period of the church. It is difficult to see the process which Glasson outlines operating in so short a time. Even if he is correct in relation to Jesus the appearance of the doctrine long pre-dates the emergence of Paul as a missionary and teacher and probably pre-dates his conversion. Paul therefore took it from tne tradition of the church.

Most scholars however trace the idea back in some form to the teaching of Jesus himself. There are those like W. G. Kümmel, *Promise and Fulfilment*, pp. 64ff, and G. R. Beasley-Murray, *Jesus and the Future*, London, 1954, pp. 183ff, who argue strongly that Jesus foresaw a period between his own death and the accomplishment of the Kingdom but that this period would not be lengthy and would come within the life-time of his disciples. It is easy to see how out of this a doctrine of the parousia would quickly emerge under the influence of the O.T. expectation of the consummation and judgement at the time of the coming of the Lord (now understood as Jesus). Other scholars argue that though Jesus foretold his own parousia he had no idea of the length of time until it would take place and therefore did not teach that it was imminent in a temporal sense (cf. A. L. Moore, *op. cit.*, pp. 175ff). If this is so then the primitive community or Paul must have taken much more seriously the shortness of the period than Jesus did for a belief in the imminence of the parousia is general in all the earlier literature of the N.T., and in particular in Paul. Yet other scholars, following the lead of Schweitzer that the End would come with the death of Jesus, have argued that the period between that death and the appearance of the kingdom would be so brief as hardly to be worthy of the name period (cf. C. K. Barrett, *Jesus and the Gospel Tradition*, London, 1967, pp. 68ff). It is easy to see how the belief in the parousia would emerge from this. Jesus' death did not produce the Son of Man; in the primitive community Jesus comes to be identified with the Son of Man and since the Son of Man is an eschatological future figure and has still to appear Jesus must return as the Son of Man; so the Gospels speak of a future coming in terms of the Son of Man and in the epistles this is interpreted either as the parousia of Christ or as the Day of the Lord. By the time of Paul this last view would have appeared to Christians to be the same as that in which Jesus expected his return in a generation or so. Either could have produced the conception in the form we find it in Paul and the primitive community. Re-inforcing this would be the contemporary Jewish belief in a consummation to come soon in history; though all Jewish belief in the consummation did not have a place for a Messiah or personal figure yet once a Messiah had been accepted, as Jesus was by the early church, he must be found a place in this consummation.

Granted that the belief in an early appearance of Jesus at the End was a part of primitive Christian tradition what is the significance of the application of the term 'parousia' to it? The term is not used consistently throughout the N.T. to describe the place of Jesus in the consummation. It is used six times in this way in the Thessalonian letters (1 Th. 2.19; 3.13; 4.15; 5.23; 2 Th. 2.1, 8) and once of the appearance of the Rebel (an anti-Christ figure; 2 Th. 2.9), but Paul uses it on only one other occasion in this sense (1 Cor. 15.23). Matthew uses it four times (24.3, 27, 37, 39); in 24.27, 37 it replaces a more original 'day' (cf. Lk. 17.24, 26); in 24.3 it is due to Matthean redaction of Mk. 13.4 and in 24.39 it may again be Matthean (cf. Lk. 17.27). It is found in some other later N.T. writings (Jas. 5.7f; 1 Jn. 2.28; 2 Pet. 1.16; 3.4, 12). But the concept is much more widespread in the N.T. than these figures suggest. In 1 & 2 Th. and even more in later letters Paul uses other expressions to render it: he writes about the coming of the Lord and uses verbal forms (1 Cor. 4.5; 11.26; 16.22; 1 Th. 5.2; 2 Th. 1.10; cf. Phil. 3.20; 4.5); he speaks of the Day of the Lord (2 Th. 2.2; 1 Cor. 5.5; cf. Rom. 13.11f; 2 Th. 1.10); he writes of the revelation of Jesus (2 Th. 1.7; 1 Cor. 1.7; cf. 2 Th. 2.8). The first two types of expression obviously depend on the O.T. (for 'the Day of the Lord' see on 1 Th. 5.2); the origin of the third is more difficult and may be Paul's creation (see notes on 2 Th. 1.7). These are also the main ways of expressing the concept in other parts of the N.T. We may reasonably assume that the expressions 'the coming of the Lord' and 'the Day of the Lord' go back to Palestinian Christianity (for the first see 1 Cor. 16.22, and for the second its appearance in so many of the 'Son of Man' eschatological sayings), but what of 'parousia'? We suggest that it did not belong to this period but comes from the time of the translation of Christian concepts into Greek. Hebrew and Aramaic prefer verbal forms to nouns for indicating motion and arrival and would therefore naturally speak of the coming of the Lord if movement was implied. Greek would tend to express the concept either verbally or substantivally. Where a verbal form appears the Greek regularly uses ἔρχεσθαι (Rev. 22.20 is the equivalent of 1 Cor. 16.22; cf. also 1 Cor. 4.5; 11.26; Mt. 10.23; 16.27f, etc.). Where other verbs are used (1 Th. 4.16; Phil. 4.5) these have been usually determined specially by the context. In view of this use of ἔρχεσθαι we would expect that a cognate noun would appear, e.g. ἔλευσις. This is used of Jesus' first coming (Acts 7.52; cf. 1 Clem. 17.1; Polycarp, *Phil.* 6.3) for which the verb was also used (Mt. 11.19; 20.28; Lk. 19.10). G. D. Kilpatrick, 'Acts VII. 52, *ΕΛΕΥΣΙΣ*', *J.T.S.* 46 (1945) 136–45, has argued that this noun was used in the cycle of prophetic pseudepigrapha in reference to the advent of the Messiah and παρουσία, with some possible late exceptions, 'always in the Greek versions of the Testaments . . . for the eschatological coming of God'. No necessary distinction would have existed in the underlying Hebrew or Aramaic. But it is difficult to know how far the choice of these two words to express different concepts is due to the influence of early Christianity since we cannot be certain that the texts Kilpatrick uses are free from Christian influence (cf. Dupont, *op. cit.*, pp. 55–9). Even if the choice of the words is post-Christian there is implied therein a recognition that parousia is unsuitable to describe the first coming of the Messiah in humility. The evidence for the use of ἔλευσις by Christians with reference to the incarnation is also much later than the evidence in 1 & 2 Th. for the use of parousia for the return of Jesus (Acts 7, even if it is a verbatim account of Stephen's speech, is in its present form a translation from a later period since Stephen will have spoken in Hebrew or Aramaic). Another possible noun that could have been used is ἄφιξις. This can mean both arrival and departure and is used in both senses by Josephus (*Ant.* 20.51; 2.18; 4.315; 7.247; cf. Acts 20.29); the meaning must be determined from the context. This ambiguity may have militated against its selection; moreover there is no reason to suppose that ἀφικνεῖσθαι was ever used of the coming of the Messiah or of the Day of the Lord. Words like ἐπιφάνεια and ἐπισκοπή do not contain the notion of motion and would not therefore have been suitable renderings, though the second would have fitted in well with the Jewish idea of God visiting his people, and is used in this way in the LXX but generally with the implication of a visitation in judgement (cf. H. W. Beyer, *T.D.N.T.* II, pp. 606f), whereas for Paul and the primitive church the coming of Christ is primarily for salvation (1 Th. 1.9f; 4.13–18; etc.). None of this suggests any particular reason why parousia was chosen. The use of the verbal form in Dan. 7.13 LXX may have suggested its equivalence to ἔρχεσθαι but the verbal form is not used there with the sense of motion but rather with its alternative meaning of 'presence'. Generally however the verbal form in the LXX has the sense 'come' and often renders בוא.

The root has two fundamental senses, 'to be present' and 'to come, arrive' and both these appear in the noun. Paul clearly uses the noun with the former sense of his own presence and without eschatological overtones of any kind in 2 Cor. 10.10; Phil. 2.12; he uses it of the coming of others again without eschatological overtones in 1 Cor. 16.17; 2 Cor. 7.6f, but this coming involves their continued presence after they have come (Phil. 1.26 is doubtful). In the Hellenistic world the word came to have particular associations in relation to the sense 'come, arrive'. It denoted the ceremonial arrival of a ruler to a city where he is greeted with honours of one kind and another; the parousia was more than the physical act of arrival; it included the attendant ceremonies in which the ruler was honoured. The word was also used of the coming of a God to help those in need, e.g. Aesculapius visits his temple to heal the sick. It is used in a somewhat similar way by Josephus of God giving help to his people, cf. *Ant.* 3.80, 202; 9.55; 18.284. (For detailed references see Rigaux, pp. 196ff; A. Oepke, *T.D.N.T.* V, pp. 858ff). These two usages are not so far apart as may seem for court and sacral language are closely linked. It is difficult to believe that those who used the term in the Hellenistic world were unaware of this significance even if the first person who rendered the concept with the word had not realized it. The word then was chosen to express the concept in Greek because it carried the nuance of movement and probably, though not certainly, because it also carried from Hellenistic culture the idea of a ceremonial visit of a ruler to his people which would be for them a joyful occasion; the description of 1 Th. 4.16–17 ('a meeting' in 4.17 has similar associations; see notes), the 'word of the Lord', which is probably non-Pauline, fits appropriately into this Hellenistic idea. In support of this we may note that where Paul uses parousia he does so always in a positive sense, i.e. it is a time of joy for believers rather than a time of destruction for unbelievers. The latter appears in 1 Th. 5.2; 2 Th. 1.7f; but in neither case is parousia used. 2 Th. 2.8 may appear to be an exception but there parousia is qualified, 'the manifestation of his parousia', and the qualification probably makes it more hostile (see notes). If we say this we must also realize that the basic imagery which goes with 'parousia' to describe the visit is drawn from apocalyptic Judaism and behind it the O.T. At times there may even be some deliberate avoidance of terms which would make the parallels with the contemporary world too strong; in 1 Th. 1.10, 'to wait for his son out of heaven . . . Jesus who delivers us from the approaching anger', a verbal form ῥυόμενον may be used instead of the noun σωτήρ for the latter would have made too strong a parallel to Aesculapius who is often described with it. The partial disappearance after 1 & 2 Th. and 1 Cor. of parousia itself as a term for the coming of Christ may have come from the realization of the danger of too close an association with Hellenistic ideas.

Although the parousia is often loosely equated with the 'second coming' of Jesus the term itself does not contain either the idea of 'return' or of 'second'. Equally it is never used of the incarnation (until Ignatius, *Philad.* 9.2) for which it would have been unsuitable with its secular associations of a ceremonial arrival. It is only in Justin Martyr, *Dial,* 14.8; 40.4; 118.2, that we begin to get the idea of a first and second coming.

The secular significance of parousia reinforces the conception of a coming of Christ which is a public event, in which he returns from 'outside' history to end history and which therefore eliminates any idea of a gradual development of events within history which themselves shape the End. Just as a king comes from elsewhere to visit a city so Jesus comes to the earth.

V PAUL AND THE THESSALONIANS

In 1 Th. we obtain a more detailed account of Paul's initial visit to a town in which he established a church than in any of his other letters; 2 Th. has a little but not much to add to the picture. It is not that Paul gives us any direct information about the time of his arrival, the length of his stay, the names of the people with whom he lodged or the steps which led to the rupture with the synagogue, but he lets us see some of his feelings towards the Thessalonians and his relationship with them at a time not very long after he left them. The brief period until the writing of his letters left little opportunity for this relationship to change.

Paul uses principally two terms to describe his message: 'gospel' is the most frequent (1 Th. 1.5; 2.2, 4, 8, 9; 3.2; 2 Th. 1.8; 2.14) but he also employs 'word' (1 Th. 1.6, 8; 2.13; 2 Th. 3.1, 14). He speaks of preaching (1 Th. 2.9; cf. 2.2) and sharing the gospel (1 Th. 2.8); it is more than human words; God makes it effective (1 Th. 1.5; 2.13). These terms do not of themselves reveal any of the content of what Paul spoke, except in so far as the gospel is defined as the gospel of Christ (1 Th. 3.2; 2 Th. 1.8), meaning certainly the gospel which is about Christ, though it may also mean the gospel which has its origin with Christ. But we learn something more of the gospel Paul preached in Thessalonica from the pieces of tradition which we find embedded in the letters; we have discovered at least three credal statements: 1 Th. 1.9f; 4.14; 5.10; the first is of very different type from the other two in that it makes no reference to the death of Christ yet it must have been part of evangelical preaching rather than catechetical instruction because of its reference to conversion (1.9). As well as 'gospel' in the narrow sense there is a great deal of other traditional material, most of it catechetical (1 Th. 4.2ff; 4.9; 4.11; 5.12ff; 2 Th. 3.10) and there are other references to it (2 Th. 2.15) which show how important a place it played in Paul's nurture of a young community. Paul is not just improvising in each community as new situations turn up but has a solid body of material to hand on. Even on one point which seems a concern of the Thessalonian community alone, the refusal of some members to work, a stray remark shows that Paul's teaching here was part of the 'tradition' (2 Th. 3.6); 3.10 was probably its content. The regular way in which he uses words like 'Father', 'Christ', 'Lord', 'Son' shows that he must have given instruction on their meaning; some like 'Christ' could not have been understood by a pagan audience without explanation; others like 'son of God' would have been too easily misunderstood. The fact of his use of 1 Th. 1.9f in his preaching is confirmed by the amount of eschatological information the Thessalonians have; they know about 'dates and times' (1 Th. 5.1); they understand what the parousia is; they have been told about the Rebel, the apostasy and the *katechon*. The extent of their knowledge and the fewer references to it in other Pauline letters suggests that Paul gave more eschatological instruction in this church than in any of the others for which correspondence still exists. The reason for this we do not know. We have seen that there are many contacts between this eschatological teaching of Paul and the Synoptic apocalypses; these did not take their present form until a period after our letters so Paul is not dependent on them; rather we see again that Paul in his eschatological teaching is using the common tradition of the church.

When he left Thessalonica a Christian community was established. It does not appear to have had any leaders who could be clearly distinguished with a title or name (Acts 14.23 reflects a later period of church history); organization was rudimentary. In the problems which face the members he expects the whole community to act (1 Th. 5.12-14; 2 Th. 3.6-15). Even if he did not appoint leaders for them he still regards himself as in some way their leader though he has been compelled to leave them. He writes to them with authority, as he does to all his other churches. This authority is not specially stressed in our letter (note the omission of the title 'apostle' in the address) but it emerges in the implicit claim that he can still advise and instruct them (cf. 1 Th. 4.1; 5.12; 2 Th. 3.4, 6) how they are to meet their present difficulties and that he has the right to answer their questions. How far we should build this up into a conscious position on Paul's part as an 'apostle' in the community is very far from certain. Anyone who has founded a new branch of an organization and left it will expect to have difficulties referred to him and will expect his advice to be accepted while the organization is still in its infancy. But Paul presents the picture of his relationship with the Thessalonians in a much more intimate and deeper way than authority suggests. He presents himself as 'father' and 'nursing-mother', though these terms would not then have sounded so paternalistic as they do today. Parents are a child's first examples and from them he begins to learn the way to live. It is in keeping with this when Paul describes himself as their example and begs them to imitate him (1 Th. 1.6; 2 Th. 3.7); he does not however imply that he is the only example to be imitated; all Christians may be examples to others and so he speaks of the imitation of the churches of Judea (1 Th. 2.14; cf. 1.7). Imitation is necessary and natural; Paul is not being presumptuous; the Christian life is so different from the pagan culture out of which the Thessalonians have come that teaching is not sufficient by itself to disclose love; only an example can show its radically new nature. Paul has therefore much more to give them than his words; he shares his very being with them (1 Th. 2.8). But the traffic is not all one way and he acknowledges that they have something as deep to give him. He and they will pray for one another (1 Th. 5.25; 2 Th. 3.1); their faith and love bring the gospel to him so that he has true joy and grows in spiritual life (1 Th. 3.6–10). Together they are 'brothers'; he repeatedly addresses them in this way; he was their father but they are now on their own and in a real sense stand on level terms with him in the one community of God. In later times 'brothers' became a meaningless term of address; when Paul used it, it still meant what it said.

And if they are brothers of Paul they are also brothers of one another. Many of the terms which we associate with Paul's teaching on the corporate nature of the church are missing; but the reality is there. In so far as Paul and his associates are also a part of the church it is seen in much of what we have written of his relationship to them but we can also see it more directly in reference to the Thessalonians themselves. They are a group clearly distinguishable from the rest of mankind (1 Th. 4.13; 5.6) to whom they must set a good example (1 Th. 4.12), and as such they are part of a much larger community (1 Th. 1.6–8; 2.14); this is seen in the common tradition to which they adhere. They have a mutual duty to build up one another in the faith (1 Th. 5.11) and to deal with those who are difficult in their membership (5.14). They are responsible for those who have become 'idle' and must win them back (2 Th. 3.13–15). Something of the depth of this mutual relationship which is founded on a relationship to Christ comes out in

357

Paul's use of the phrase 'in Christ' with its allied forms (cf. 1 Th. 2.14; 3.8; 4.1, 16; 5.12; 2 Th. 3.12); the phrase would have been in large part meaningless to them unless they had entered into the experience which it describes.

VI THE RETURN OF CHRIST

The eschatological atmosphere of the Thessalonian letters, and indeed of the whole primitive church, is very far removed from today. Throughout the centuries there have been recrudescences of expectation that Jesus was about to return but all who placed their trust in its imminence were cruelly disappointed (for a brief résumé of these revived hopes, cf. U. Simon, *The End Is Not Yet*, London, 1964, pp. 38ff).

Have we any right to speak at all about a return of Christ at any time let alone one within the foreseeable future? Is this belief that Jesus will come from God's right hand to judge the quick and the dead something which ought to be written out of Christian faith? Is there something important behind it to be found by transmuting it into other terms or by demythologizing it? Before it is written off too glibly we should recall the increasing amount of attention which theologians are again paying to the future. The germinal thought of Bloch has inspired the work of Pannenberg, Metz and Moltmann; the title of Moltmann's best known book—*Theology of Hope* (London, 1967)—exemplifies this interest in the future. From another angle we have the mystic and scientific approach of Tielhard de Chardin, and from yet another the American school of process theologians who base their work on the philosophy of A. N. Whitehead and for whom the future is still open, both for the world and for God. This ought to encourage us to look again at the significance of the parousia.

First, then, what is its significance for the N.T., and in particular for Paul? Christian eschatological expectation originated in Christianity's Jewish matrix, though necessarily there were large differences. The expectation of a personal Messiah, whether an earthly king or a heavenly saviour, was not an essential element of Jewish eschatology. Even where this belief was accepted it was still different from the Christian idea: the Jew believed the Messiah was still to come; the Christian believed he was due to return. But whether a personal Messiah was envisaged or not in all of it the End is viewed as a dateable, public and cosmic event. In particular Paul's Thessalonian converts are to see Christ as he descends from the skies and they will be taken up to meet him. No matter how

359

much we argue that Paul's language is poetical, symbolical or metaphorical, and much of it certainly is, we cannot eliminate the conception of a public and cosmic event taking place at a definite date in history; men will take part in it and be aware of it. For them and their world one state of existence will come to an end and another will begin. Even those parts of the N.T. which do not expect the parousia immediately still believe it will be a public and historical event affecting the cosmos and not just individuals.

One of the striking features of N.T. belief in the parousia is its nearness. While this is not found in all the N.T. books it is not encountered solely in those which are generally recognized as early. It is in 1 Peter (e.g. 4.7, 17; 1.5f) which probably dates from the final quarter of the first century; 1 Jn. 2.18, 28 testifies to its appearance in the Johannine literature which is at least as late as this; Rev. in its final form also comes from the same period and in it the belief is widespread. The history of the church shows that where belief in the parousia has been strong it has almost always been accompanied by an expectation of its immediacy; where men have not expected it soon they have taken little interest in it. We have seen that belief in the immediacy of the End is certainly found in the earlier Paul (1 Th. 4.15; Rom. 13.11; 1 Cor. 7.25–9; see on 1 Th. 4.15). It is also present in the teaching of Jesus, or entered the church tradition of that teaching very early (cf. Mk. 9.1; 13.30; Mt. 10.23). While the post-Paulines and the Lukan writings do not stress it and allow for a more lengthy period before it they do not abandon belief in it (e.g. Acts 1.11; 1 Tim. 6.14). Obviously few people today expect a quick return of Christ. They also know that the expectancy of the early church was erroneous. Does this then mean that the conception of the End or parousia must itself go?

How far does the immediacy of the End penetrate and affect the thought of the N.T.? Very little! Those writers of the N.T. who believe in its immediacy do not allow this belief to affect in any real degree the lines of conduct and belief which they set down as correct. There appear to be only two points at which the nearness of the End can be said to be a factor affecting conduct, though Mk. 1.15, 'the kingdom of God is at hand, repent and believe in the gospel', i.e. the nearness of the kingdom creates the need for repentance, may also seem a possible case; this is not so for repentance remains a necessity even though the parousia is not regarded as near; indeed Luke is the writer in the N.T. who emphasizes repentance most and he has come to terms with the non-imminence of the parousia and expects an indefinite continuance of the church. Like repentance other virtues and duties of the Christian and the non-Christian are sometimes linked to the nearness of the parousia but in other places appear without this connection. The two points where the connection seems essential are: (i) The warning to watchfulness, e.g. Mt. 24.42 (cf. v. 44 and 25.13); once the imminence of the End is removed the need for watchfulness disappears; thus Luke who does not expect an imminent End changes the whole tenor of the verse into a need for watchfulness at all times (Lk. 21.36). (ii) Paul's instructions on marriage are affected by his belief in the nearness of the parousia; it is imminent and therefore it is better to remain unmarried (1 Cor. 7.25–31); if we remove the pressure of the End the argument collapses, and indeed those who argue for celibacy today do not use this argument.

This may be taken a little further. When eschatological sects have over-stressed watchfulness history has shown that other more essential virtues tend to be neglected. While watchfulness does not feature prominently in Thessalonica yet we have seen that eschatological over-excitement did lead to neglect of one ordinary duty—working for a living. But nearness ought not to have this affect. 1 Pet. 4.7ff can be roughly paraphrased: 'The End is imminent; do not therefore go to extremes of worship; love each other; give a cup of tea to your neighbour; use your God-given talents for the good of the church.' Whether the parousia is near or far that summary of Christian duty would not require to be altered. In Rom. 13.11–13 Paul makes one of his clearest statements about the nearness of the End but this is also the chapter in which he expresses his view on the duty of the Christian towards the state (which is soon to pass away at the End) and in which he emphatically expounds the duty of brotherly love. Thus, taken as a whole, belief in the imminence of the End does not lead to changes in the structure of Christian ethics. (An *Interimsethik* could therefore be valid for an indefinite period.)

It is impossible to stop here. A few Christian bodies may still take seriously the imminence of the End but after the passage of two thousand years most Christians do not think about the End at all though their official creeds still contain statements about it.

361

If we allow that N.T. Christians may have erred in respect of the date of the parouisa we might argue that this is all in which they erred, especially since we have seen that the removal of imminence makes no difference to essential Christian belief and practice. Luke who did not believe in the nearness of the parousia still thinks of a real End—of a cosmic and public event at the end of history in which Jesus will return. But supposing we do not believe in such a public, cosmic and dateable event, what then?

It is a commonplace of all Jewish and early Christian eschatological literature that the End will bear some resemblance to the beginning. If the beginning is the creation of the heaven and the earth the End is the creation of the new heaven and the new earth. Christian faith has never, of course, held that the End is a simple restoration of the beginning, if for no other reason than that the End comes after Jesus Christ. The comparison between End and Beginning was more easily grasped by those who accepted a cosmology which viewed God as creating the universe at a dated period a few thousand years before Christ and as about to end it at a dated period some ten or hundred or thousand years after him. Both were then public cosmic events and were comparable because they belonged to the same order of reality. Such a belief in respect of the Beginning has now disappeared. First, our time scale has shifted from the order of thousands of years to billions. When it was believed the world was only a few thousand years old it was possible to believe that its end was very near, within perhaps a few thousand years of the other side of the mid-point, Jesus. But the stretching of the time scale towards a supposed point of creation permits us to stretch the time scale beyond Christ and ourselves in the same way—and the End may be pushed so far away that it may be thought there is no need to reckon with it any longer at all. The End in this connection means the End of the universe and not just the termination of life on this planet or the destruction of the planet itself; life here may end at any time through the mis-use of science, the approach of an unknown star breaking up the solar system, or some other way we have not even imagined. But this is not the end of the universe; it may not even be the end of life, if there is life elsewhere in the universe. Secondly, and more importantly, if there is some similarity between creation and consummation, Beginning and End, the way in which we think of the origin of the universe may help us to understand its End.

Scientists entertain different views of the beginning, some envisaging continuous, others instantaneous creation. In either case they attach no significance to the manner or time of creation; it is not conceived of as a 'public' event. Each of these theories has some bearing on the End. Those who accept the idea of instantaneous creation, the 'big bang' theory, probably accept some form of a gradual dying of the universe, its energy being dissipated into less and less useful forms (increasing entropy) until eventually everything ends in a dead, flat, meaningless sameness. Those who accept the idea of continuous creation probably never think of an end at all; new energy is always appearing and both end and beginning may be infinitely far away. It is not for the Christian to settle the problems of scientists but only to see what they have to say which is relevant to his own. If we take what they say of the End as seriously as we now do of what they say about the Beginning then we have to conclude that the End is something with which men will never have to reckon in practical terms, again excluding the possible destruction of our own planet, and that it is as wrong to think of a real physical End which God achieves in some public way as it is to think of a real physical Beginning. We must therefore exclude the conception of the End in the physical sense. Is there then nothing which the Christian may say in relation to the End? To help us reach an answer we shall look at the work of three N.T. theologians. Two current schools of N.T. interpretation deny the importance of the End: Dodd's realized eschatology and Bultmann's existentialism.

As classically stated realized eschatology held Jesus to have taught that with himself the Kingdom of God had come; there was to be no further coming; however the early church under the influence of Jewish apocalyptic introduced the concept of the second advent (cf. Glasson, *op. cit.*, and pp. 349f *supra*). John recovered the primitive view by transmuting the second advent into the coming of the Spirit, the other Paraclete, whom Jesus sent in his own place. If in this way we lay all the stress on a past event and say that the kingdom of God is realized in Jesus Christ, what is to be made of the future? C. H. Dodd writes, 'the thought of Jesus passed directly from the immediate situation to the eternal order lying beyond all history, of which he spoke in the language of apocalyptic symbolism' (*The Parables of the Kingdom*, London, 1943, p. 207). This Platonistic view lacks any conception of a real end. History is real and 'the whole series of events remains plastic to the will of God, and serves to bring men again and again face to face with the eternal issues' (*ibid.* p. 209), but history has no goal. 'Our destiny lies in the eternal order' (*ibid.*, p. 210, see also *The Apostolic Preaching*, 2nd edn., London, 1944, pp. 79-96, and *History and the Gospel*, London, 1938). Whatever triumph the End represents has already been attained in the Cross and Resurrection (*History and the Gospel*, p. 170). Such a view leaves no place for the parousia. How then is it and its associated ideas to be interpreted? Neil, another adherent of this school of thought, answers: The Day of the Lord 'is God's timeless Judgement which is past, present, and future. In a sense it is always to come, in a sense it is always present, and in a sense it has already been passed' (p. xli). 'Thus the Parousia is, like Creation, in a real sense timeless; not an historical event, but the underlying purpose of history and the summing up of all things in Christ' (p. xlii). 'That—Paul following our Lord—regarded the Second Advent as a religious truth rather than an historical prophecy is clear' (p. xliv). (As our exegesis of 1 & 2 Th. has shown Neil here falsely imposes his own view on Paul.) We have already suggested that the view of realized eschatology is inadequate as an interpretation of the N.T. evidence (see pp. 349f) and if it is to be accepted this must be on grounds other than its faithfulness to Scripture.

Bultmann's approach is much more thorough, consistent and deadly than Dodd's, for while Dodd can be refuted by a better understanding of the teaching of Jesus Bultmann accepts that Jesus was an apocalyptic prophet who looked to the future for the fulfilment of God's plan but denies that this has relevance for us or is true. For Bultmann Jesus lived in an apocalyptic culture and therefore could not escape being an apocalyptic, but men today do not live in such a culture and therefore require to demythologize Jesus' apocalypticism. Paul began the process of demythologization and John carried it further (Bultmann eliminates from the latter all the features of traditional eschatology by attributing them to a redactor; cf. R. Bultmann, *History and Eschatology*, Edinburgh, 1957, pp. 37ff and 'History and Eschatology in the New Testament', *N.T.S.* 1 (1954) 5–16). 'The true solution of the problem lies in the thought of Paul and John, namely in the idea that Christ is the ever present or ever becoming present eschatological event' (*N.T.S.* p. 15). He becomes this event when he is preached and a man

364

moving from inauthentic to authentic existence becomes a Christian in response to that preaching (*History and Eschatology*, p. 151). As a Christian he is a new being and there is no need to think of any other new event at the end of the world; indeed the end of the world may be abandoned to science; it is a purely natural phenomenon and does not concern the Christian as Christian. 'The mythical eschatology is untenable for the simple reason that the parousia of Christ never took place as the New Testament expected. History did not come to an end, and, as every schoolboy knows, it will continue to run its course. Even if we believe that the world as we know it will come to an end in time, we expect the end to take the form of a natural catastrophe, not of a mythical event such as the New Testament expects. And if we explain the parousia in terms of modern scientific theory, we are applying criticism to the New Testament, albeit unconsciously' ('New Testament and Mythology' in *Kerygma and Myth*, I, London, 1953, p. 5). For Bultmann history though real has neither goal nor meaning (*History and Eschatology*, p. 120); all meaning lies in the life of the individual (*ibid.*, pp. 120ff; *N.T.S.*, p. 13). Consequently Bultmann ends like Dodd in an individualistic position but unlike Dodd he sees no 'other world' to which the individual may ultimately belong. He cannot however be answered as easily as Dodd; the latter believes the primitive community misunderstood Jesus and tries to recover a truer understanding and make that normative for us. The former does not believe that a truer understanding of Jesus' teaching will really help us. If Bultmann is to be refuted we must start further back and ask whether the existentialist approach within which he interprets the N.T. is a valid, or the only valid, approach, and whether the excessive individualism which we find in that approach is at all possible in terms of any faithfulness to N.T. thought. It is interesting to notice how many preachers solve the problem of the parousia and judgement in a similar individualistic way by making each man's death the moment of the parousia and judgement.

Bultmann has in fact been challenged on the very point of existentialist interpretation by Cullmann, our third typical interpreter, who in effect argues that salvation-history is the category which the N.T. itself provides for its own interpretation. He himself uses this category to elucidate the N.T. conception of the parousia and the End. Cullmann views time not as circular or spiral but as moving in a straight line from creation to consummation; yet its true End lies not at the consummation but in the middle, in the Christ-event. Here the real and essential victory has been won and the remainder of history is only a mopping-up operation. Cullmann contrasts with this views which argue that world history obtains its meaning from its End, e.g. Judaism (cf. *Christ and Time*, London, 1951, p. 140); this idea also exists in secularized form in Marxism and Scientific Humanism. But for the Christian the present is itself an eschatological period since it follows Christ and is characterized by a tension between the 'already fulfilled' and the 'not yet fulfilled' (*Christ and Time*, p. 212; *Salvation in History*, London, 1967, p. 172). At the End this tension will be resolved in what appears for Cullmann to be a public and cosmic event: cosmic, in so far as it is not just an affair of an individual's fully realized reconciliation with God but involves the universe (*Christ and Time*, pp. 177ff); public, in so far as Cullmann appears to envisage a real parousia of Christ and a new though transformed creation. He writes: 'the coming of the end *cannot* fail to materialize' (*Salvation in History*, p. 181; italics Cullmann's); the consummation 'will be nothing less than the creation of a new heaven and new earth (II Pet. 3.13). This is why Christ will return to earth. The decisive event, like the first decisive event which took place under Pontius Pilate, will take place on earth, because matter itself has to be re-created' ('The Return of Christ' in *The Early Church*, London, 1956, p. 147; cf. p. 156, 'Christ reigns today invisibly except to the eye of faith, but when the final struggle and the last judgement which precede the beginning of the coming age take place, he will reign before all eyes'; see also *Christ and Time*, pp. 141–3). Although he acknowledges that the primitive church expected this End almost immediately, he allows that for us it is undateable (cf. *Salvation in History*, pp. 181f). Yet even if it is indefinitely postponed it will eventually come for 'every passing minute brings us nearer to the end point' (*Christ and Time*, p. 148). During this prolonged period the signs of the End are continuous, e.g. the preaching to the Gentiles (Mk. 13.10) is the church's ever-present task, the anti-Christ is often at work (*Christ and Time*, pp. 158ff; *Salvation in History*, pp. 309f).

Cullmann's interpretation certainly keeps closer to the N.T. picture than Dodd's or Bultmann's, at least in so far as he depicts a cosmic event and not just an event in the life of the individual.

It can indeed be said that Cullmann describes fairly accurately the theology of the N. T. as its writers intended it to be understood and then takes it over as his own with one major (he would probably term it 'minor') emendation: the indefinite extension of the interim period. Cullmann is open to severe criticism at this point for he has not taken sufficient account of the significance of this extension. He still operates with a pre-scientific conception of time. The parousia is delayed; 2 Pet. 3.8ff postponed it beyond what earlier Christians expected; Cullmann postpones it still further—but he still expects a parousia at some precise though indefinite moment. This implies that time is limited in a fairly rigid way. If we cannot really put a date to the beginning of the universe and no longer want to, can we put a date to the End? It is not that science does not yet know enough to put such a date but rather that it lies outside the realm of what is possible. To keep on extending the interim period does not deal with this problem for it still expects that at some point God will intervene by sending back his Son to wind up the universe; such a solution really ignores the genuine difficulty. If we are to deal with it we must retrace our steps and ask about the relationship of the parousia to the End.

It was perfectly natural for the primitive church to associate these two ideas. Jesus was the Messiah; wherever a Messiah was accepted in Judaism he was linked to the End; but the End had not come with Jesus, nor had many of the terrors and blessings associated with it; therefore he must come again. So we find that his parousia is regarded as the time when judgement will be enacted, the evil and righteous separated and go to their respective rewards, Satan destroyed and the heavens and the earth re-created, i.e. what Judaism expected at the End is transferred to the parousia. Just as the thought of judgement at the End was used in Judaism as a motive for conduct so we find Christians using the parousia in the same way. All this means that the parousia was an integral part of an existing framework which thought of the world as created a few thousand years earlier and ending in at least a comparable, if not a much shorter, period in the future. If we jettison this framework, as jettison it we must today, does any place remain for the parousia? As such there is no place, but the parousia is the parousia of Christ and a place must remain for him. If the first Christians inserted the parousia of Christ into an existing Jewish framework they did so not just because some elements of Judaism believed in an eschatological Messiah but because they themselves believed that the meaning of existence was to be found in him: an End envisaged apart from him was not a Christian End, and the simplest way in which they could make the End Christian was to set him as the central figure in it. It was the simplest way, and it was perfectly natural for them to do so but, as we shall see shortly, it was not the only way they took.

A somewhat similar problem existed in relation to the Beginning and we know that the early Christians solved it by setting Christ alongside God as creator (cf. Jn. 1.1–3; Col. 1.15–17); here again they used Jewish ideas (and probably also Hellenistic) developing the role of Wisdom in creation. While John does not explore the nature of the End as he does the Beginning, this is done in Col. 1 and a surprisingly different picture emerges from the traditional parousia conception. If Christ is the creator of all he is also the reconciler of all (Col. 1.20) and this reconciliation is attached not just to the moment of the cross but to the End: through Christ God reconciles all things to himself. In the normally accepted parousia teaching Christ judges men at that time and takes those who are his to be with him for ever in a new heaven and earth which he has created. In this Colossian passage there is no reference to the parousia or to judgement and yet Christ is quite firmly made the centre of the End. This new role in relation to the End is found also in Eph. 1.10; Rom. 8.19–21; Phil. 2.9–11. It is often argued that the last passage fits in with the parousia conception in so far as it is perfectly satisfied by a separation of men at the parousia, so that those in hell eventually realize their folly and while there acknowledge Christ as their victor. This is not so, for: (i) It operates with a wrong conception of victory; for a man to stand on another's neck and compel him to confess he has been vanquished is not a victory compatible with the God of the cross. (ii) The text makes no distinction between the ways in which those in hell and those who have been redeemed by Christ would hail him as Lord, and surely they would not do it in the same way? 1 Cor. 15.22 also belongs to this series of texts; Paul is forced here (but perhaps not unwillingly) into a position in which no distinction is made between men in relation to their ultimate fate, because at this point (cf. Rom. 5.12–21) he parallels the Beginning, Adam, with the End, Christ—though, it must be acknowledged, in the succeeding verses he goes back on this. It should be noted that a number of these passages are not concerned only with men but with the End of the whole creation in relation to Christ. In this they follow a trend already present in the O.T. (cf. Isa. 11.6–9; 35). If it is asked why these relatively few passages in the Bible are preferred to the many which envisage a final End, a real return of Christ and a judgement of men, and to the few which may suggest annihilation of the wicked, the answer can only be given by developing a hermeneutic of Scripture, and for this there is no space here. The choice in our problem is only part of a much wider one, for there are few doctrines in the N.T. which are presented uniformly throughout it.

Here then we have a teaching which links Christ to the End but makes no reference to the parousia, and in each of the quoted passages Christ occupies a more central position than he does in the parousia. His role there as judge could as easily have been filled by an angelic being and indeed in Judaism various 'mechanisms' did exist to carry out the functions fulfilled by Christ as Messiah at the parousia. In this other conception the End is given a quite definite Christological basis. It is fair to observe here that the three schools of interpretation at which we previously looked all attempted to make the End Christological. Dodd set the End in the past Christ-event. Bultmann made the individual's response to the preaching of Christ an eschatological event. Cullmann made Christ the mid-point of history. It is worth following this up in respect of Cullmann for he alone retains the cosmic dimension of the End. Having made Christ the mid-point of history he has some difficulty in explaining what there is over and above this in the End. He argues repeatedly that in the End something new emerges (e.g. *Salvation* in *History*, p. 177) but it is difficult to see what this is other than an unveiling of what is already true: 'The events of the Revelation belong to the beginning of the world to come, when the present but invisible lordship of Christ will become visible' ('The Return of Christ', p. 156, and cf. the quotation from the same page on p. 366). Is this adequate? A new creation in being is qualitatively different from a new creation in process of realization; God is the God who raises the dead and calls into being the things that are not (Rom. 4.17). We have the Holy Spirit now, but he is only an 'earnest' of what will be. The new is thus more than an accomplishment or completion of the old. There is always an 'overplus of promise' coming from 'the inexhaustibility of the God

369

of promise' (J. Moltmann, *op. cit.*, p. 106). There was an overplus in the O.T. promises of a saviour to come; will there not be also in the promise of the consummation that takes place through him? 'The fulfilments can very well contain an element of newness and surprise over against the promise as it was received' (p. 104). Something new has begun to appear in the resurrection of Jesus which will reach its fulfilment in the End. In passing we may note that such a view leaves the future open-ended in a way that the traditional view does not. The End is with Christ and it involves all things but we cannot say how or when; it will be richer and fuller than we can anticipate: 'No eye has seen, nor ear heard, nor the heart of man conceived, what God has prepared for those who love him' (1 Cor. 2.9). This open-endedness fits more easily into the newer theologies which in contrast to existentialism are beginning to take the End more seriously. ('End' may be a misleading term since it seems to imply a temporal limitation and then a changed condition and this is not what we intend; perhaps we should use 'Consummation' instead.)

The End then is not to be conceived as the End of history, as a public event which can be seen, as an intervention of God into the world process. Christ bears a similar relation to the End as to the Beginning: he is creator and consummator. But in neither case is he to be tied to the universe in any way which science would find recognizable or which the historian could record. The End is not an event in history but outside it. And the End is something more than the Beginning; it is not just the growth of the acorn into the oak, the unfolding of what was always present in essence. It is new in the same way in which Christ is new. But the nature of that newness we cannot predict; we can only say it lies with the God who gave something new in Christ and it will accord with what we know of God through Christ.

There are two further points. First, in the traditional teaching there are signs preceding and heralding the End, of which the most obvious is the expectation of a period of great evil before the Messiah returns; when things are at their worst God intervenes. Such a view with its idea of intervention must go. It looked for God to intervene because man could do no more. Does the view we have expounded mean that man can do something more; can he advance the End? This is to think of the End in temporal terms and is probably therefore a wrong question. What can be said is this: if ultimate reconciliation is part of the End then what advances that advances the End. Thus the Christian mission has its continuing place. The Church which results from it and lives by it reaches its fulfilment in the consummation and already foreshadows that consummation.

Secondly, what is the relation of the End to the event of the cross and resurrection? Against Cullman we must say that the End is more than an unveiling of what was true in the cross and resurrection. It is interesting that the N.T. uses the idea of 'revelation' in relation to the parousia but is hesitant to use it of the Christ-event; there is a wholeness in the End which is not present in the Christ-event for a purpose has been accomplished. All history will have been caught up in this purpose and come to glory. The universe will know fully and completely who God is and what he is and what his love and glory are; these could only be glimpsed in the cross. But it is more than an unveiling of what was half-seen, more than a restoration of a past Golden Age. Because of Christ, because of the response of men and the universe to God in him, something will have come into existence which did not exist before. What that will be will only be known when the End is accomplished.

INDEX OF MODERN AUTHORS

INDEX OF MODERN AUTHORS